P9-CFV-231

The Haynes
Fuel Injection
Diagnostic
Manual

by Mike Stubblefield
and John H Haynes

Member of the Guild of Motoring Writers

The Haynes Automotive Repair Manual
for maintaining, troubleshooting and
repairing fuel injection systems

(2Z3 - 10220)

(2111)

ABCDE
FGHIJ
KLM

Haynes Publishing Group
Sparkford Nr Yeovil
Somerset BA22 7JJ England

Haynes North America, Inc
861 Lawrence Drive
Newbury Park
California 91320 USA

629.253
STU

Acknowledgements

We are grateful for the help and cooperation of the Chrysler Corporation, Ford Motor Company, Nissan Motor Company, Volvo North America Corporation and Robert Bosch Corporation for assistance with technical information and certain illustrations. We also wish to thank Milton Webb for consultation on this project. Technical authors who contributed to this project are Larry Warren, Robert Maddox and Mark Ryan.

© **Haynes North America, Inc. 1994, 1997**

With permission from J.H. Haynes & Co. Ltd.

A book in the Haynes Automotive Repair Manual Series

Printed in the U.S.A.

All rights reserved. No part of this book may be reproduced or transmitted in any form or by any means, electronic or mechanical, including photocopying, recording or by any information storage or retrieval system, without permission in writing from the copyright holder.

ISBN 1 56392 233 9

Library of Congress Catalog Card Number 96-78642

While every attempt is made to ensure that the information in this manual is correct, no liability can be accepted by the authors or publishers for loss, damage or injury caused by any errors in, or omissions from, the information given.

94-352

Contents

Chapter 1 Introduction

Chapter 2 Fuel injection tools

Chapter 3 Part A Basic troubleshooting

Chapter 3 Part B Computer trouble codes

Fuel Injection Diagnostic Manual

Chapter 4 Fuel system pressure relief

Chapter 5 Fuel filters, lines and fittings

Chapter 6 Component check and replacement

Glossary

Index

1 Introduction

1 Why fuel injection?

Today, every new vehicle sold in this country is fuel injected. But it wasn't always that way. For over 75 years, carburetors were used by virtually every manufacturer on all but a tiny handful of special models. Low production costs and high power, not low emissions and high mileage, were the priorities. Even after the original Clean Air Act in 1963, the Big Three stuck with the carburetor. By the mid-Eighties, pushed by increasingly stringent emissions legislation, electronic feedback carburetors had reached a degree of refinement unthinkable 20 years ago. But, despite this undeniable progress, time finally ran out for the venerable carburetor. It simply couldn't meet State or Federal emissions standards. There were five major problems with carburetors:

1   The venturi constriction limits the amount of mixture available at higher engine speeds, which causes power to fall off. The solutions are twofold: Either multiple carburetion, which results in an excessively rich mixture at lower engine speeds, or progressively linked secondaries. The second solution is the better choice, but the result is a more complicated carburetor.

2   The distance between the carburetor and the combustion chambers results in a poorly distributed and uneven mixture. This problem is compounded by the limited amount of space usually available for the intake manifold. So the shape of the intake manifold is usually less-than-ideal for getting the air-fuel mixture to the combustion chamber.

3   Cold starts can be difficult on a carburetor-equipped vehicle. A choke mechanism helps, but because its opening angle is never a perfectly accurate response to the actual operating conditions of the engine during warm-up, it always wastes fuel and diminishes driveability. The use of a choke mechanism also necessitates the addition of a fast idle cam, which opens the throttle plate slightly while the engine is "on choke." The fast idle cam promotes a slightly faster idle during warm-up; without it, the engine might stall.

4   Transient enrichment during acceleration is poor. When the throttle is opened suddenly, it leans out the mixture because fuel flow doesn't keep up with air velocity. The addition of an accelerator pump alleviates this problem by squirting extra fuel into the throat of the carburetor, but the pump wastes fuel and increases emissions.

5   During hard cornering, the fuel in the float bowl may try to "climb" the walls of the bowl, lowering the fuel level in the bowl, raising the float, closing the float valve and blocking fuel delivery. Properly-designed baffles installed in the float bowl can mitigate this tendency.

Vehicles with fuel-injection systems have none of these problems. Fuel is metered much more precisely under all operating conditions because it's sprayed out of an injector, or injectors, under pressure, instead of being drawn through carburetor tubes and passages by pressure differential. When fuel is sprayed under pressure, instead of sucked by pressure differential, the amount of fuel delivered can be increased or decreased much more rapidly. In other words, a fuel injection system responds to changes in engine operating conditions more quickly than a carburetor. And that's why it has totally replaced the carburetor.

2 What is fuel injection?

There are many types of fuel injection, and some of the components differ from one system to another, but the principle is always the same: Pressurized fuel is squirted into the bore of a throttle body by one or two injectors, or directly into each intake port by an injector. Besides the injectors, most of the other components used on one injection system are found on all fuel injection systems. We'll look at each of those components in a moment. But first, let's look at what happens in a fuel injected engine: Fuel is pumped from the fuel tank by an electric fuel pump, through the fuel lines and fuel filter, to the throttle body (throttle body injection systems) or the fuel rail (port fuel injection systems), then through the fuel injector(s) into the airstream. Each injector contains a tiny valve that's opened and closed by a small solenoid. A small computer "fires" the injector by turning on this solenoid, which lifts the valve and allows the pressurized fuel to exit the injector through a precisely machined nozzle that "sprays" the fuel in a manner similar to the nozzle on your garden hose. When the computer deenergizes the solenoid, the valve closes, shutting off the spraying fuel. This cycle of operation occurs over and over, many times a second, as long as the engine is running. Injectors are designed - and warrantied - to last a very long time, at least five years or 50,000 miles. Obviously, injectors are manufactured to a very high degree of precision.

There are two basic types of fuel injection now in use on production vehicles, electronic and mechanical. Mechanical injection, generally referred to as continuous injection, or simply CIS (continuous injection system), was manufactured by Robert Bosch, but is no longer installed on today's vehicles. However, over 6,000,000 vehicles built by European manufacturers for sale in the United States and Canada were equipped with various versions of CIS, and many of those vehicles are still on the road. So we will include them in this book. But first, lets look at the basic components in a typical electronic injection system.

3 Electronic fuel injection systems

Throttle body injection (TBI)

A throttle body injection(TBI) system utilizes a single injector (some units use two) located inside a carburetor-like casting which is installed just like a carburetor, i.e. in the center of the manifold on V6 and V8 engines, or to the side, on inline motors. Because the fuel mist sprayed out of an injector into the airstream has better atomization properties than fuel drawn from a float bowl, and because pressurized fuel is sprayed in a consistently uniform pattern, throttle body injection systems offer more power, better fuel economy and lower emissions than carburetors. However, because of the throttle body's centralized location, some of the air-fuel mixture can still drop out of suspension as it travels from the throttle body to the intake ports, so in this sense it's not that much better than a carbureted vehicle. Still, a lot less fuel droplets fall out of suspension and cling to the walls of the intake manifold, wasting less fuel and resulting in a better-than-a-carburetor mixture. TBI systems are a popular compromise between carburetors and port fuel injection systems because they're inexpensive (they're probably cheaper than most electronic feedback carburetors), they're vastly superior to carburetors for cold starts and they offer better driveability during engine warm-up.

Port fuel injection

A port fuel injection system **(see illustration)** sprays pressurized fuel through an injector at each intake port. Because no fuel is lost in the intake manifold, port injection systems offer more power, better mileage and lower emissions than throttle body injection systems.

Now let's look at the typical components found in an electronic fuel injection system.

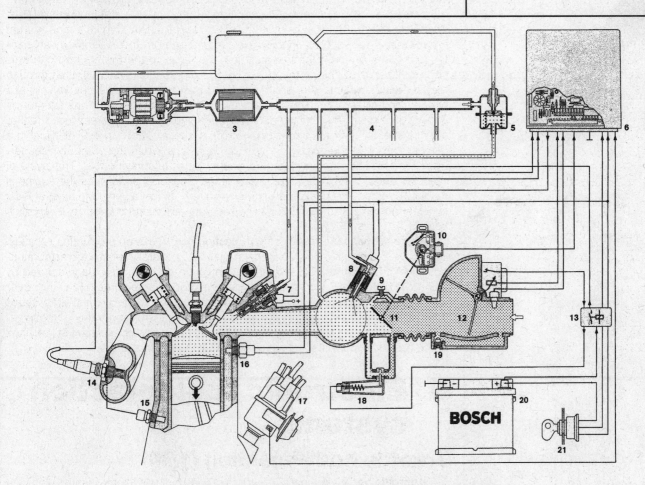

3.1 Schematic of a typical electronic port fuel injection system

1	Fuel tank	9	Idle speed adjusting screw	16	Thermo-time switch
2	Electric fuel pump	10	Throttle valve switch	17	Distributor
3	Fuel filter	11	Throttle valve	18	Auxiliary air valve
4	Distributor pipe	12	Airflow sensor	19	Idle mixture adjusting screw
5	Pressure regulator	13	Relay combination	20	Battery
6	Control unit	14	Lambda (oxygen) sensor	21	Ignition switch
7	Injector	15	Engine coolant temperature		
8	Cold start injector		sensor		

Electric fuel pump

Fuel must be delivered to the fuel injectors at the right pressure, in the right volume and within a fairly consistent temperature range. There must be no fuel vapor or air bubbles in the fuel at the point of delivery. The electric fuel pump **(see illustrations)**, with a little help from the fuel pressure regulator, makes all this happen.

Electric fuel pumps have a number of advantages over mechanical pumps:

1   A mechanical pump, because it's driven by the camshaft or crankshaft, must be bolted to the block. An electric fuel pump can be located anywhere.

2   The speed at which a mechanical pump operates is determined by engine speed; it pumps more slowly at idle, more quickly at higher rpm. An electric pump runs at a constant speed.

3   Engine heat is transferred through a mechanical pump to the fuel; This doesn't happen with an electric pump, which is actually cooled and lubricated by the fuel passing through it.

4   A mechanical pump must create a strong enough vacuum to draw the fuel from the tank, through the fuel filter, through the fuel lines, and into the float bowl of the carburetor. An electric pump pushes fuel to the injectors;

5   An electric pump can be insulated to reduce noise; it can also be located inside the fuel tank, to further reduce noise.

Now, let's look at how the typical pump works: Most electric fuel pumps are the roller vane type, consisting of an electric motor and a rotor inside an integral housing. The rotor has pockets (slots) machined into its outer circumference. A roller (something like a roller bearing) is installed in each pocket. The diameter of the roller is only a few thousandths of an inch less than the distance between the walls of the pocket. Which means the roller is free to move up and down - but not sideways - in its pocket. As the rotor is turned by the electric motor, the rollers are forced outward by centrifugal force, and roll along the inside wall of the pump housing. Because the bearing surfaces (the sides) of the rollers contact both the pump housing wall and the pocket walls, they create a seal. The rotor itself is round; but the pump housing is an oblong shape which allows the rollers to move out farther from the rotor on the suction side than they do on the pressure side. In other words, the space between the rotor and the pump housing on the suction side is larger than the space between the rotor and the housing on the pressure side. So as the rotor turns, a pressure differential, or vacuum, is created on the suction side of the pump.

Air pressure inside the top of the fuel tank is pushing against the surface of the fuel. This is what forces the fuel into that low-pressure area at the suction side of the pump. As the rotor continues to rotate, fuel is trapped in the space between the two adjacent rollers, the rotor and the housing. As this space moves closer to the pressure side, it gets smaller and smaller, raising the pressure of the fuel, which is finally forced out the pump outlet. Of course, when this little sequence is repeated 3500 to 4500 times per minute (the speed of the typical pump), a good deal of pressure can be created. A spring-loaded check valve near the pump outlet maintains fuel pressure at whatever level it's adjusted

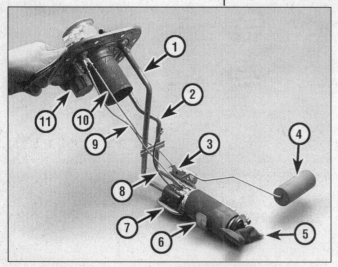

3.2a A typical in-tank fuel pump assembly

1	Fuel feed line	7	Pulsation damper
2	Fuel return line	8	Fuel pump ground wire
3	Fuel level sender	9	Fuel pump hot wire
4	Fuel level float	10	Fuel level sender hot
5	Fuel pump intake		wire
	strainer	11	Splash cup liquid vapor
6	Fuel pump		separator

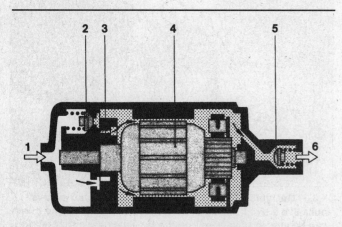

3.2b Cutaway of a typical electric fuel pump for a fuel injection system

1	Fuel inlet	4	Electric motor armature
2	Pressure relief valve	5	Non-return valve
3	Roller cell pump	6	Fuel outlet

for at the factory. The check valve also prevents the fuel pressure from reaching a level so high that it might damage some part of the system.

These pumps can develop a lot of heat. The rollers, which are the hottest parts, are cooled and lubricated by the fuel itself as it travels through the pump. Fuel is even pumped through the electric motor part of the pump, to help cool the motor.

The electric motor uses permanent magnets to create a stationary magnetic field. The armature, the part of the motor that turns, is wound with wire and has a commutator section which gets its current from brushes. The typical pump operates at speeds of 3500 to 4500 rpm. The outlet pressure can be set as low as 10 psi for some throttle body injections systems, to as high as 90 psi for some CIS systems.

Fuel injection systems are equipped with at least one electric fuel pump. High-pressure systems such as Bosch K-Jetronic (CIS) may have two pumps: a transfer pump inside the fuel tank (to prevent cavitation), and a main pump outside the tank. Some GM pumps accomplish the same thing with only one pump by adding an impeller, or centrifugal, pump to the roller vane type described above. The impeller separates vapor out of the fuel before it's delivered to the roller vane pump. And it adds some pressure to the fuel before it enters the roller vane section, thus ensuring a consistent output pressure.

Pressurized fuel is pumped through the fuel filter, fuel lines, fuel rail (port injection) and out the injectors. Because the pump delivers more fuel than the injectors can use, the excess fuel is returned to the fuel tank via the fuel pressure regulator and a return line.

Fuel pump relay

The electric motor in a fuel pump draws several amperes of current. The pump motor is turned on, controlled and turned off by the fuel injection or engine management computer. The pump current is too high for the circuitry in the computer to handle. So a relay **(see illustration)** is used for the actual switching. The computer simply controls the relay. A relay is an electrically operated switch with an input magnetic coil, an armature (spring arm) and output switch contacts. Fine wire is wound around the laminated iron core of the input coil. The laminated core increases the coil's magnetic field strength. The armature is a spring-loaded iron bar in close proximity to the electromagnet. The armature arm itself is usually the spring. The armature is electrically insulated from the relay base.

One electrical output contact is attached to the armature; the other output contact is mounted on a stationary arm. Power from the battery is always available to the stationary arm contact. When the computer sends a small current through the electromagnet coil, its magnetic field pulls down the armature arm, the two contacts close and the large current needed to run the fuel pump moves through the contacts. The relay allows battery current to go to the fuel pump without going through the ignition switch or computer.

Fuel pump relays can be located almost anywhere in the engine compartment or in the passenger area. If you can't find the fuel pump relay, check the owner's manual, or refer to Chapter 4 or Chapter 12 in your Haynes Automotive Repair Manual.

3.3 The typical fuel pump relay usually - but not always - looks like a small plastic or metal box. The relay for the pump can be almost anywhere - on the firewall, near either fender, even under the dash. Sometimes it's by itself; sometimes it's in an array with other relays. The fuel pump relay (A) shown here, on a Lumina APV, is right next to the cooling fan relay (B) and the air conditioning relay (C). If you have difficulty finding the fuel pump relay, refer to Chapter 4 in your Haynes Automotive Repair Manual

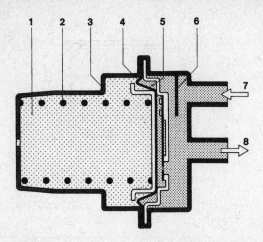

3.4 Cutaway of a typical fuel accumulator assembly

1	Spring chamber	5	Accumulator volume
2	Spring	6	Baffle plate
3	Stop	7	Fuel inlet
4	Diaphragm	8	Fuel outlet

Fuel accumulator

Engines equipped with certain types of fuel injection systems start better if there's already residual pressure and volume in the system during starting. The purpose of an accumulator (see illustration) is to store the requisite amount of fuel at its normal delivery pressure. The accumulator can be installed anywhere in the fuel line between the fuel pump and the injectors. The typical accumulator consists of a housing with a bladder and spring inside. The housing is a two-piece metal stamping. A single pipe serves as a combination inlet and outlet. The inlet/outlet pipe is connected to the fuel line with a T-fitting. The bladder is a balloon-like container made of rubber or plastic-covered fabric. A metal plate is fastened to the back side of the bladder for the spring to push against.

When the fuel pump is energized, the accumulator fills with pressurized fuel in about one second. As fuel pressure in the fuel line builds, fuel flows into the accumulator and pushes the bladder back, compressing the spring. Once the bladder is full, it remains filled, even after the system is turned off (unless it's depressurized). Think of the fuel stored in the accumulator as an emergency reservoir. Should the need arise - for instance, the engine suddenly consumes more fuel than the pump can deliver - fuel at the right pressure and in sufficient volume is available. As soon as this event is over, the pump fills the accumulator once more for the next time.

Let's look at a typical situation: Let's say the car hasn't been operated for several days. Fuel is still being stored in the accumulator under full operating pressure. When you turn the key to start the engine, several things happen. Of course, the cranking circuit is activated. And so is the ignition circuit. And so is the fuel pump circuit. Almost immediately, the fuel pump brings the system up to its operating pressure. But it may take an instant longer before the volume is adequate because the pulse width of the injectors during a cold start is wide enough to bleed off the fuel as it's being pumped. Not to worry. Fuel from the accumulator supplies the injector as soon as the engine is cranked! The engine starts immediately. Shortly after that the fuel pump resupplies the fuel used from the accumulator.

Finally, it should be noted that the accumulator also serves as an anti-vapor lock device by maintaining high residual pressure in the fuel lines, after the vehicle has been turned off, long enough for the fuel to cool off.

Fuel filter

There are actually two types of fuel filters. The first type (see illustration) is a woven plastic screen, strainer or "sock," located inside the fuel tank at the fuel pickup point. Filters must have a known, uniform porosity. In other words, they must possess a specified ability to stop materials down to a certain size. That size is usually expressed in microns. A micron is 4/1,000,000 of an inch (0.00000394 inch).The screen/strainer/sock type filter has a porosity of about 70 microns. It can filter larger dirt particles and can stop water from passing through unless completely submerged. This type of filter isn't usually replaced as a maintenance item, but should the tank ever be filled with dirty gasoline, it could become clogged. If this happens, the filter must be removed and cleaned, or replaced.

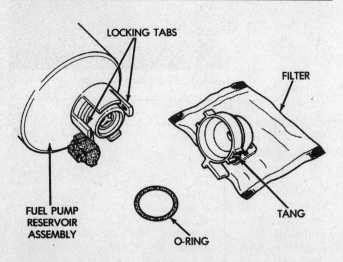

3.5 This sock-type fuel "filter" is the first line of defense for the fuel injection system; it protects the pump itself from debris in the bottom of the fuel tank

The other type of fuel filter **(see illustration)** is a replaceable metal canister which must be changed at the interval specified by the manufacturer. This filter contains a porous material that allows fuel - but not solid particles - to pass through. The filter element in a fuel filter is usually a fibrous or paper-like material; some filters even use a porous metal. A filter must be able to do several things. It must let the fuel pass through, yet it must catch all particles of dirt above a certain size, and it must prevent these particles from working their way through the filter for the service life of the filter.

The engine can't run without the proper supply of fuel at the right pressure. So the size of the filter pores must be large enough to allow fuel to flow through easily. Yet the pores must be small enough to trap dirt that will damage or clog the fuel injectors. Typically, the best compromise is around 10 to 20 microns.

Filters hold on to the dirt by using a chemically-treated porous paper. The chemical treatment makes the paper sticky. When a particle of dirt contacts the paper, it's unable to break free. The filter element is also folded into an accordion shape to increase the surface area of the filter and help trap dirt particles in the folds so they can't break loose. The increased surface area afforded by the accordion arrangement also means fuel can pass through easily even if part of the filter becomes clogged.

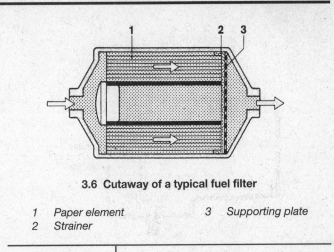

3.6 Cutaway of a typical fuel filter

1	Paper element	3	Supporting plate
2	Strainer		

Fuel pulsation damper

This device **(see illustration)** is similar in appearance to a fuel pressure regulator. It's usually mounted on the fuel rail near the fuel inlet line fitting. A spring-loaded diaphragm inside the damper smoothes out the rhythmical pressure surges from the fuel pump. Think of it as a "shock absorber" for fuel pump pulsations. The damper also muffles fuel pump noise.

Fuel rail

The fuel rail **(see illustration)** serves two purposes. It's a pressurized reservoir for delivering fuel to the injectors, and it stabilizes the fuel pressure at the injectors. The pressure rapidly rises and falls inside the fuel rail as the injectors open and close. If the volume inside the fuel rail is too small, this rapidly fluctuating pressure can affect the amount of fuel injected. On older tubular type fuel rails - they look sort of like big fuel lines - the fuel pressure fluctuates wildly as the injectors open and close because the interior volume of these units is too small. As manufacturers have learned more about this phenomenon, fuel rails have grown larger. On these newer, larger units - generously oversized square section tubing - pressure is steadier at the injectors.

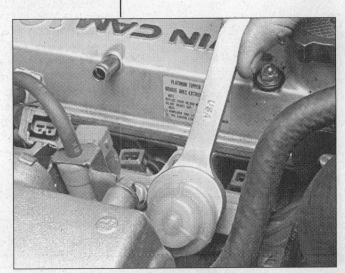

3.7 A typical fuel pulsation damper

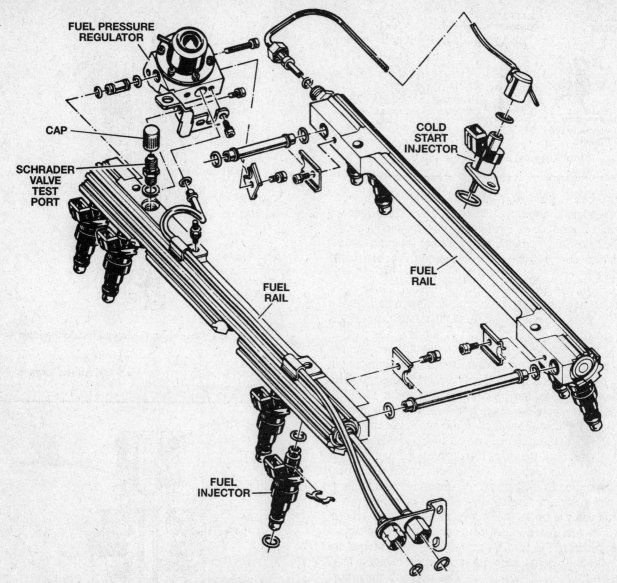

FUEL PRESSURE REGULATOR

CAP

SCHRADER VALVE TEST PORT

COLD START INJECTOR

FUEL RAIL

FUEL RAIL

FUEL INJECTOR

3.8 An exploded view of a typical fuel rail assembly

3.9 A typical throttle-body injector; compared to port type fuel injectors, throttle body injectors are always shorter and larger in diameter, just like this unit

Fuel injector

A throttle-body type injector (**see illustration**) is installed in the mouth of the throttle body. Port type fuel injectors (**see illustration**) are installed between the fuel rail and the intake port. The upper end of each port injector is press-fitted into the fuel rail; an O-ring forms a seal between the injector and the fuel rail. The lower end is also fitted with some sort of O-ring or sealing ring that's supposed to prevent air leaks and protect the injectors from heat and vibration (if these lower O-rings crack, air leaks into the combustion chamber, leans out the mixture and increases idle rpm). Most injectors are protected internally by an inlet fuel screen or filter in the fitting for the fuel line connection. Electronic injectors also have a plug-type electrical connection on top (if there's no electrical connection to the injector, you're looking at a Bosch CIS injector!).

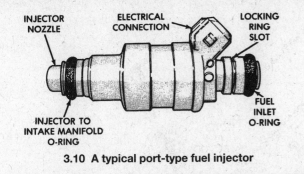

3.10 A typical port-type fuel injector

INJECTOR NOZZLE

ELECTRICAL CONNECTION

LOCKING RING SLOT

FUEL INLET O-RING

INJECTOR TO INTAKE MANIFOLD O-RING

An injector is a solenoid valve **(see illustration).** A coil surrounds a metal armature. On signal from the electronic control unit, current flows through the coil, creating a strong magnetic field. This magnetic field pulls the solenoid toward the armature, compressing the return spring. A needle valve is attached to, or is part of, the solenoid. When the solenoid moves up, the needle valve is lifted off its seat, allowing the pressurized fuel inside the injector to spray out through the orifice or nozzle. A pintle on the tip of the needle valve helps to atomize and distribute the fuel; the shape of the needle, the valve seat, the pintle and the nozzle all determine the spray pattern. When the control unit cuts the current to the injector, the field collapses and spring force slams the valve shut. Some older solenoids must lift up about 10 to 30 thousandths of an inch to open the valve; they take about 2 milliseconds to do so. The lift on some newer injectors is as little as 0.006-inch; opening time on these low-lift units is about 1 millisecond. Because the distance it must travel is so short, the valve responds very quickly. An injector may be held open for as long as 20 milliseconds. Fuel is delivered to the injector at a relatively constant pressure, so the longer the valve is open, the more fuel will be sprayed out. Very precise fuel delivery control is possible with injectors.

The injector(s) in throttle body injection systems are somewhat larger in size than the typical port injector. They must deliver more fuel at a given time because they must serve either all of the engine cylinders (single injector) or half of the engine cylinders (dual injector). The spray pattern is usually broader too.

Electronic solenoid injectors all work the same way. Their differences are primarily in the area of valve design, so that's how injectors are usually classified. Three basic types of injector valves have emerged as the most common on modern vehicles.

The pintle-valve injector **(see illustration)** uses a spring-loaded armature that is magnetically attracted by the solenoid coil when it is energized. (Remember that "armature" and "solenoid" are two different names for the same part of the injector). The armature is pulled up against the return spring by magnetic attraction, lifting a finely-ground pintle out of a tiny spray orifice. The design of the pintle and seat gives the injector the ability to provide a relatively narrow spray pattern. The pintle-valve injector is the original injector design; it's used on most older EFI engines. But you'll still find it on many newer ones as well.

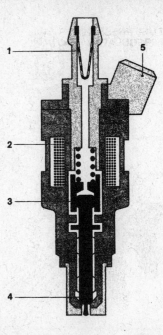

3.11 Cutaway showing the solenoid inside the injector

1 Filter	4 Valve
2 Solenoid winding	5 Electrical terminal
3 Solenoid armature	

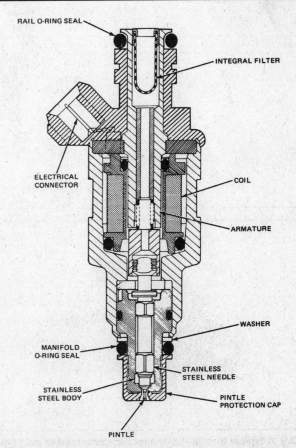

RAIL O-RING SEAL

INTEGRAL FILTER

ELECTRICAL CONNECTOR

COIL

ARMATURE

WASHER

MANIFOLD O-RING SEAL

STAINLESS STEEL NEEDLE

STAINLESS STEEL BODY

PINTLE PROTECTION CAP

PINTLE

3.12 Cutaway of a typical pintle-valve type injector (this is still the most common injector design)

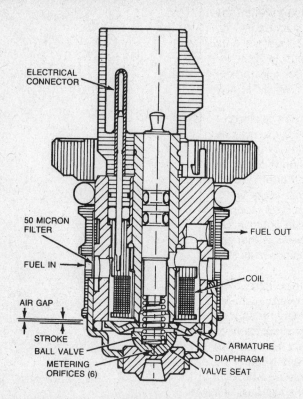

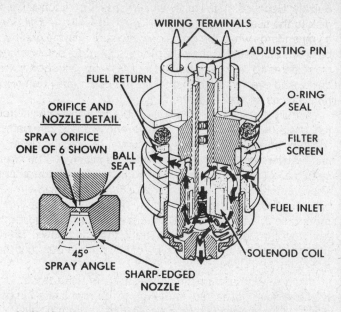

3.13b Another cutaway of the same ball-type injector: Note the fuel flow path through the injector, the multiple-orifice design which allows a greater volume of fuel to be sprayed and the wide spray angle

3.13a Cutaway of a typical ball-type injector (this design is commonly used in throttle body injection systems)

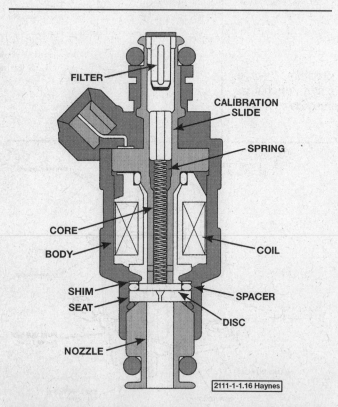

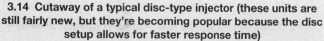

3.14 Cutaway of a typical disc-type injector (these units are still fairly new, but they're becoming popular because the disc setup allows for faster response time)

Despite its widespread use, there are a couple of problems with the pintle-valve injector. First, because of the small contact surface area between the needle and the valve seat, even modest fuel deposits which build up in those areas can create a major restriction to fuel flow through the orifice, which eventually leads to lean fuel delivery problems. Second, the armatures on pintle-valve injectors are usually heavier and larger than the valves used in other injector designs. So their response time is slower. And wear is greater, so the service life of the typical pintle valve injector is shorter than that of other designs.

The ball-type injector (see illustrations) is typically used in throttle body injection systems. The electrical part of a ball-type injector is similar to that of a pintle-valve injector. But its armature (solenoid) is smaller and has a rounded valve tip that mates with a conical seat.

The ball-type injector has several things going for it. The smaller armature design of the ball-type injector allows quicker response time and means less seat wear and fuel fouling. The spray pattern is typically wider. The multiple-orifice design (there are six orifices in the unit shown in the accompanying illustrations) also allows a higher fuel flow rate for a given firing time. And more fuel can be delivered while the valve is open.

The disk-type injector (see illustration) looks similar to pintle-valve and ball-type injectors, except it doesn't have an armature. The magnetic field produced by the coil is directed toward the valve area by the shape of the injector core. The valve itself is a disk-and-seat arrangement with the spray orifice in the center of the seat.

The disk in this type of injector is a much smaller mass to move with a magnetic field, so it's able to respond more quickly. Because of its lighter weight, less spring tension is needed to return the disk to the seat to stop fuel flow. Which means the disk doesn't slam down with as much force when the coil is deenergized. And the greater contact surface area between the disk and the seat reduces point-to-point contact pressure. This design seems to resist the build-up of fuel deposits better than other injector designs. And even when such deposits do occur, they don't restrict fuel flow as significantly as in other designs.

Finally, a few words of warning about injector-driver circuitry: Early electronic fuel injection systems, and a few current systems, use battery voltage to operate the injector solenoids. However, many fuel injection driver circuits now use ballast resistors wired in series with the fuel injectors. The combination of these resistors and the redesigned circuitry inside the injector produces a better injector. The injector solenoid coil winding uses a larger-diameter wire with fewer turns, so it has less electrical resistance. This design allows the solenoid to respond more quickly when energized. And less voltage is required to attain optimal current flow through the solenoid. That's the good news. The bad news is that applying battery voltage to this type of injector will burn out the windings in as little as a tenth of a second.

And wiring ballast resistors in series with injector solenoids also introduces wasteful heat losses. So, in the latest, current-limited injector-driver circuit designs, these resistors have been eliminated with no apparent loss in response time. How did they do it? The driver current rises rapidly to a level sufficient to open the injector, then it's reduced to the minimum level of current necessary to keep the injector valve open. The current rise time, from the moment at which the valve opens to the moment at which the current reaches the maximum safe level (about 6 to 8 amps), is very quick, about 1.2 milliseconds, and it's fixed, i.e. it's always about 1.2 ms. The part of the pulse width that's altered occurs during the second, current-limited (to about .5 amp) phase. So, once again, don't apply battery voltage to a current-limited injector (unless you plan to do so for less than 1.2 milliseconds!).

Fuel pressure regulator

An electric fuel pump doesn't always pump at the same pressure. Voltage and current to the pump vary in accordance with the battery's state of charge. Fuel pressure is also affected by the temperature. The fuel pressure regulator **(see illustration)** helps maintain an even pressure despite these deviations. The latest regulators alter the fuel pressure in accordance with engine operating conditions, such as changes in manifold pressure or vacuum, some are even computer controlled.

A fuel pressure regulator is a fairly simple device. It consists of a metal housing with a spring-loaded diaphragm and a valve attached to the fuel side of the diaphragm. A fuel inlet tube directs fuel to the valve; the inlet tube and the fuel side of the housing are usually an integral piece. An outlet pipe extends into the fuel side of the housing and serves as the seat for the valve. When the valve is seated, fuel is blocked; when it's open, fuel flows through the outlet pipe. A vacuum or pressure reference tube connects the back (spring) side of the diaphragm housing to the intake manifold.

Here's how it works: Fuel from the pump fills the fuel lines, the fuel rail, the fuel injectors and the fuel side of the pressure regulator. The diaphragm spring which holds the valve against its seat is designed to compress when the pressure against the diaphragm reaches the upper limit of the operating range of the system. When fuel pressure ex-

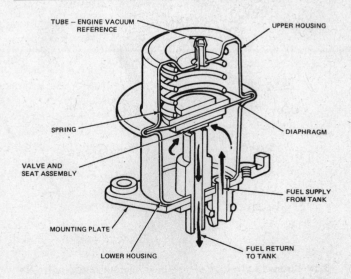

3.15 Cutaway of a typical fuel pressure regulator assembly

ceeds this upper limit, the diaphragm is pushed back against the compressed spring, the valve, which is attached to the diaphragm, is lifted off its seat, fuel flows through the outlet pipe and returns to the fuel tank. As fuel flows out of the regulator, the fuel pressure in the fuel rail and the regulator drops back within its operating range, and below spring pressure. The spring pushes the diaphragm back to its normal position, seating the valve and blocking fuel flow.

The vacuum or pressure port on the back side of the diaphragm also affects the total force applied against the diaphragm. If pressure from the intake manifold is routed through the port to the back side of the diaphragm, it acts like an extra spring applying additional force to the diaphragm. So it will take a higher fuel pressure to open the regulator valve. Until that higher pressure is reached, the fuel pressure at the injector nozzles is higher. So they spray more fuel in a given amount of time, resulting in a richer air-fuel mixture.

Let's look at some typical examples: At low speed, the throttle is only partially open, so there's a vacuum in the intake manifold. A vacuum signal is transmitted to the pressure regulator, lowering the pressure on the spring side of the diaphragm. So less fuel pressure is needed to push the diaphragm against its spring and open the regulator valve. Which means less fuel will be sprayed out the injector nozzles. But when you step on the gas, the throttle plates open, intake manifold vacuum drops, the vacuum signal to the regulator vanishes, and there's greater pressure pushing against the diaphragm. Now it takes more pressure to push the diaphragm against its spring, so the valve stays seated until a higher pressure is reached. In the meantime, the injector nozzles have more fuel pressure available, resulting in a richer air-fuel mixture.

The vacuum line between the manifold and the pressure regulator on turbocharged vehicles carry pressure as well as vacuum. When you mash the throttle on a turbo, the engine revs build, the turbo pumps air into the intake manifold and pressure in the manifold goes up to, say, seven pounds of boost. A seven psi pressure signal is transmitted to the pressure regulator through the connecting hose from the intake manifold. So the valve in the regulator has an extra seven pounds psi forcing it closed. Which means more fuel pressure will be needed to overcome the pressure holding the regulator valve closed. So the fuel pressure at the injectors increases, and more fuel is sprayed through the injector nozzles each time they're opened. The result is a richer mixture, which is just what a turbocharged vehicle needs under boost conditions.

Fuel hoses and lines

Pressurization of the fuel provides a nice spray pattern at each injector nozzle, but it poses special problems for fuel hoses and lines. The pressure in a carbureted system is typically no more than 4 to 6 psi, but a throttle body injection system is typically pressurized to around 9 to 15 psi, a port fuel injection system, to about 30 to 50 psi. Which is why fuel injection systems use specially designed fuel hoses and lines to connect components like the fuel pump, fuel filter, accumulator and fuel rail (port systems) or throttle body (TBI systems). Fuel injected vehicles use rigid steel tubing under the vehicle, which can be securely attached to the frame or pan. Steel lines can withstand high pressure easily. They're also coated or plated to resist corrosion. If you ever have to replace metal fuel lines, don't substitute copper or aluminum - they'll crack.

Flexible synthetic hoses are used for bridging the gap between the rigidly mounted steel fuel lines and the fuel injection system. Because the engine shakes and vibrates, it's not feasible to run metal lines directly to the fuel injection system. Two types of flexible hoses are used. One type has three layers: The inner layer is a fuel-resistant, rubber-like, synthetic material made by DuPont. This material, known commercially as Neoprene, doesn't swell or dissolve when it comes in contact with fuel the way rubber does. The next layer is a woven polyester fabric which gives the hose strength against pressure and flexing. The outer layer of the hose is another synthetic rubber material, such as Hypalon, which allows it to resist abrasion and weathering. The other type of "hose" is really an extruded plastic (nylon) tubing. Nylon tubing is commonly found on fuel-injected vehicles because of its ability to withstand higher pressures.

There are many types of hoses designed for different applications on automobiles. When servicing a fuel-injected vehicle, NEVER substitute hoses or lines designed for use on carbureted vehicles. Carburetor hoses will not stand up to the higher operating pressures of fuel injection systems. Always use the same type and size hose or line specified by the manufacturer.

Throttle body

This carburetor-like aluminum casting **(see illustrations)** houses the throttle plate, or throttle valve, which regulates airflow to the engine. The more it's open, the greater the airflow into the engine. On the outside, you'll see the throttle linkage, a throttle position sensor, some vacuum ports and, on some systems, an idle air system of some sort. If the throttle body is for a throttle body injection system, it also houses one or two injectors and a fuel pressure regulator.

Input: Information sensors

A sensor is an input device that converts one form of energy to another. Since a computer can only read voltage signals, an information sensor must convert motion, pressure, temperature, light and other forms of energy to voltage. Automobile sensors come in many forms - switches, timers, resistors, transformers and generators. Sensors monitor various engine operating conditions such as air

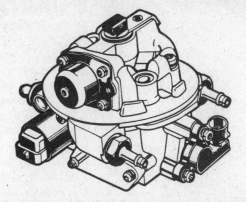

3.16a A typical throttle body designed for a throttle-body injection system: This unit was part of a GM Digital Fuel Injection system, once used on Buicks, Oldsmobiles and Cadillacs

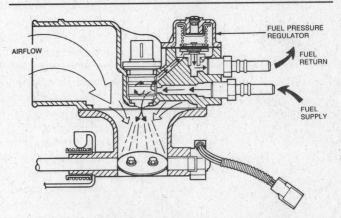

3.16b Cutaway of a typical throttle-body assembly for a throttle-body injection system

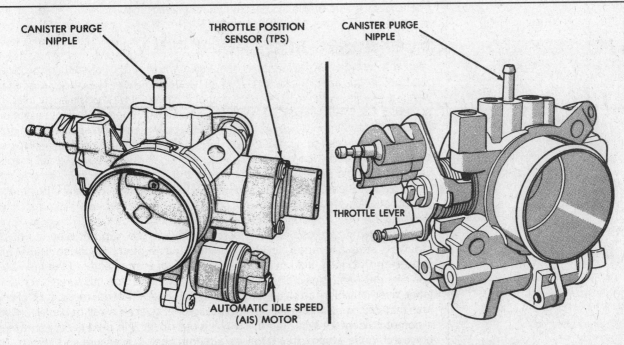

3.16c Typical (Chrysler) throttle body unit for a port-type fuel injection system

flow, air mass, air temperature, coolant temperature, exhaust oxygen content, manifold absolute pressure, throttle position, etc. and transmit this information to a computer in the form of low-voltage signals. Some information sensors are simply digital switches, i.e. they're "on-off" devices. They send no signal to the computer until a certain threshold in coolant temperature, throttle position, etc. has been exceeded. Most information sensors are analog devices, that is, they react to changes in the condition they're monitoring by altering a continuous voltage signal to the computer.

Most information sensors are resistors. A resistor can send an analog signal that's proportional to temperature, pressure, motion or other variables. A resistor, however, cannot generate its own voltage. It can only modify a voltage applied to it. Therefore, automobile resistive sensors must operate with a reference voltage from the computer. This is a fixed voltage applied by the computer to the resistor. Most engine control systems operate with a five-volt reference voltage (Bosch, Chrysler, GM, Ford EEC-IV, for example). Some operate with a nine-volt reference voltage (Ford EEC-I, II and III). In any case, reference voltage must be less than minimum battery voltage to prevent inaccurate sensor signals.

Let's look at how a typical sensor works: The computer sends a reference voltage to the sensor. As sensor resistance changes, so does the return voltage. Okay. Now, let's assume that a temperature sensor can be calibrated to send a 0-volt return signal at 0 degrees F. and a 5-volt return signal at 250 degrees F.. Every 1-degree temperature change causes a 0.02-volt change in the return voltage. The computer reads these 20-millivolt increments and computes them to "air temperature" or "engine coolant temperature."

Manifold pressure sensor

The manifold pressure sensor was Introduced by Bosch in 1967 on its Electronically Controlled Gasoline Injection (ECGI). In 1969, the ECGI system was renamed Bosch D-Jetronic and installed in the VW Type 3 (fastback, notchback and squareback). For the next six years, the D-Jet system was installed on a wide variety of European vehicles. It was last used on the 1975 Volvo 164E and the 1975 Mercedes 450 (the next year, both switched to K-Jetronic).

Manifold pressure sensors, often referred to as MAP sensors, are still used on some fuel injection systems as an alternative to air-flow or air mass sensors. The idea behind a manifold pressure sensor is that manifold pressure is an indication of engine load. How does it work? A pressure sensor is connected to the intake manifold between the throttle and the intake valves (see illustration). The sensor houses two diaphragm cells that expand and contract in accordance with changing pressure. The inside of one diaphragm cell is vented to the atmosphere; the space surrounding both cells is vented to intake manifold pressure. When manifold pressure goes up, the cells compress, and pull an iron core armature into a coil, changing the electrical signal to the control unit. A rising manifold-pressure indicates an increasing load, so the control unit increases the pulse-width of the injectors. This signal is a succession of analog actions requiring no digital computation (D-Jetronic control units are analog computers!). When manifold pressure goes down, as it does at idle, for instance, the diaphragm cells expand, pushing the core out of the coil. Now, the analog voltage signal tells the control unit to reduce the pulse-width, reducing the amount of fuel injected.

The manifold pressure sensor has a couple of corrective features to account for differences in temperature and altitude. An air-temperature sensor signals the control unit to correct the injector pulse width for colder, denser air. Altitude compensation is provided by the venting of one cell

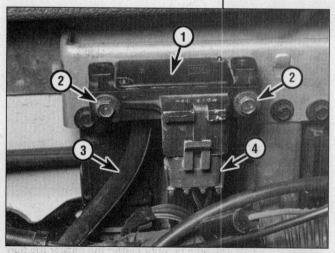

3.17 A typical manifold absolute pressure sensor assembly (this one's mounted on the firewall on a Chevy Corsica

1 MAP sensor assembly
2 Mounting screws
3 MAP sensor vacuum line
4 MAP sensor electrical connector

to the atmosphere. In the part-load range, both manifold pressure and atmospheric pressure are reduced as the altitude increases, so the fuel injection signal must be adjusted for the thinner air.

Bosch no longer regards manifold-pressure sensing as a sufficiently accurate measurement of engine load. Modern systems measure air flow (L-Jetronic and K-Jetronic, for example), or they measure air mass (LH-Jetronic). Manifold pressure sensing was still widely used by GM, Chrysler, AMC and some Toyotas until fairly recently, but most manufacturers have now abandoned it.

Vane, or flap-type, airflow sensor

The vane or flap type airflow meter was introduced by Bosch during the 1970s, and was used on many electronic fuel injection systems during the 1970s and 1980s, such as Bosch L-Jetronic and Motronic, as well as many Ford and Japanese applications.

The vane sensor is positioned somewhere in the intake tract between the air cleaner housing and the throttle body. It's easily identified by the unique shape of its housing, which always has a semi-circular bulge in its housing (see illustrations). The sensor consists of a hinged vane, or flap, positioned in the air stream, which deflects, or swings open, when pushed by the mass of incoming air drawn into the engine through the throttle valve. The greater the airflow, the greater the movement of the flap. When the air vane is pushed open by incoming air, a damper flap cushions the movement of the air vane by pressing against the air in the damping chamber (the semi-circular portion of the meter housing). This reduces fluttering caused by manifold pressure variations from the opening and closing of the intake valves. The damper flap is cleverly designed: It's the same area as the vane and it pivots on the same axis, at a right angle to the vane. Even the slightest pulse of pressure (a pressure drop of as little 0.017 psi) rotates the air vane. But it also rotates the damper flap into the damping chamber, neutralizing the effect of the pressure change. During a sudden throttle opening, the air vane snaps open but its final travel is cushioned by the damper flap as it pushes against the air in the damping chamber. The vane is also lightly spring-loaded to insure that it returns to its closed position when no air is moving through the sensor.

3.18a A typical vane-type airflow sensor (this is a Japanese unit, but American and German ones look virtually identical). You can always spot a vane-type sensor because of its unique semicircular housing for the damper flap

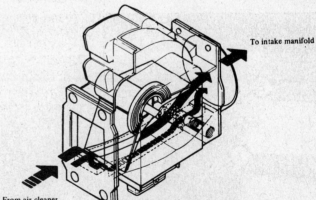

3.18b Cutaway of a typical vane-type airflow sensor: As air flows through the sensor, it opens a spring-loaded flap that rotates the wiper arm on a potentiometer; the farther the flap opens, the greater the resistance through the potentiometer circuit, and the lower the voltage. The control unit interprets this inverse voltage signal to determine the volume of air entering the engine

3.19 As the vane or flap opens, this arm, known as a *wiper*, also rotates, crossing a series of resistors and conductor straps, which increases resistance and alters the voltage signal back to the computer, letting it know that airflow has increased, so that the computer can alter the pulse width of the injectors accordingly

Air flow measurements are more critical at low speeds. So the shape of the airflow sensor housing opposite the air vane is designed to produce a logarithmic relationship between air passing through and the angle of the flap. In other words, a doubling of the air vane angle means that air flow has increased 10 times (maximum air flow is 30 times the minimum). This clever design allows the airflow sensor to make its most sensitive measurements at low air flows.

A potentiometer **(see illustration)** is mounted on the same shaft as the air vane. As the vane rotates, a moving electrical contact known as a wiper also rotates, crossing a series of resistors and conductor straps on a ceramic base, and increasing resistance. These resistors oppose current flow from a fixed-voltage input from the control unit. So as the amount of air passing through the meter increases, the voltage signal to the electronic control unit decreases. The control unit interprets this inverted analog voltage signal by increasing the width of the injection pulse to enrichen the air-fuel mixture ratio.

Vane-type airflow sensors admit extra air through a bypass channel to permit adjustment of the idle mixture. When the screw is turned counterclockwise, more air is allowed to pass through the channel, and the mixture is richened. When the screw is turned clockwise, less bypass air is admitted, leaning the mixture.

The vane-type airflow sensor provides direct measurement of the air intake by the engine. Because it measures air flow, it compensates for changes which occur in the engine during its service life. Factors such as normal engine wear, combustion chamber deposits, valve settings, etc. influence air flow. And recirculation of EGR gases has no effect on the air measured by the meter.

But there are some limitations to this design. Vacuum leaks can be caused by a loose clamp or gasket, or by a tear in the flexible intake duct or in the vacuum hoses. The airflow sensor is usually mounted some distance from the intake manifold, so any air that enters the intake system between the sensor and the valves is unmeasured, or false air. The engine gets no fuel to match that air. The result can be lean mixtures that can cause driveability problems such as hard starting, rough idle, low CO and stumbling.

Another problem with the vane-type airflow sensor: It measures the volume of the air intake, but the engine burns weight, or mass of air. Colder air is heavier and requires more fuel than the same volume of warm air. An air temperature sensor mitigates this problem somewhat, but not entirely.

In most vehicles (those without an anti-backfire valve in the air vane), the vane can be damaged by backfires. The best thing you can do to prevent this situation from occurring is keep your foot off the accelerator during starting!

Air-mass ("hot-wire") sensor

An air-mass sensor **(see illustration)**, also known as a hot-wire sensor, is an unobtrusive black plastic or cast aluminum cylinder located in the intake tract between the air cleaner housing and the throttle body. If you remove the sensor for a better look, you'll see small platinum resistance wires suspended inside the cylinder. The wires are smaller in diameter than a human hair - about 70 micrometers, or less than 1/10 of a millimeter. Each wire looks - and is - delicate. It looks like it could break rather easily just from nor-

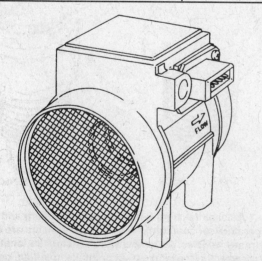

3.20 A typical mass airflow ("hot wire") sensor; this type of sensor measures air mass, or weight, by monitoring the cooling effect of the air as it moves across the heated wires

mal vibration. But in actual service, this type of sensor has proven more reliable than the vane-type sensor. An ingenious suspension system prevents the wires from snapping in two, and a pair of mesh protective screens at either end of the sensor cylinder protect the wires from damage from incoming particulate matter as well as from backfires. In the unlikely event that a wire should break, the engine will run - albeit in a "limp-home" mode - well enough to get you home. (You can simulate limp-home mode by unplugging the air-mass sensor connector on a warmed-up engine, then driving the vehicle).

The air-mass sensor is completely electronic. It "measures" air flow as a function of the amount of current flowing through heated wires. (It gets its hot-wire name from this heated-wire design; this is also the source of the "H" in Bosch LH Motronic systems). The air-mass sensor has several significant advantages over the vane-type air flow sensor used on L-Jetronic type systems.

First, it measures air mass, or weight (in physics, mass and weight aren't exactly the same thing, but they're proportional, so for the purposes of this discussion, we'll use them more or less interchangeably). The air-fuel mixture ratio is really the ratio of the masses of the substances involved. A certain mass of fuel is mixed with a certain mass of air. Measuring the mass also eliminates the need for compensation sensors for air temperature and altitude. And eliminating compensation corrections simplifies the control unit program.

An air-mass sensor has no moving parts. The system monitors the cooling effect of intake air as it moves across the heated wires. Imagine a fan blowing across an electric heater. If the fan motor is set too its Low position, the cooling effect on the heater wires is minimal; turn the fan motor to its High position and the cooling effect increases. The control circuit uses this effect to measure how much air is passing over the hot wires. The wires are heated to a specific temperature differential which is 180 degrees F. above the incoming air when the ignition is turned on. As soon as air begins to flow over the wire, the wire cools. The control circuit applies more voltage to keep the wire at its original temperature differential. This creates a voltage signal which the control unit monitors. The greater the air flow, the more the wire cools and the greater the voltage signal.

A hot-wire sensor responds much more quickly than the moving vane of an air-flow sensor. Changes in air-mass are followed by corrected measurements within 1 to 3 milliseconds. The wire in an air-mass sensor offers virtually zero resistance to the air moving past it. Even at maximum airflow, the drag on the wire, measured in milligrams, is insignificant. Air mass measurement by hot wire improves driveability, stability and reliability. Even racers use it! Soon, it will totally replace air flow measurement by vane-type sensors.

Air and coolant temperature sensors

All fuel injection systems use temperature sensors to measure air and engine temperature because temperature affects intake air density and air-fuel mixture ratio. A temperature sensor can be a simple on-off switch that opens or closes when a certain threshold temperature is reached. Most temperature sensors, however, are thermistors. A thermistor **(see illustration)** , also known as a negative temperature coefficient (NTC) resistor, is a special kind of variable resistor whose resistance decreases as the temperature increases. The bimetal element used in a thermistor has a highly predictable and repeatable property: The amount of current and voltage it conducts at a certain temperature is always the same. This characteristic makes the thermistor an excellent analog temperature sensor. As the

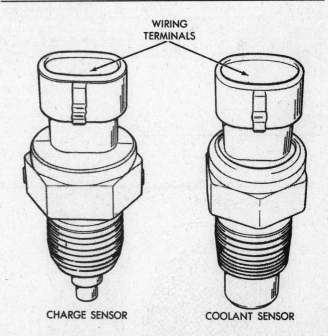

WIRING TERMINALS

CHARGE SENSOR   COOLANT SENSOR

3.21 Typical air (charge) temperature sensor (left) and coolant temperature sensor (right). Both of these sensors are used on many vehicles. Air temperature sensors are located somewhere in the intake tract or intake manifold; coolant temperature sensors are often located near the thermostat. Refer to the VECI label to find the air and coolant temperature sensors on your vehicle.

temperature increases, the resistance decreases, and the current and voltage increase. The control unit uses this rising voltage signal, along with signals from other sensors, to alter the injector pulse width or the fuel pressure as the engine warms up.

Oxygen sensor

The oxygen sensor **(see illustration)**, also referred to as a Lambda sensor (Bosch), an exhaust gas oxygen (EGO) sensor (Ford) or simply an O2 sensor, is the most important information sensor on a fuel-injected vehicle. The oxygen sensor compares the difference between the amount of oxygen in the exhaust and the amount of oxygen in the ambient air, and it expresses the results of this comparison as an analog voltage signal that varies between 0 and 1 volt.

The oxygen sensor is based on the Lambda concept pioneered by the Robert Bosch Corporation. Lambda is the Greek symbol which engineers use to indicate the ratio of one number to another. When discussing the control of the air-fuel ratio, lambda refers to the ratio of excess air to stoichiometric air quantity. (That's why Bosch calls the oxygen sensor a lambda sensor).

At the stoichiometric (ideal) air-fuel ratio of 14.7:1, the maximum amount of air available combines with fuel. There's no air left over, and there's no shortage of air. Lambda, therefore, equals 1. But if the mixture ratio is lean, say 15, 16 or 17:1, there's air left over after combustion. The lambda ratio of excess air to the ideal amount of air is now greater than 1, say, 1.05, 1.09, 1.13, etc. And if the mixture is rich, say, 12, 13 or 14.:1, there's a shortage of air, so the lambda ratio is less than 1, say, 0.95, 0.91, 0.87, etc. If the air-fuel ratio is richer than

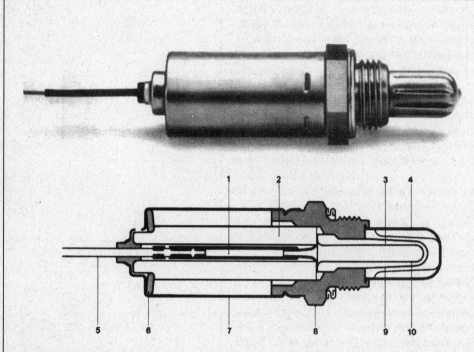

3.22 Typical oxygen sensor (also known as a Lambda sensor or simply an O_2 sensor)

1	Contact	6	Disc spring
2	Supporting ceramic	7	Protective sleeve (air side)
3	Sensor ceramic	8	Housing (-)
4	Protective tube (exhaust side)	9	Electrode (-)
5	Electrical connection	10	Electrode (+)

11.7:1 or leaner than 18:1 (lambda ratios of less than 0.8 or greater than 1.20, respectively) the engine won't run.

The oxygen sensor is really a galvanic battery which generates a low-voltage signal between 0.1 and 0.9 volt (100 to 900 millivolts). When oxygen content in the exhaust is low (rich mixture), sensor voltage is high (450 to 900 millivolts). When exhaust oxygen content is high (lean mixture), sensor voltage is low (100 to 450 millivolts). The oxygen sensor voltage changes fastest near a lambda ratio of 1 (air-fuel ratio of 14.7:1), making it ideal for maintaining a stoichiometric ratio.

The oxygen sensor consists of two platinum electrodes separated by a zirconium dioxide ($ZrO2$) ceramic electrolyte. $ZrO2$ attracts free oxygen ions, which are negatively charged. One electrode is exposed to ambient (outside) air through vents in the sensor shell and collects many O2 ions, becoming a more negative electrode. The other electrode is exposed to exhaust gas and it too collects O2 ions. But it collects fewer ions and becomes more positive, compared to the other electrode. When there's a large difference between the amount of oxygen in the exhaust and the amount of oxygen in the air (rich mixture), the negative oxygen ions on the outer electrode move to the positive inner electrode, creating a direct current. The sensor then develops a voltage between the two electrodes. When there is more oxygen in the exhaust (lean mixture), there is less difference between O2 ions on the electrodes and a lower voltage.

The important thing to remember here is that an oxygen sensor measures oxygen; it doesn't measure air-fuel ratio. Which is one reason why the sensor, and the computer, can be fooled. For example, let's say the engine misfires, which means no oxygen is consumed in combustion. Most of the oxygen is still in the unburned exhaust mixture, so the sensor delivers a "lean mixture" signal. The computer reads this false signal and logically, but mistakenly, richens the fuel mixture!

All oxygen sensors work on the principle explained above, but construction details differ. Some sensors have a single-wire connector for the output signal. The ground connection exists between the sensor shell and the exhaust manifold or pipe. Other sensors have a 2-wire connector that provides a ground connection through the computer. Single-wire and 2-wire sensors are not interchangeable.

Most sensors have a silicone boot that protects the sensor and provides a vent opening for ambient air circulation. The boot position is important for these sensors. If it is pushed too far down on the body, it will block the air vent and create an inaccurate signal voltage. In 1986, Chrysler introduced an oxygen sensor that has no air vent. Ambient air for the inner electrode is absorbed through the insulation on the connector wiring.

The typical unheated oxygen sensor must warm up to at least 572 degrees F. before it generates an accurate signal, and its fastest switching time doesn't occur until it reaches a temperature of about 1472 degrees F. This is why the engine management system must remain in open-loop fuel control when the engine is cold. Some manufacturers have solved this problem by installing heated oxygen sensors. These sensors have an extra wire that delivers 1 ampere or less current to the sensor electrodes whenever the ignition switch is turned to On. Heated sensors warm up more quickly during cold-engine starts and they stay warm enough to provide an accurate voltage signal regardless of operating conditions. Heated oxygen sensors are a must on turbocharged vehicles, where the oxygen sensor is installed downstream from the turbo. The turbo absorbs so much of the heat energy in the exhaust that it prolongs sensor warm-up on a cold engine. On turbo vehicles, an unheated oxygen sensor can also cool off to a temperature below its minimum operating temperature during long periods of idling and low-speed operation. A heated oxygen sensor solves these problems.

Oxygen sensors are always installed in the exhaust manifold(s) or in the exhaust pipe very close to the manifold, but exact locations vary for different engines. Some V6 and V8 engines have a sensor in each manifold; others use only a single sensor. Some sensors are difficult to reach because they're located in the lower regions of the engine compartment. Others are installed in the center of the exhaust manifold, and access is easy.

Throttle position sensor

The throttle position sensor (TPS) **(see illustration)** tells the electronic control unit whether the engine is at idle, at wide open throttle or at some point in between. A TPS can be a simple wide-open throttle (WOT) switch or idle position switch which indicates the extremes of throttle travel with a high or low voltage. However, the typical TPS is a potentiometer.

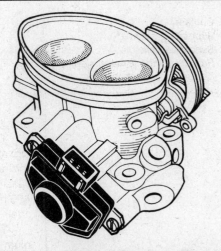

3.23 You can always find the throttle position sensor because, like the unit shown here, it's always a small, (usually) black, plastic box attached to the end of the throttle valve shaft

A potentiometer is a variable resistor with three terminals. A reference voltage is applied to one end of the resistor, and the other end is grounded. The third terminal is connected to a movable wiper, or contact, that slides across the resistor. Depending on the position of this sliding contact - near the supply end or the ground end of the resistor - return voltage will be high or low. Since the current through the resistor remains constant, so does the temperature. So the resistance doesn't change because of variations in temperature. The result is a constant voltage drop across the resistor so that the return voltage changes only in relation to sliding contact movement. A potentiometer-type TPS is both a load and a speed sensor. It tells the control unit not only the position of the throttle, but the speed with which it's being opened or closed.

Processing: The electronic control unit

Also known as the electronic control module, this small microcomputer **(see illustration)** is the "brain" of the fuel injection system. It receives analog (continuously variable) voltage signals from the information sensors, converts them to digital (on-off signals) and processes this information in accordance with its program or "map." Despite its complexity, the control unit is one of the most reliable components in the entire system. The failure rate of computers is remarkably low. Which means it should be the last component you suspect in the event there's a problem with your fuel injection system.

3.24 The typical electronic control unit is a compact rectangular box, usually aluminum, sometimes plastic; you'll find it behind the left or right kick panel, under the dash, under a seat or inside the console

Output: System actuators

The outputs, or actuators, of the electronic engine management system are those computer-controlled devices - fuel injectors, idle speed motor, EGR solenoid, EVAP canister purge solenoid, etc. - which can be altered in some way to change the operating conditions of the engine. Fuel injectors are the principal actuators in electronic fuel injection systems. Two factors influence the quality and accuracy of their delivery: When they're opened, and how long they're open.

Timing the injection system

Not all electronic fuel injection systems "fire" (open) the injectors in the same sequence. A popular misconception is that injectors open every time the intake valve opens. While it's true that each injector must open every other crankshaft revolution, it doesn't necessarily open at the instant before the intake valve opens on the intake stroke. Three distinct strategies are employed by manufacturers for timing their injectors; of course, there are many more names for these three groups than there are real differences. Figuring out exactly what kind of injector timing a system uses can be tricky.

Group injection - In this type of system, half of the injectors are fired at the same time. For example, on a four-cylinder engine, two injectors are fired during one crankshaft revolution, then the other two injectors are fired during the next crank revolution. On a V8 engine, four injectors fire during the first revolution of the crank; then the other four fire on the next go-round. When a group of two, or four, injectors fire, they fire simultaneously. In this type of system, when a group of injectors fires, clouds of injected fuel vapor wait momentarily in each intake port for the intake valve to open because not all the intake valves served by that group are going to be opening at the same time.

Group injection was used on many VW, Porsche, Saab, Volvo and Mercedes models equipped with Bosch D-Jetronic during the late 1960s and early 1970s. Cadillacs of the 1970s also used a similar system. Some current Ford and Nissan engines are equipped with contemporary systems which utilize group injection. The Nissan system uses a program that fires like a conventional group injection system under normal operating conditions, but it switches to simultaneous double fire (see below) for very rich fuel requirements.

Except for the Nissan system, group injection systems require a less complex computer program than other pulsed electronic port injection systems. The control unit used on D-Jetronic and early L-Jet systems was an analog computer; simple programs are a must on analog computers. Other components on early group injection systems were similarly rudimentary: D-Jet systems used an injector timing device similar to a pair of mechanical ignition points! Crankshaft position sensors are used on modern group injection systems.

Simultaneous double-fire injection - In a simultaneous double-fire system, all the injectors are fired together as one big group every crankshaft revolution. But only half of the fuel needed by each cylinder is injected each time its injector opens. In other words, each injector fires twice before its corresponding intake valve opens to admit the air/fuel mixture. Again, as in a group injection system, the injected fuel vapors form a cloud outside their respective valve while they wait for it to open.

Double-fire systems use less computer power than sequential systems, yet still manage to deliver very good performance and response. The only disadvantage to this system is that the fuel pressure in the fuel rail tends to drop when all the injectors open at once. The addition of a fuel accumulator (previously described) to the system usually solves this problem.

Sequential fuel injection - In a sequential system, the injectors are fired one at a time, in the spark plug firing order. Each fuel injector delivers fuel just outside its assigned intake valve. Fuel delivery is timed to occur immediately before, during or after intake valve opening, depending on engine rpm and intake manifold air velocity. This system currently produces the highest performance and fuel efficiency.

Fuel injector pulse width

Injector "on-time," known as pulse width **(see illustration)**, is controlled by the electronic control unit. Pulse width is the length of time - measured in milliseconds - that the injector is energized. The electronic control unit alters injector pulse width in relation to the amount of fuel the engine needs. It takes into account such factors as airflow, air temperature, throttle position, coolant temperature, oxygen content in the exhaust, crankshaft position, vehicle speed, and even fuel temperature. The control unit samples these conditions many times a second, so the pulse width changes constantly. A short pulse width delivers less fuel, a longer pulse width, more. Basically, when the oxygen sensor detects a rich condition in the exhaust gas stream, the electronic control unit shortens the pulse width to lean out the air-fuel mixture; when a lean condition is detected, the control unit lengthens the pulse width to enrichen the mixture. But keep in mind that this basic feedback loop is also influenced by the other variables mentioned above.

The pulse width is related to the duty cycle. The duty cycle is the ratio of injector on-time to total on-and-off time. In other words, it's a variable percentage of one complete injector operating cycle. A simple example will make this relationship clearer: Let's say that the pulse width is 1 mil-

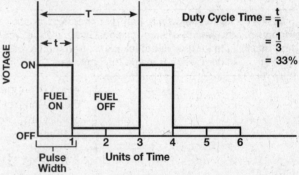

T = Complete Cycle Time
t = Duty Cycle Time (Pulse Width)

$$\text{Duty Cycle Time} = \frac{t}{T}$$
$$= \frac{1}{3}$$
$$= 33\%$$

SHOT DUTY CYCLE (PUSLE WIDTH), MINIMUM FUEL INJECTION

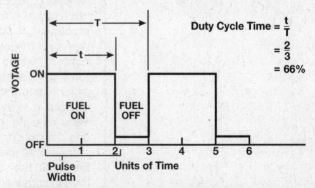

$$\text{Duty Cycle Time} = \frac{t}{T}$$
$$= \frac{2}{3}$$
$$= 66\%$$

LONG DUTY CYCLE (PUSLE WIDTH), MAXIMUM FUEL INJECTION

3.25 Pulse width is the length of time - measured in milliseconds - that the injector is energized; pulse width is controlled by the electronic control unit

lisecond and the total cycle time is 3 milliseconds. Therefore, the duty cycle is the pulse width divided by the total cycle time, or 1/3, or 33 percent. Another example: The pulse width is 2 milliseconds and the total cycle time is 3 milliseconds. So the duty cycle is 2/3, or 66 percent. The duty cycle changes in response to changes in engine loads and in response to the amount of oxygen present in the exhaust stream. The pulse width, and the total cycle time, change in relation to engine speed. The higher the engine rpm, the higher the frequency of the pulse width and the total cycle time. In other words, as engine rpm goes up, the time available for pulse width and total cycle time shortens. To keep from getting confused, just remember that pulse width and total cycle times are always expressed as units of time (milliseconds), while duty cycle is always expressed as a percentage of the total cycle time.

4 Continuous injection system (CIS)

The Bosch Continuous Injection System **(see illustration)** is found only on European automobiles, such as Audi, BMW, Ferrari, Lotus, Mercedes-Benz, Peu-

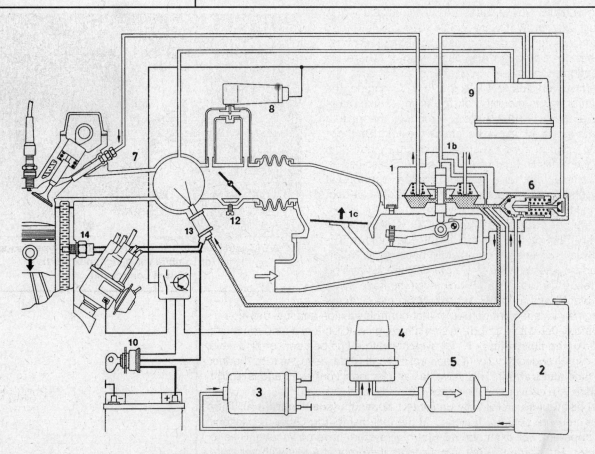

4.1 Schematic of a typical Bosch Continuous Injection System (CIS)

1	Mixture control unit	5	Fuel filter	11	Mixture adjustment screw
1b	Fuel distributor	6	Pressure regulator		and lever
1c	Airflow sensor plate	7	Fuel injector	12	Idle speed screw
2	Fuel tank	8	Auxiliary air valve	13	Cold start injector
3	Electric fuel pump	9	Warm-up regulator	14	Thermo-time switch
4	Fuel accumulator	10	Ignition switch		

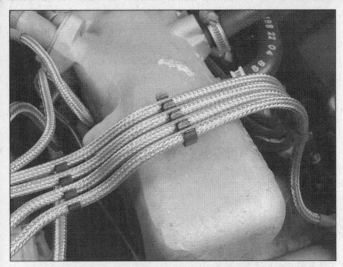

4.2 CIS systems are easy to identify because they use braided stainless steel hoses to withstand a higher operating fuel pressure

4.3 You can distinguish a CIS or CIS-with-Lambda system from a CIS-E or CIS-E Motronic system by the black cast-iron fuel distributor (the distributor is unpainted aluminum on the latter two systems)

geot, Porsche, Rolls-Royce, Saab, Volkswagen and Volvo. The quickest way to tell if your vehicle uses CIS is to pop the hood and look for 4, 6 or 8 braided stainless steel hoses between the fuel distributor and each injector. There are some exceptions: On some Mercedes and on Peugeot, Renault and Volvo vehicles that use the PRV V6 engine, the mixture control unit is mounted on top of the intake manifold. On 1976 through 1982 Volvo 240 models, the mixture control unit is mounted below the intake manifold. On these vehicles, no braided steel lines are visible; they use rigid metal or plastic lines. To identify the type of CIS installed on any other vehicle, look for a separate mixture control unit (usually) mounted on a fender panel, with a flexible air duct leading to the throttle body.

There are basically three types of CIS: K-Jetronic, K-Jetronic-with-Lambda (O2 sensor) and KE-Jetronic or KE-Motronic. K-Jet systems are completely mechanical; K-Jet-with-Lambda systems have a simple O2 sensor/analog computer feedback loop; KE-Jetronic systems have some additional electronic controls; and KE-Motronic systems have an engine management computer that controls ignition and fuel delivery.

4.4 A CIS with Lambda system has a solenoid-type frequency valve (or Lambda valve) right next to the mixture control unit

K-Jet and K-Jet-with-Lambda systems have a cast iron fuel distributor that's painted black **(see illustration)**. K-Jet systems with a Lambda sensor also have a solenoid-type frequency valve (Bosch calls it a lambda valve) next to the fuel distributor **(see illustration)**. This valve has an electrical connector and is similar in appearance to a conventional electronic fuel injector.

KE fuel distributors are usually unpainted aluminum **(see illustration)**. They also have a pressure actuator fastened to the fuel distributor. Other distinctions are not so apparent. For example, KE-Motronic system have no vacuum lines to the distributor. But some KE-Jetronic systems (late-model Audis with separate electronic ignition-timing, for instance) have no vacuum lines to the distributor either.

Some parts of the Bosch continuous injection system (CIS) - the electric fuel pump, the fuel accumulator, the fuel filter and the system pressure regulator - aren't that different from the components used in an electronic port injection system. Most applications since 1977 have also used a pre-pump in the fuel tank

4.5 On KE-Jetronic and KE-Motronic systems, the fuel distributor is an unpainted aluminum casting instead of cast iron

(the main pump is usually outside the tank, right in front of it, under the vehicle). And the fuel filter and system pressure regulator are of sturdier construction, to deal with the higher pressures of continuous injection.

However, the rest of a CIS system is completely different. Let's start with the mixture control unit.

Mixture-control unit (airflow sensor and fuel distributor)

A fuel injection system must measure the amount of air drawn in by the engine and meter the correct amount of pressurized fuel to match that air. The mixture-control unit **(see illustration)** is the component where those two functions come together. The mixture-control unit measures engine intake air, then meters fuel in proportion to that air flow. The mixture-control unit is actually two components - the airflow sensor and the fuel distributor - integrated into a single assembly: The airflow sensor measures the air entering the engine. The fuel distributor delivers a proportional amount of pressurized fuel to the injectors. Now let's look at how they work.

The round airflow sensor plate is located in the intake tract, so that all air entering the engine must flow past it. The plate is attached to a lever which pivots, allowing the plate to move up and down. When intake air flows through the mixture-control housing, it raises the plate. The movement of the sensor plate and lever is in direct proportion to the volume of the incoming air.

This airflow measurement is converted to a fuel injection quantity by the control plunger **(see illustrations)** in the fuel distributor. The plunger, which rests on the airflow sensor lever, rises and falls with the airflow sensor plate. The position of the plunger controls fuel flow to the injectors. When airflow increases, it raises the airflow sensor plate, which raises the lever, which raises the plunger. When the plunger rises, fuel flow is proportionally increased, maintaining the correct air-fuel ratio.

In electronic fuel injection systems, fuel metering is controlled by the opening and closing of the injectors. In continuous injection systems, no fuel metering takes place at the fuel injectors. While the engine is running, fuel flows through them continuously; their only function is atomization of the fuel.

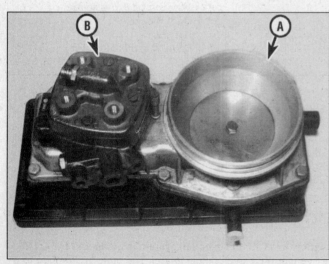

4.6a A typical mixture control unit

A   *Airflow sensor*   B   *Fuel distributor*

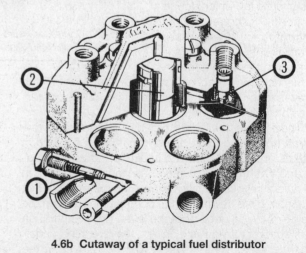

4.6b Cutaway of a typical fuel distributor

1   *Line pressure regulator*   3   *Pressure-differential*
2   *Control plunger*   *valve*

Continuous injection systems are sometimes referred to as "mechanical" fuel injection, because basic fuel metering is controlled by this mechanical relationship between the airflow sensor plate and the control plunger in the fuel distributor. CIS is also known as "hydraulic" fuel injection, because its control systems alter the basic air-fuel mixture ratio for different operating conditions by altering fuel pressures in various parts of the system.

Airflow system

The airflow system includes the airflow sensor, the ducting to the throttle body, the throttle valve and the intake manifold. The throttle valve controls the amount of air entering the engine. The airflow sensor is deflected by that air and the amount of this deflection is converted into a lifting force which raises the control plunger inside the fuel distributor. The airflow system also provides an adjustment for engine idle speed.

The heart of the airflow sensor operation is a round sensor plate sitting inside a conically-shaped air funnel (see illustration). When the engine is off, the sensor plate rests on a spring support; this is known as the zero position. The plate is attached to one end of a lever that pivots from its other end. The control plunger inside the fuel distributor sits directly atop the lever, right next to the pivot.

As the engine draws in air, the sensor plate rises. The greater the airflow, the higher the plate and lever rise (see illustration). Because of its position on the lever, the control plunger rises at the same rate as the sensor plate. The relationship between the rate of rise of the sensor plate and the control plunger is linear: Doubling the airflow doubles the sensor-plate lift, which doubles the control plunger lift. The height of the plunger regulates the fuel flow to the injectors, so the higher it rises, the greater the fuel flow. This mechanical relationship between the airflow sensor and the control plunger is what determines basic fuel metering.

There are actually two types of airflow sensors - updraft and downdraft - used in continuous injection systems. In updraft sensors, intake air flows from below and lifts the sensor plate, as describe above. In downdraft sensors, air flows from above and pushes the sensor plate down. But the control plunger is on the far side of the pivot point of the lever. So, even though the direction of airflow is different, the operating principle is the same: As the sensor plate is deflected, the control plunger rises and increases fuel flow.

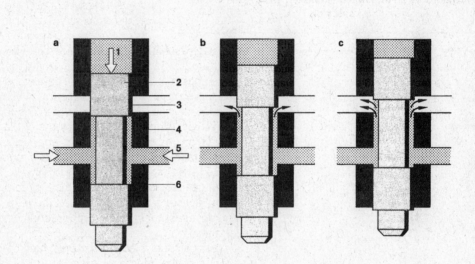

4.7 Barrel with metering slits and control plunger

a	"Zero" (inoperative) position	3	Metering slit in the barrel
b	Part load	4	Control edge
c	Full load	5	Fuel intake
1	Control pressure	6	Barrel with metering slits
2	Control plunger		

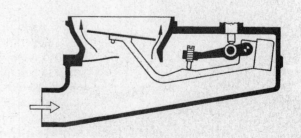

4.8 Airflow in a CIS fuel injection system is measured by a disc-shaped sensor plate in a conical funnel. The plate is attached to a lever arm which pivots as the plate rises, raising and lowering the control plunger inside the fuel distributor

In both types of airflow sensors, the weight of the sensor plate and lever is counterbalanced by a weight on the other end of the lever. So the plate acts as though it were weightless in the intake air stream. In fact, the force of the airflow lifts the sensor plate so easily that a counteracting force is necessary to stabilize the movement of the plate. (That force is fuel pressure, applied to the top of the control plunger, which we'll get to in a moment.) Later systems use a balance spring instead of the counterweight. The spring has less inertia than the weight, so the sensor plate adjusts more quickly to changing airflow, which means fuel metering and throttle response are faster.

The operation of the airflow sensor plate is based on the floating body principle, which means that, under the right conditions, a column of pressurized air will support and move an object, and that the movement of this object will be in direct proportion to the volume of air flowing past. Intake air flows through the sensor air funnel to create the air column. The counterweighted sensor plate "floats" on this air column. As the engine uses more air, the flow through the funnel increases, and the sensor plate rises on the column of air moving through the funnel. The shape of the funnel - which is different on different engines - is determined by the power characteristics of the engine on which the system is installed. For a given airflow, the strength of the column of air is less or more, and the lift of the sensor plate is lower or higher, depending on the shape of the funnel.

Funnel angles can be changed to affect the air-fuel ratio for a given air flow. In K-Jetronic (no Lambda) systems, the funnel is usually shaped with different angles to meet different operating conditions. A steeper wall section near the top of the funnel causes the sensor plate and plunger to lift higher for a given airflow, providing a richer mixture for full-load conditions. A shallower angle wall in the middle of the funnel means less lift for a leaner mixture at part-load. At the bottom of the funnel, another steep wall section provides more lift and a richer mixture for idle/off-idle conditions. (In K-Jetronic systems with Lambda and in KE-Jetronic systems, the funnel shape is usually conical, so the proportion of the basic fuel metering is constant for the entire range of sensor plate lift.)

The clearance between the edge of the sensor plate and the small part of the funnel is about .10 mm. Because the plate effectively blocks the intake tract, any backfire in the intake manifold could build up reverse pressure and blow the ductwork, bend the sensor plate or damage vacuum-operated systems. To prevent damage in the event of a backfire, the airflow sensor is designed with a secondary relief area in the funnel. Any backfire in the manifold drives the sensor plate against its spring support and rubber bumper so that the pressure is vented around the edge of the plate. The sensor plate is driven past the zero position, down against its stop. (In downdraft designs, the plate is driven up against its stop).

Control plunger counterforce

Some extra force is needed to balance the airflow force that raises the sensor plate and control plunger. Without it, the movement of the plate would be too quick, and when the engine is started, the plunger would rise to the top of its travel and stay there.

Fuel pressure, applied to the top of the control plunger in the fuel distributor, supplies this counterforce. Resisting the upward force of the airflow sensor and the upward movement of the control plunger, fuel pressure regulates their movement and allows the sensor plate to "float" in the air stream. It also pushes the plunger back down when there is less airflow, and returns the control plunger to its rest position when the engine stops running. This fuel-pressure counterforce can be varied to affect control-plunger lift for a given airflow, changing the proportion of fuel injected, thus changing the basic air-fuel ratio. In K-Jetronic and K-Jetronic-with-Lambda systems, this fuel pressure counterforce is known as the control pressure (which we'll get to in a moment).

On 1983 and later models, a return spring on top of the control plunger ensures that the plunger follows the movement of the airflow sensor during starting and engine deceleration. This improves starting and reduces hydrocarbon emissions during coasting.

Sensor plate positions

In K-Jetronic and K-Jetronic-with-Lambda systems, the control plunger rests on the lever when the engine is off and the sensor plate is at its zero (rest) position. When the plate is at its zero position in KE-Jetronic and KE-Motronic systems, the plunger rests on an O-ring seal in the fuel distributor. There's a small amount of clearance between the plunger and the lever to insure that the plunger seats firmly against the O-ring. When the engine is turned off, this design seals off fuel pressure more effectively, reducing the likelihood of vapor lock in the fuel lines. So there are actually two sensor plate positions in KE systems. One is the zero position described above, where a wire clip supports the sensor plate when the engine is off and there is clearance between the control plunger and the lever. The second position, found only on KE systems, is the position of the plate in the air funnel when it's lifted, so that the lever just touches the control plunger.

Incorrect clearance between the sensor plate lever and the control plunger will cause problems on KE systems. If there's no clearance, the plunger will not seal against the O-ring, and residual fuel may dribble down into the mixture control unit while the engine is turned off. This can cause flooding-type restart problems and, worst case, a potential fire hazard. If there's too much clearance between the sensor plate lever and the plunger, you'll have a different kind of starting problem. During cranking, airflow must lift the sensor plate a certain amount before the lever contacts the plunger. If there's too much clearance, the lever will not lift the plunger soon enough for the airflow, so fuel metering won't be in the correct proportion to airflow.

Mixture (CO) adjustments

Continuous injection systems have a mixture screw for fine-tuning the basic air-fuel mixture to insure compliance with emission regulations. The adjustment is made at idle, but it affects the relationship between the sensor plate and the control plunger over their entire operating range. For a given amount of sensor plate lift, control plunger lift is adjusted to alter the amount of fuel injected, i.e. the air-fuel mixture. The mixture adjustment is known as the "CO adjustment" because changing the air-fuel mixture changes the amount of CO (carbon monoxide) in the exhaust.

The mixture is adjusted by means of a mixture-control screw in the end of a mixture lever located inside the mixture control unit. The air-flow sensor lever actually consists of two parts: the aforementioned lever between the sensor plate and the control plunger, and the smaller mixture lever immediately above the sensor-plate lever. The mixture lever pivots from the same point at the sensor-plate lever, but the distance between the two levers is determined by the mixture screw. Turning the mixture screw in or out moves the mixture lever only. But the control plunger rests on the mixture lever, so when you raise or lower the mixture lever, you raise or lower the control plunger, without changing the position of the sensor-plate lever or sensor plate.

Let's say the engine is at idle and airflow is constant. Turning the mixture screw clockwise raises the mixture lever and lifts the control plunger, so more fuel is injected for the same airflow, enriching the mixture. Turning the mixture screw counterclockwise lowers the control plunger and leans the mixture.

Because the mixture screw is located inside the mixture control unit, you'll need a long 3 mm Allen wrench to reach it. Also, generally speaking, the only way to check the accuracy of a mixture adjustment is by measuring exhaust CO with a gas analyzer. However, later we'll show you how to check the accuracy of the mixture adjustment with a dwellmeter.

Throttle body

The throttle body in a continuous injection system is not unlike the throttle body in an electronic port injection system. It's downstream from the mixture control unit, usually bolted to the intake manifold plenum. It houses the throttle valve, which regulates airflow to the engine.

The throttle valve doesn't control the idle speed on continuous injection systems. The idle speed is adjusted by controlling a small amount of air that is allowed to bypass the throttle. This is a more reliable method than controlling the idle with the throttle valve because it's not influenced by a stretching throttle cable or by a worn throttle valve mechanism. The idle air bypass is regulated by an idle screw. Turning the screw in or out changes the amount of bypass air. Since the screw is downstream from the airflow sensor, altering the amount of air allowed to bypass results in a corresponding change in the amount of fuel injected, so idle speed adjustments don't affect the mixture adjustment.

Auxiliary air valve

During cold starts, the added friction of all those cold metal parts rubbing against each other can stall the engine. So some means of increasing engine idle speed during cold warm-ups is needed. The auxiliary air valve **(see illustrations)**, which bypasses the throttle valve, provides enough extra air to the engine to keep it from stalling until it's sufficiently warmed up.

When the engine is started up cold, the valve is initially open. Current flows through a heating element which, over a two-to-four-minute period, gradually heats up the bimetallic strip, which bends, and closes the valve. On most applications, voltage is available as long as the engine is running. Thus the valve remains closed until the engine is switched off. What if you start up the engine again while it's still warm? The auxiliary air valve relies on two factors for its operation: the electrical heating element and engine heat. Even though no current heats up the element while the engine is turned off, engine and underhood heat are still sufficient to keep the bimetallic element bent enough to keep the valve closed. So the engine won't resume a fast idle if you restart it while still warm.

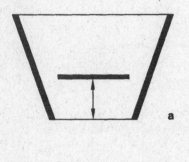

4.9a The airflow sensor plate is lifted slightly by a smaller amount of air (a), more by a larger amount of air (b)

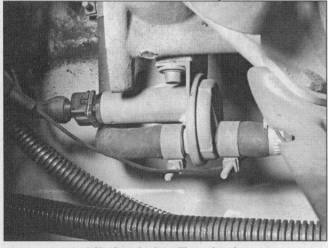

4.9b A typical auxiliary air valve

Fuel system

Controlling the fuel pressure is even more important in continuous injection systems than it is in electronic injection systems. Fuel pressure opens the injectors and the control systems regulate fuel pressure to alter the basic air-fuel mixture in compensation for different operating conditions. The fuel system must not only supply adequate fuel, it must also pressurize the fuel, maintain it and control it within a narrow range.

The fuel system includes the fuel tank, the electric fuel pump, the fuel accumulator, the filter, the fuel distributor, the pressure regulator and the fuel injectors. With the exception of the fuel distributor and system-pressure regulator, these components are similar to those used in an electronic injection system.

The fuel distributor is the part of the mixture control unit that meters the fuel and then distributes it to the individual injectors. All fuel metering takes place in the center of the fuel distributor at the control plunger as it rises and falls. Secondary mixture control by the control systems to fine-tune the basic air-fuel mixture takes place through the manipulation of fuel pressures in the fuel distributor.

System-pressure regulator

Continuous injection systems use fuel pressure to manipulate the air-fuel mixture, so that pressure must be regulated precisely. The system-pressure regulator maintains system pressure (also known as primary pressure) at the specified level. There are two types of system-pressure regulators. K-Jetronic and K-Jetronic-with-Lambda systems use a pressure-relief valve located in the fuel distributor housing. KE systems have an external diaphragm-type system-pressure regulator. Both types regulate fuel pressure by recirculating excess fuel back to the fuel tank.

In K-Jetronic and K-Jetronic-with-Lambda systems, the system-pressure regulator **(see illustration)** is integral with the fuel distributor. System pressure is regulated by a spring pushing against the regulator relief valve. When the electric fuel pump is energized, fuel pressure builds until it overcomes spring pressure and opens the relief valve, returning excess fuel to the tank. There are actually two versions of the system-pressure regulator. The first version was used on all units through 1977 and on some 1978 units; it controls only system pressure. A second version - used on some 1978 and on all later units - does this too, and it also performs another pressure-control function. This newer regulator contains a device known as a push valve. In this design, opening the relief valve also opens the push valve. The push valve controls the return of fuel from the control-pressure regulator (which we'll get to in a moment). The push valve O-ring shuts off fuel returning from the control-pressure regulator in order to preserve more residual system pressure. This difference between these two types of system-pressure regulators - push valve or no push valve - affects how you measure fuel pressure.

You can identify a regulator by its size and its position on the system-pressure regulator on the fuel distributor. The system-pressure regulator is built into the fuel distributor casting on both types. But those units manufactured prior to 1978 are not equipped with a push valve, and are a little smaller. 1978 and later units are equipped with a push valve and are therefore a little larger in size than the older units.

On KE systems, the system-pressure regulator **(see illustration)** is mounted externally. System pressure is maintained by a diaphragm-type regulator, a device that operates in a fashion similar to a regulator in an electronic injection system. When the fuel pump is running, fuel pressure builds until it overcomes spring pressure in the regulator and moves a diaphragm. This opens the regulating valve to return excess fuel to the tank and maintain pressure at the specified level. The thinner return line carries fuel from the fuel distributor to the regulator; the thicker line supplies fuel from the pump.

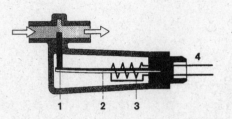

4.10 Cutaway of a typical auxiliary air valve

1 Blocking plate	3 Electric heating element
2 Bimetallic strip	4 Electrical connection

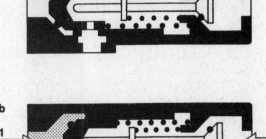

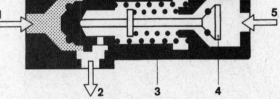

4.11 Cutaway of a typical system-pressure regulator valve (later style, with push valve)

a Zero (inoperative) position - engine not running
b Engine running
1 Primary pressure intake
2 Return
3 Plunger
4 Push valve
5 Control pressure inlet (from warm-up regulator)

Fuel injectors

The fuel injectors **(see illustration)** used on continuous injection systems are purely mechanical. There is no electrical signal from the computer to the injector, as in an electronic injection system. Fuel pressure overcomes spring pressure and opens the injector. Opening pressure is preset by the strength of the spring.

4.12 The system pressure regulator on KE-Jetronic and KE-Motronic systems is mounted externally, right next to the mixture control unit

The injectors do not meter the fuel; they just continually inject fuel and atomize it. When an injector is working, you can hear a chatter as fuel pressure vibrates the open valve pins to atomize the fuel. When fuel pressure drops below the preset spring opening, the injector closes and delivery stops.

Some 1984 and all later KE system injectors have air-shrouded injectors, which offer improved fuel atomization. Better atomization means more efficient combustion, which saves fuel and reduces exhaust emissions. Each injector is mounted in a special air shroud in the intake manifold. At idle, lower manifold pressure at the injector tips induces air flow from upstream of the throttle to flow around the injected fuel stream.

Fuel metering

Fuel metering - matching a proportional amount of fuel to the air entering the engine to create the correct air-fuel mixture - takes place inside the fuel distributor in continuous injection systems. The basic air-fuel mixture is altered by the control system to compensate for different operating conditions. The control systems for each type of K-Jetronic system are different. We'll look at them in a moment. First, let's look at a little more closely at fuel metering.

Control plunger

You've already seen how fuel metering occurs when air entering the engine lifts the sensor plate, which in turn lifts the control plunger in the fuel distributor, allowing fuel to the injectors. Now let's look at how the control plunger and the fuel distributor turn that airflow measurement into a proportional fuel quantity. The control plunger resides in a precision housing called the "barrel," which is located inside the fuel distributor. The fuel pump supplies fuel at system pressure to the lower part of the barrel. As the control plunger is lifted, fuel flows out of the barrel through slits, and through the fuel lines to the injectors. There is one slit for each injector.

The control edge of the plunger is the key element here **(see illustration)**; its position in the barrel determines how much cross-sectional area of the upper slits is exposed, and therefore available, for flowing fuel. As the plunger is lifted in the barrel, the control edge exposes a greater portion of each slit. Low airflow into the engine causes only a small lift of the sensor plate and plunger; so only a small amount of each slit is exposed, and only a small amount of fuel is delivered through each slit. As airflow increases sensor-plate and plunger lift; more of each slit is exposed, and fuel flow increases.

Pressure drop

Fuel flow to the injectors is determined not just by the size of the exposed slit, but by the pressure drop at the metering slits. Pressure drop is the difference between the system pressure inside the slit, pushing fuel out, and the pressure outside the slit, inside the fuel distributor. Should the pressure drop for a given airflow and plunger lift change, then fuel flow through the slit also changes. For example, an increase in pressure drop forces more fuel to flow through the slit; and fuel delivery increases.

A changing pressure drop at the slits interferes with the

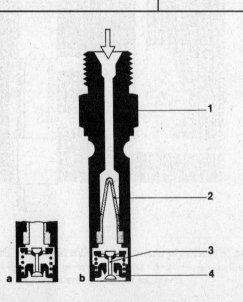

4.13 Cutaway of a typical CIS fuel injector

a	Engine turned off	2	Filter
b	Engine running	3	Valve needle
1	Valve housing	4	Valve seat

linear relationship between airflow and fuel flow. When the control plunger rises, a more exposed slit reduces the pressure drop and upsets the basic proportional relationship between airflow and fuel flow. So, even though increased airflow produces a linear increase in plunger lift, it doesn't necessarily produce a linear increase in fuel flow. At a certain point, the pressure change will cause the air-fuel mixture to be incorrect. To maintain a steady pressure drop at the slits throughout the range of plunger lift, continuous injection systems are equipped with differential-pressure valves in the fuel distributor.

Differential pressure valves

There is one differential-pressure valve per injector **(see illustrations)**. Each valve is installed in its own chamber inside the fuel distributor. The upper and lower halves of each chamber are separated by a flexible metal diaphragm.

Differential-pressure valves maintain a constant pressure drop at the metering slits of the control plunger by reacting to the increased fuel flow that accompanies a larger slit opening. As the control plunger rises, fuel flows out of the slit and into the differential-pressure valve, and the rising fuel pressure deflects the diaphragm, causing a proportional increase in the area of the fuel outlet to the injector and maintaining the same pressure drop at the control-plunger slit. Even though there is more fuel flow through a more open slit, the differential between pressure inside the slit and pressure outside the slit remains constant.

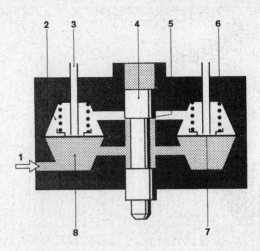

4.14a The position of the control edge of the plunger determines how much cross-sectional area of the slits is exposed to allow fuel to flow out of the barrel and into the differential-pressure valve chambers

1 *Fuel inlet (primary pressure)*
2 *Upper chamber of the differential-pressure valve*
3 *Fuel line to the injector*
4 *Control plunger*
5 *Control edge and metering slit*
6 *Pressure-differential valve spring*
7 *Pressure-differnetial valve diaphragm*
8 *Lower chamber of the differential-pressure valve*

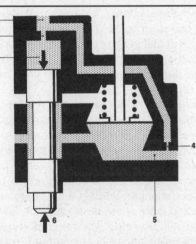

4.14b The upper and lower chambers inside each differential-pressure valve are separated by a spring-loaded metal diaphragm that moves up and down in response to the pressure in the lower chamber; when lower chamber pressure (supply pressure or primary pressure) is high, the diaphragm is pushed up against spring pressure and the upper chamber outlet to the fuel injector is closed

1 *Control pressure*
2 *Damping orifice (restriction)*
3 *Line to warm-up regulator*
4 *Decoupling restriction bore*
5 *Primary pressure (supply pressure)*
6 *Mechanical pressure from the airflow sensor lever arm pushes control plunger up*

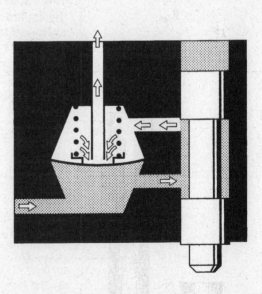

4.14c When lower chamber pressure is low, the diaphragm is pushed down by the spring, allowing the fuel in the upper chamber to flow to the injector

Since the deflection of the diaphragm enlarges the outlet to the fuel injectors, it might seem that fuel metering is a function of how close the diaphragm is to the outlet. But that's not what's happening here. Fuel metering takes place at the control-plunger slits. The movement of the diaphragm acts only to maintain a constant pressure drop - to eliminate pressure drop as a variable and maintain accurate metering to each injector, regardless of changing fuel flow rates.

Inside each differential-pressure valve, the diaphragm separates the flow of injector fuel through the lower chamber from the fuel in the upper chamber. The upper chamber is separated so that the pressure-drop regulating function is independent for each injector and its injector hose.

In K-Jetronic and K-Jetronic-with-Lambda systems, a spring in the upper chamber pushes down on the diaphragm to reduce the pressure in the upper chamber by 0.1 bar (1.5 psi). It's this pressure drop which causes fuel to flow out through the slits to the upper chamber and from there to the injectors. In K-Jet systems, the lower chambers are always at system pressure, so the job of each diaphragm is to flex up and down to maintain the constant 0.1 bar pressure drop regardless of flow in the upper chamber. In K-Jetronic systems with Lambda, the flexible diaphragms still move up and down to equalize the pressures in the upper and lower chambers, but electronic control systems can also change the lower-chamber pressure.

Control systems

Were it not for emissions regulations, the continuous fuel injection system just described would be sufficient. But a modern fuel injection system must make many fine adjustments to the mixture to maintain the stoichiometric air-fuel ratio and to compensate for the demands of different operating conditions. So a number of control systems have been added to fine-tune the basic air-fuel mixture. Basically, these controls enrich or lean the basic mixture as necessary. Two methods are used - changing slit size and changing pressure drop at the slits. The control systems used on each type of continuous injection achieve these two objectives in different ways.

One way to adjust fuel metering is to alter the position of the control plunger for a given airflow by changing the amount of counterforce opposing the plunger. Remember that fuel pressure counterforce is used to oppose the lift of the control plunger against the airflow force. Reducing the counterforce allows the sensor plate to lift the plunger higher for the same airflow, exposing more of the slits and allowing more fuel to flow for a richer mixture. Increasing the counterforce reduces plunger lift for a given airflow, exposing less of the slits and resulting in less fuel flow for a leaner mixture.

Another method used by the control systems for mixture adjustment is the manipulation of pressures on either side of the differential-pressure valves. This changes the deflection of the diaphragm which, in turn, changes the pressure drop at the slit. Remember, pressure drop is the difference between pressure inside the slit and pressure outside the slit. For a given airflow and plunger lift, a change in the pressure drop changes the amount of fuel flowing through the slit, enriching or leaning the mixture.

K-Jetronic

K-Jetronic systems use pressurized fuel as a hydraulic control fluid to impose a counterforce against the control plunger. This counterforce is known as control pressure. K-Jetronic systems make adjustments to basic fuel metering by varying the control pressure, which changes the counterforce on the control plunger. This changes the lift of the plunger, and the size of the metering slits, for a given airflow. The K-Jetronic control system has no effect on the differential-pressure valves. They deflect in the normal fashion to maintain a constant pressure drop at the control plunger metering slits.

Control pressure is applied through passages in the fuel distributor. A flow restrictor transfers fuel pressure from the system-pressure side to the control-pressure side without delivering fuel system pressure to the top of the plunger. A damping restrictor admits control-pressure force to the top of the plunger in order to balance the airflow force of the airflow sensor plate. The damping restrictor is large enough to allow a transfer of pressure, but small enough to dampen oscillation of the sensor plate and plunger which could be caused by pulsating airflow.

The control-pressure regulator alters control pressure by returning excess fuel from the control-pressure circuit to the fuel tank. If more fuel is bled off to the tank, control pressure is reduced. If less fuel is bled off, control pressure is increased. The control-pressure regulator consists of a valve mounted on a bimetal arm, which is constructed from two different metals of different expansion rates. This arm changes the control pressure in response to temperature by bending one way when it's cold and the other way when it's warm. When it's cold, the natural shape of the bimetal arm pulls the diaphragm away from the valve. So the valve increases the amount of fuel returned to the tank and reduces control pressure. But as the regulator warms up, the bimetal arm bends the other way, and the spring closes the valve, which decreases the amount of fuel returned to the tank and increases control pressure.

Basically, the fuel-pressure counterforce on the plunger balances the force of the airflow entering the engine, so the movement of the sensor plate is opposed by the plunger. If this counterforce is altered while airflow remains constant, the amount that the sensor plate and plunger lift will also change.

The control-pressure regulator enriches the basic mixture for cold starts and engine warm-up by reducing the control-pressure counterforce on the control plunger. When the control-pressure regulator is cold, control-pressure counterforce on the plunger is low; it can be lifted higher for a given airflow force, uncovering more of the metering slits so more fuel flows for the same amount of air. This enriches the mixture and improves cold driveability. As the control-pressure regulator and its bimetal arm warm up, control-pressure increases, increasing counterforce on the plunger and holding it lower for a given airflow. This reduces the size of the slits and leans the mixture. The regulator eventually reaches a temperature at which it no longer compensates the mixture for cold operating conditions; when this point is reached, only the basic sensor-plate lift of the control plunger determines the mixture.

The best way to check the operation of the regulator as pressures change with temperature is to measure the control pressure. For instance, the control pressure at freezing might be 1 bar (14.5 psi), and warm control pressure 3.5 bar (51 psi).

The control-pressure regulator **(see illustrations)** is usually installed on the engine block, where its bimetal arm can react to engine-block temperature. If you have trouble finding it, look for its two fuel lines to the distributor: One of them is the control-pressure line to the regulator, and one returns fuel to the tank. On vehicles built prior to 1978, the return fuel flows uncontrolled through a "tee" into the return line from the system-pressure regulator. On 1978 and later vehicles, return fuel flow is controlled by the push valve, through the system-pressure regulator and back to the tank.

4.15a The control pressure regulator is mounted on the block, where its temperature-sensitive bimetal arm can react to engine heat

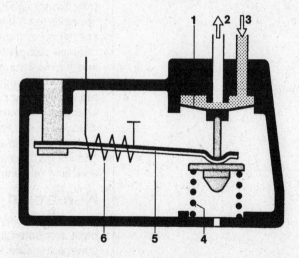

4.15b Cutaway of a typical control-pressure regulator (K-Jetronic systems)

1 Valve diaphragm
2 Return
3 Control pressure (from mixture control unit)
4 Valve spring
5 Bimetal spring
6 Electrical heating

After a cold start, fuel enrichment must gradually taper off over a one or two-minute period. However, the engine block can take 10 minutes to warm up to the point where it affects the bimetal arm in the control-pressure regulator. So, to insure that the mixture isn't enriched for too long, an electric heating coil warms the arm when the ignition is turned on. Warm-up specs are different for each make and model, so do NOT interchange regulators.

K-Jetronic-with-Lambda

The K-Jetronic-with-Lambda system adjusts the basic air-fuel mixture by combining two methods. First, using the control-pressure regulator for (primarily) cold running, it changes slit size for a given airflow, just like a K-Jetronic-without-Lambda system. Second, it adjusts the basic air-fuel mixture by altering the pressure drop at the control-plunger slit so that the fuel flow changes for a given plunger lift. It does this by manipulating pressures in the differential-pressure valves. Pressure in the valves' lower chambers is controlled by the Lambda Control System, in response to the signals from a lambda sensor in the exhaust system.

Differential-pressure valves on K-Jetronic systems without Lambda hold the pressure drop constant at the control plunger metering slits. The deflection of the valve diaphragm increases with fuel flow for this pressure-drop function. If airflow and control plunger lift are constant, but the deflection of the diaphragm is altered, the pressure drop, and the amount of fuel flowing through the slits, also changes. Let's look at a typical example: For a certain amount of plunger lift, and fuel flow through the slits, the pressure drop at the slits is constant. But if the lower-chamber pressure of the differential-pressure valves is lowered, the diaphragms deflect more. This extra deflection of the diaphragms decreases the pressure in the upper chambers and increases the pressure drop at the slits; so more fuel flows for the same amount of plunger lift, enriching the mixture.

K-Jetronic-with-Lambda control systems use this same method to adjust the air-fuel mixture. Except the lower-chamber pressure of the differential-pressure valves is not system pressure, as it is in K-Jet-without-Lambda systems. The pressure in the lower chambers (and, therefore, the pressure drop at the slits) is controlled by a separate pressure circuit which in turn is controlled by the Lambda Control System. Fuel is admitted to these lower chambers through a restrictor, and flows back to the tank through the frequency valve (also known as the lambda valve, or the timing valve) and the fuel return lines. In other words, the pressure of all lower chambers is controlled by the lambda valve.

The Lambda Control System includes an oxygen sensor, an electronic control unit and a frequency valve. The frequency valve is similar in appearance to an electronic injector. And it opens and closes like an injector, but it doesn't meter fuel. The amount of time the frequency valve is open controls the pressure in the lower chambers of the differential pressure valves, which alters the upper chamber pressure to alter the pressure drop and change enrichment.

The frequency valve is a solenoid valve that is opened and closed by the electronic control unit, which monitors a signal from the oxygen sensor. The oxygen sensor signal to the control unit is based on the oxygen content in the exhaust. The control unit sends on-off voltage pulses to the frequency valve. The frequency of these pulses determines the amount of time the valve is open and, therefore, the amount of fuel that is returned to the tank. The on-off cycle of these pulses is known as the duty cycle. Duty cycle is measured on a scale of 0 to 100 percent. When the duty cycle is 50 percent, that means the frequency valve is open 50 percent of the time and closed the rest of the time. Duty cycle can also be measured using a dwell meter scale of 0 to 90 degrees. If you read a 50 percent duty cycle on a dwell meter set to the 4-cylinder scale, it will read 45 percent degrees (50 percent of 90 degrees).

When the frequency valve's duty cycle increases, it's open longer and returns more fuel to the tank, so lower-chamber pressure decreases. The differential-pressure valve diaphragms deflect more, which reduces upper-chamber pressure and increases the pressure drop at each metering slit, allowing more fuel to flow through the slits for any given plunger lift. In other words, the longer the duty cycle, the richer the mixture. Conversely, a shorter duty cycle means that less fuel is bled off from the lower chamber, so lower chamber pressure increases and the diaphragm deflects less. This reduces the pressure drop and fuel flow at the slits. So, a shorter duty cycle means a leaner mixture.

The Lambda Control System controls enrichment of the basic mixture via a closed-loop between the control unit and the oxygen sensor. The control system continuously corrects the air-fuel mixture for the amount of plunger lift in order to maintain the mixture near the stoichiometric ratio necessary for catalytic converter operation. As exhaust gases pass over the oxygen sensor, oxygen-content signals are sent to the control unit, which alters the duty cycle of the frequency control valve to change the pressure drop at the slits and adjust the mixture. The resulting change in exhaust-gas oxygen content alters the oxygen-sensor signal again. The control unit senses this new change and changes the duty cycle of the frequency valve again. And so on. The cycle is continuous. Because the oxygen content in the exhaust is continuously changing, the Lambda-Control System tries to average the ideal mixture, i.e. it corrects to one side or the other of the stoichiometric ratio, but in a very narrow range.

The oxygen sensor doesn't begin to operate until the temperature is high, so the system must operate in open loop until the sensor warms up. Because of the less-than-perfect mixture control during open loop, driveability problems and increased exhaust emissions can and do occur. To mitigate this situation, many vehicles are equipped with a lambda thermoswitch located in the coolant (or on the cylinder head in air-cooled Porsches) to give the control unit some idea what's going on during engine warm-up.

When you crank a cold engine, the thermoswitch is closed. The control unit sends a fixed, slightly-rich (60 percent) duty-cycle signal to the frequency valve. When the thermoswitch warms up enough to open, the control unit sends a fixed middle (50 percent) duty cycle signal. When the lambda sensor reaches operating temperature, the control unit switches to closed-loop operation. Remember that in closed-loop, the duty-cycle signals are constantly changing, cycling back-and-forth between about 45 percent and 55 percent, so that the air-fuel ratio is maintained near stoichiometric (lambda = 1).

KE-Jetronic and KE-Motronic

KE-Jetronic and KE-Motronic control systems **(see illustration)** alter the basic air-fuel mixture by altering the pressure drop at the control-plunger slits. The KE control system consists of a series of information sensors similar to those used in electronic injection systems, a control unit and a computer-controlled pressure actuator on the fuel distributor. KE control systems don't use a control-pressure regulator or frequency valve.

In KE systems, slit size for any airflow is determined solely by the lift of the sensor plate. The KE control system alters pressures in the chambers of the differential-pressure valves - and therefore the pressure drop at the slits - should any adjustments be necessary to compensate for warm-ups, emissions requirements, etc.

On KE systems, the counterforce above the plunger that balances airflow force is constant system pressure. In other words, for a given airflow, plunger lift and slit size is constant, unlike K-Jetronic and K-Jetronic with Lambda systems which reduce control pressure to allow the plunger to rise higher for a certain airflow, increasing slit size to increase fuel delivery.

KE control systems achieve more accurate pressure control by using two fuel-flow paths into the chambers of the differential-pressure valves. Fuel enters the control plunger barrel at system pressure through one path. Then it flows through each slit into each separate upper chamber at reduced pressure, and out to the injectors. The basic rate of fuel flow to the injectors is determined by the lift of the control plunger and by the airflow sensor, like other systems.

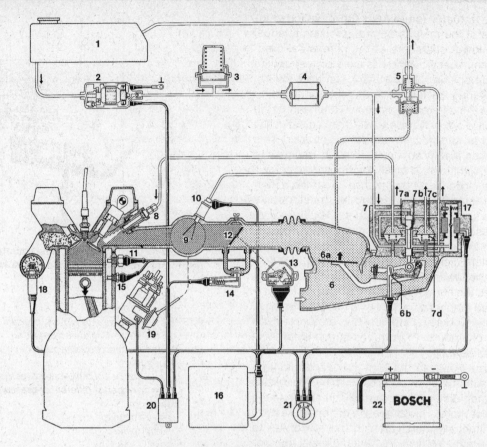

4.16 Schematic of a typical Bosch CIS-E Jetronic system

1	Fuel tank	7b	Control edge	15	Engine temperature sensor
2	Electric fuel pump	7c	Upper chamber	16	Electronic control unit (ECU)
3	Fuel accumulator	7d	Lower chamber	17	Electro-hydraulic pressure actuator
4	Fuel filter	8	Injector		
5	Primary pressure regulator	9	Intake manifold	18	Lambda (oxygen) sensor
6	Airflow sensor	10	Cold-start injector	19	Ignition distributor
6a	Sensor plate	11	Thermo-time switch	20	Control relay
6b	Potentiometer	12	Throttle valve	21	Ignition switch
7	Fuel distributor	13	Throttle valve switch	22	Battery
7a	Control plunger	14	Auxiliary air valve		

In the other path, fuel - at system pressure - flows first to the pressure actuator. Then it flows - at reduced pressure - through the lower chambers, through a restrictor and back to the tank. The restrictor controls the rate of flow out of the lower chambers. The pressure actuator controls the amount of fuel flowing into the lower chambers, so it also controls the lower-chamber pressure, and the pressure drop at the slits.

In KE systems, pressure drop at the slits (and therefore the basic fuel metering adjustment), is controlled by the pressure drop at the entrance to the pressure actuator. This difference, between actuator pressure in the lower chambers and system pressure entering the pressure actuator, is known as differential pressure.

Differential pressure has a direct effect on the deflection of the differential-pressure valve diaphragms, which means it affects the pressure drop at the slits. And remember, by changing the pressure drop at the metering slits of the control plunger, fuel flow is altered for a given airflow and slit size. Differential pressure is altered by changing the flow of fuel (from the actuator) through the lower chambers.

The pressure actuator **(see illustration)**, which is located on the side of the mixture control unit, controls fuel flow through the lower chambers of the differential-pressure valves. For any specific airflow and its corresponding control-plunger slit opening, the actuator can alter the air-fuel mixture by altering the flow of fuel to the lower chambers, thus altering the differential pressure. The heart of the pressure actuator is a small plate valve that regulates the amount of fuel that can flow through the actuator. This valve is very small so that it can move rapidly in response to changing engine conditions. A small electromagnet causes the plate to move closer to or farther away from the actuator fuel inlet. The magnet is controlled by the electronic control unit. Let's say that fuel is flowing to the actuator inlet at system pressure. If the control unit increasing the current flow through the electromagnet, the greater magnetic force pulls the plate closer to the inlet, reducing the flow and pressure of the fuel in the lower chambers. If the control unit decreases the current flow through the electromagnet, the diminished magnetic force allows the plate to move closer to the inlet, decreasing the flow and pressure of the fuel in the lower chambers. In both cases, the differential pressure is altered as well.

When the plate is pulled down by the electromagnet, it's closer to the actuator inlet, so it restricts the flow of fuel through the actuator, differential pressure increases and the diaphragms deflect more. This increases the pressure drop at the control-plunger slits and increases the flow of fuel to the injectors for a given plunger lift. When the electromagnetic attraction is less, the plate moves further away from the inlet, the differential-pressure decreases and the diaphragms deflect less. This decreases the pressure drop at the slits and reduces the flow of fuel to the injectors for a given plunger lift.

Here's another way to look at the pressure function of the actuator: The pressure drop at the metering slits equals system pressure minus upper-chamber pressure. Upper-chamber pressure equals system pressure plus the 2.94 psi (0.2 bar) spring pressure, minus the differential pressure. Remember that differential pressure is the difference between system pressure and pressure in the lower chambers controlled by the pressure actuator. You can't test differential pressure directly. First, you'll have to measure system pressure, then subtract your measurement for lower-chamber pressure to get the differential.

The amount of current supplied to the pressure-actuator electromagnet is determined by the KE control unit. To determine the correct current, the control unit relies on inputs from information sensors similar to those used on electronic injection systems. These inputs include engine speed (from the ignition circuit), the lambda sensor, the engine-temperature sensor, the intake-air temperature sensor (1986 and later Mercedes-Benz), the sensor plate potentiometer for acceleration, and the throttle switch for closed and wide-open throttle indications. Control-unit outputs include the pressure-actuator signal and, on some vehicles, the signal to an idle-speed stabilizer.

You'll need a high-impedance digital multimeter to troubleshoot this circuit, because the control-unit actuator current is measured in milliamps (mA). Current levels this low are even affected by oxidation on the connectors, so make sure all connectors are clean. And make sure you don't bend connectors when you insert probes into them to take a reading. Here are some examples of how the control current relates to pressure-actuator mixture adjustment. If you can grasp the following three operations, you'll have the basic idea of how the KE-Jetronic control system adjusts the basic fuel mixture.

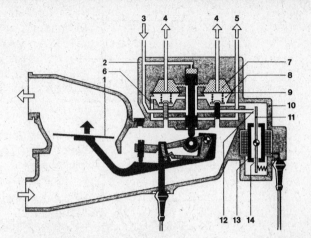

4.17 Cutaway of a typical pressure actuator-equipped fuel distributor on KE-Jetronic and KE-Motronic systems

1   Sensor plate
2   Fuel distributor
3   Fuel inlet (primary, or supply, pressure)
4   Fuel to injectors (injection pressure)
5   Fuel return to pressure regulator
6   Fixed orifice
7   Upper chamber of differential-pressure valve
8   Lower chamber of differential-pressure valve
9   Diaphragm
10 Pressure actuator
11 Actuator plate
12 Nozzle
13 magnetic pole
14 Air gap

During engine warm-up, a richer mixture is needed. Current flow is increased to about 70 mA and the plate is pulled closer to the actuator inlet. Differential pressure goes up, to about 14.7 psi (1 bar), so the amount of fuel going to the injectors increases. More actuator current means more differential pressure, greater deflection of the pressure-differential valve diaphragms, and more pressure drop at the metering slits, so more fuel is injected.

During warm-engine operation, current flow is typically about 10 mA. This causes only a small deflection of the plate valve, and a small difference between system pressure and lower-chamber pressure. The indicated differential pressure on a fuel pressure gauge will be about 5.88 psi (0.4 bar). Pressure drop and injector fuel flow at the slits is normal.

Should it become necessary to lean out the mixture (during deceleration, for example), current is reduced to maybe 1 mA, allowing the plate to move away from the actuator inlet. The differential pressure falls to a mere 2.94 psi (0.2 bar), so the amount of fuel going to the injectors decreases.

Should the control-unit current be interrupted, the actuator plate is designed to rest at a "limp-home" position. The engine will keep running, but at a slightly-leaner-than-normal mixture ratio, since the actuator current is no longer fine-tuning the mixture. In this limp-home mode, the air-fuel mixture is controlled solely by the basic mechanical metering of the airflow sensor and control plunger, just like an older K-Jetronic system. The uncontrolled plate inside the pressure actuator allows just enough pressure drop at the slits to keep a warm engine running. But don't let it die! The engine may not start again. You can simulate the limp-home mode on a running warm engine by unplugging the electrical connector to the pressure-actuator.

Some 1986 and later KE systems also have logic circuits in the control unit which help it identify - and ignore - signal errors. The computer recognizes a sudden change in input from certain sensors as incorrect, and switches to a default value, i.e. a pre-programmed output, when it detects such a signal. For example, the coolant temperature signal shouldn't change quickly. If it does, the computer recognizes it as a short or an open circuit, and switches to the default value for a warm engine. Because this capability is so new and so vehicle-specific, you'll have to refer to the factory service manual for more information.

Cold-start injector and thermo-time switch

A cold-start injector (see illustrations) supplies extra fuel during cold cranking and, briefly, during warm-up. Although the main system already provides enrichment, some of the fuel initially injected into a cold engine condenses on the intake ports and the cylinder walls. Some additional fuel is still needed. The cold-start injector supplements the standard enrichment. On some applications, the injector is also operated during warm starts to mitigate poor fuel vaporization. Its operation is carried out via an electrical relay.

Although there are some variations in the circuitry used on different vehicles, the basic operation is the same for all applications. The cold-start injector is installed in the plenum chamber, where its spray mixes with the air in the plenum before being drawn into the cylinders. The cold-start injector is opened by a solenoid inside the injector body, just like a typical electrically-operated solenoid injector in an electronic injection system. When current flows, the injector valve opens, injecting fuel at primary pressure.

A temperature-sensitive switch - Bosch calls it a thermo-time switch (see illustrations) - is installed in or near the cylinder head so that its tip protrudes into a cooling passage. The thermo-time switch is wired to the cold start injector, or to a relay which operates the injector. During cranking, the injector operates as long as the

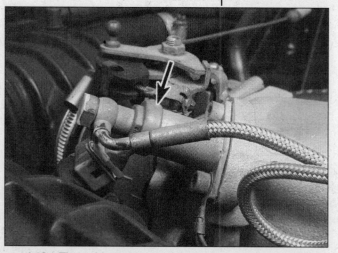

4.18a The cold-start injector (arrow) is usually located somewhere on the intake plenum

thermo-time switch completes the circuit. The thermo-time switch is designed to complete the circuit when the temperature is below a certain level. If, however, the coolant temperature is above that level, the thermo-time switch will open, thus preventing the injector from operating.

The thermo-time switch contains a pair of contacts which close the circuit when the coolant is below the preset temperature, but current also flows through a heating element inside the switch during cranking. If the temperature is just below or at the preset level, the heating element heats the contacts rapidly, causing them to open. If the temperature is lower, the heating element takes longer to open the contacts, allowing the cold-start injector to operate for a little while longer. Typical time periods for cold-start injector operation range from 1 to 12 seconds, depending on the initial temperature. A typical preset temperature for thermo-time switch operation is around 86 degrees F.

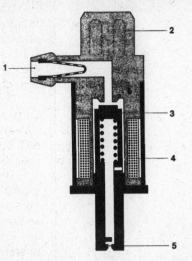

4.18b Cutaway of a typical cold-start injector

1 Fuel inlet
2 Electrical terminal
3 Solenoid armature
4 Solenoid winding
5 Swirl nozzle

4.19a The thermo-time switch is always installed somewhere near a coolant passage. On this VW, it's screwed into the thermostat housing (arrow)

Lines and hoses

Bosch continuous injection systems operate in the neighborhood of 70 to 90 psi! Mechanical injection systems must run at higher pressures than electronic injection systems because the injectors are continuously open and because the regulated pressure is what determines the amount of fuel sprayed out the injector nozzles. Braided stainless steel hoses are the first thing you notice on an engine equipped with CIS when you pop the hood. These hoses are virtually indestructible. Unless they rub against a sharp corner on the head, or something similarly abrasive, they'll last the life of the vehicle. However, it's not a bad idea to check the hose fittings at the fuel distributor and at the injectors once in a while to make sure they're snug. Should you ever have to replace one or all of the injector hoses, make sure you use nothing but OEM quality replacements.

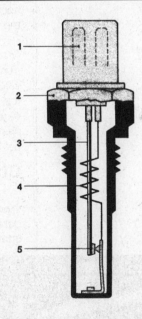

4.19b Cutaway of a typical thermo-time switch

1 Electrical terminal
2 Housing
3 Bimetallic element
4 Heating coil
5 Switch contact

Notes

 Fuel injection tools

You don't need a lot of special tools to service fuel injection systems. Most parts and components can be removed and installed with the same tools you use to work on the rest of your vehicle. But there are a few special diagnostic tools that you will need. Here are some of the important ones.

1 Vacuum gauges and hand-operated vacuum pumps

Many fuel injection systems, particularly older ones, use vacuum-operated diaphragms and other devices that depend on a good source of vacuum for proper operation. This vacuum comes from the intake manifold. A good vacuum gauge **(see illustration)** is a handy tool for measuring the amount of vacuum available under various operating conditions.

Sometimes, you'll need to check a vacuum-operated device on the bench. For this kind of testing, you'll need a hand-operated vacuum pump **(see illustration)**. With this instrument, you can apply a specific amount of vacuum to a device and test its ability to hold, bleed down or delay a certain amount of vacuum for a specified period of time.

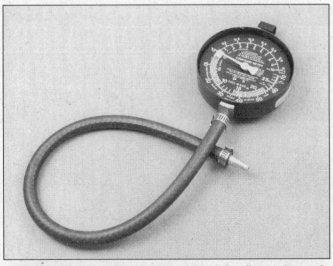

1.1 A vacuum gauge is an essential tool for diagnosing and troubleshooting any fuel-injected system that utilizes ported or intake vacuum for controlling various devices

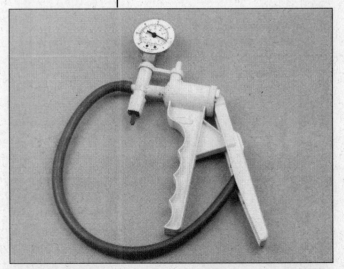

1.2 A hand-operated vacuum pump with a vacuum gauge is more versatile than a regular vacuum gauge because it can create its own vacuum source if necessary

2 Fuel pressure gauge

In a continuous injection system, the fuel pressure is the critical factor in determining the amount of fuel injected. And fuel pressure is one of the important operating variables in any electronic fuel injection system. So one of the most important tools you'll need for troubleshooting is a good fuel pressure gauge designed for use with fuel injection systems.

Electronic injection

With the exception of some low-pressure systems, the fuel pressure in an electronic fuel injection system is generally higher than the pressure in a carbureted system. In some low-pressure systems (usually throttle-body injection systems), fuel pressure might be only 9 or 10 psi, so a fuel pressure gauge designed for use with a mechanical fuel pump (range of 1 to 15 psi) may be adequate. But most fuel injection systems operate at higher pressures, so you'll need a special gauge designed for higher operating pressures.

A typical fuel-pressure gauge (see illustration) for fuel injection work has a range of 1 to 100 psi. The finest quality gauges are available from OEM suppliers such as Kent-Moore, OTC and Miller, and from professional-quality tool manufacturers such as Mac, Snap-On or Lisle. These generally run from $100 to $200. However, less expensive units, generally under $100, are available at most auto parts stores. These gauges will work just fine for the do-it-yourselfer. They're just not designed for the same level of abuse as a more expensive unit. When buying a gauge, try to verify that at least one of the adapters included with the kit will enable you to hook up the gauge to the system you're going to diagnose. Because Murphy's Law is always an important element of every "adapter search," you'll probably discover that none of the adapters included will fit your system! This is why some people simply pay the piper and purchase a factory gauge, because they know it will fit. But don't despair! You can usually find or make something that will work for far less than the difference between a factory gauge and a good aftermarket gauge.

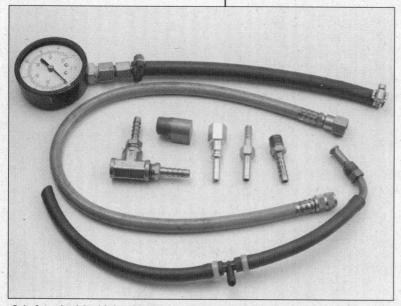

2.1 A typical fuel injection fuel pressure gauge with assorted fittings and hoses; most gauges come equipped with several fittings, but eventually you'll probably have to fabricate some of your own

You can use hose clamps to hook up a fuel pressure gauge to a carbureted vehicle, but, generally speaking, this isn't a good idea on a fuel-injected vehicle (except for a few very-low-pressure throttle-body injection systems). Systems designed to run at 30 or 40 psi will generally leak past a hose-clamp fitting, squirting fuel everywhere when the engine is started. It's no fun trying to read a fuel-pressure gauge and dodging flying fuel being sprayed in your face.

Fuel injection systems usually provide a *test port, pressure tap*, or *pressure relief valve* of some sort. The test port, which is usually a Schrader valve, looks just like a tire valve. It's usually located somewhere on the fuel rail. A screw-off cap keeps out dirt when the port's not in use. To hook up your fuel pressure gauge to a test port, simply remove the cap and screw on the adapter attached to the gauge test hose. Most gauges are sold with a variety of adapters. But that doesn't mean you won't have to buy a special adapter or make your own. If possible, try to obtain the correct adapter for your vehicle when you purchase a gauge.

Adapters

In theory, there should be enough adapters available to provide some means of hooking up virtually any aftermarket fuel pressure gauge to any fuel injection system test port. In practice, this isn't always the case. Test ports are not yet standardized, nor are they even included on every system. Every manufacturer, it seems, has its own way of letting you tap into the system.

Some fuel injection systems have no test port. If the system you're servicing has no port, your only option is to relieve the system fuel pressure, disconnect a fuel line from the fuel rail and hook up the fuel pressure gauge with a "T" type fitting. This can be tricky on some Ford and GM models equipped with spring-lock couplings. If you're servicing one of these models, you'll have to obtain a T-fitting with the special spring-lock couplings on either end, either from the manufacturer or from a specialized tool company that makes its own line of specialized adapters.

Systems that provide threaded test ports are easier to tap into. These ports are simply a threaded hole in the fuel rail, with a bolt or threaded plug screwed into the hole. The factory gauge for this setup comes equipped with an adapter that screws into the test port. Or, you can purchase the special adapter fitting and hose and use it with your gauge. Or you can fabricate your own adapter by obtaining a bolt with the correct thread diameter and thread pitch and drilling it out on a drill press.

Some systems provide Schrader-valve type test ports. For these systems, all you need to tap into the test port is a test hose with the right threaded adapter on the end that attaches to the Schrader valve. Manufacturers usually sell adapter hoses through their own suppliers, such as OTC, Kent-Moore, Miller, etc. These units are the best quality, but they're often pricey and difficult to obtain unless you're on very good terms with a savvy dealership partsman. There's only one way around this quandary.

It's not that difficult to fabricate your own adapter for this type of fuel injection system. We have fabricated our own adapters here at Haynes for various project vehicles for years. Here's how we do it: Relieve the fuel pressure, remove the Schrader valve, remove the core from the valve stem and install the hollow valve. Now, push a short section of rubber hose down over the valve and clamp it tightly with a hose clamp. Finally, attach the other end of the hose to the fuel pressure gauge and clamp it tightly as well with another hose clamp. You're in business!

Continuous injection

Fuel-pressure gauges for continuous injection systems (see illustration) are different from those used on electronic injection systems. First, they're more expensive! Nearly all of them are in the $200 to $300 range. Second, they're more difficult to obtain. You'll have to buy this type of instrument either directly from Robert Bosch or from an aftermarket tool company, such as Assenmacher, that specializes in tools for European vehicles (Assenmacher doesn't sell tools to the public directly; it sells through companies such as Snap-On) Third, not all CIS systems can be accessed with the same adapters. You must obtain special adapters to hook up one of these gauges to certain models. Your local Snap-On dealer can show you an As-

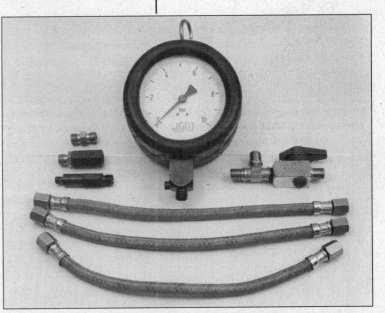

2.2 A typical continuous injection system (CIS) type fuel pressure gauge with assorted fittings and hoses; the main difference between the CIS fuel pressure gauge and the conventional unit shown in the previous illustration is its ability to read much higher pressures (although some regular gauges can also read to 100 psi), and the specially-designed high-pressure braided hoses (which closely resemble the injector lines on a CIS equipped vehicle)

senmacher tool catalog with the fittings available for various fuel injection systems. Fourth, you can't use gauges intended for electronic injection systems on CIS. The pressure range for most non-CIS gauges is from 0 to 70 psi. This isn't high enough for CIS work. You need a gauge that reads to 100 psi. But even if you have a conventional gauge that does read to 100 psi, there's no way to safely hook it up to a high-pressure system.

3 Special tools for disconnecting special connections

The fuel lines on many newer Ford fuel injection systems are now attached to each other and to other components in the fuel injection system with *spring lock couplings*. Some GM vehicles, Saturn for instance, are also starting to use special *duckbill* fuel line connections. If you're servicing a Ford or GM system with funny-looking fuel line connections, do NOT try to disconnect them without a special fuel line disconnect tool **(see illustration)**.

4 Injector harness testers ("noid" lights)

Noid lights **(see illustration)** tell you whether an injector harness is working properly or not. To use one, simply unplug the harness connector from the injector, plug the noid light into the connector and run the engine. The noid light will flash on and off as the computer sends pulses to the injector. Or it won't, if there's something wrong with the harness wire for that injector. Quick and simple. Noid lights are available in a wide variety of configurations for various port and throttle body injectors.

3.1 **Typical spring-lock couplings**

4.1 **These special injector harness testers, known as** *noid lights***, can quickly tell you the status of the harness to each injector**

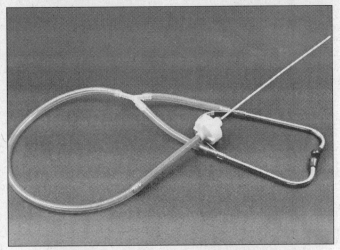

5.1 An automotive stethoscope is handy for isolating the subtle sounds of irregular injectors

6.1 Typical GM throttle body idle speed adjustment tool (arrow)

5 Stethoscope

An automotive stethoscope (see illustration) looks just the one your doctor uses, except that it's equipped with a noise attenuator to dampen the harsh sounds of the engine. When you want to isolate the sound of one injector, listen to a fuel pump, an idle speed control motor, etc., a stethoscope if the only way to go.

6 Idle speed adjustment tools

Fuel injection systems are equipped with a wide variety of idle speed controls. Many systems use some sort of idle air bypass controlled by an idle speed control motor. The minimum idle speed on most modern fuel-injected vehicles is pre-set at the factory and should not require adjustment under normal operating conditions. However, if certain components (such as the throttle body) have been replaced, or if you suspect the idle speed adjustment has been tampered with, it may be necessary to adjust the idle speed. On many vehicles you'll need special tools to adjust these devices. For instance, you can only set the minimum idle speed on most GM vehicles equipped with TBI (throttle body injection) with a special idle speed adjusting tool (see illustration).

7 Fuel tank spanner wrenches

In-tank fuel pump/sending unit assemblies are usually mounted inside the tank. To remove a defective pump and install a new unit, you must work through a small hole in the top of the tank. This hole is sealed with a circular base plate, the flange of which uses a bayonet-type locking ring that must be turned counterclockwise to unlock it before you can remove the fuel pump/sending unit assembly. If you don't mind removing the fuel tank, this is a fairly simply procedure. In fact, you can knock the locking ring loose with a hammer and a brass punch (*never* use a steel punch on one of the lock rings - it could cause sparks which could ignite the gasoline in the tank). Nowadays, many fuel-injected vehicles are equipped with an access plate in the floor of the trunk or hatch area that allows you to get at this lock ring/baseplate *without* dropping the fuel tank. Which means you can replace a fuel pump/sending unit without removing the tank from the vehicle! The trouble is, on many of these vehicles with an access plate, the distance between the access plate and the lock ring/baseplate makes it virtually impossible to knock that ring loose with a hammer and punch. In order to loosen the lock ring through the hole in the trunk, you'll need a special wrench **(see illustration)**.

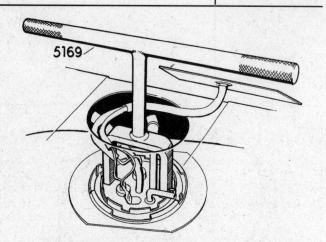

7.1 The easy way to loosen the locking bayonet ring that secures the fuel pump/sending unit assembly to the tank is with a special spanner like this one

8 Diagnosing and correcting circuit faults

The goal of electrical diagnosis is to find the faulty component which prevents current from flowing through the circuit as originally designed. As fuel injection systems are equipped with more and more electrical and electronic components, devices and subsystems, the potential for electrical and electronic problems increases dramatically. Because of the complexity of these electrical parts and subsystems, and because of the high cost of replacing them, a "hit-and-miss" approach to troubleshooting is expensive. An organized and logical approach to diagnosis is essential to repair fuel injection electrical circuits in a prompt and cost effective manner.

You'll need a few pieces of specialized test equipment to trace circuits and check components. Accurate methods of measuring current, voltage and resistance are essential for finding the problem without unnecessary parts replacement and wasted time.

Jumper wires

Jumper wires **(see illustration)** are used mainly for finding open circuits and for finding excessive resistance by bypassing a portion of an existing circuit. They can also be used for testing components off the vehicle. You can purchase them in completed form, or you can fabricate your own from parts purchased at an automotive or electronics supply store.

Jumper wires can be equipped with various types of terminals for different uses. If you're jumping current from the battery to a component, make sure your jumper wire is equipped with an inline fuse to avoid a current overload, and make sure it has insulated boots over the terminals to prevent accidental grounding.

Warning: *Never use jumpers made of wire that is thinner (of lighter gage) than the wiring in the circuit you are testing. Always use a fuse with the same (or lower) rating as the circuit had originally.*

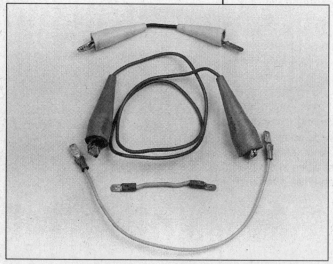

8.1 Jumper wires can be equipped with various types of terminals for different uses

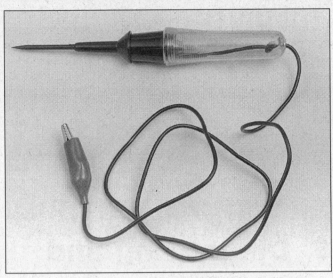

8.2 A test light is a must for automotive electrical testing

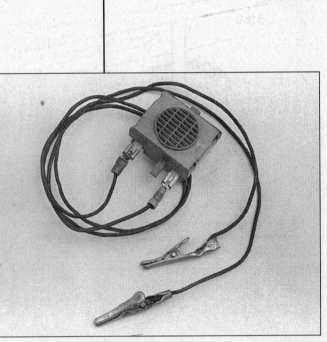

8.3 This test buzzer was made from a key reminder buzzer salvaged from a junked car

Test lights

Test lights are handy for verifying that there's voltage in a powered circuit. A test light **(see illustration)** is one of the cheapest electrical testing devices available; it should be the first thing you purchase for your electrical troubleshooting tool box. Test lights can also be fabricated from parts purchased at an automotive or electronics supply store. Test lights come in several styles, but all of them have three basic parts: a light bulb, a test probe and a wire with a ground connector. Six, 12, or 24-volt systems may be tested by changing the bulb to the appropriate voltage. Although accurate voltage measurements aren't possible with a test light, large differences can be detected by the relative brightness of the glowing bulb. **Note:** *Before using a test light for diagnosis, check it by connecting it to the battery, ensuring the bulb lights brightly.*

Test Buzzers

A test buzzer **(see illustration)** works the same way as a test light; but it offers the advantage of remote operation. For example, one person working alone may test a fuel pump circuit by turning the key to On and listening for the sound of the buzzer connected to the fuel pump circuit. A test buzzer can be fabricated at home from parts purchased at an electronics store or made with jumper wires and a key reminder buzzer. Test buzzers are used in the same manner described for test lights. Additionally, they can be used to find shorts to ground.

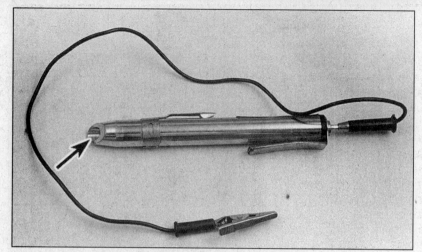

8.4 This continuity tester uses its own batteries to power the light bulb located in its tip (arrow)

Continuity testers

A continuity tester **(see illustration)**, also known as a self-powered test light, is used to check for open or short circuits. The typical continuity is nothing more than a light bulb, a battery pack and two wires combined into one unit. These parts can be purchased from any auto parts or electronics store. Continuity testers must be used only on non-powered circuits; battery voltage will burn out a low-voltage tester bulb.

Caution: *Never use a self-powered continuity tester on circuits that contain solid state components, since damage to these components may occur.*

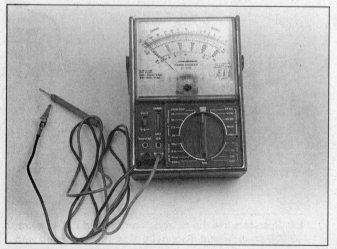

8.5 Short finders consist of a pulse unit and a separate hand-held meter

Short finders

A short finder **(see illustration)** is an electromagnetic device designed to trace short circuits quickly and easily. One part of the short finder is a pulse unit, which is installed in place of the fuse for a circuit in which a short is suspected. The other part of the short finder is a hand-held meter which is moved along the faulty wiring harness. Meter deflections indicate the area in the harness where the short is located. Short finders are available from most tool manufacturers for a moderate price. The savings from one use usually offsets the purchase price.

Analog (gauge-type) multimeters

Analog multimeters **(see illustration)** are used for a variety of test functions requiring the measurement of volts, ohms or amperes. Many brands and varieties are available at tool and electronics supply stores and by mail order. The units offering the most features and scales are usually the costliest. Analog multimeters can't be used to test solid state circuits, such as computers and electronic ignition control modules. But they're handy for outputting the trouble codes on certain vehicle makes.

If you're planning to purchase a new multimeter, get a digital unit. It can perform all the same tests as an analog unit, and it's suitable for use with electronic circuits and devices.

8.6 Analog multimeters can be used to measure volts, amps and ohms in non-solid state circuits - and they're handy for outputting the engine trouble codes on Fords and some other vehicles

Digital multimeters

A digital multimeter **(see illustration)** doesn't necessarily measure volts, ohms and amperes with a higher degree of accuracy, but it can display its measurements in tenths, hundredths and even thousandths of a volt, ohm or ampere. When working with electronic circuits, which are often very low-voltage, this kind of reading is essential for a meaningful diagnosis. A digital meter is somewhat more expensive than an analog unit, but it's the only game in town if you want to troubleshoot electronic circuits and devices. That's because a digital meter has a *high-impedance* circuit inside; the resistance of a digital meter's internal circuitry is 10 million ohms (10 M-ohms). Because a voltmeter, or a multimeter being used as a voltmeter, must be hooked up in parallel to the circuit or load whose voltage drop it's measuring, it's vital that none of the voltage being measured should be allowed to travel the parallel path set up by the meter itself. This is exactly what happens to analog meters (most of which don't have this high-impedance circuitry) when they're used to measure low-voltage circuits. If a fraction of a volt goes through the meter when you're measuring a 12-volt circuit, it doesn't much matter; your reading is still close enough to be considered accurate. But if you're measuring an extremely low-voltage circuit, an oxygen sensor circuit, for example, a fraction of a volt may be a significant chunk of what you've got to work with. Allowing any voltage to sneak through the meter will upset the accuracy of your reading. That's why a digital meter is essential for many of the circuits you'll have to work with on a fuel-injected vehicle.

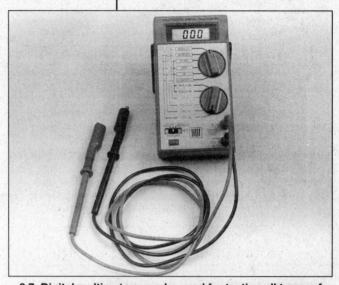

8.7 Digital multimeters can be used for testing all types of circuits; because of their high impedance, they're much more accurate than analog meters for measuring millivoltages in low-voltage computer circuits

9 Scanners, software and trouble-code tools

Scanners (computer analyzers)

Hand-held digital scanners **(see illustration)** are the most powerful and versatile tools for analyzing engine management systems used on later models vehicles. Unfortunately, they're also the most expensive. In this manual, we're going to show you how to troubleshoot sensors and actuators without resorting to analyzers.

8.8 Scanners like the Actron Scantool and the AutoXray XP240 are powerful diagnostic aids - programmed with comprehensive diagnostic information, they can tell you just about anything you want to know about your engine management system, but they're expensive

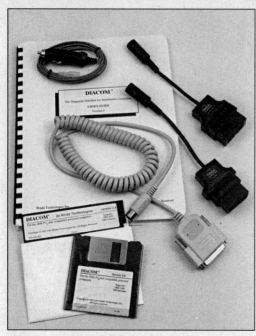

8.9 Diagnostic software, such as this kit from Diacom, turns your IBM compatible computer into the scan tool, saving the extra cost of buying a scanner but providing you with all the same information

Software

Software **(see illustration)** is available that enables your desktop or laptop computer to interface with the engine management computer on many 1981 and later General Motors and Chrysler vehicles.

Such software can output trouble codes, identify problems without even lifting the hood, solve intermittent performance problems and even help you determine the best repair solutions with on-line technical help. We tested Rinda Technology's Diacom software. It runs on any IBM PC, XT, AT or compatible. The kit includes the software, an instruction manual and the interface cables you need to plug in your computer.

8.10 Trouble code tools simplify the task of extracting trouble codes

Trouble-code tools

A new type of special tool - we'll call it the trouble code tool - has recently become available to the do-it-yourselfer **(see illustration)**. These tools simplify the procedure for extracting trouble codes from your vehicle's engine management computer. Of course, you can extract trouble codes without special tools. And we'll show you how to get those codes with nothing fancier than a jumper wire or an analog multimeter or voltmeter. But trouble code tools do make the job a little easier and they also protect the diagnostic connector terminals and the computer itself from damage.

3 Basic
Part A troubleshooting

1 General information

A malfunctioning fuel injection system or component can cause a variety of problems. While some may be obvious, others are not. The obvious symptoms might include a vehicle that won't start or stay running, sluggish performance or a lack of power, pinging, backfiring or excessive exhaust smoke. Symptoms that are more difficult to diagnose include an occasional fuel smell, an intermittent misfire or decreased fuel mileage.

Many of the symptoms described can also be caused by malfunctions of the basic fuel, ignition or mechanical systems of the vehicle. More often than not, the cause of a problem can be found through inspecting and testing one of these basic systems. You may actually find that performing the basic troubleshooting procedures found in this Chapter may correct the symptoms thought to be fuel injection or computer related.

This Chapter provides a guide to the most common problems, and their corrections, diagnosed with the basic tools common to today's automotive industry.

The fundamentals of all basic engine and fuel systems being dealt with in this Chapter are similar enough, among manufacturers, that the basic tests and specifications given will help you correctly track down the reason(s) for the problem(s) being experienced.

2 Safety precautions

Regardless of how enthusiastic you may be about getting on with the job at hand, take the time to ensure that your safety is not jeopardized. A moment's lack of attention can result in an accident, as can failure to observe certain simple safety precautions. The possibility of an accident will always exist, and the following points should not be considered a comprehensive list of all dangers. Rather, they are intended to make you aware of the risks and to encourage a safety conscious approach to all work you carry out on your vehicle.

Essential DOs and DON'Ts

DON'T rush or take unsafe shortcuts to finish a job.

DON'T allow children or pets in or around the vehicle while you are working on it.

DON'T start the engine without first making sure that the transmission is in Neutral (or Park where applicable) and the parking brake is set.

DON'T touch any part of the engine or exhaust system until it has cooled sufficiently to avoid burns.

DON'T use poorly maintained trouble lights/shop lights that may have exposed wiring, broken insulation or a bad ground

DON'T open any connection in the fuel system without properly releasing the pressure

DON'T siphon toxic liquids such as gasoline, antifreeze and brake fluid by mouth, or allow them to remain on your skin.

DON'T remove the radiator cap from a hot cooling system - let it cool sufficiently, cover the cap with a cloth and release the pressure gradually.

DON'T attempt to drain the engine oil until you are sure it has cooled to the point that it will not burn you.

DON'T use loose fitting wrenches or other tools which may slip and cause injury.

DON'T push on wrenches when loosening or tightening nuts or bolts. Always try to pull the wrench toward you. If the situation calls for pushing the wrench away, push with an open hand to avoid scraped knuckles if the wrench should slip.

DO keep loose clothing and long hair well out of the way of moving parts.

DO get someone to check on you periodically when working alone on a vehicle.

DO carry out work in a logical sequence and make sure that everything is correctly assembled and tightened.

DO keep chemicals and fluids tightly capped and out of the reach of children and pets.

DO remember that your vehicle's safety affects that of yourself and others. If in doubt on any point, seek professional advice.

Gasoline and fuel injection cleaners

Warning: *Gasoline and fuel injection cleaners are extremely flammable, so take extra precautions when you work on any part of the fuel system or hook up external connections to clean the system. Don't smoke or allow open flames or bare light bulbs near the work area, and don't work in a garage where a natural gas-type appliance (such as a water heater or a clothes dryer) with a pilot light is present. Since gasoline and fuel injector cleaners are carcinogenic, wear latex gloves when there's a possibility of being exposed to fuel or cleaners, and, if you spill any fuel on your skin, rinse it off immediately with soap and water. The vapors are harmful. Avoid prolonged breathing of vapors or contact with eyes or skin. Always work in an area with adequate ventilation. If using a fuel injector cleaner, follow all additional instructions and warning on the product being used. Mop up any spills immediately and do not store fuel-soaked rags where they could ignite. The fuel system on fuel-injected models is under constant pressure, so, if any fuel lines are to be disconnected, the fuel pressure in the system must be relieved first (see Chapter 4 for more information). When you perform any kind of work on the fuel system, wear safety glasses and have a Class B type fire extinguisher on hand.*

Fire

Warning: *We strongly recommend that a fire extinguisher suitable for use on fuel and electrical fires be kept handy in the garage or the workshop at all times. Never try to extinguish a fuel or electrical fire with water. Post the phone number for the nearest fire department in a conspicuous location near the phone.*

A spark caused by an electrical short circuit, by two metal surfaces contacting each other, or even by static electricity built up in your body under certain conditions, can ignite gasoline or battery vapors, which in a confined space are highly explosive. Do not, under any circumstances, use gasoline for cleaning parts. Use an approved safety solvent.

Fumes

Warning: *Certain fumes are highly toxic and can quickly cause unconsciousness and even death if inhaled to any extent. Gasoline vapor falls into this category, as do the vapors from some cleaning solvents. Any draining or pouring of such volatile fluids should be done in a well ventilated area.*

When using cleaning fluids and solvents, read the instructions on the container carefully. Never use materials from unmarked containers.

Never run the engine in an enclosed space, such as a garage. Exhaust fumes contain carbon monoxide, which is extremely poisonous. If you need to run the engine, always do so in the open air, or at least have the rear of the vehicle outside the work area.

If you are fortunate enough to have the use of an inspection pit, never drain or pour gasoline and never run the engine while the vehicle is over the pit. The fumes, being heavier than air, will concentrate in the pit with possibly lethal results.

In the event of an emergency, be sure to post the phone number for a poison control center in a conspicuous location near the phone.

Battery

Warning: *Never create a spark or allow a bare light bulb near a battery. They normally give off a certain amount of hydrogen gas, which is highly explosive.*

Always disconnect the battery ground/negative(-) cable at the battery before working on the fuel or electrical systems. If disconnecting both cables for any reason, always disconnect the ground/negative cable first, then disconnect the positive cable. This will avoid the spark, that could ignite fuel or battery fumes, that would occur if the positive cable was removed first.

If possible, loosen the filler caps or cover when charging the battery from an external source (this does not apply to sealed or maintenance-free batteries). Do not charge at an excessive rate or the battery may burst.

Take care when adding water to a non maintenance-free battery and when carrying a battery. The electrolyte, even when diluted, is very corrosive and should not be allowed to contact clothing or skin.

Always wear eye protection when using compressed air.

Always wear eye protection when cleaning the battery to prevent the caustic deposits from entering your eyes.

Household current

When using an electric power tool, inspection light, etc., which operates on household current, always make sure that the tool is correctly connected to its plug and that, where necessary, it is properly grounded. Do not use such items in damp conditions and, again, do not create a spark or apply excessive heat in the vicinity of fuel or fuel vapor.

Secondary ignition system voltage

A severe electric shock can result from touching certain parts of the secondary ignition system (such as the spark plug wires, coil, etc.) when the engine is running or being cranked, particularly if components are damp or the insulation is defective. In the case of an electronic ignition system, the secondary system voltage is much higher and could prove fatal.

3 Vehicle identification

Changes, modifications and corrections are a continuing process in vehicle and replacement parts manufacturing. Don't rely on information that is 'thought' to be correct. Always find the **correct** specification and procedure. It may have been correct for one model year and not the next, even if everything in the vehicle appears the same in all other respects.

Since spare parts manuals and lists are compiled on a numerical basis, the individual vehicle numbers are essential to correctly identify the part needed when going to the local parts store or when checking the specifications to be used.

Vehicle Identification Number (VIN)

This very important identification number is stamped on a plate attached to the left side of the dashboard just inside the windshield on the driver's side of the vehicle (see illustration). The VIN also appears on the Vehicle Certificate of Title and Registration. It contains information such as where and when the vehicle was manufactured, the model year and engine codes.

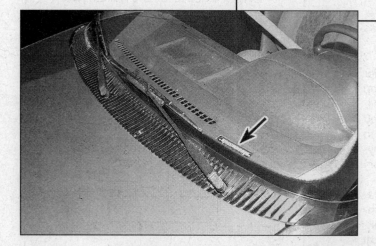

3.1 The Vehicle Identification Number (VIN) is important for identifying the vehicle and engine type - it is on the front of the dash, visible from outside the vehicle, looking through the windshield on the driver's side. The chart shows the information conveyed by the VIN (on 1981 and later vehicles). The eighth digit identifies the engine and the tenth digit denotes the model year - (on almost all vehicles) see the text for further explanation

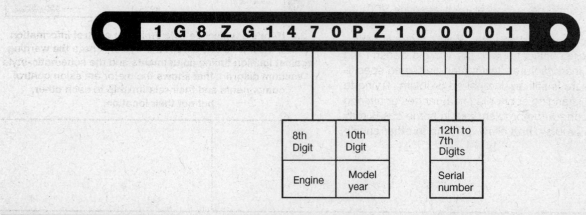

8th Digit	10th Digit		12th to 7th Digits
Engine	Model year		Serial number

Finding the correct information is the usual starting point and two important pieces to find first are the model year and engine codes. On models through 1980 the VIN has 11, 12 or 13 digits, depending on manufacturer. On Chrysler and General Motors products the engine code is the fifth digit (counting from the left) and the model year code is the sixth digit. On AMC vehicles the second digit is the model year code and the seventh digit is the engine code. On Ford cars the first digit is the model year code and the fifth digit is the engine code. On Ford trucks the fifth digit is the engine code and the sixth digit is the model year code. On Jeep vehicles the second digit is the model year and the sixth digit is the engine code. On 1981 and later models the VIN has 17 digits - the 8th digit is the engine code and the 10th digit is the model year code. The exception to this is on some AMC and Jeep vehicles. On some of these models the fourth digit is the engine code and the tenth digit is the model year code.

Caution: *It's possible the original engine may have been "swapped" for a different engine somewhere in the life of the vehicle. This information may or may not have been passed on from owner to owner. If the engine has been replaced it will be necessary to know what engine (year, size, emissions, etc.) is in the vehicle, in order to find the correct specifications to use for repairs or adjustments.*

The Vehicle Emissions Control Information (VECI) label

The VECI label **(see illustrations)** identifies the engine, the fuel system and the emission control systems used on your specific vehicle. It also provides essential tune-up specifications, such as the spark plug gap, slow-idle speed, fast-idle speed, initial ignition timing setting (if adjustable) and components that originally came on the vehicle such as Exhaust Gas Recirculation (EGR), Three way catalyst converter (TWC), Fuel Injection (FI), etc.

Some VECI labels simply provide the specifications for these adjustments; others even include brief step-by-step adjustment procedures. Most labels also provide a simplified vacuum diagram of the emissions control devices used on your vehicle and the vacuum lines connecting them to each other and to engine vacuum. You won't find everything you need to know on the VECI label, but it's a very good place to start.

The information on the VECI label is specific to your vehicle. Any changes or modifications authorized by the manufacturer will be marked on the label by a technician making the modification. He may also indicate the change with a special modification decal and place it near the VECI label.

It can't be emphasized enough, DON'T make substitutions for parts or specifications. If the vehicle doesn't run well with all the manufacturer designated parts and specifications used, there is still an unrepaired problem. Trying to compensate by changing spark plug heat ranges or altering timing doesn't correct the problem and in some cases may actually mask a problem and allow damage to other engine components.

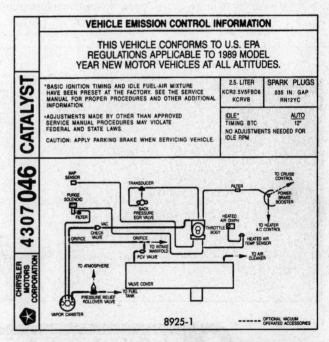

3.2 Here's a typical Vehicle Emission control Information (VECI) label (this one's from a Chrysler) - note the warning against ignition timing adjustments and the schematic-style vacuum diagram that shows the major emission control components and their relationship to each other, but not their location.

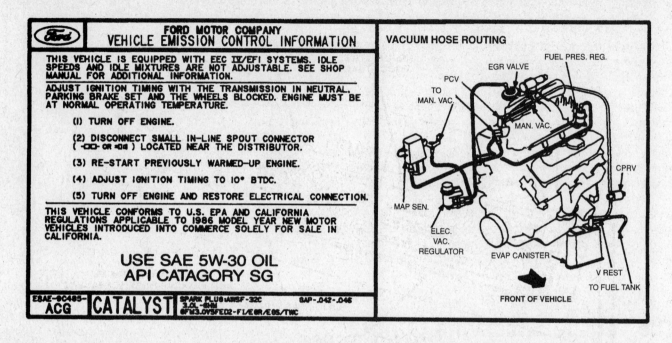

3.3 This VECI label is from a Ford - note the brief ignition timing procedure and the line-art style vacuum diagram that shows not only what emissions components are on the engine, but also what they look like and where they're located.

What does a VECI label look like?

The VECI label is usually a small, white, adhesive-backed, plastic-coated label about 4 X 6 inches in size, located somewhere in the engine compartment. It's usually affixed to the underside of the hood, the radiator support, the front upper crossmember, the firewall or one of the inner wheel wells.

What if you can't find the VECI label?

If you're not the original owner of your vehicle, and you can't find the VECI label anywhere, chances are it's been removed, or the body part to which it was affixed has been replaced. Don't worry - you can buy a new one at a dealer parts department. **Note:** *They normally have to be ordered from the assembly plant at which the vehicle was manufactured.*

Be sure to give the parts department the VIN number, year, model, engine, etc. of your vehicle; be as specific as possible. For instance, if it's a high-altitude model, a 49-state model or a California model, be sure to tell them, because each of these models may have a different fuel system and a unique combination of emission control devices.

Don't just forget about the VECI label if you don't have one. Intelligent diagnosis of the fuel injection system on your vehicle begins here. Without the VECI label, you can't be sure every component is still installed and connected, as originally manufactured.

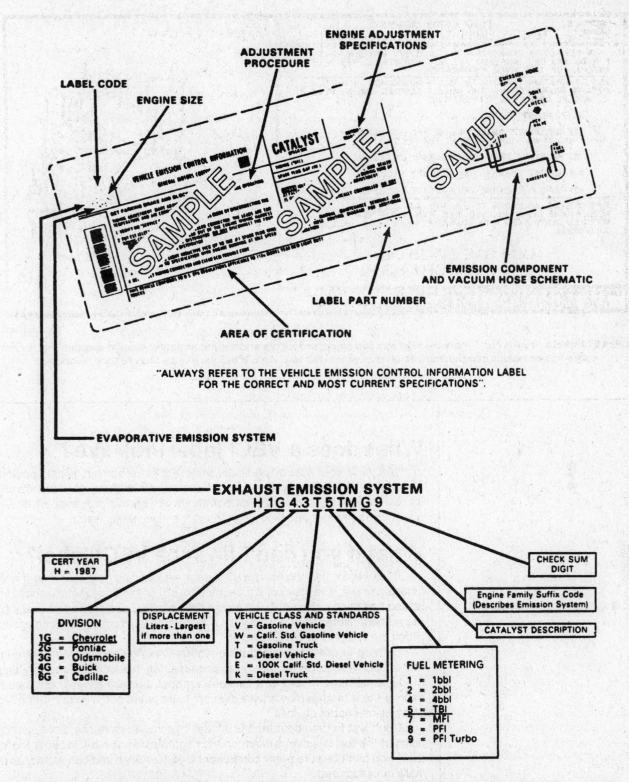

3.4 No matter what vehicle they're used on, General Motors VECI labels are all formatted the same way, even though the information provided at each location on the label is specific to the make and model.

4 Problem identification

Identifying the problem, or symptom, is the first step in using your time wisely, getting to the basis for the problem quickly and dealing with it effectively.

The most inexpensive and easiest way to keep your vehicle operating properly is simply to check it over on a regular basis. This is the best to way spot individual problems before other component problems occur and compound the symptoms. When maintenance is ignored, over a period of time, multiple repairs usually become necessary. This makes diagnosing the symptoms more difficult than if they had been discovered individually during periodic checks.

The emissions, fuel, ignition, and engine management systems are interrelated, a minor problem in one can have a ripple effect on others. These minor malfunctions among several systems can eventually lead to a breakdown which could have been avoided by a simple check and maintenance program.

When you've taken a vehicle to a dealership or auto shop in the past, you'll probably remember how difficult it was to make the service advisor clearly understand the problem being experienced. Some times the written repair order described something completely different than what you were trying to convey. So the explanation and problem, many times, was mis-diagnosed or the problem may not have been addressed completely. A return visit to the shop now becomes necessary. This example of poor communication is the stuff that the highly advertised Customer Satisfaction Index (CSI) ratings are made of. Repeat repairs and return visits to a shop don't make for a happy customer.

Follow simple guidelines like:

Don't ignore the basics! (spark, fuel, air, etc.).

Don't overlook the simple or obvious problems that can be found upon visual inspection (vacuum line disconnected, air intake hose cracked, etc.).

Never assume that someone else's diagnosis is correct.

Start out the repair procedure correctly by questioning yourself, or the driver that experienced the symptoms, these essential pieces of information:

WHAT are the problems or symptoms being experienced?

Does the engine stall, surge, misfire, or does it idle rough? . . . etc.

WHEN are these symptoms experienced?

Is the engine hot or cold? Does the problem happen immediately, or only after an extended drive? Is the vehicle moving at a constant speed or idling at a stop when the problem occurs? Does the problem occur under easy or hard acceleration? Is the weather wet or dry? . . . etc.

WHERE do the symptoms seem to be most obvious or severe?

Are they most severe under a load (possibly pulling a trailer or boat), going up a grade, at sea level or high altitude (such as Denver, Albuquerque, etc.)?

Did the vehicle emit any out-of-the-ordinary noises or unusual smells at the time the problem was being experienced?

Noises from pre-ignition (pinging) or the smell of sulfur (rotten eggs) could help pinpoint the problem system or component.

Has another shop or person worked on the vehicle recently?

If so ,what problems was the vehicle taken in for? What was the diagnosis? What was actually done to repair the vehicle?

Everyone has heard, at one time or another, that there is no such thing as a dumb question. Getting all the information possible to repair a problem, in a timely and effective manner, an instance time when that old saying really holds true. Ask all the questions necessary that will help clarify the problem. This can only help narrow the search for the cause of the problem. Even ask questions like; is tire inflation correct? . . . was the parking brake applied? . . .what is the quality of gasoline used? . . .when was the last time the vehicle was serviced, and what was done? . . . etc. If you think these questions sound dumb, imagine how sluggish a vehicle would feel with tires at half pressure, or with a parking brake that is partially applied.

5 Basic system checks

General engine condition

The term "tune-up" is used in this manual to represent a combination of individual operations rather than one specific procedure.

If, from the time the vehicle is new, the routine maintenance schedule is followed closely and frequent checks are made of fluid levels and high wear items, as suggested throughout this manual, the engine will be kept in relatively good running condition and the need for additional work will be minimized.

More likely than not, however, there will be times when the engine is running poorly due to lack of regular maintenance. This is even more likely if a used vehicle, which has not received regular and frequent maintenance checks, is purchased. In such cases, an engine tune-up will be needed outside of the regular routine maintenance intervals.

The following general list of components and tests are those most often needed to bring a generally poor running engine back into a proper state of tune:

Air intake system
Cooling system
Underhood hoses
Check all engine-related fluids
Adjustment of the drivebelts
Check engine vacuum and hoses
Clean, inspect and test the battery, cables and starter
Charging system output
Primary ignition system
Secondary ignition system
Computer power and grounds
Emissions related components
Fuel pump pressures

Any of these areas or components found to be excessively worn, damaged or out of specifications should be repaired replaced before proceeding with other diagnosis.

The vehicle being worked on may have a problem with one or more of these items or systems, so take the time to be thorough and use the procedures in the following Sections.

Since you are now at this point in the repair procedure, questions should have been asked and the visual inspection should have been completed. If the symptom or problem still exists, follow the procedures described to more closely examine the individual components making up the fundamental engine systems.

Disable the ignition system, either by grounding the ignition coil or disconnecting the primary (low voltage) wires from the coil, so that the vehicle won't start.

Crank the engine over and listen to the sound it is making. A smooth, even rhythm to the engines rotation, with no slowing at spots during cranking, is a good general indicator that there is even compression in all cylinders. High or low compression, in comparison to other cylinders, would cause individual piston strokes to be harder or easier than others, thereby causing uneven rotating speed.

Now this isn't, by any stretch of the imagination, as accurate as actually performing a compression test. For purposes of saving time, finding the source and correcting the problem, this quick check will indicate whether more time should be spent on this area or should you go on to look elsewhere for the source of the driveability problem being experienced.

A good general rule of thumb would be if fluctuations or surging are noted of more than 40 or 50 rpm, then there is a significant difference between the compression of the cylinders. A more in-depth look at each individual cylinder should be taken with a compression gauge to more accurately determine the cause for the compression differences.

Airflow, filters, hoses and connections

Inspect the outer surface of the filter element. Even if the surface looks fairly clean it needs to checked further. Place a shop light on one side of the element and see if light can be see when looking through the filter towards the light. If it is dirty, replace it. If it is only moderately dusty, it can be reused by blowing it clean, from the back to the front surface, with compressed air. If it is a pleated paper type filter, it cannot be washed or oiled. If it cannot be cleaned satisfactorily with compressed air, discard and replace it.

High temperatures in the engine compartment can cause the deterioration of the rubber and plastic components and/or hoses used for engine, accessory and emission systems operation. Periodic inspection should be made for soft deteriorating hoses, cracks, loose clamps, material hardening and leaks.

Some, but not all, hoses are secured to the fittings with clamps. Where clamps are used, check to be sure they haven't lost their tension, allowing the hose to leak. If clamps aren't used, make sure the hose has not expanded and/or hardened where it slips over the fitting.

Airleak check

The term "airleak" refers to outside air that has entered the system downstream (after) from the airflow meter or mass airflow sensor (where the airflow is metered and fuel flow is calibrated accordingly) but before the intake valves. This un-metered air makes the correct air/fuel calculations difficult, if not impossible. The computer can't measure the additional air to so it's unable to compensate for the change, which results in a lean air/fuel mixture. Although the oxygen sensor does send a signal to adjust for what is indicated by the exhaust gas, it can't command a large enough adjustment to overcome the problem.

Look for air inlet hoses, and rubber ductwork that has broken, split or cracked from age and/or underhood heat. One other possibility may be from a previous repair. Sometimes connections don't always get aligned or reassembled quite right. Handling of original hoses or lines sometimes causes them to crack because they have become so brittle with age and heat.

Check for leaks in the air intake system spraying water or carburetor spray in the area of suspected leaks and listen for an rpm change. **Warning:** *Carburetor spray is flammable and can ignite if sprayed on hot manifolds or comes in contact with an open spark. For the sake of safety, it's recommended that water be used to check for air leaks.*

Oil level and condition

The proper level of good clean oil must be maintained in the engine at all times for a number of reasons. Everyone knows that the first and foremost reason is lubrication, which prevents engine damage. But dirty oil has an affect on other systems as well.

Poorly maintained engine oil will allow sludge and moisture to build up within the lubrication system. Over a period of time this can lead to blockages in the oil passage ways or PCV systems. This can increase crankcase pressure and as a result increase blow-by gases. Excessive blow-by combined with marginal ignition parts can combine to create an engine misfire that may be hard to locate.

Many modern vehicles have protection built into the engine management system. If for any reason oil pressure drops below a set lower limit, the oil pressure switch will indicate this lack of pressure and the computer will shut the engine off. Hopefully before any damage can take place.

The lubrication system could often be overlooked as a cause of a stalling problem. Here again, regular maintenance and awareness of the overall condition of the engine may help find a simple solution to a problem, rather than allowing matters more complicated than they really are.

Coolant level, condition and circulation

The level, condition and circulation of the coolant has a direct affect on engine operation. Of course, the engine must not be allowed to overheat, but it must also reach the correct operating temperature for proper fuel control to take place. Therefore, a thermostat that operates within the temperature range the vehicle was originally designed for, must be installed in the cooling system at all times. Never install a "cooler" thermostat in your engine in an attempt to solve an overheating problem, and never, ever, completely remove the thermostat. With the thermostat removed, the engine may remain in the "open loop" mode (no computerized fuel control) and fuel economy and performance will suffer.

The cooling system must be maintained properly to keep the engine from overheating. Overheating the engine can cause many problems, none of which would seem to be fuel injection related. But when an engine is overheated it can not only damage the engine mechanically, it can also damage sensors, electrical solenoids and output actuators, all of which have a impact on how the computer senses the operating condition of the engine. The damaged condition of these components and the ECM's attempt to manage all the systems, without accurate information, will cause a driveability problem. This is one of those items that, although unrelated, can indirectly affect other systems, such as fuel injection, of the vehicle.

The cooling system should be checked with the engine cold. Do this before the vehicle is driven for the day or after the engine has been shut off for at least three hours. Remove the cooling system cap and inspect the condition of the coolant. **Note:** *Some later vehicles no longer have a cap on the radiator itself. In these systems the coolant expansion tank/reservoir is part of the pressure system. The pressure cap is located on the expansion tank.* If you hear a hissing sound (indicating there is still pressure in the system), wait until it stops before proceeding with the cap removal.

The coolant inside the radiator will have some color, probably light green or pink, but should be relatively transparent. If it's rust colored, the system should be drained and refilled. If the coolant level isn't up to the proper level, add additional antifreeze/coolant mixture until it is.

Thoroughly clean the cap, inside and out, with clean water. Pressure check the radiator cap to be sure it maintains the specified pressure (14-to-18 lbs, and is usually stamped on the cap). Pressurizing the system allows the operating temperature of the coolant to reach a temperature above the normal boiling point of 212 degrees.

Make sure that all hose clamps are tight. A small leak in the cooling system, if not large enough to have a noticeable drip, will usually show up as white or rust colored deposits on the areas adjoining the leak. If older style wire-type clamps are used at the ends of the hoses, it may be a good idea to replace them with more secure screw-type clamps.

If rust or corrosion is excessive, or if the coolant is due to be replaced, consider flushing the cooling system at this time. If corrosion is found at the connections or at the radiator cap it is an indication that the coolant should be flushed from the engine, and refilled with a fresh coolant/water mixture. Flushing kits and/or cooling system additives to clean the inside of the system, are available at local auto parts stores.

Vacuum hoses, fittings and connections

The fuel injection and engine emission systems often use engine vacuum to operate various switches and control devices on the engine. Vacuum may also be used to alter the spark timing at the distributor, if equipped. Accessories such as power brake boosters, automatic transmission vacuum modulators, cruise control systems and heating-ventilation-air conditioning air distribution systems also use engine vacuum to operate their various systems. A vacuum leak in any one of these systems could seriously affect engine performance.

Most emission control systems depend on vacuum for proper operation. These systems use numerous vacuum-operated devices that respond to vacuum to activate and deactivate output actuators which control emissions by altering engine operation in accordance with changing loads and operating temperatures.

It's quite common for vacuum hoses, especially those in the emissions system, to be color coded or identified by colored stripes. Various systems require hoses with different wall thickness, collapse resistance and temperature resistance. When replacing hoses, be sure the new hoses meet the same specifications as the original.

Often, because the routing of the hose may be under other components, the only effective way to check a hose is to remove it completely from the vehicle. If more than one hose is removed, be sure to label the hoses and fittings to ensure correct installation. When checking vacuum hoses, be sure to include all plastic connectors and T-fittings in the inspection. Look at the fittings for cracks, and check the hose where it fits over the fitting for distortion, hardening or cracking, which could cause leakage. Check the entire hose, but especially at spots where the hose may make contact with hot engine components and/or oil leakage areas. A hot engine can melt through or bake a hose until it crumbles. Likewise, oil leakage will rot a hose until it disintegrates.

The major cause of vacuum-related problems is damaged or disconnected vacuum hoses, lines or tubing. Vacuum leaks can cause many engine performance related problems. It can cause an engine to idle rough or erratic, or misfire. Vacuum leaks in the emission system can cause spark knock or "pinging", or cause an engine to backfire. If large enough leak is present, the engine may stall repeatedly and of course, fuel economy will suffer drastically.

If you suspect a vacuum problem because one or more of the above symptoms occurs, the following visual inspection may get you to the source of the problem with no further testing:

Make sure all the vacuum hoses are routed correctly - kinked lines block vacuum flow at first, then cause a vacuum leak when they crack and break.

Make sure all connections are tight. Look for loose connections and disconnected lines. Vacuum hoses and lines are sometimes accidentally knocked loose by an errant elbow during an oil change or some other maintenance.

Inspect the entire length of every hose, line and tube for breaks, cracks, cuts, hardening, kinks and tears **(see illustration)**. Replace all damaged lines and hoses.

When subjected to the high under hood temperatures of a running engine, hoses become brittle (hardened). Once they're brittle, they crack more easily when subjected to engine vibrations. When you inspect the vacuum hoses and lines, pay particularly close attention to those that are routed near hot areas such as exhaust manifolds, EGR systems, reduction catalysts (often right below the exhaust manifold on modern front-wheel drive vehicles with transverse engines), etc.

Inspect all vacuum devices for visible damage (dents, broken pipes or ports, broken tees in vacuum lines, etc.)

Make sure none of the lines are coated with coolant, fuel, oil or transmission fluid. Many vacuum devices will malfunction if any of these fluids get inside them.

If none of the above steps eliminates the vacuum leak problem, using a vacuum pump, apply vacuum to each suspect area, then watch the gauge for any loss of vacuum.

And if you still can't find the leak? Well, maybe it's not in the fuel injection/engine control system; maybe it's right at the source, at the intake manifold or the base gasket under the throttle body. To test for leaks in this area, spray aerosol carburetor cleaner along the gasket joints with the engine running at idle. If the idle speed smoothes out momentarily, you've located your leak. Tighten the intake manifold or the throttle body fasteners to the specified torque and recheck. If the leak persists, you may have to replace the gasket.

A small piece of vacuum hose (1/4-inch inside diameter) can be used as a stethoscope to detect vacuum leaks. Hold one end of the hose to your ear and probe around vacuum hoses and fittings, listening for the "hissing" sound characteristic of a vacuum leak. **Warning:** *When probing with the vacuum hose stethoscope, watch where you are placing your hands! be very careful not to come into contact with moving engine components such as the drivebelts, cooling fan, etc.*

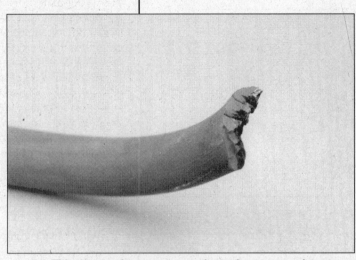

5.1 This vacuum hose was routed too close to an exhaust manifold - after being overheated repeatedly, it finally cracked and broke.

Where can you find vacuum diagrams?

The quickest way to determine what vacuum devices are used in the emission control systems on your vehicle is to refer to the Vehicle Emission Control Information (VECI) label located in the engine compartment. Most vehicles have a vacuum diagram (or "schematic") located on or near the label. The label is usually affixed to the radiator core support, inner fender panel, engine air cleaner assembly or the underside of the hood for convenient reference when working on your vehicle.

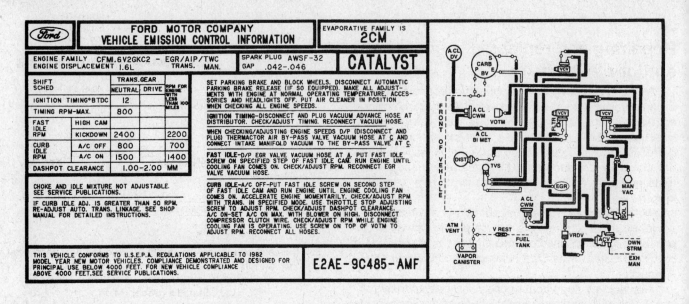

Ford Motor Company Vehicle Emission Control Information label

Ford	FORD MOTOR COMPANY VEHICLE EMISSION CONTROL INFORMATION	EVAPORATIVE FAMILY IS **2CM**

ENGINE FAMILY CFMI.6V2GKC2 - EGR/AIP/TWC
ENGINE DISPLACEMENT 1.6L   TRANS. MAN.

SPARK PLUG AWSF-32   GAP .042-.046

CATALYST

SHIFT SCHED		TRANS.GEAR		RPM FOR ENGINE WITH LESS THAN 100 MILES
		NEUTRAL	DRIVE	
IGNITION TIMING°BTDC		12		
TIMING RPM-MAX.		800		
FAST IDLE RPM	HIGH CAM			
	KICKDOWN	2400	2200	
CURB IDLE RPM	A/C OFF	800	700	
	A/C ON	1500	1400	
DASHPOT CLEARANCE		1.00-2.00 MM		

CHOKE AND IDLE MIXTURE NOT ADJUSTABLE. SEE SERVICE PUBLICATIONS.

IF CURB IDLE ADJ. IS GREATER THAN 50 RPM, RE-ADJUST AUTO. TRANS. LINKAGE. SEE SHOP MANUAL FOR DETAILED INSTRUCTIONS.

SET PARKING BRAKE AND BLOCK WHEELS. DISCONNECT AUTOMATIC PARKING BRAKE RELEASE (IF SO EQUIPPED). MAKE ALL ADJUSTMENTS WITH ENGINE AT NORMAL OPERATING TEMPERATURE. ACCESSORIES AND HEADLIGHTS OFF. PUT AIR CLEANER IN POSITION WHEN CHECKING ALL ENGINE SPEEDS.

IGNITION TIMING-DISCONNECT AND PLUG VACUUM ADVANCE HOSE AT DISTRIBUTOR. CHECK/ADJUST TIMING. RECONNECT VACUUM HOSE.

WHEN CHECKING/ADJUSTING ENGINE SPEEDS D/P (DISCONNECT AND PLUG) THERMACTOR AIR BY-PASS VALVE VACUUM HOSE AT C AND CONNECT INTAKE MANIFOLD VACUUM TO THE BY-PASS VALVE AT C.

FAST IDLE-D/P EGR VALVE VACUUM HOSE AT A. PUT FAST IDLE SCREW ON SPECIFIED STEP OF FAST IDLE CAM. RUN ENGINE UNTIL COOLING FAN COMES ON. CHECK/ADJUST RPM. RECONNECT EGR VALVE VACUUM HOSE.

CURB IDLE-A/C OFF-PUT FAST IDLE SCREW ON SECOND STEP OF FAST IDLE CAM AND RUN ENGINE UNTIL ENGINE COOLING FAN COMES ON. ACCELERATE ENGINE MOMENTARILY. CHECK/ADJUST RPM WITH TRANS. IN SPECIFIED MODE. USE THROTTLE STOP ADJUSTING SCREW TO ADJUST RPM. CHECK/ADJUST DASHPOT CLEARANCE. A/C ON-SET A/C ON MAX. WITH BLOWER ON HIGH. DISCONNECT COMPRESSOR CLUTCH WIRE. CHECK/ADJUST RPM WHILE ENGINE COOLING FAN IS OPERATING. USE SCREW ON TOP OF VOTM TO ADJUST RPM. RECONNECT ALL HOSES.

THIS VEHICLE CONFORMS TO U.S.E.P.A. REGULATIONS APPLICABLE TO 1982 MODEL YEAR NEW MOTOR VEHICLES. COMPLIANCE DEMONSTRATED AND DESIGNED FOR PRINCIPAL USE BELOW 4000 FEET. FOR NEW VEHICLE COMPLIANCE ABOVE 4000 FEET.SEE SERVICE PUBLICATIONS.

E2AE-9C485-AMF

5.2 Raise the hood and find your VECI label - many manufacturers place the vacuum diagram right on the VECI label

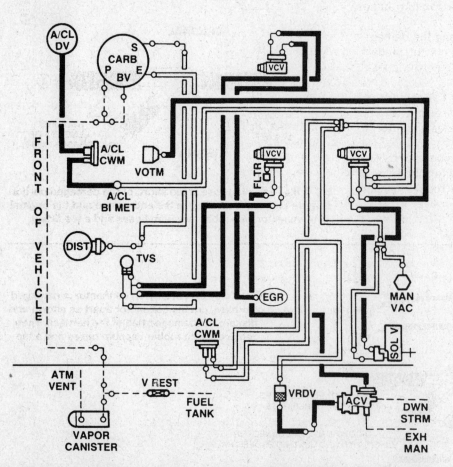

Raise the hood and find your VECI label. Most manufacturers place the vacuum diagram right on the VECI label **(see illustration)**. Some put it on a separate label, near the VECI label **(see illustration)**. **Note:** *The diagrams in this manual are typical examples of the type you'll find on your vehicle's VECI label, in a Haynes Automotive Repair Manual or in a factory service manual. But they're instructional - they DON'T necessarily apply to your vehicle. When you're working on fuel injection/engine control systems, if you notice differences between the vacuum diagram affixed to your vehicle and those in the owner's manual, a Haynes Auto Repair Manual for the specific vehicle or a factory manual, always go with the one on the vehicle. It's always the most accurate diagram.*

If the VECI label has been removed from your vehicle, replacement labels are available at your authorized dealer parts department. (Of course, as mentioned above, sometimes the vacuum diagram is part of the VECI label, sometimes they're not).

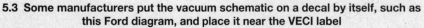

5.3 Some manufacturers put the vacuum schematic on a decal by itself, such as this Ford diagram, and place it near the VECI label

Repairing and replacing vacuum hose and/or plastic lines

Replace defective sections one at a time to avoid confusion or misrouting. If you discover more than one disconnected line during an inspection of the lines, refer to the vehicle vacuum schematic to make sure you reattach the lines correctly. Route rubber hoses and nylon lines away from hot components, such as EGR tubes and exhaust manifolds, and away from rough surfaces which may wear holes in them.

Most factory-installed vacuum lines are rubber, but some are nylon. Connectors can be plastic, bonded nylon or rubber. Nylon connectors usually have rubber inserts to provide a seal between the connector and the component connection.

Replacing nylon vacuum lines can be expensive and tricky. Using rubber hose may not be as aesthetically pleasing as the OEM nylon tubing, but it's perfectly acceptable, as long as the hoses and fittings are tightly connected and correctly routed (away from rough surfaces and hot EGR tubes, exhaust manifolds, etc.).

Here are some tips for repairing nylon vacuum hoses and lines:

If a nylon hose is broken or kinked, and the damaged area is 1/2-inch or more from a connector, cut out the damaged section (don't remove more than 1/2-inch) and install a rubber union **(see illustration)**.

If the remaining hose is too short, or the damage exceeds 1/2-inch in length, replace the entire hose and the original connector with rubber vacuum hoses and a tee fitting **(see illustration)**.

If only part of a nylon connector is damaged or broken, cut it apart and discard the damaged half of the harness **(see illustration)**. Then replace it with rubber vacuum hoses and a tee.

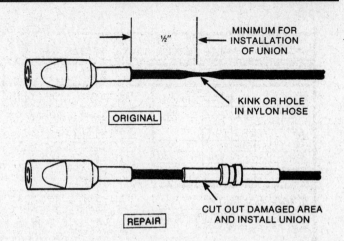

5.4 If nylon hose is broken or kinked, and the damaged area is 1/2-inch or more from the connector, cut out the damaged section (don't remove more than 1/2-inch) and install a rubber union

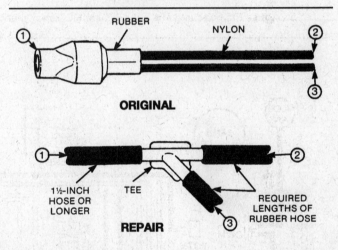

5.5 If the remaining hose is too short, or the damaged portion is more than 1/2-inch, replace the entire hose and the original connector with rubber vacuum hoses and a tee fitting

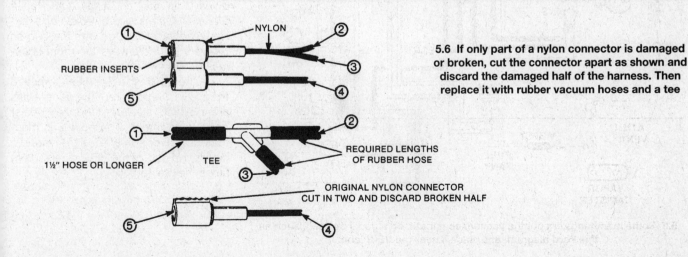

5.6 If only part of a nylon connector is damaged or broken, cut the connector apart as shown and discard the damaged half of the harness. Then replace it with rubber vacuum hoses and a tee

Battery, cables, electrical connections and grounds

Battery warnings and precautions:

a)   Batteries give off hydrogen gas constantly. During charging, they give off even more. Hydrogen gas is highly explosive.

b)   Always disconnect the battery cable from the negative terminal **first,** and hook it up **last**.

c)   Sulfuric acid is the active ingredient in battery electrolyte (the fluid inside the battery). It's a powerful acid that will corrode all common metals, destroy paint finishes and clothing and inflict serious burns when it contacts skin and eyes.

d)   If you spill electrolyte on your skin, rinse it off immediately with water.

e)   If you get electrolyte in your eyes, flush them with water for 15 minutes and get prompt medical attention.

f)   If you accidentally ingest electrolyte, immediately drink large amounts of water or milk. Follow with milk of magnesia, beaten eggs or vegetable oil. Call a doctor immediately.

g)   When you service, charge or jump start a battery, make sure the area is well ventilated.

h)   Never allow flames, cigarettes or any device that might cause a spark anywhere near a battery being charged or jump started.

i)   When inspecting or servicing the battery, always turn the engine and all accessories off.

j)   Never break a live circuit at the battery terminals. An arc could occur when the battery, charger or jumper cables are disconnected, igniting the hydrogen gas.

k)   Always wear safety goggles when performing any work on the battery.

l)   When loosening cables or working near a battery, keep metallic tools away from the battery terminals. The resulting short circuit or spark could damage the battery or ignite the hydrogen gas around the battery.

m)   Never move a battery with the vent caps removed. Electrolyte can easily splash out.

n)   Always use a battery carrier when lifting a battery with a plastic case or place your hands at the bottom and end of the battery. If you're not careful, too much pressure on the ends can cause acid to spew through the vent caps.

o)   Use fender covers to protect the vehicle from acid spillage.

p)   Keep sharp objects out of the battery tray to avoid puncturing the case, and don't over tighten the battery hold-down.

Maintenance

All batteries, although later batteries are called "maintenance free," do require some attention. Poor battery and cable connections **(see illustration)** can cause starting problems and poor operation of the electrical system. The high current requirement of the starting system means that voltage loss through the cables (voltage drop) must be minimized. The voltage drop, caused by the resistance in the cable, the ends and all their connections, reduces the amount of available voltage for cranking, starting and sometimes even computer functions. Inspect the entire length of each battery cable. Inspect the clamps and all connections. Examine the positive and negative terminals and cables for corrosion or loose connections (usually these two problems are found together, so check for both). Clean and/or replace the cables as necessary.

5.7 Battery terminal corrosion usually appears as light, fluffy powder

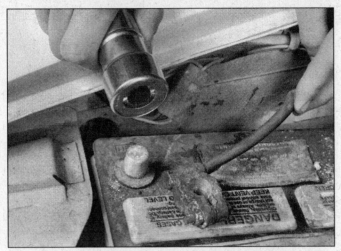

5.8 Regardless of the type of tool used on the battery posts, a clean, shiny surface should be the result

5.9 When cleaning the cable clamps, all corrosion must be removed (the inside of the clamp is tapered to match the taper on the post, so don't remove too much material)

Clean the cable clamps thoroughly with a battery brush or a terminal cleaner **(see illustrations)** and a solution of warm water and baking soda. Wash the terminals and the top of the battery case with the same solution but make sure that the solution doesn't get into the battery. When cleaning the cables, terminals and battery top, wear safety goggles and rubber gloves to prevent any solution from coming in contact with your eyes or hands. Wear old clothes too - even diluted, sulfuric acid splashed onto clothes will burn holes in them. If the terminals have been extensively corroded, clean them with a terminal cleaner. Thoroughly wash all cleaned areas with plain water. **Note:** *Although cables can be repaired and replacement ends are available, it is a good idea to replace the entire cable. Replacement cables have connections that are sealed and resist corrosion much better, and thereby give the cable a longer life, than repaired connections.*

Earlier batteries, with removable vent caps, must be checked periodically for low electrolyte (battery fluid) in each of the cells. **Note:** *If you have a maintenance free battery with removable caps, it's a good idea to occasionally check the electrolyte level, regardless of the manufacturers recommendations. If any of the cells are found to be low, water can be added to bring them up to the correct level.*

Battery condition

On models not equipped with a sealed battery, check the electrolyte level of all six battery cells. Remove the filler caps and check the level of each individual cell. - they must be at or near the split ring. If the level is low, add distilled water. Install and securely re-tighten the caps.

Use a hydrometer **(see illustration)**, that can be purchased at local automotive parts stores, and the accompanying chart **(see illustration)**, to check the state of charge of each battery cell.

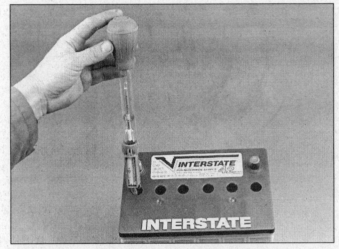

5.10 Use a hydrometer to measure the specific gravity of each individual cell

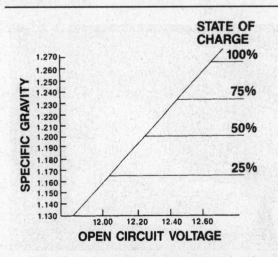

5.11 Use the specific gravity to determine the state of charge of the battery

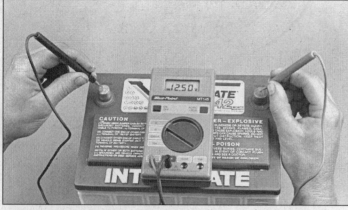

5.12 Measure the battery voltage by using the voltmeter, with a test lead at each battery post, Place the positive lead to the positive post and the negative lead to the negative post

If the battery has a sealed top and no built-in hydrometer to check the state of the batteries charge, you can hook up a digital voltmeter across the battery terminals to check the charge **(see illustration)**. A fully charged battery should read 12.6 volts or higher (engine off). If the voltage is less than 12.6 volts, charge the battery fully and retest.

Battery Charging

Warning: *Battery handling and servicing involves two hazardous substances: sulfuric acid and hydrogen gas. When batteries are being charged, sulfuric acids creates hydrogen gas, which is very explosive and flammable, is produced. Do not smoke or allow open flames near a charging or a recently charged battery. Wear eye protection when near the battery during charging. Also, make sure the charger is unplugged before connecting or disconnecting the battery from the charger.*

Slow-rate charging is the best way to restore a battery that's discharged to the point where it will not start the engine. It's also a good way to maintain the battery charge in a vehicle that's only driven a few miles between starts. Maintaining the battery charge is particularly important in the winter when the battery must work harder to start the engine and electrical accessories that drain the battery are in greater use.

It's best to use a one or two-amp battery charger (sometimes called a "trickle" charger). They are the safest and put the least strain on the battery. They are also the least expensive. For a faster charge, you can use a higher amperage charger, but don't use one rated more than 1/10th the amp/hour rating of the battery. Rapid boost chargers that claim to restore the power of the battery in one to two hours are hardest on the battery and can damage batteries not in good condition; this type of charging should only be used in emergency situations.

The average time necessary to charge a battery should be listed in the instructions that come with the charger. As a general rule, a trickle charger will fully charge a battery in 12 to 16 hours.

Remove all the cell caps (if equipped) and cover the holes with a clean, damp cloth to prevent spattering electrolyte. Disconnect the negative battery cable and hook the battery charger leads to the battery posts (positive to positive, negative to negative), then plug in the charger. Make sure it is set at 12 volts if it has a selector switch.

If you're using a charger with a rate higher than two amps, check the battery regularly during charging to make sure it doesn't overheat. If you're using a trickle charger, you can safely let the battery charge overnight after you've checked it regularly for the first couple of hours.

If the battery has removable cell caps, measure the specific gravity with a hydrometer every hour during the last few hours of the charging cycle. Hydrometers are available inexpensively from auto parts stores - follow the instructions that come with the hydrometer. Consider the battery charged when there's no change in the specific gravity reading for two hours and the electrolyte in the cells is gassing (bubbling) freely. The specific gravity reading from each cell should be very close to the others. If not, the battery probably has a bad cell or cells.

Some batteries with sealed tops have built-in hydrometers on the top that indicate the state of charge by the color displayed in the hydrometer window. Normally, a bright-colored hydrometer indicates a full charge and a dark hydrometer indicates the battery still needs charging. Check the battery manufacturer's instructions to be sure you know what the colors mean.

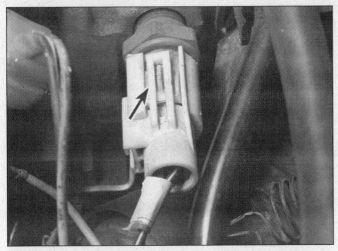

5.13 Most connectors have one or more tabs like this (arrow) that must be lifted before the halves can be separated

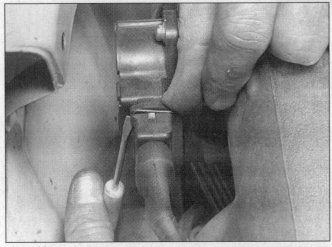

5.14 Some connectors, such as this one on a Toyota throttle position sensor, have a spring clip that must be pried up before the connector can be unplugged

Cables

Battery cables can be deceptive by their appearance. The obvious signs of cracks or corrosion may not be evident, but the cable can still need replacement. Feel the cable. Has it become extremely hard? Is it no longer flexible? Cut back the insulation at little, near the ends and examine the cable. If it shows signs of corrosion that weren't showing on the outside, replace the cable(s). **Note:** *It is recommended that battery cables be replaced in pairs. If one is bad the other is probably very close to the same condition, or shortly will be.*

Connections and electrical grounds

The electrical grounds, both the battery-to-engine block and the engine block-to-body/chassis, are usually overlooked as a source for problems. Inspect all connections, they must be clean on all contacting surfaces and the connection must be tight. Make sure there is a ground strap from the engine to the body and/or chassis.

Once the battery, cables and connections have been checked, repaired, replaced or cleaned, seal the connections from the elements using either a small amount of petroleum jelly or grease to coat the connections. There are products available at local parts stores made specifically for this purpose.

Check the electrical connections to the computer, all sensors and actuators and all other emissions devices. Make sure they're mated properly and tightly connected. Shake and wiggle the connectors to ensure they're tight. Loose connectors should be unplugged and inspected for corrosion **(see illustrations)**. Look closely at t he connector pins and tabs. If corrosion is present, clean it off with a small wire brush and electrical contact cleaner. Some connectors might require use of a special conductive grease to prevent corrosion.

5.15 Many modern engine-management system connectors have flexible seals (arrow) to keep moisture off the terminals and prevent corrosion - make sure the seal isn't damaged in any way

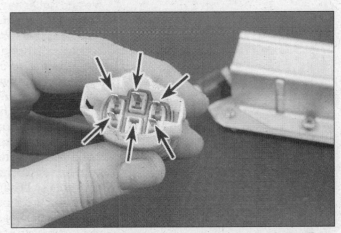

5.16 Check the terminals (arrows) in each connector for corrosion that will cause excessive resistance in the circuit, or even an open circuit

5.17 With your hand, try turning the pulley to see if the belt slips

Charging system

Check the alternator drivebelt tension and condition. Replace the belt if it's worn or deteriorated. If the drivebelt tension is correct, try turning the alternator pulley with your hand to see if the belt is slipping **(see illustration)**. If it slips, replace the belt. When replacing a belt, adjust the tension, then make sure the alternator mounting bolts are tight.

Inspect the alternator wiring harness and the connectors at the alternator. They must be in good condition, tight and have no corrosion.

Start the engine and check the alternator for abnormal noises (a shrieking or squealing sound indicates a bad bearing).

If the alternator is to be replaced, consider a rebuilt unit from the local parts store. Older alternators are rebuildable and most parts are readily available at auto parts stores. Some later model vehicles use alternators, referred to by the manufacturer and aftermarket parts books, as "non-serviceable." This usually means that parts are only available to an authorized rebuilder. Many times parts are soldered or crimped in place. Some fasteners may even be the type that must be broken to disassemble the unit, requiring the same type fastener for reassembly. Don't just blindly start overhauling your alternator. Check for the availability of parts first!

For specific voltage and amperage tests see Section 8 of this Chapter.

Fuel system

Warning 1: *Gasoline is extremely flammable, so take extra precautions when you work on any part of the fuel system. Don't smoke or allow open flames or bare light bulbs near the work area, and don't work in a garage where a natural gas-type appliance (such as a water heater or a clothes dryer) with a pilot light is present. Since gasoline is carcinogenic, wear latex gloves when there's a possibility of being exposed to fuel, and, if you spill any fuel on your skin, rinse it off immediately with soap and water. Mop up any spills immediately and do not store fuel-soaked rags where they could ignite. The fuel system on fuel-injected models is under constant pressure, so, if any fuel lines are to be disconnected, the fuel pressure in the system must be relieved first (see Chapter 4 for more information). When you perform any kind of work on the fuel system, wear safety glasses and have a Class B type fire extinguisher on hand.*

Warning 2: *Many of the rubber fuel lines/hoses used for fuel injection systems are **high-pressure** lines with special crimped on connections. When replacing a hose, use only hose that is specifically designed for your fuel-injection system.*

This Section is to be used as a preliminary check of the fuel system before any disassembly or repairs. For more specifics on inspection, depressurization, disconnection, removal and testing refer to Chapters 4 and 6.

If you smell gasoline while driving or after the vehicle has been sitting in the sun, inspect the fuel system immediately.

Remove the gas filler cap and inspect it for damage and corrosion. The gasket should have an unbroken sealing imprint. If the gasket is damaged or corroded, remove it and install a new one.

Inspect the fuel feed and return lines for cracks. Make sure that all the fittings and connectors, which secure the metal fuel lines to the fuel injection system, and the in-line fuel filter, are properly connected and/or tightened correctly.

Since some components of the fuel system - the fuel tank and part of the fuel feed and return lines, for example - are underneath the vehicle, they can be inspected more easily with the vehicle raised on a hoist. If that's not possible, raise the vehicle and support it securely on jackstands.

Check all rubber fuel lines for deterioration and chafing. Check especially for cracks in areas where the hose bends and just before fittings, such as where a hose attaches to the fuel filter.

With the vehicle raised and safely supported, inspect the fuel tank and filler neck for punctures, cracks and other damage. The connection between the filler neck and the tank is particularly critical. Sometimes, a rubber filler neck will leak because of loose clamps or deteriorated rubber. These are problems a home mechanic can usually rectify. **Warning:** *Do not, under any circumstances, try to repair a fuel tank (except rubber components). A welding torch or any open flame can easily cause fuel vapors inside the tank to explode.*

Carefully check all rubber hoses and metal lines leading away from the fuel tank. Check for loose connections, deteriorated hoses, crimped lines and other damage. Carefully inspect the lines from the tank to the fuel injection system. Repair or replace damaged sections as necessary.

6 Fuel pump pressure check

Key components of the fuel injection system are the fuel pump and the fuel pressure regulator. Incorrect fuel pressure could cause such symptoms as an engine that is hard to start or won't start, to one that hesitates, surges, or misfires. Any basic troubleshooting procedures should include a fuel pump pressure check. Fuel pump pressures and testing procedures are covered in Chapter 6.

7 Troubleshooting with a vacuum gauge

General information

A vacuum gauge provides valuable information about what is going on inside the engine at a low cost. You can check for many internal engine problems such as rings and valves, leaking intake manifold gaskets, restricted exhaust, improper ignition or valve timing and ignition problems.

Vacuum system problems can produce, or contribute to, numerous driveability problems. These include, but aren't limited to:

Deceleration backfiring
Detonation
Hard starting
Knocking or pinging
Overheating
Poor acceleration
Poor fuel economy
Rich or lean stumbling
Rough idling
Stalling
Won't start when cold

Unfortunately, vacuum gauge readings are easy to misinterpret, so they should be used in conjunction with other tests to confirm the diagnosis.

Both the absolute readings and the rate of needle movement are important for accurate interpretation. Most gauges measure vacuum in inches of mercury (in-Hg). The following typical vacuum gauge readings assume the diagnosis is being performed at sea level. As elevation increases (or atmospheric pressure decreases), the reading will decrease. From sea level to approximately 2,000 feet, the gauge readings will the remain the same. For every 1,000 foot increase in elevation above 2,000 feet, the gauge readings will decrease about one inch of mercury. **Example:** *Let's say a vehicle, at sea level, has engine vacuum of 17 to 18 in-Hg. This would be a "normal" reading and not be any indication of internal engine trouble. Now, suppose the same vehicle was driven to Denver, Colorado (5,280 feet above sea level). The vacuum reading would be approximately 14 to 15 in-Hg. This reading would be a concern at sea level, but at a mile above sea level this is an indication of "normal" engine vacuum.*

Connect the vacuum gauge directly to intake manifold vacuum, not to ported vacuum. You want to read full engine vacuum, uncontrolled by the throttle body. Be sure no hoses are left disconnected during the test or false readings will result.

Before you begin the test, allow the engine to warm up completely. Block the wheels and set the parking brake. With the transmission in neutral (or Park, on automatics), start the engine and allow it to run at normal idle speed. **Warning:** *Keep your hands, the vacuum tester and hose clear of the fan and do not stand in front of the vehicle or in line with the fan when the engine is running.*

Read the vacuum gauge and, as a general rule, apply the following guidelines:

What is "normal" vacuum?

Internal combustion engines, regardless of the number of cylinders, all have approximately the same range for acceptable vacuum -f about 15 to 20 inches of mercury (in-Hg).

At wide-open-throttle (WOT) the vacuum reading will be 0 in-Hg, and on deceleration vacuum may go as high, very briefly, as 25 to 28 in-Hg.

Vacuum diagnostic checks

The following guidelines for vacuum are approximate and will be affected by the overall condition of the engine and related systems:

Cranking vacuum

Disable the ignition system and hold the throttle in the wide open position. Take a reading of the engine vacuum while only cranking the engine, don't start the engine at this time. There should be approximately 1-to-4 in-Hg during cranking.

Operating readings

Start the engine and read the gauge. A healthy engine should produce approximately 15-to-20 in-Hg at idle, with a fairly steady needle.

Raise the engine speed to about 2500 rpm and hold rpm steady, a reading of approximately 19-to-21 in-Hg should be seen on the gauge.

Rev the engine up and down, watch the gauge during both increasing and decreasing rpm. At wide open throttle (hard acceleration), vacuum approaches zero. While on deceleration, the vacuum should jump up to somewhere around 21-to-27 in-Hg as the throttle is released.

If the readings you are seeing aren't at the appropriate level or steady, refer to the following vacuum gauge readings and what they indicate about the engine:

Low steady reading

This usually indicates a leaking gasket between the intake manifold and carburetor or throttle body, a leaky vacuum hose, late ignition timing or incorrect camshaft timing **(see illustration)**. Check ignition timing with a timing light and eliminate all other possible causes, utilizing the tests provided in this Chapter, before you remove the timing chain cover to check the timing marks.

7.1 Low, steady reading

7.2 Low, fluctuating needle

7.3 Regular drops

7.4 Irregular drops

Low, fluctuating reading

If the needle fluctuates about three to eight inches below normal **(see illustration)**, suspect an intake manifold gasket leak at an intake port or a faulty injector(s) (on port-injected models only).

Regular drops

If the needle drops about two to four inches at a steady rate **(see illustration)**, the valves are probably leaking. Perform a compression or leakdown test to confirm this.

Irregular drops

An irregular down-flick of the needle **(see illustration)** can be caused by a sticking valve or an ignition misfire. Perform a compression or leakdown test and read the spark plugs.

7.5 Rapid vibration

Rapid vibration

A rapid four in-Hg vibration at idle **(see illustration)** combined with exhaust smoke indicates worn valve guides. Perform a leakdown test to confirm this. If the rapid vibration occurs with an increase in engine speed, check for a leaking intake manifold gasket or head gasket, weak valve springs, burned valves or ignition misfire.

Slight fluctuation

A slight fluctuation, say one inch up and down, may mean ignition problems. Check all the usual tune-up items and, if necessary, run the engine on an ignition analyzer.

Large fluctuation

If this occurs **(see illustration)**, perform a compression or leakdown test to look for a weak or dead cylinder or a blown head gasket.

7.6 Large fluctuation

Slow hunting

If the needle moves slowly through a wide range, check for a clogged PCV system, incorrect idle fuel mixture, carburetor/throttle body or intake manifold gasket leaks.

Slow return after revving

Quickly snap the throttle open until the engine reaches about 2,500 rpm and let it shut. Normally the reading should drop to near zero, rise above normal idle reading (about 5 in-Hg over) and then return to the previous idle reading **(see illustration)**. If the vacuum returns slowly and doesn't peak when the throttle is snapped shut, the rings may be worn. If there is a long delay, look for a restricted exhaust system (often the muffler or catalytic converter). An easy way to check this is to temporarily disconnect the exhaust ahead of the suspected part and redo the test.

7.7 Slow return after revving

Restricted or blocked exhaust

When an exhaust system becomes restricted, usually the catalytic converter, it typically causes a loss of power and backfiring through the throttle body. A vacuum gauge can be used to check for a restricted exhaust by checking for excessive exhaust backpressure and observing any vacuum variation. Follow the steps described:

1   Block the wheels and set the parking brake.
2   Disconnect a vacuum line connected to an intake manifold port, plug the line (so you don't create your own vacuum leak) and install a vacuum gauge to the intake manifold port.
3   Start the engine and record the vacuum at idle. If the vacuum reading slowly drops toward zero, there is a restriction.
4   Gradually increase speed to 2,000 rpm with the transmission in Neutral or Park. The reading from the vacuum gauge should quickly rise above the level recorded at idle, somewhere around 16 in-Hg. If not, there could be excessive backpressure in the exhaust system.
5   While at approximately 2000 rpm, quickly close the throttle. The vacuum reading should return to normal idle vacuum as quickly as it rose above it in the previous step.
6   If the vacuum reading is 5 in-Hg or more higher than the normally observed reading, there is an exhaust restriction.

Once it has been determined that the exhaust system is the cause of the problem, the exact cause must be pinpointed. Perform the following:

7   Turn the ignition key OFF.
8   Disconnect the exhaust system at the exhaust manifold.
9   Start the engine (despite the loud exhaust roar) and gradually increase the engine speed to 2,000 rpm.
10 The reading from the exhaust manifold vacuum gauge should be above 16 in-Hg.
11 If 16 in-Hg. is not reached, the exhaust manifold may be restricted (or the valve timing or ignition timing may be late, or there could be a vacuum leak).
12 If 16 in-Hg. is reached, the blockage is most likely in the muffler, exhaust pipes, or catalytic converter. Also, if the catalytic converter debris has entered the muffler, have it replaced too.

8 Starting and charging circuits

Battery

Warning: *Certain precautions must be followed when checking and servicing the battery. Hydrogen gas, which is highly flammable, is always present in the battery cells, so keep all open flames and sparks away from the battery. The electrolyte inside the battery is actually diluted sulfuric acid, which will cause injury if splashed on your skin or in your eyes. It will also ruin clothes and painted surfaces. See additional warnings and precautions in Section 5 of this Chapter.*
Caution: *Overfilling the cells may cause electrolyte to spill over during periods of heavy charging, causing corrosion or damage. When removing the battery cables, always detach the negative cable first and hook it up last!*

Charging and maintenance

See Section 5 of this Chapter.

Cranking voltage

The next check is cranking voltage. Cranking voltage is used to determine if the battery has enough reserve capacity.

1   Disable the ignition.

2   Hook up a voltmeter across the battery **(see illustration 5.12)**. Now, crank the engine for a few seconds and watch the battery voltage. This will use the starter, cranking the engine, as the load for the battery. **Note:** *In a shop the technicians would use a machine to place an artificial load on the battery with what is called a "carbon pile", a calibrated resistance, to duplicate the starters effect.*

3   The low limit for this test is 9.6 volts. If the voltage falls to 9.6 volts or lower, it doesn't have enough reserve power and will never keep up with the demands of the starting system. Replace the battery. **Note:** *The low limit of 9.6 volts is based upon a outside temperature of approximately 70-degrees Fahrenheit. The acceptable voltage goes down as the temperature drops. If, when testing a battery, the temperature is less than 70-degrees F, refer to the table* **(see illustration)** *for the correct minimum voltage.*

Approximate temperature (degrees Fahrenheit)	Minimum voltage
70	9.6
60	9.5
50	9.4
40	9.3
30	9.1
20	8.9
10	8.7
0	8.5

8.1 Follow this chart to determine the acceptable minimum battery voltage, adjusting for the outside side temperature

Battery ground circuit check

1   The other value to check, while cranking, is the voltage of the battery ground circuit. Hook up the voltmeter positive lead to the battery ground at the engine block or starter and the negative lead to the negative terminal of the battery. **Note:** *Be sure to touch the voltmeter probe directly to the battery post, not the clamp. If touched to the clamp, any additional resistance at that connection to the post would not be measured.* With the ignition still disabled, crank the engine for a few seconds and note the reading on the voltmeter.

2   Readings will probably be somewhere between 0.1 and 0.3 volts. Anything above 0.3 volts is an indication of a bad ground connection. Inspect, clean and replace parts as necessary.

Voltage drops

1   The next concern is the voltage drop (the amount voltage lost from one point to another in an electrical circuit) in the battery terminals, cables, starter and connections. Hook up a voltmeter so the meter is connected across the connection where the voltage drop is to be checked, example: If the voltage loss between the battery post and connecting clamp is to be checked, the voltmeter probes should be connected to the post and the clamp **(see illustration)**.

2   Have the meter set on the volt scale and read the amount of voltage drop on the gauge, it should be 0.2 volts maximum, across any of the individual connections tested.

3   A greater reading than this would indicate an excessive voltage drop. Caused by a loose connection, corroded end or cable, rusty connection, etc. If found, repair any of these conditions and recheck the connections to be sure the problem has been corrected.

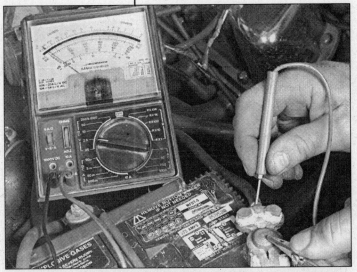

8.2 Here's a battery cable connection being checked for a voltage drop that could be caused by corrosion or a loose connection

8.3 Simple inductive ammeters like this are available from auto parts stores at reasonable prices

8.4 This is another simple inductive ammeter being used to check starter draw while cranking the engine

8.5 To find out whether there's a drain on the battery, simply disconnect the negative battery cable and hook up a test light between the cable clamp and the battery post - if the light comes on, with all the accessories off, there's an electrical drain

Starter

Cranking amperage (starter draw)

1   Checking the amount of cranking amperage required to operate the starter will require the use of an inexpensive inductive amp gauge **(see illustration)** which can be found at most auto parts stores.

2   Disable the ignition system, if not already done from previous tests.

3   Place the gauge directly on the battery cable **(see illustration)**. **Note:** *In order for the reading to be accurate, the use of this gauge requires that it placed directly on the battery cable with about 3-to-4 inches of clearance from all other components to avoid magnetic interference.*

4   Crank the starter and take a reading after the starter reaches a steady cranking speed. This usually takes about 2-to-3 seconds. **Caution:** *Don't continuously operate the starter for more than 15 seconds - it can be damaged by overheating.* Compare your readings to these general guidelines:

   Four cylinder engine - 120-to-180 amps
   Six cylinder engine - 150-to-200 amps
   Eight cylinder engine - 180-to-220 amps

Note: *Large cubic inch or high-compression eight cylinder engines, as well as engines using high-performance starters, may normally use 300-to-350 amps.*

Alternator

1   If a malfunction occurs in the charging system, do not automatically assume the alternator is causing the problem. First check the visual and maintenance items (refer to Section 5, Charging system).

2   Check the battery, as described in the previous Section.

3   With the key off, remove the cable from the negative battery terminal. Connect a test light **(see illustration)** between the negative battery post and the disconnected negative cable clamp:

   a) If the test light does not come on, reattach the clamp and proceed to the next step.

   b) If the test light comes on, there is a short (drain) in the electrical system of the vehicle. The short must be repaired before the charging system can be checked.

4   Disconnect the alternator wiring harness:

   a) If the light goes out, there's a problem in the alternator. Repair or replace it.

   b) If the light stays on, pull each fuse until the light goes out. When the light goes out it indicates which circuit has the problem.

   c) Now, replace the fuse and inspect and/or disconnect each individual component of that circuit to find the cause of the current drain **Note:** *Many owners manuals have a section describing the fuse block and list of the components that are handled by each circuit.* Repair and/or replace as necessary.

5   Reconnect the cable to the negative battery terminal. Start the engine, increase engine speed to approximately 2000 RPM and check the battery voltage again. It should now be approximately 13.5 to 14.7 volts.

6   Turn on the headlights. The voltage should drop, and then come back up, if the charging system is working properly.

7   If the voltage reading is more than approximately 14.7 volts, check the regulator ground connection (vehicles with remotely mounted regulators). If the ground is OK, the problem lies in the regulator, the alternator or the wiring between them. If the vehicle has an internal regulator, replace the alternator. If the vehicle has a remotely mounted regulator, remove the electrical connector from the regulator and repeat checking the voltage at 2000 rpm. If the voltage drops with the regulator disconnected, replace the regulator. If the voltage is still high, there's a short in the wiring between the alternator and regulator or there's a short in the rotor or stator within the alternator. Check the wiring. If the wiring is OK, replace the alternator.

8   If the voltage is less than 13 volts, an undercharging condition is present. If the vehicle is equipped with an indicator light, turn the ignition key to ON and see if the light illuminates. If it does, proceed to the next Step. If it doesn't, check the indicator light circuit. In some vehicles, a faulty circuit could cause the alternator to malfunction.

9   If the indicator light circuit is OK, check for a bad ground at the voltage regulator. If the ground is OK, the problem lies in the alternator, regulator or the wiring between them. If the vehicle has an internal regulator, replace the alternator. If the vehicle has a remotely mounted regulator, check the wiring. If necessary, disconnect the cable from the negative battery terminal and check for continuity, using the vehicle's wiring diagram for reference. If the wiring is OK, you'll have to determine whether the problem lies in the alternator or regulator.

10   A good way to determine whether an undercharging problem is caused by the alternator or regulator is with a full-field test. **Caution:** *Full-fielding sends high voltage through the vehicle's electrical system, which can damage components, particularly electronic components. Carefully monitor the charging system voltage during full-fielding to be sure it doesn't exceed 16 volts. Also, do not operate a full-fielded alternator for an extended period of time. Operate it only long enough to take the voltage reading.* Basically, the full-field test bypasses the regulator to send full battery voltage to the alternator's field (the rotor). If the charging voltage is normal when the alternator is "full-fielded," you know the alternator is OK. If the voltage is still low, the problem is in the alternator. It's best to obtain wiring diagrams for the vehicle to determine the best way to send battery voltage to the field. However, the following gives some general guidelines which may help you in determining how to full-field the alternator:

  a) On older Delco (GM) alternators with remotely mounted regulators ("B" circuit type), disconnect the electrical connector from the regulator and connect a jumper wire between the BAT and F terminals of the connector.

  b) On Ford Motorcraft alternators with remotely mounted regulators ("B" circuit type), disconnect the electrical connector from the regulator and connect a jumper wire between the A and F terminals of the connector.

  c) On Chrysler alternators with remotely mounted electronic voltage regulators ("A" circuit type), disconnect the regulator connector and connect a jumper wire between the green wire terminal of the connector and ground.

11   Make the connections with the ignition turned OFF, then repeat Step 3, above. The voltage reading should be high (about 15 to 16 volts). If it's not, the alternator is faulty. If it is, the regulator is probably bad.

Alternator output amperage

1   To check the amount of output amperage, an inductive amp gauge will be required **(see illustration 8.3).** These are inexpensive and can be found at most local auto parts stores. In order for the reading to be accurate, the use of this gauge only

8.6 This is a typical example of how the identifying information will look on an alternator

requires that it is placed on the output wire of the alternator.

2   Place a load on the electrical system of the vehicle. Do this by turning on all lights and accessories for approximately one minute before and during testing.

3   Start the engine and accelerate to about 1500-to-2000 rpm. Hold the gauge in place and read the amps, it should be within a few amps of the rated output of the alternator **(see illustration)**. **Note:** *The output amperage of an alternator is stamped either in the housing or on a tag attached to the housing.*

Alternator voltage "AC (alternating current) bleed-off"

1   A last check is to look for AC voltage "leaks" or voltage "bleed off". **Note:** *Voltage spikes that are cause by a failed or weak diodes can fool the ECM and create an engine misfire.* Diodes in the alternator are supposed to direct all electrical flow into DC (direct current) voltage. A failed or weakened diode can allow small amounts of AC voltage to surge back through the circuit.

2   AC bleed-off can be checked for in two ways:

a) To check the condition of the alternator output, even if no symptoms are occurring currently, hook up a voltmeter to the alternator output wire and ground. Set the selector to AC voltage. With the engine running there should be no more than 0.5 AC volts. Any reading any higher than 0.5 volts indicates replacement or repairs to the alternator are necessary.

b) Start the engine and see if there is an engine miss. If there is, turn off the engine and disconnect the alternator output wire (wire from the alternator to the battery). Restart the engine with the wire disconnected. If the miss has stopped, perform a thorough check and test of the charging system.

9 Ignition system

General information

With the introduction of electronic ignition (breakerless ignition) many of the areas that could create a problem, such as points and condensers, were eliminated. If information on detailed diagnosis, overhaul or removal and installation is needed, refer to the specific *Haynes Automotive Repair Manual* for the vehicle being worked on.

Distributor (if equipped)

The distributor is a key component that determines engine operation and performance. The distributor is made up of a mechanical, electrical and, on some models, a vacuum system. Each of these need to be inspected, repaired and/or replaced as necessary.

Note: *Many later model vehicles don't use mechanical advance above idle (they do have some mechanical timing built in for initial timing), these vehicles have computer controlled timing advance.*

Make sure the wires are numbered before removal, then remove the spark plug wires from the distributor cap. Remove the distributor cap and rotor and inspect the parts for cracks, carbon tracking between terminals, pitting or corrosion buildup on electrodes, etc. **(see illustrations)**. If any of these are evident r place the necessary parts. **Note:** *Always replace the cap and rotor together as a set. The air gap between the tip of the rotor and the terminal in the cap is critical to delivering correct firing voltage.*

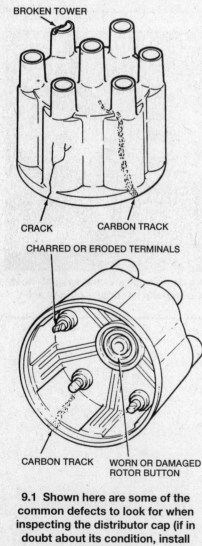

9.1 Shown here are some of the common defects to look for when inspecting the distributor cap (if in doubt about its condition, install a new one)

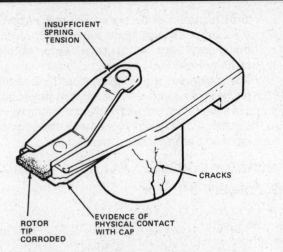

9.2 The ignition rotor should be checked for wear and corrosion as indicated here (if in doubt about its condition, install a new one)

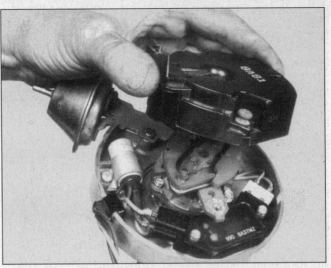

9.3 To detach the rotor, in order to get to the centrifugal weights and springs (arrows), remove the two screws on top and lift off the rotor

Mechanical advance

1   Most distributors use weights and springs to mechanically advance the ignition timing as rpm increases. Once the cap and rotor are removed, the mounting positions of the weights and springs can be easily seen **(see illustration)**.

2   With the rotor removed - turn the shaft - it will only move slightly, and let it snap back. If it is operating properly the weights should move out from their rest positions, when turned, and the spring tension should snap them back into place when the shaft is released.

3   Watch to make sure the weights don't stick. A very thin film of lubrication between the weights and the top of the shaft should be all that is needed to allow the weights to move freely.

9.4 An example of a worn centrifugal advance weight - note the elongated hole showing the need for replacement

Vacuum advance

Note: *Computer controls have done away with vacuum advance on many later model vehicles. This information only applies to models with vacuum operated advance.*

1   The diaphragm assembly is attached to the distributor breaker plate. A vacuum line attaches the diaphragm housing to a ported vacuum source. As vacuum changes from idle to acceleration through deceleration and back to idle, the timing changes accordingly.

2   With the engine off, check the condition of the vacuum hose from the distributor to the vacuum source. Make sure the hose is connected and the connections seal well (see Section 5).

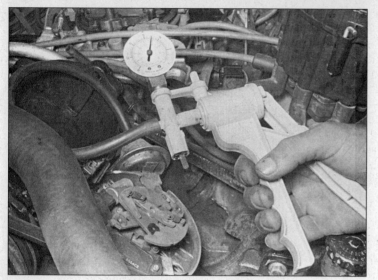

9.5 Apply vacuum to the vacuum advance unit and observe movement of the distributor plate

3   Disconnect and plug the vacuum hose to the distributor. Connect a vacuum pump to vacuum diaphragm **(see illustration)**. Apply between 15-to-20 in-Hg and make sure the diaphragm assembly holds vacuum. If it bleeds down, replace the diaphragm assembly. **Note:** *This assembly can be replaced without removal of the distributor.*

4   Connect a timing light to the engine according to the manufacturers instructions.

5   Start the engine and allow it to idle. Shine the timing light on the scale and while watching the timing indicator, apply 5-to-10 in-Hg to the diaphragm.

6   As the vacuum is applied, does the timing change? If it does, the advance is working properly. The engine will probably stumble or stall as more vacuum is applied. If the assembly holds vacuum when applied, but no timing advance takes place, the advance plate inside the distributor is stuck.

7   If the vacuum advance is functioning as described, it may be wise to inspect and test other components or systems in this general way first, in order to look for obvious failures. Then if the cause isn't found, inspect different systems with an emphasis on looking for components out of specifications.

Ignition module and coil

1   In the previous tests for available coil voltage and available spark plug firing voltage, the end check for voltages would verify that the components of the ignition system are working properly. If not, there would no voltage readings for any of the tests performed.

2   The condition of the coil and module and any tests to be conducted, although important, are beyond the scope of this manual. If there is no voltage readings the problem(s) will need to be diagnosed further. The primary concern of this manual is fuel injection related problems and corrections. **Note:** *There are many variations of manufacturers wiring, connections, components, locations and appropriate test procedures for ignition modules, coils or Distributorless Ignition Systems (DIS). If further information is needed to diagnose or repair the vehicle electrical system, beyond the information given in Section 5 and 9 of this manual, refer to the specific* Haynes Automotive Repair Manual *for the vehicle being repaired.*

Spark plug wires

1   The spark plug wires should be checked at the recommended intervals and whenever new spark plugs are installed in the engine.

2   Using a clean rag, wipe the entire length of the wire to remove built-up dirt and grease. Once the wire is clean, check for burns, cracks and other damage. Do not bend the wire sharply, because the conductor might break.

3   Make a visual check of the spark plug wires while the engine is running. In a darkened garage (make sure there is adequate ventilation) start the engine and observe each plug wire. Be careful not to come into contact with any moving engine parts. If there is a break in the wire, you will see arcing or a small spark at the damaged area. If arcing is noticed, stop the engine, allow the engine to cool and replace the necessary parts.

4   The wires should be further inspected, if necessary, one at a time to prevent

mixing up the order, which is essential to proper engine operation.

5   Disconnect the plug wire from the spark plug. A removal tool can be used for this purpose or you can grasp the rubber boot, twist the boot half a turn, to break it loose from the spark plug, and pull the boot free **(see illustration)**. Do not pull on the wire itself.

6   Disconnect the wire from the distributor or coil pack. Again, pull only on the rubber boot.

7   Check inside the boot for corrosion, which will look like a white crusty powder. **Note:** *Don't mistake white dielectric grease for corrosion. Many manufacturers use this grease during assembly to prevent corrosion.*

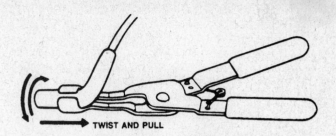

TWIST AND PULL

9.6 When removing the spark plug wires, pull only on the boot and twist it back-and-forth - a spark plug wire removal tool makes this job easier and safer

Spark plug wire resistance check

8   Spark plug wires, some times referred to as ignition cables, should to be checked for continuity to determine if they should be replaced. **Note:** *Spark plug wires can be replaced separately. It sometimes is all that is needed to correct a problem. But it is suggested that if any need replacement, they all be replaced as a set. Even if not all wires test bad, their condition is probably very similar to the ones that are already in need of replacement.*

9   There are some general resistance (ohms) values used to test spark plug wires. Remove each spark plug wire, one at a time, and hook up an ohm meter (see Chapter 2). Measure the resistance of each wire. Use the following guidelines for interpreting your vehicle's resistance readings:

  a) When measuring the resistance value of the spark plug wires there should be approximately 1K (1,000) ohms per inch of length.

  b) There should be a maximum resistance of 30K (30,000) ohms for any complete spark plug wire, regardless of length.

10   These resistance values are for new or used spark plug wires. If your test values are outside these ranges, replace the spark plug wires.

11   Inspect the remaining spark plug wires, making sure that each one is securely fastened at the distributor, or coil pack, and spark plug when the check is complete.

12   Push the wire and boot back onto the end of the spark plug. It should fit tightly onto the end of the plug and 'snap' into place, indicating a proper connection. If it doesn't, remove the wire and use pliers to carefully crimp the metal connector inside the wire boot until the fit is correct.

13   If new spark plug wires are required, purchase a set for your specific engine model. Pre-cut wire sets with the boots already installed are available or spark plug cable and terminal ends of many different angles can be purchased for anyone that wants to route the wires to fit a custom application. Remove and replace the wires one at a time to avoid mix-ups in the firing order.

Spark plugs

Removal

14   The spark plugs provide a sort of window into the combustion chamber and can give a wealth of information about engine operation to a savvy mechanic. Fuel mixture, heat range, oil consumption and detonation all leave their mark on the tips of the spark plugs.

15   Before you begin the check, drive the vehicle at highway speed, allowing it to warm up thoroughly without excessive idling. Shut the engine off and wait until it cools sufficiently so you won't get burned if you touch the exhaust manifolds.

Common spark plug conditions

NORMAL

Symptoms: Brown to grayish-tan color and slight electrode wear. Correct heat range for engine and operating conditions.

Recommendation: When new spark plugs are installed, replace with plugs of the same heat range.

WORN

Symptoms: Rounded electrodes with a small amount of deposits on the firing end. Normal color. Causes hard starting in damp or cold weather and poor fuel economy.

Recommendation: Plugs have been left in the engine too long. Replace with new plugs of the same heat range. Follow the recommended maintenance schedule.

CARBON DEPOSITS

Symptoms: Dry sooty deposits indicate a rich mixture or weak ignition. Causes misfiring, hard starting and hesitation.

Recommendation: Make sure the plug has the correct heat range. Check for a clogged air filter or problem in the fuel system or engine management system. Also check for ignition system problems.

ASH DEPOSITS

Symptoms: Light brown deposits encrusted on the side or center electrodes or both. Derived from oil and/or fuel additives. Excessive amounts may mask the spark, causing misfiring and hesitation during acceleration.

Recommendation: If excessive deposits accumulate over a short time or low mileage, install new valve guide seals to prevent seepage of oil into the combustion chambers. Also try changing gasoline brands.

OIL DEPOSITS

Symptoms: Oily coating caused by poor oil control. Oil is leaking past worn valve guides or piston rings into the combustion chamber. Causes hard starting, misfiring and hesitation.

Recommendation: Correct the mechanical condition with necessary repairs and install new plugs.

GAP BRIDGING

Symptoms: Combustion deposits lodge between the electrodes. Heavy deposits accumulate and bridge the electrode gap. The plug ceases to fire, resulting in a dead cylinder.

Recommendation: Locate the faulty plug and remove the deposits from between the electrodes.

TOO HOT

Symptoms: Blistered, white insulator, eroded electrode and absence of deposits. Results in shortened plug life.

Recommendation: Check for the correct plug heat range, over-advanced ignition timing, lean fuel mixture, intake manifold vacuum leaks, sticking valves and insufficient engine cooling.

PREIGNITION

Symptoms: Melted electrodes. Insulators are white, but may be dirty due to misfiring or flying debris in the combustion chamber. Can lead to engine damage.

Recommendation: Check for the correct plug heat range, over-advanced ignition timing, lean fuel mixture, insufficient engine cooling and lack of lubrication.

HIGH SPEED GLAZING

Symptoms: Insulator has yellowish, glazed appearance. Indicates that combustion chamber temperatures have risen suddenly during hard acceleration. Normal deposits melt to form a conductive coating. Causes misfiring at high speeds.

Recommendation: Install new plugs. Consider using a colder plug if driving habits warrant.

DETONATION

Symptoms: Insulators may be cracked or chipped. Improper gap setting techniques can also result in a fractured insulator tip. Can lead to piston damage.

Recommendation: Make sure the fuel anti-knock values meet engine requirements. Use care when setting the gaps on new plugs. Avoid lugging the engine.

MECHANICAL DAMAGE

Symptoms: May be caused by a foreign object in the combustion chamber or the piston striking an incorrect reach (too long) plug. Causes a dead cylinder and could result in piston damage.

Recommendation: Repair the mechanical damage. Remove the foreign object from the engine and/or install the correct reach plug.

16   If compressed air is available, blow any dirt or foreign material away from the spark plug area before proceeding (a common bicycle pump will also work).

17   Check the spark plug wires to see if they have the cylinder numbers on them. Label them if necessary so you can reinstall them on the correct spark plugs.

18   Never remove the spark plug wire connector from the spark plug by pulling the wire. Be sure, even when grabbing the boot, that the connector is being grasped before pulling it off the plug. There are some helpful spark plug removal tools available at local automotive parts stores.

19   Once the spark plug wires have been disconnected, proceed with removing the spark plug(s).

Heat range

20   Remove the spark plugs and place them in order on top of the air cleaner or on the workbench. Note the brand and number on the plugs. Compare this to the VECI label, which is the manufacturers recommendation for that vehicle, to determine if the correct type and heat range is being used.

21   Spark plug manufacturers make spark plugs in several heat ranges for different vehicle applications and driving conditions. These have been determined by working with the vehicle manufacturers to come up with the proper match of spark plug to engine requirements.

22   The engine must have the correct heat range spark plugs before you can read the tips accurately. Plugs that are too hot will mask a rich fuel mixture reading; conversely, cold plugs will tend to foul on a normal mixture. On most European and Japanese spark plugs, the higher the number, the colder the heat range. American plugs are just the opposite.

23   There are several "old mechanic's tales" about heat range that need to be dispelled. Hotter heat range plugs don't make the engine run hotter, they don't make a hotter spark and they don't increase combustion chamber temperature (unless the colder plug wasn't firing). The plugs themselves retain more heat, which helps resist fouling in climates where richer mixtures or different fuel blends are used.

24   If a change in spark plug heat range is being considered, first ask - what is causing the engine to run in a way that necessitates a change? Manufacturers go to a great deal of trouble to determine the correct plug type, heat range and gap for every vehicle on the market. It's recommended that the spark plug requirements found on the VECI label under the hood be followed at all times. After the conditions that were causing the spark plug to fire poorly are corrected, the original spark plug recommendation will work as it was intended. **Note:** *Non-resistor spark plugs can add electrical interference or "noise" to the ECM and/or sensor circuits. This is sometimes referred to as "spark echo" (think of all that static that solid, non-resistor, plug wires caused on the radio of your old hot rod). This can have a direct affect on the low amperage current used by computer control vehicles to monitor and control engine functions, such as fuel ratios, spark timing, etc. or any circuit that is controlled by low voltage impulses.*

Reading spark plugs

25   Examine the plugs for hints about the engine's internal condition and state of tune **(see illustration 9.32)**. If any of the plugs are wet with oil, engine repairs are needed right away. If the plugs have significant gray or white deposits, it means that a moderate amount of oil is seeping into the cylinders and repairs will be needed soon, or you've been doing a lot of short trip driving.

26   The ideal color for plugs used in engines run on leaded gasoline is light brown on the insulator cone and beige on the ground (side) electrode. Engines that run on unleaded gasoline tend to leave very little color on the plugs. Late-model emission-controlled engines run very lean. Normally, the plugs range from almost white to tan on the porcelain insulator cone and the ground electrode should be light brown to dark gray. **Note:** *If a spark plug is worn to the extent that replacement is necessary, it's recommended that all spark plugs be replaced at the same time.*

27 Excessively rich fuel mixtures cause the spark plugs tips to turn black and lean mixtures result in light tan or white tips. You can tell by the color if the fuel mixture is in the ballpark by reading the plugs.

28 If the engine has a misfire and one or more plugs are carbon fouled, look for an ignition problem or low compression in the affected cylinder(s). Sometimes the spark plugs will vary among each other in color because of improper mixture distribution. Look for a leaky intake manifold gasket if one or more adjoining cylinders are running very lean. If the plugs are burning unevenly, you may have a vacuum leak or a fuel distribution problem in the fuel injection system.

29 Detonation, preignition and plugs that are too long can result in physical damage to the tip. Check the accompanying photos to help identify these problems.

30 You will also need a gauge. Different types are available to check and adjust the spark plug gap, and a torque wrench to tighten the new plugs to the specified torque.

31 If you are replacing the plugs, purchase the new plugs, adjust them to the proper gap and then replace each plug one at a time. **Caution:** *When buying new spark plugs, it's essential that you obtain the correct plugs for your specific vehicle. Don't substitute spark plugs, use what was designed for the vehicle. This information can be found on the Vehicle Emissions Control Information (VECI) label located on the underside of the hood or in the owner's manual (see Section 3). Many people, even professionals, sometimes substitute heat ranges for the ones called for by the manufacturer. This is a mistake and misses the underlying reason for the condition of the spark plugs. If the spark plug change is to correct a problem (not just a tune-up) the new plug may mask the real cause of the driveability problem, which still exist. Correct the cause and the recommended spark plugs will work as they were originally designed. Incorrect spark plug selection can cause engine damage.*

32 Inspect each of the new plugs for defects. If there are any signs of cracks in the porcelain insulator of a plug, don't use it. Check the electrode gaps of the new plugs. Check the gap by inserting the gauge of the proper thickness between the electrodes at the tip of the plug **(see illustration)**. The gap between the electrodes should be identical to the manufacturers specifications, which are listed on the VECI label. If the gap is incorrect, use the notched adjuster to bend the curved side electrode slightly.

33 If the side electrode is not exactly over the center electrode, use the notched adjuster to align them **(see illustration)**. **Caution:** *If the gap of a new plug must be adjusted, bend only the base of the side electrode - do not touch the tip.*

9.8 An example of a wire-type gauge for checking the gap - if the wire does not slide between the electrodes with a slight drag, adjustment is required

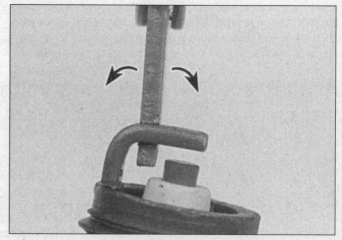

9.9 To change the gap, bend the side electrode as shown to specification, be careful not to chip or crack the porcelain insulator

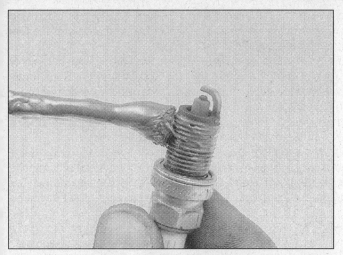

9.10 Apply a very thin coat of anti-seize compound or a few drops of oil, to the spark plug threads to ease installation and prevent the spark plug from seizing in the cylinder head

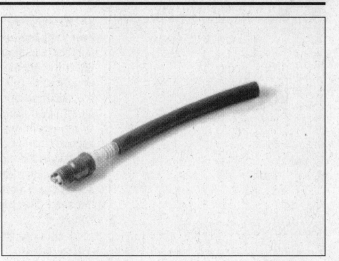

9.11 A length of 3/8-inch rubber hose will save time and prevent damaged threads when installing the spark plugs

Installation

34   Prior to installation, apply a light film of anti-seize compound or a drop of oil on the spark plug threads **(see illustration).Note:** *A handy source of oil for this purpose is the dipstick - just pull it out and touch the end to the threads of the plug*. It's often difficult to insert spark plugs into their holes without cross-threading them. To avoid this possibility, fit a short piece of 3/8-inch, inner diameter rubber hose, or an old spark plug boot, over the end of the spark plug **(see illustration)**. The flexible hose, or boot, acts as a universal joint to help align the plug with the plug hole. Should the plug begin to cross-thread, the hose will slip on the spark plug, preventing thread damage. Follow the manufacturers recommendations for torque when tightening the plugs on installation. If that information isn't readily available, use the following guidelines:

a) Spark plugs with a gasket require only 1/4-additional turn, after the gasket makes contact with the cylinder head, to seal properly.

b) Tapered seat spark plugs, ones that have no gasket, require only 1/16-additional turn, after the spark plug seat contact the cylinder head, to seal properly.

35   Attach the plug wire to the new spark plug, again using a twisting motion on the boot until it is firmly seated on the end of the spark plug.

36   Follow the above procedure for the remaining spark plugs, replacing them one at a time to prevent mixing up the spark plug wires.

Available spark plug firing voltage

Warning 1: *Before starting these procedures, make sure the vehicle is in park or in neutral with the parking brake set. Always perform all tests while standing at the sides of the vehicle - never from the front.*

Warning 2: *To avoid electric shock, always use insulated pliers* **(see illustration 9.6)** *when it's necessary to grasp the high voltage spark plug wire with the engine running.*

Note: *The purpose of the following voltage tests are to verify that the ignition system is functioning properly, which must be done before a proper fuel injection diagnosis can be continued. Although these tests would normally be performed on an engine analyzer or oscilloscope, they can successfully be performed with a far less expensive hand-held digital kilovolt tester with an inductive pick-up.*

1   Spark plug firing voltage is a measurement of the available output of the entire ignition circuit, checked at the spark plugs. Checking for the correct end result, such as the firing voltages within their specifications, is a quick confirmation of all the parts of the primary and secondary ignition circuits are functioning properly.

2   Using an inductive digital kilovolt tester, attach the meter to each individual spark plug wire, one at a time, perform the tests and record the voltage readings described in the following steps to determine the condition of the entire ignition circuit.

3   Start the vehicle and read the meter at idle and on a "snap-test". **Note:** *Called snap-tests because the voltage reading is taken as the throttle is quickly opened and let return to idle, "snapped", for a short, hard acceleration burst.* The general guidelines for the voltage readings, of an engine in good operating condition, are:

a) Idle - 10-to-12kv

b) Snap-test - 15-to-25kv (up to 30kv on distributorless ignition systems)

4   Look for consistency between cylinder at both idle and on the snap-test. Variations would indicate the ignition system components are worn to different degrees. Inspect the components in question and repair or replace as necessary.

5   If there is no voltage reading, the problem will need to be diagnosed further which is beyond the scope of this manual. The primary concern of this manual is fuel injection related problems and corrections. If further information is needed to diagnose or repair the electrical system beyond the information given in Sections 5 and 9 of this manual, refer to the specific *Haynes Automotive Repair Manual* for the vehicle being repaired.

Available coil voltage

1   This test will check the available coil voltage to verify the condition of the coil(s).

2   Attach the inductive kilovolt tester to one of the spark plug wires as in the previous tests. Disconnect the spark plug wire from the spark plug and secure it away from the engine. **Caution:** *Never pull the on the spark plug wire itself, it can be internally damaged. Grasp the boot over the tip of the spark plug. The open created by disconnecting the spark plug wire causes the build up of voltage that the coil is trying to send to ground through the spark plug. The available coil voltage goes to maximum buildup when this open in the circuit is made.*

3   Disable the fuel system so the engine wont start (see Chapter 4) and crank the engine over long enough to take the reading.

4   A general guideline of 30-to-50kV (30,000-to-50,000 volts) of available coil voltage indicates a coil with sufficient reserve capacity for times of greater demand.

5   If there is no voltage reading, the problem will need to be diagnosed further which is beyond the scope of this manual. The primary concern of this manual is fuel injection related problems and corrections. If further information is needed to diagnose or repair the electrical system beyond the information given in Sections 5 and 9 of this manual, refer to the specific Haynes Automotive Repair Manual for the vehicle being repaired.

Rotor tip-to-cap terminal air gap voltage check

1   Another important test to perform is the rotor tip-to-cap terminal air gap voltage (the voltage required for spark to "jump" the air gap between the rotor tip and the distributor cap terminal). This test checks the condition of the distributor cap and rotor without removing the cap. **Note:** *The visual check of parts for cracks, carbon tracking, etc. should have been done in the previous inspection steps.*

2   Different manufacturers have different specifications when manufacturing their parts. So the voltage required to jump the gap inside the distributor cap, even with new parts, can vary. But as a general rule it only takes 2000-to-3000 volts to jump from the rotor tip to the distributor cap terminal. Normally voltages higher than approximately 5000-to-6000 volts would indicate an excessive gap or very pitted, deteriorated condition of the parts. Replace all necessary parts based on voltage readings and visual inspection.

3   To perform the test attach the inductive kilovolt tester to the spark plug wires, as in the previous tests. Disable the fuel system so the engine wont start (see Chapter 4).

4   Disconnect the spark plug wire from the spark plug and ground the terminal against the block or cylinder head. Crank the engine over and read the voltage on the meter.

5   With the wire connected directly to ground, the only air gap remaining in the circuit is the gap from the rotor tip to the terminal post. So the voltage reading is what is required to bridge the air gap.

Timing and idle speed

1   The first thing to do, before actually pulling out your timing light, is to look up the **correct specifications and adjustment procedures**. **Caution:** *Don't just read that sentence - it's important to actually follow the procedures to the letter. One of the most overlooked or misadjusted items in the diagnosis of driveability problems or a tune-up is setting the timing either to the wrong specification or not following the proper steps necessary to correctly set the timing.*

2   This information can be found in several places. First find and read the VECI label (see Section 3) under the hood. If this label is affixed to the vehicle, always use this information before any other source. If the label is missing, a possibility if the vehicle has been repaired previously, contact the auto dealership to order another to be put back in the originals place. If more information is needed refer to the specific Haynes Automotive Repair Manual that applies to your vehicle.

3   Next, locate the timing marks on the vibration damper (crankshaft pulley) and engine cover **(see illustration)**. **Note:** *Some manufacturers have the timing marks on the flywheel, and an inspection cover must be removed to see the marks for Top Dead Center (TDC) location or timing adjustment.* Clean them off so no mistake it made when aligning the marks during the timing procedure. If the marks are faint or there are multiple marks to choose from, paint the correct marks so it will make location of the correct marks easier when timing is set. Typing correction fluid works great. It has a small brush in the bottle and isn't easily washed off, so it will be there for the next tune-up.

9.12 Align the notch in the pulley with the 0 on the timing scale then check to see if the distributor rotor is pointing to the number 1 cylinder

Base timing (initial advance)

4   Base timing is made up of two forms of advance, base timing and built in mechanical advance. Together they give the engine the base timing, before any centrifugal or computer control timing advance, above idle, is added by the computer.

5   The following guidelines are general and will be close for most vehicles. If more information is needed, refer to the Haynes Automotive Repair Manual specifically for your vehicle:

6   Advance, at idle, will generally be between 15 and 25-degrees BTDC. This is the advance that is seen at the timing marks with your timing light, and the built-in mechanical advance of the distributor.

Total advance

7   Advance at about 2500 rpm will generally be between 30 and 50-degrees BTDC, of total advance. This is the initial, built-in advance plus base timing, and the centrifugal advance of either the mechanical weights and springs, or a computer controlled amount of timing advance.

Timing adjustment and idle speed

Caution: *By not following correct procedures, and guessing where timing and idle speed should be set, the timing and idle speed are probably the two major causes for most driveability problems found in a tune-up. The computer system takes many of it's readings and makes its adjustments using this information as a basis. If these are wrong, the subsequent engine management will also be wrong. Many times the end result will appear to be a fuel injection problem, when in fact it's only a misadjustment of the fundamentals.*

8   Many times, when tuning a vehicle, the timing is adjusted to try and offset some other problem (idles too slow, pings on acceleration, etc.). A slight deviation of approximately 2 or 3-degrees is usually all right. Be careful, if the timing has to be moved, maybe 5-degrees or more, then it should raise a warning flag that there is probably something else to be corrected, or replaced, before the timing changes should even be considered. Again don't take it upon yourself to re-engineer the specifications. Follow the VECI label that is found on the vehicle and don't deviate.

9   This is one of the most commonly ignored or misadjusted specifications of any repair work done. Some "mechanics" think they know better. Better the people who designed and tested it? Doubtful. **Always** adjust the base idle speed, fast idle, minimum air rate, etc. to the specification listed, and exactly follow the procedures outlined on the VECI label of the vehicle being worked on.

10   For correct adjustment procedures and specifications of minimum idle speed, refer to the VECI label of your vehicle and Chapter 6 of this manual.

10 EGR (Exhaust Gas Recirculation) system

General information

To reduce oxides of nitrogen emissions, a small amount of exhaust gas is recirculated through the EGR valve **(see illustration)** into the intake manifold. The introduction of the inert gas lowers the combustion temperatures, which reduces the oxides of nitrogen.

The EGR system **(see illustration)** typically consists of the EGR valve, the EGR modulator, vacuum switching valve, the Electronic Control Module (ECM) and the EGR gas temperature sensor (found on some California models only).

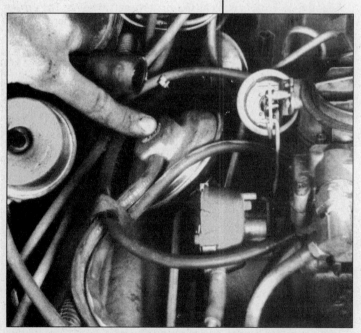

10.1 On most models, the EGR valve is located on the intake manifold, adjacent to the throttle body

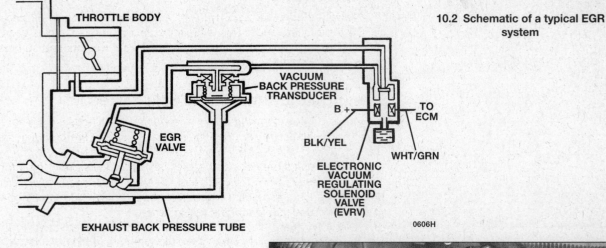

10.2 Schematic of a typical EGR system

THROTTLE BODY

VACUUM BACK PRESSURE TRANSDUCER

EGR VALVE

B +

TO ECM

BLK/YEL

WHT/GRN

ELECTRONIC VACUUM REGULATING SOLENOID VALVE (EVRV)

EXHAUST BACK PRESSURE TUBE

0606H

Early EGR systems are made up of a vacuum-operated valve that admits exhaust gas into the intake manifold (EGR valve), a hose that is connected to a ported vacuum source. A Thermostatic Vacuum Switch (TVS) is spliced into a pipe that is threaded into the radiator or, more typically, into the coolant passage near the thermostat. The TVS detects the operating temperature of the engine and doesn't allow the EGR to operate until the correct temperature is reached.

At idle, the throttle plate blocks the vacuum port, no vacuum reaches the valve and it remains closed. As the throttle opens and uncovers the port, a vacuum signal is sent to the EGR valve which slowly opens the valve, allowing exhaust gases to circulate into the intake manifold.

Since the introduction of the exhaust gas leans the fuel mixture and causes a rough idle and stalling when the engine is cold, the TVS only allows vacuum to the EGR valve when the engine is at normal operating temperature.

Also, when the throttle is opened on full acceleration, there is little or no ported vacuum available to the EGR valve, resulting in little or no EGR flow, which would cause mixture dilution and interfere with power output.

On later vehicles there are additional sensors and actuators included in the EGR system. The EGR valve acts on direct command from the computer after it (the computer) has determined that all the working parameters (air temperature, coolant temperature, EGR valve position, fuel/air mixture etc.) are correct.

Later model EGR valves are often controlled by a computer-controlled solenoid in line with the valve and vacuum source **(see illustrations)**. Some models also often have a position sensor on the EGR valve that

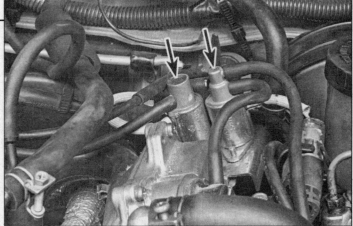

10.3 Some EGR solenoids (left arrow) are installed on a bracket near the EGR valve, such as this on a Nissan Maxima. The arrow on the right points to the air injection system solenoid

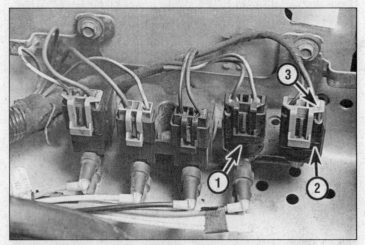

10.4 Some EGR solenoids are installed on the firewall, in an array of other solenoids, such as these units on a Ford Thunderbird - the vacuum valve (1) supplies vacuum to the electronic EGR valve when energized; when de-energized, the vent valve (2) vents the EGR valve to the atmosphere through a small vent (3)

10.5 Some EGR valves are also equipped with a position sensor like this unit on a Ford Thunderbird - the position sensor is almost always mounted on top of the EGR valve

10.6 Apply vacuum to the EGR valve and check with the tip of the finger for movement of the diaphragm. It should move smoothly without any binding with vacuum applied

informs the computer what position the EGR valve is in **(see illustration)**

The EGR valve could be either a negative or positive backpressure type of valve. For the purposes of replacement you may need to know which type it is, but for a function check it really isn't that important. The biggest concern is that the valve has movement, indicating a good vacuum signal to the EGR valve is present. Also, that with the movement of the EGR the engine rpm is changing, indicating that the EGR command, and exhaust gases are getting to the engine. If more detailed information is needed for any reason, refer to the *Haynes Automotive Emissions Control Manual* or the *Haynes Automotive Repair Manual* for the specific vehicle.

Checking EGR systems

1   There are several basic EGR system checks that you can perform on your vehicle to pinpoint problems. To perform these checks you will need a vacuum pump **(see illustration)** and a vacuum gauge.

2   Check for a vacuum source **(see illustration)** by hooking up a vacuum gauge to the line going to the EGR valve.

3   If no vacuum if found, the vehicle may have computer controlled solenoids, which regulate the vacuum to the EGR valve **(see illustrations 10.3 and 10.4)**, depending upon conditions such as the transmission being in drive, engine at operating temperature, open or closed loop computer operation, etc.

4   If the EGR valve diaphragm is accessible, lightly push it up or down slightly (against spring pressure) to see if it can move and operate freely **(see illustration)**.

5   If it is stuck proceed to step 13.

6   If the EGR valve stem moves smoothly and the EGR system continues to malfunction, check for a pinhole vacuum leak in the diaphragm of the EGR valve. Obtain a can of carburetor cleaner spray and attach the flexible "straw" to the nozzle. Aim carefully into the diaphragm areas of the EGR valve and spray around the actuator shaft while the engine is running. Listen carefully for any changes in engine rpm. If there is a leak, the engine rpm will increase and surge

10.7 With the engine running, check for vacuum to the EGR valve

10.8 use your finger to check for free movement of the diaphragm within the EGR valve

temporarily, then it will smooth back out to a constant idle. The only way to properly repair this problem is to replace the EGR valve with a new unit.

7   After the engine has been warmed up to normal operating temperature, open the throttle to approximately 2,500 rpm and observe the EGR valve stem as it moves with the rise in engine rpm. Use a mirror or even a finger placed on the diaphragm to feel movement, if necessary. If it doesn't move, remove the vacuum hose and check for vacuum with a gauge. Raise the rpm of the engine and see or feel if the valve opens up and/or flutters approximately 1/8 inch. Larger abrupt, jerky movements and/or opening all the way will cause a driveability problem and is not correct operation, replace the EGR valve. **Warning:** *A computer-controlled EGR valve needs to have the vehicle placed into gear in order for the computer to signal the valve to work. Have an assistant in the vehicle apply the parking brake and press firmly on the brake pedal before placing the transmission in gear for this check.*

8   This test will tell you if the gas flow passages are open and if the gas flow is proper. Remove the vacuum line from the EGR valve and plug the line. Attach a hand vacuum pump to the EGR valve. With the engine idling, slowly apply approximately 8-to-10 in-Hg to the valve and watch the valve stem for movement. If the gas flow is good, the engine will begin to idle rough or it may even stall. **Note:** *If the valve is a positive backpressure type, it will be necessary to create an exhaust restriction. This can be done by folding a thick towel over a few times, soaking it in water then having an assistant hold it over the end of the exhaust pipe (don't do this any longer than necessary to perform the test).* If the stem moves but the idle does not change, there is a restriction in the valve spacer plate or passages in the intake manifold (*see Cleaning the EGR valve*). If the valve stem does not move or the EGR valve diaphragm does not hold vacuum, replace the EGR valve with a new part.

9   The thermostatic vacuum switch (TVS) should also be checked, if equipped. This switch is usually regulated by a bi-metal core that expands or contracts according to the temperature. The valve remains closed and does not operate as long as the coolant temperature is below 115 to 129-degrees F. As the coolant temperature rises, the valve will open and the EGR system will operate. Remove the switch and place it in a pan of cool water and check the valve for vacuum - vacuum should not pass through the valve. Heat the water to the specified temperature (over 129-degrees F) and make sure the valve opens and allows the vacuum to pass. If the switch fails the test, replace it with a new part.

EGR vacuum modulator valve (if equipped)

10   Remove the valve.
11   Pull the cover off and check the filters **(see illustrations)**.
12   Replace the filters or clean them with compressed air, reinstall the cover and the modulator.

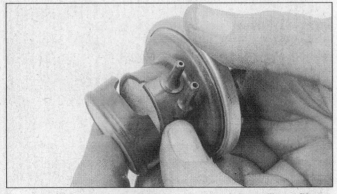

10.9 To remove the EGR vacuum modulator filters (if equipped) for cleaning, remove the cap . . .

10.10 . . . then pull out the filter(s) and blow it out with compressed air - be sure the coarse side of the outer filter faces the atmosphere (out) when reinstalling the filters

10.11 Depress the EGR valve diaphragm and inspect the full length of the pintle (arrow) and the seat at its base for carbon deposits

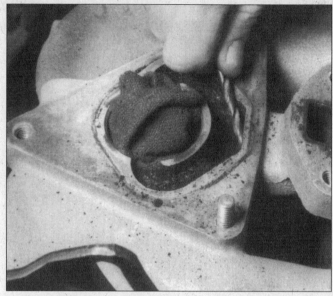

10.12 With a rag in the passage opening, the exhaust gas passages can be scraped clean of deposits

Cleaning the EGR valve

13 The bottoms of EGR valves often get covered with carbon deposits **(see illustration)**, causing them to restrict exhaust flow or leak exhaust. The valve must be removed so the bottom of the valve and the passages in the manifold can be cleaned **(see illustration)**. **Caution:** *When removing the EGR valve be sure to replace the gasket upon reassembly* **(see illustration)**. *There is generally more heat at this location, because of exhaust gases, and the gasket deteriorates quickly. If not replaced, the gasket, can be the source of a vacuum leak after reassembly.*

14 There are important points that must be observed when cleaning EGR valves:

a) Never use solvent to dissolve deposits on EGR valves unless you are extremely careful not to get any on the diaphragm.

b) Clean the pintle and valve seat with a dull scraper and wire brush and knock out loose carbon by tapping on the assembly.

c) Some EGR valves can be disassembled for cleaning, but be sure the parts are in alignment before assembly.

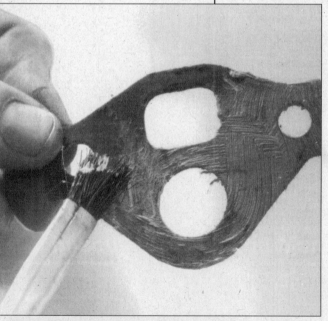

10.13 Coat the new EGR base gasket with a lithium-based grease to help preserve the gasket

11 Positive Crankcase Ventilation (PCV) system

General description

The Positive Crankcase Ventilation (PCV) system reduces hydrocarbon emissions by scavenging crankcase vapors. It does this by circulating blow-by gases and then rerouting them to the intake manifold by way of the air cleaner **(see illustration)**.

The PCV system is a sealed system. The crankcase blow-by vapors are routed directly to the air cleaner or air collector with crankcase pressure behind them.

The main components of the PCV system are:

a) PCV valve or a 'fixed-size orifice' in the PCV line
b) Air cleaner assembly and filters
c) Crankcase inlet hose
d) Oil filler cap and hose

If abnormal operating conditions (such as piston ring problems) arise, the system is designed to allow excessive amounts of blow-by gases to flow back through the crankcase vent tube into the intake system to be consumed by normal combustion. **Note:** *Some vehicles don't use a filtering element, it's a good idea to check the PCV system passageways for clogging from sludge and combustion residue.*

The Positive Crankcase Ventilation (PCV) system requires maintenance at regular intervals, which are specified by the manufacturer, to prevent, carbon, sludge and gum from clogging the PCV valve. orifice and/or hoses. A clogged PCV system can cause:

a) Increased oil consumption
b) Contaminated or diluted, dirty oil from sludge, moisture, and acid build-up in the crankcase and valve covers.
c) Blow-by vapors from the oil filler tube or breather cap, valve cover gasket, dipstick tube and other openings in the crankcase.
d) Rich or erratic operation at idle and low speeds.

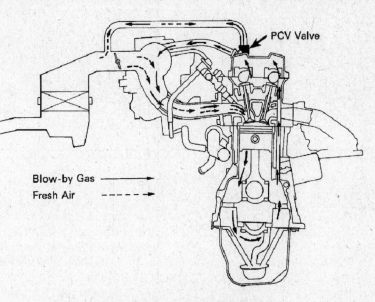

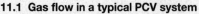

11.1 Gas flow in a typical PCV system

Inspection

1 Check all PCV hoses for proper routing and connections.
2 Inspect the PCV hoses for cracks, deterioration, rotting, and/or clogging.
Note: *Squeeze the hose, near the PCV valve, and see if it is mushy enough to collapse or stick closed. If the hose is in this kind of shape, replace it and any others found to be in this condition.*
3 Remove the air cleaner cover and check the air filter element. Crankcase blow-by can frequently clog the filter with oil. This filter may or may not be able to be washed out and reused.

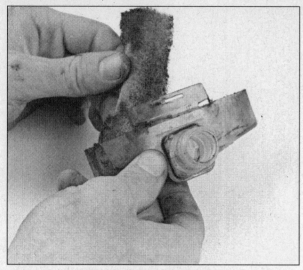

11.2 On some models the PCV filter can be pulled out and replaced separately

11.3 On this type of PCV filter, the filter and housing are taken out and replaced together by removal of a clip

4   Check the crankcase inlet air filter for clogging **(see illustrations)**, and clean or replace the filter as needed. The filter is normally located in the air cleaner housing, at the point where the crankcase air inlet hose is attached to the housing. **Note:** *High mileage vehicles may need this filter checked or replaced more often than regular maintenance schedules suggest, due to increased blow-by.*

5   Check the PCV inlet for deposits. Make sure the hose connects tightly to the inlet fitting.

6   Inspect the PCV valve or orifice for clogging and deposits. The valve/orifice may be located in or attached to **(see illustrations):**

a) The intake manifold
b) A valve cover
c) The crankcase vent hose
d) A vent line between the charcoal canister and the valve cover

11.4 A common location for PCV valves is right in the rubber grommet in the rocker arm cover

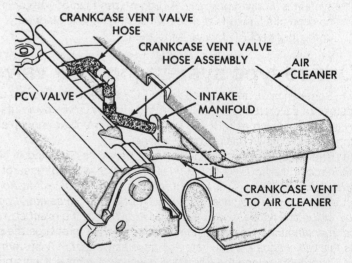

11.5 Some PCV valves are located in-line with the hoses connecting the crankcase to the intake manifold

7 Shake the PCV valve and listen for a rattle **(see illustration)**, indicating that the plunger inside moves freely. If it does, spray the inside of the valve thoroughly with carburetor cleaner and allow it to air dry. If the plunger does not rattle, replace the PCV valve.

PCV functional test

8 Several special testers are made to check overall PCV system operation. Some measure pressure in the crankcase. Others test the flow rate at engine idle speed. Follow the instructions that come with the tester you are using.

9 On some vehicles, the charcoal canister is purged through the PCV line. If a PCV system fails either of the tests, disconnect and plug the canister purge hose, and repeat the test. If the system then passes the test, the purge hose connection is loose, or there is a leak in the hose.

10 If a PCV tester is unavailable, hold a small piece of stiff paper over the oil filler opening with the engine idling. Crankcase vacuum should pull the paper against the opening if the PCV system is working properly. If the paper is not pulled against the opening or is blown up, there is a problem in the system. This may be the result of too much blow-by, which often happens to older engines. **Note:** *A lower than normal vacuum reading can be caused by a clogged PCV valve.*

11 The following method can also be used to test the PCV system when you do not have a PCV tester or when the results of the vacuum test are inconclusive:

a) Connect an accurate tachometer, then start the engine and run it at idle.

b) Disconnect the PCV valve and the line to the throttle body. This can usually be done by pulling the PCV valve out of the valve cover.

c) If the PCV valve is not clogged, you should hear a hissing noise as air passes through the valve and the idle speed should increase slightly.

d) Place your finger over the end of the PCV valve **(see illustration)**. You should feel a strong vacuum, and the engine speed should drop approximately 50 rpm, or more, if the system is working properly. A drop of less than 50 rpm or no drop at all, means the PCV valve or a hose is clogged, or the incorrect PCV valve is installed.

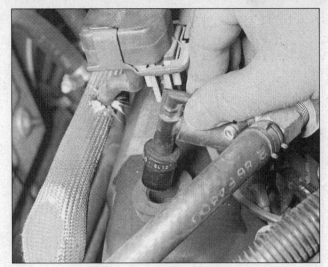

11.6 Shake the PCV valve, it should rattle

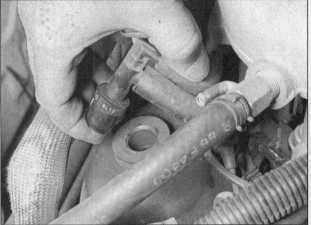

11.7 With the engine running, put your finger over the end of the PCV valve, you should feel vacuum

Orifice type system (no PCV valve)

12 Some engines are equipped with PCV systems that do not use a PCV valve. Instead, a calibrated orifice, which may be in the valve cover, intake manifold or a system hose (such as a Bosch system used on Volkswagens), allows crankcase vapors to be drawn back into the engine.

13 The orifice must be cleaned when it becomes restricted or clogged. If possible remove the housing or the hose the orifice is in, for ease of cleaning. **Note:** *The orifice MAY be able to be removed from the line that houses it. Using a rounded end (Phillips style) screwdriver, push the orifice out, if possible. To clean the calibrated orifice, use solvent and a drill bit of the exact size specified by the car manufacturer.* **Caution:** *Take special care not to enlarge the calibrated orifice as this will change the flow rate and adversely affect PCV system operation.*

14 Thoroughly clean the calibrated orifice and reinstall it in its original location. If it cannot be cleaned satisfactorily it must be replaced.

Parts replacement

15   Both the inlet hose to the crankcase and the hose to the throttle body should be replaced if damaged or deteriorated. PCV systems use only special hoses that are fuel and oil resistant, made for PCV and fuel system service. Federal regulations prohibit the use of any hose not specifically approved for use in PCV systems. **Caution:** *Ordinary heater hose or water hose will not withstand the affect of blow-by vapors.*

16   To replace a PCV valve, install the new part in place of the old one. Make sure the valve is the correct one for the vehicle being worked on. If the valve is mounted in a rubber grommet, make sure the grommet fits the valve cover correctly and the PCV valve fits snugly in the grommet. If the grommet is hardened or cracked, replace it. Make sure it seals tightly so there are no air leaks.

12 Evaporative emissions control (EVAP) system

General description

The evaporative emissions control system **(see illustration)** stores fuel vapors generated in the fuel tank in a charcoal canister **(see illustration)** when the engine isn't running. When the engine is started, the fuel vapors are drawn into the intake manifold and burned. The crankcase emission control system works

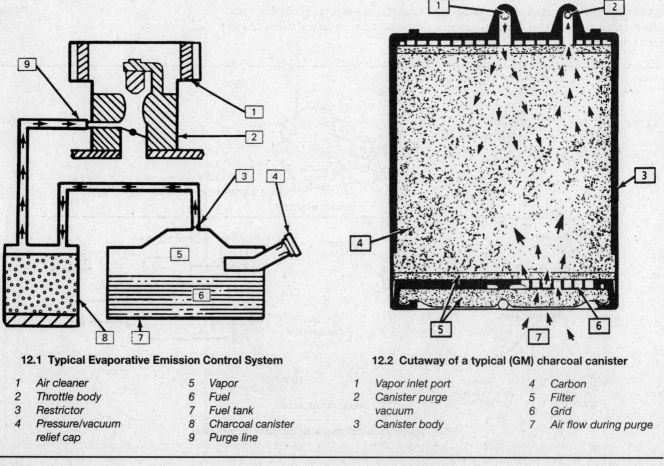

12.1 Typical Evaporative Emission Control System

1	Air cleaner	5	Vapor
2	Throttle body	6	Fuel
3	Restrictor	7	Fuel tank
4	Pressure/vacuum	8	Charcoal canister
	relief cap	9	Purge line

12.2 Cutaway of a typical (GM) charcoal canister

1	Vapor inlet port	4	Carbon
2	Canister purge	5	Filter
	vacuum	6	Grid
3	Canister body	7	Air flow during purge

like this: When the engine is cruising (not under load), the purge control valve (bypass valve) is opened slightly and a small amount of blow-by gas is drawn into the intake manifold and burned. When the engine is starting cold or idling, the bypass valve prevents any vapors from entering the intake manifold causing an excessively rich fuel mixture.

Two types of purge valves or bypass valves are used on these models; an electrically operated valve or a vacuum-operated valve **(see illustration)**. To find out which type is on your vehicle, follow the hose from the charcoal canister until you locate the purge valve. Some are located on the intake manifold and others near the charcoal canister. Look for an electrical connector **(see illustration)** to the purge valve (electrically operated) or vacuum lines (vacuum-operated).

A faulty EVAP system affects the engine driveability only when the temperatures are warm. The EVAP system is not usually the cause of hard cold starting or any other cold running problems.

12.3 A common location for the canister purge solenoid valve is on the firewall or an inner fender, where it's often installed as part of an array of other solenoids

Check

Vacuum-operated purge valve

1   Remove the vacuum lines from the purge valve and blow into the larger port of the valve. It should be closed and not pass any air. **Note:** *Some models are equipped with a thermo-vacuum valve that prevents canister purge until the coolant temperature reaches approximately 115-degrees F. Check this valve to make sure that vacuum is controlled at the proper temperatures. The valve is usually located in the intake manifold, near the thermo-time switch and the coolant temperature sensor.*

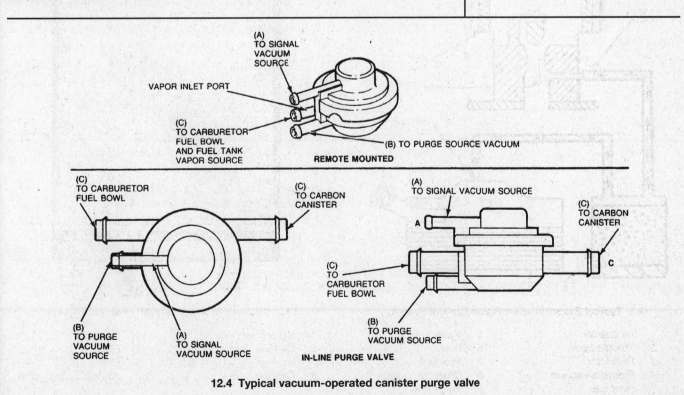

12.4 Typical vacuum-operated canister purge valve

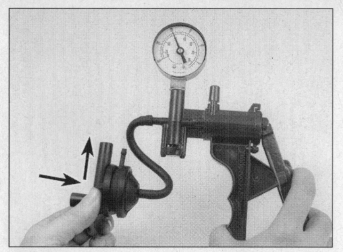

12.5 Apply vacuum and blow air through the purge control valve - air should pass through

12.6 Example of a typical canister location. To remove the charcoal canister, label and detach the vacuum lines, then remove the canister clamp bolt and lift the canister out (some canisters may come out from underneath the vehicle)

2   Disconnect the small vacuum hose from the purge valve and apply vacuum with a hand-held vacuum pump (see illustration). The purge valve should be open and air should be able to pass through.

3   If the test results are incorrect, replace the purge valve with a new part.

Electrically operated purge valve

1   Disconnect any lines from the purge valve and without disconnecting the electrical connector, place it in a convenient spot for testing. Check that the valve makes a 'click' sound as the ignition key is turned to the On position.

2   If the valve does not 'click', disconnect the valve connector and check for power to the valve using a test light or a voltmeter.

3   If there is battery voltage, replace the purge valve. If there is no voltage present, check the control unit and the wiring harness for any shorts or faulty components.

Canister

1   Label, then detach all hoses to the canister (see illustration).
2   Slide the canister out of its mounting clip.
3   Visually examine the canister for leakage or damage.
4   Replace the canister if you find evidence of damage or leakage.

13 Computer function

General information

Note: For more information and testing on this, or other, engine management sensors and components refer to Chapter 6.

The actual internal functions of the computer can't be checked without expensive diagnostic equipment. Dealerships have the luxury of "replacing with a known good unit", a popular step in factory service manuals, but for practical diagnosis it really doesn't matter. Even dealerships don't "fix" computers, they check power, grounds and closed loop operation. They are simple checks to verify that the computer is functioning properly.

The electronic fuel injection and engine management components are really

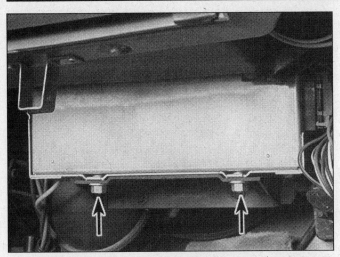

13.1 Computers can be anywhere there's room, but there are some common locations: Many are installed beneath the right side of the dash - usually right under the glove box as on this Pontiac Grand Am

13.2 Another likely location is behind the kick panel (usually the right side) just ahead of the door and underneath the dash, as on this Chevrolet Corsica

quite reliable. There are actually many more problems with wiring, vacuum hoses and connections. Even very small amounts of rust, oxidation or corrosion can, and will, interfere with the small milliamp current that is used in computer circuits.

When first assembled and run, as a new vehicle, any ECM problems would have normally shown up at that time. But over the years, and miles, sometimes failures do occur. Heat, moisture, corrosive salt air, previous inspections, repair or maintenance could all have an affect on the condition of the computer and related system.

Locate the computer (see illustrations) and check the harness connections and electrical grounds. If necessary, take the connectors apart and check for corrosion or a bent pin. **Caution:** *Make sure the ignition key is in the off position before disconnecting or connecting the computer electrical connector(s).* Clean the connectors with electrical contact cleaner and reconnect the computer, making sure that all the terminals are securely seated in the connectors. Check all the computer grounds for corrosion and make sure they're clean, tight and secure.

13.3 A third computer location is between the seats, as on this Pontiac Fiero, or even underneath one of the front seats (arrows point to electrical connector mounting bolt locations)

13.4 In recent years some manufacturers have been placing the computer in the engine compartment (BMW shown here) for ease of access and actually cooler operation than when sandwiched inside an insulated body panel with no airflow

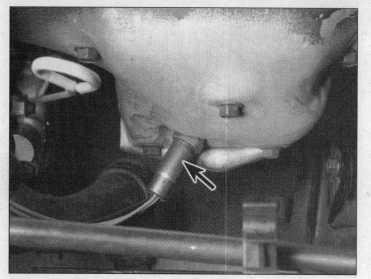

13.5 The oxygen sensor is located in the exhaust manifold ahead of the catalytic converter (some later models now have an additional sensor after the converter to monitor catalytic converter efficiency)

Oxygen sensor

General information

The oxygen sensor, which is located in the exhaust manifold(s) or exhaust pipe **(see illustration)**, monitors the oxygen content of the exhaust gas stream. The oxygen content in the exhaust reacts with the oxygen sensor to produce a voltage output which varies from 0.1-volt (high oxygen, lean mixture) to 0.9-volts (low oxygen, rich mixture). The ECM constantly monitors this variable voltage output to determine the ratio of oxygen to fuel in the mixture. **Note:** *On later vehicles, a dual-stage system may used. A second oxygen sensor is placed in the exhaust stream after the catalytic converter to monitor the change in the exhaust gases.*

There is a timer built into most computer controlled systems that acts as a delay, approximately 90 seconds, before allowing sensor information to be used by the computer.

The timer, along with operating temperature, controls closed loop operation. So even if the engine is up to operating temperature, on a restart for example, there will be a slight delay before the computer closed loop operation will take over engine management from sensor feedback information.

When there is a problem with the oxygen sensor or its circuit, the ECM operates in the "open loop" mode - that is, it controls fuel delivery in accordance with a programmed default value instead of feedback information from the oxygen sensor.

The proper operation of the oxygen sensor depends on four conditions:

a) Electrical - The low voltages generated by the sensor depend upon good, clean connections which should be checked whenever a malfunction of the sensor is suspected or indicated.

b) Outside air supply - The sensor is designed to allow air circulation to the internal portion of the sensor. Whenever the sensor is removed and installed or replaced, make sure the air passages are not restricted.

c) Proper operating temperature - The ECM will not react to the sensor signal until the sensor reaches approximately 600-degrees F. The oxygen sensor produces no voltage when it is below its normal operating temperature. During this initial period before warm-up, the ECM operates in "open loop" mode. This factor must be taken into consideration when evaluating the performance of the sensor.

d) Unleaded fuel - The use of unleaded fuel is essential for proper operation of the sensor. Make sure the fuel you are using is of this type.

In addition to observing the above conditions, special care must be taken whenever the sensor is serviced.

a) The oxygen sensor has a permanently attached pigtail and electrical connector which should not be removed from the sensor. Damage or removal of the pigtail or electrical connector can adversely affect operation of the sensor.

b) Grease, dirt and other contaminants should be kept away from the electrical connector and the louvered end of the sensor.

c) Do not use cleaning solvents of any kind on the oxygen sensor.

d) Do not drop or roughly handle the sensor.

e) The silicone boot must be installed in the correct position to prevent the boot from being melted and to allow the sensor to operate properly. See Chapter 6 for more information on the oxygen sensor.

Oxygen sensor - voltage check (verifying open or closed loop)

1   Locate the oxygen sensor electrical connector and using a straight pin, backprobe the connector with the positive probe of a digital voltmeter. Connect the negative probe of the meter to ground.

2   Warm up the engine to normal operating temperature and let it run at idle. **Note:** *Readings at the oxygen sensor while the engine is cold will only show a fixed voltage signal of approximately 0.2 volt.*

3   Increase and decrease the engine speed and monitor the voltage.

4   When the vehicle goes into closed loop the sensor voltage will begin to vary, normally between 0.1 and 0.9 volts. **Note:** *This shows that the sensor is reacting to the changes in the exhaust gases and is sending a varying signal to the computer to adjust and maintain correct fuel mixture.* If this movement is noted, the ECM has gone into closed loop. It can be concluded from the end result seen here that the power, ground and function of the ECM is working properly, since it is actively trying to monitor and control fuel mixture.

5   If the computer isn't going into closed loop the voltage will remain "fixed" and will not vary. The voltage for open loop will remain fixed at approximately 0.2 volt.

6   There is a condition known as a "lazy sensor", where the voltage does fluctuate as previously described, but it does so very slowly. If voltage readings are changing, but only every 2 or 3 seconds, it's reacting too slowly to exhaust gas changes, and should be replaced.

7   If the voltage reading remains fixed, there are other problems. Power to the computer and all connecting grounds should be checked. There is also a possibility that the oxygen sensor is bad and needs to be replaced.

Electrical grounds

8   Grounds for all the electrical systems are important, but for computer systems they are critical. Computer systems operate on extremely small voltages called millivolts (thousandths of a volt). Even very small changes in resistance can affect the operation of the system.

9   Manufacturers don't always do things the same way. Some have grounded their components through the mounting of the part, others may have used a wire in the harness to lead off to a common ground with other components. But whatever method is used, a good ground is essential to proper operation.

10 To find the computer, remove it and then check for grounds can be time consuming. It isn't always practical, when all that was necessary was to verify that it was going into closed loop operation. So the way many experienced technicians check computer function and closed loop operation is to use the operation of the oxygen sensor as the telltale sign. If the computer isn't receiving power or being sufficiently grounded, it cannot go into closed loop operation.

14 Symptom-based troubleshooting

Note: *The problem symptoms and driveability complaints listed in this Section are primarily related to the fuel injection, emissions and engine management systems. For other possible causes of vehicle problems, refer to the* Haynes Automotive Repair Manual *for your specific vehicle.*

This Section provides an easy reference guide to the more common problems that may occur during the operation of your vehicle. Various symptoms and their probable causes are grouped under headings denoting components or systems, such as Engine, Cooling system, etc.

Remember that successful troubleshooting isn't a mysterious art practiced only by professional mechanics, it's simply the result of knowledge combined with an intelligent, systematic approach to a problem. Always use a process of elimination, starting with the simplest solution and working through to the most complex - and never overlook the obvious. Anyone can run the gas tank dry or leave the lights on overnight, so don't assume that you're exempt from such oversights.

Finally, always establish a clear idea why a problem has occurred and take steps to ensure that it doesn't happen again. If the electrical system fails because of a poor connection, check all other connections in the system to make sure they don't fail as well. If a particular fuse continues to blow, find out why - don't just go on replacing fuses. Remember, failure of a small component can often be indicative of potential failure or incorrect functioning of a more important component or system. If and/or when a check engine light should appear on the instrument panel of your vehicle, don't automatically assume that the faulty component is the computer. A majority of the driveability related complaints so often turn out to be corrected by simply attending to the basics. Concentrate on fundamental items such as airflow, fuel flow, adequate voltage and good grounds to operate the ignition system and sensor/relay systems, good engine mechanical condition - i.e. good vacuum, minimal blow-by gases, good maintenance schedule for oil and coolant changes, etc. All these items make up the whole picture that the computer bases system operations upon.

The following is a list of symptoms and driveability complaints most often experienced with fuel injection systems. The list has been put together to try and cover the majority of all fuel injection systems. Not all the possibilities listed may apply to all types of fuel injection systems. Following each symptom are the components and/or general systems to more closely look at in order to correct the experienced problem:

1 Engine noise

Hiss - vacuum leak(s) (see Section 5).
Electrical arcing (snapping noise) (see Section 9).

2 Engine cranks but won't start

Carbon (charcoal) canister full of fuel (see Section 12).
Faulty MAP, MAF (if equipped) or coolant sensor or circuit (see Chapter 6).
EGR valve stuck open (see Section 10).
Faulty canister vent valve (see Section 12).
Lack of or incorrect fuel pressure (see Chapter 6).
Fuel tank empty.
Water in fuel.
Cold start injector not opening (see Chapter 6)

Battery discharged (engine rotates slowly) (see Section 8).
Battery terminal connections loose or corroded (see Section 8).
Water/excessive moisture inside the distributor cap (particularly in foul weather).
Fouled spark plugs or bad spark-plug wires (see Section 9).
Faulty distributor components (see Section 9).
Faulty distributor pick-up coil or ignition module.
Severe vacuum leak (see Sections 5 and 7).
Severely restricted injectors (see Chapter 6).
Broken, loose or disconnected wires in the starting circuit (see Section 8).
Loose distributor (changing ignition timing) (see Section 5).
Jammed or sticking air flow sensor (Bosch CIS systems) (see Chapter 6).
Auxiliary air valve sticking (Bosch CIS systems) (see Chapter 6).
Sticking control plunger (Bosch CIS systems) (see Chapter 6).

3 Engine is hard to start - cold

Leaking injectors (see Chapter 6).
Distributor rotor carbon tracked (see Section 9).

4 Engine is hard to start - hot

Battery discharged or low (see Section 8).
Air filter clogged (see Section 5).
PCV valve stuck open (see Section 11).
Vacuum leak (see Section 7).
Defective coolant sensor or circuit (see Chapter 6).
Defective air temperature sensor or circuit (see Chapter 6).
Defective MAF (if equipped) sensor or circuit (see Chapter 6).
Defective MAP (if equipped) sensor or circuit (see Chapter 6).
Faulty TPS or circuit (see Chapter 6).
Corroded battery connections (see Section 8).
Bad engine ground connection (see Section 8).
Worn or fouled spark plugs (see Section 9).
Fuel pressure incorrect (see Chapter 6).
Insufficient residual fuel pressure (see Chapter 6).
Airflow meter faulty (see Chapter 6).
Cold start valve leaking or operating continuously (see Chapter 6).

5 Engine starts but won't run

Faulty canister vent valve (see Section 12).
EGR valve stuck open (see Section 10).
Loose or damaged wire harness connections at distributor, coil or alternator (see Section 9).
Intake manifold vacuum leaks (see Section 7).
Insufficient fuel flow (see Chapter 6).

6 Engine 'lopes' while idling, rough idle or idles erratically (cold or warm)

Clogged air filter (see Section 5).
Incorrect ignition timing (see Section 9).
Dirty throttle plate or throttle bore (see Chapter 6).

Minimum idle speed adjustment out of specification (refer to the VECI label) (see Section 3 and Chapter 6).

EGR valve stuck open or leaking (see Section 10).

Vacuum leak (see Section 7).

Air leak in intake duct and/or manifold (false air) (see Section 5).

Idle system faulty (see Chapter 6)

Lean injector(s) (see Chapter 6).

Rich injector(s) (see Chapter 6).

Fuel pump not delivering sufficient pressure (see Chapter 6).

Cold only:

PCV valve stuck open or closed (see Section 11).

Heat control valve stuck open (see Chapter 6).

EFE heater (if equipped) inoperative (see Chapter 6).

Warm only:

Heat control valve stuck closed (see Chapter 6).

TPS or circuit malfunctioning or out of adjustment (see Chapter 6).

MAF (if equipped) sensor or circuit out of adjustment or malfunctioning (see Chapter 6).

7 Engine misses at idle speed

Spark plugs fouled, faulty or not gapped properly (see Sections 3 and 9).

Faulty spark plug wires (see Section 9).

Wet or damaged distributor components (see Section 9).

Sticking or faulty EGR valve (see Section 10).

Clogged fuel filter and/or foreign matter in fuel (see Chapter 5).

Vacuum leaks at intake manifold or hose connections (see Section 5).

Incorrect ignition timing (see Section 9).

Low or uneven cylinder compression.

Cold start injector (if equipped) operating incorrectly (see Chapter 6).

8 Excessively high idle speed

Vacuum leak (see Section 5).

Idle speed incorrectly adjusted (see Chapter 6).

Sticking throttle linkage (see Section 5).

9 Engine misses throughout driving speed range

Fuel filter clogged and/or impurities in the fuel system (see Chapter 5).

Low fuel pump pressure (see Chapter 6).

Fouled, faulty or incorrectly gapped spark plugs (see Section 9).

Incorrect ignition timing (see Section 9).

Cracked distributor cap, disconnected distributor wires or damaged distributor components (see Section 9).

Spark plug wires shorting to ground (see Section 9).

Low or uneven cylinder compression pressures.

Weak or faulty ignition system (see Section 9).

Vacuum leaks (see Section 5).

Leaky EGR valve (see Section 10).

Lean injector(s) (see Chapter 6).

10 Hesitation, stumbles or stalls on acceleration

Spark plugs fouled (see Section 9).
Fuel filter clogged (see Section 5).
Faulty TPS or circuit (see Chapter 6).
Malfunctioning air temperature sensor or circuit (see Chapter 6).
MAP (if equipped) sensor or circuit faulty (see Chapter 6).
Air leak in intake duct and/or manifold (false air) (see Section 5).
Faulty MAF (if equipped) sensor or circuit (see Chapter 6).
Ignition timing incorrect (see Section 9).
Dirty throttle plate or throttle bore (see Chapter 6).
Faulty spark-plug wires, distributor cap or ignition coil (see Section 9).
Low fuel pump pressure (see Chapter 6).
Lean injector(s) (see Chapter 6).

11 Engine lacks power or has sluggish performance

Clogged air filter (see Section 5).
Restricted exhaust system (most likely the catalytic converter) (see Section 7).
Vacuum leak (see Sections 5 and 7).
EGR valve stuck open or not functioning properly (see Section 10).
EFE heater (if equipped) inoperative (cold engine) or restricted (see Chapter 6).
Heat control valve stuck open (during cold engine operation) (see Chapter 6).
Heat control valve stuck shut (during warm engine operation) (see Chapter 6).
Incorrect ignition timing (see Section 9).
Low or uneven cylinder compression pressures.
MAP (if equipped) sensor or circuit malfunctioning (see Chapter 6).
Faulty or incorrectly gapped spark plugs (see Sections 3 and 9).
Fuel filter clogged and/or impurities in the fuel system (see Chapter 5).
Vacuum leak at the intake manifold (see Section 7).
Lean injector(s) (see Chapter 6).

12 Stalls on deceleration or when coming to a quick stop

EGR valve stuck or leakage around base (see Section 10).
Idle speed incorrect (refer to the VECI label under the hood).
TPS misadjusted or defective (see Chapter 6).
Idle Speed Control or Electronic Air Control Valve misadjusted or malfunctioning (see Chapter 6).
Fuel filter clogged and/or water and impurities in the fuel system (see Chapter 5).
Damaged or wet distributor cap and wires (see Section 9).
Emissions system components faulty (see Chapter 6).
Faulty or incorrectly gapped spark plugs. Also check the spark plug wires (see Sections 3 and 9).
Vacuum leak (see Section 5).

13 Surging at steady speed

Clogged air filter (see Section 5).
Vacuum leak (see Sections 5 and 7).
Air leak in intake duct and/or manifold (false air) (see Section 5).
EGR valve stuck or leakage around base (see Section 10).
Problem with oxygen sensor or circuit (see Chapter 6).
Misadjusted or defective TPS or circuit (see Chapter 6).
Defective Mass Air Flow (MAF) (if equipped) sensor or circuit (see Chapter 6).
Defective MAP (if equipped) sensor or circuit (see Chapter 6).
Loose fuel injector wire harness connectors (see Section 5).
Torque Converter Clutch (TCC (if equipped)) engaging/disengaging (may feel similar to fuel starvation).
Fuel pressure incorrect (see Chapter 6).
Fuel pump faulty (see Chapter 6).
Lean injector(s) (see Chapter 6).
Defective computer or information sensors (see Chapter 6).

14 Engine diesels (runs on) when shut-off or idles too fast

Vacuum leak (see Sections 5 and 7).
EGR valve not operating properly or stuck closed, causing overheating (see Section 10).
Heat control valve stuck closed (see Chapter 6).
Idle speed too high - check for correct minimum idle speed (refer to the VECI label under the hood) (see Chapter 6)
Excessive engine operating temperature, check for causes of over heating (see Section 5).
Ignition timing incorrect (see Sections 3 and 9).
Incorrect spark plug selection - too hot (see Sections 3 and 9).
Fuel shut-off system not operating properly (see Chapter 6).

15 Backfiring (through the intake or exhaust)

Vacuum leak in the PCV or canister purge line (see Section 11 or 12).
Vacuum leak at fuel injector(s), intake manifold, air control valve or vacuum lines (see Section 7).
Incorrect ignition timing (see Section 9).
Faulty secondary ignition system, (cracked spark plug insulators, bad plug wires, distributor cap or rotor) (see Section 9).
EGR system not functioning properly (see Section 10).
Emission control system not operating properly (see Chapter 6).
Faulty air injection valve (see Chapter 6).
Valve clearances incorrectly set (on some vehicles this is a required maintenance item or is done during tune-up procedures).
Damaged valve springs, sticking or burned valves - a vacuum-gauge check will often reveal this problem.

16 Poor fuel economy

Clogged air filter (see Section 5).
EFE heater (if equipped) inoperative (see Chapter 6).
Heat control valve stuck open or closed (see Chapter 6).
PCV problem - valve stuck open or closed, or dirty PCV filter (see Section 11).
Emission system not operating properly (see Chapter 6).
Defective oxygen sensor (see Chapter 6).
Incorrect ignition timing (see Section 9).
Incorrect idle speed (see Chapter 6).
Fuel leakage (see Section 5).
Fuel injection internal parts excessively worn or damaged (see Chapter 6).
Cold start injector (if equipped) sticking or leaking/dripping (see Chapter 6).
Sticking/dragging parking brake (see Section 5).
Low tire pressure (see Section 5).

17 Pinging (spark knock)

Ignition timing incorrect.
EGR valve inoperative (see Section 10).
Vacuum leak (see Sections 5 and 7).
Worn or damaged distributor components (see Section 9).
Incorrect or damaged spark plugs or wires (see Sections 3 and 9).
Poor quality fuel

18 Exhaust smoke

Black (overly rich fuel mixture) - Dirty air filter or restricted intake duct (see Section 5).
Blue (burning oil) - PCV valve stuck open or PCV filter dirty (see Section 11).

19 Fuel smell

Fuel tank overfilled (see Section 5).
Fuel tank cap gasket not sealing (see Section 5).
Fuel lines leaking (see Chapter 5).
Fuel injector(s) stuck open (see Chapter 6).
Fuel injector(s) leaks internally (see Chapter 6).
Fuel injector(s) leaks externally (see Chapter 6).
EVAP canister filter in Evaporative Emissions Control system clogged (see Section 12).
Vapor leaks from Evaporative Emissions Control system lines (see Section 12).

Notes

3 Computer trouble codes

Part B

General information

When diagnosing problems on engines controlled by computer systems, remember that many driveability symptoms and/or problems may not necessarily be caused by the computer. The computer is only responding to the input (or change of input information) of the many sensors controlled by the fundamental systems previously discussed in this Book. Unless all of the basic engine systems are properly functioning, the electronic controls have inaccurate information to manage the engine fuel and emissions systems properly.

Condemning a computer, input sensor or output actuator, before verifying that the fundamental systems are operating correctly usually leads to an incorrect diagnosis. Besides wasting your time, you'll find that the electronic components of engine management systems are generally expensive and usually not returnable, even if a mistake has been made in diagnosis.

Before proceeding to the electronic control system tests make the following general checks:

1   The engine is in good overall mechanical condition, as indicated by compression and vacuum tests.

2   The battery is clean and free of connection corrosion, in good condition and fully charged.

3   The starting and charging systems operate properly.

4   All fuses and fusible links are intact.

5   All electrical connectors are free of corrosion and connected securely.

6   All vacuum lines are in good condition, correctly routed, and attached securely.

7   The air and fuel supply systems are free of restrictions and working properly.

8   The PCV, EGR and EVAP and other emissions systems are working properly and maintained as required.

9   The coolant level and condition is good, and the thermostat is in place and is of the correct operating temperature.

10 The engine oil level and condition are good.

11 The ignition system is in good condition with no signs of cross-firing, mis-firing, carbon tracks, corrosion, or wear.

12 The base timing and idle speed are set to specifications found on the VECI label.

13 The computer is going into closed loop operation.

Note: *If in doubt about the condition of any of these items, refer to the appropriate Sections of Chapter 6 and recheck the component(s) or systems in question.*

On-board computer systems not only control the engine fuel, ignition and emission functions in an attempt to achieve optimum efficiency, but on most systems they also have a built-in diagnostic feature. When the computer detects a fault, it stores a **trouble code** in its memory. The code can usually be retrieved from the computer's memory by following a certain procedure. A trouble code doesn't necessarily indicate the exact cause of a problem, but it will direct you to a particular component, circuit or system, which may simplify diagnosis.

While it may not be possible for the home mechanic to repair all of these faults, the codes can allow you to be better informed when explaining a problem to a mechanic, if the need arises.

Operating modes

If, after all the basic troubleshooting procedures have been performed, the tune-up meets specifications, and the driveability problem still exists, it is time to look more closely at the computer/engine management systems.

Computer controlled engine management takes place in two modes, "open-loop" and "closed-loop". The computer must be able to get from "open-loop" to "closed-loop" operation, in order to properly monitor and control the engine management systems.

Open-loop is the operating mode of the system when the vehicle is first started and the engine and the oxygen sensor are warming up. Until all the required criteria are met, such as time and temperature, the computer will remain in "open-loop". This means that all computer controlled functions will stay "fixed" at the manufacturers predetermined default settings. **Note:** *These default settings may also be used in the event of a component failure. They allow the vehicle to run, although poorly, in the "limp-in" mode until repairs can be made.*

Although previously discussed, closed-loop is the normal operating mode of a warmed-up engine and an oxygen sensor warm enough to generate a working signal to the computer (the system also waits a predetermined amount of time before going into closed-loop even if the engine and oxygen sensor are already at operating temperature).

On some vehicles, a few minutes at idle can cause the oxygen sensor to cool enough to allow the system to return to open-loop; on these vehicles, the system may even switch back and forth as the oxygen sensor temperature rises and falls.

Retrieving codes

There are a variety of methods of trouble code retrieval, depending on the manufacturer. Most systems work in conjunction with a light on the dash which illuminates when a fault is detected and a code is stored. The light is marked - "CHECK ENGINE", "POWER LOSS", "SERVICE ENGINE SOON" - or something similar, and is used to blink the codes stored in the computer when manually triggered through the diagnostic connector, if the vehicles computer allows access to trouble codes in this manner.

On other models, the code can be accessed by connecting a voltmeter to the diagnostic connector and counting the needle sweeps or in an LED readout on the computer itself.

Each manufacturer's procedure for retrieving and clearing trouble codes is described at the beginning of the following tables.

Once the codes are retrieved, check them against the chart for your vehicle. **Caution:** *Because engine management systems may differ by year and model, certain trouble codes indicate different problems, depending on the vehicle being repaired. Since this is the case, it would be a good idea to consult your dealer or* *other qualified repair shop before replacing any electrical component, as they are usually expensive and can't be returned once they are purchased.*

Some models require a special diagnostic scanner or tool to retrieve the codes. These scanners are easy to use to gather information, but they're very expensive, making their use beyond the scope of this manual. Consequently, in this manual code retrieval procedures will be limited to those vehicles which don't require such scanners or tools.

Note 1: *When the battery is disconnected, vehicle computer and memory systems may lose memory data. Driveability problems may exist until the computer systems have completed a relearn cycle.*

Note 2: *If the stereo in your vehicle is equipped with an anti-theft system, make sure you have the correct activation code before disconnecting the battery.*

OBD II systems

For some years there has been a gradual process of making and enforcing a "universal" set of computer codes that would be applied by all auto manufacturers to their self-diagnostics. One of the first automotive applications of computers was self-diagnosis of system and component failures. While early on-board diagnostic computers simply lit a "CHECK ENGINE" light on the dash, present systems must monitor complex interactive emission control systems, and provide enough data to the technician to successfully isolate a malfunction.

The computer's role in self-diagnosing emission control problems has become so important that such computers are now required by Federal law. The requirements of the "first generation" system, nicknamed OBD I for On-Board Diagnostics, have been incorporated into 1993 through 1995 models. The purpose of On Board Diagnostics (OBD) is to ensure that emission related components and systems are functioning properly to reduce emission levels of several pollutants emitted by auto and truck engines. The first step is to detect that a malfunction has occurred which may cause increased emissions. The next step is for the system to notify the driver so that the vehicle can be serviced. The final step is to store enough information about the malfunction so that it can be identified and repaired.

The latest step has been the establishment of the OBD II system, which further defines emissions performance, and also regulates the code numbers and definitions.

The basic OBD II code is a letter followed by a four-digit number. Most manufacturers also have many additional codes that are *specific* to their vehicles. Although many of the self-diagnostic tests performed by early OBD systems are retained in OBD II systems, they are now more sensitive in detecting malfunctions. Where there may have been only one code for an oxygen sensor malfunction, there are now six codes that narrow down where the performance discrepancy is. OBD II systems perform many additional tests in areas not required under the earlier OBD. These include monitoring for engine misfires and detecting deterioration of the catalytic converter.

OBD II systems started appearing on a few models in 1994, a few more in 1995 and almost all models in 1996. The only problem with the codes is that a very expensive scan tool is required to read them. It remains for the aftermarket to come up with an inexpensive scan tool for the home mechanic to use. For most OBD II vehicles, the scan tool is the only way to extract and clear trouble codes. For some OBD II vehicles, however, the manufacturer has kept the count-the-blinks method of using the Malfunction Indicator Light (MIL) or Check Engine Light, in addition to the mandated five-character scanner codes, so these vehicles can still be diagnosed by the do-it-yourself mechanic. However, the blinking light codes will not give the detailed information now available from the mandated Federal OBD II codes. **Note:** *To determine if your vehicle is OBD II or not, look at the VECI (Vehicle Emission Control Information) decal on the top of the radiator fan shroud. If it's OBD II, the decal will indicate "OBD II certified".*

Acura

Retrieving codes

The Engine Control Unit (ECU) stores the codes which are accessed by reading the flashing Light Emitting Diode (LED) on the unit (early models) or the CHECK ENGINE light on the dash (later models). If the ECU has two LED's, the red one is for codes. The ECU on 1990 and earlier Legend sedans and Integra models through 1989 is located under the front passenger seat **(see illustration)**. On Legend coupes, 1991 and later Legend sedans, 1990 and later Integras and all Vigor models, the ECU is found under the dashboard on the passenger's side behind the carpet; 1990 Legends incorporate a flip-out mirror so the LED can be seen.

1990 and earlier Legend, 1991 and earlier Integra

When the ECU sets a code, the Check Engine light on the dashboard will illuminate. To access the codes, turn the ignition switch On, then count and record the number of times the LED flashes. On 1986 through 1989 models, the light will blink a sequence the sum total representing the code number (for example, 14 short blinks is code 14). On 1990 Legends and 1990 and 1991 Integras, the light will hold a longer blink to represent the first digit of a two-digit number and then will blink short for the second digit (1 long and 8 short blinks is 18). If the system has more than one problem, the codes will be displayed in sequence, pause, then repeat.

1991 and later Legend, 1992 and later Integra and Vigor models

To access the codes on these models, locate the two-terminal diagnostic connector. On Legend and Integra models it's located under the right side of the dash, behind the glove box. On Vigor models it's located behind the right side of the center console, under the dash. With the ignition On (engine not running), bridge the two terminals of the diagnostic connector with a jumper wire. Any stored codes will be displayed on the CHECK ENGINE light on the dash, in a series of flashes. For example, a code 14 would be indicated by one long flash, a pause, then four short flashes. If more than one code is present, the codes will be displayed in numerical order, with a pause between each code. **Note:** *The self-diagnostic system switched to OBD II on some models in 1994, others in 1995, and all are OBD II in 1996, but DTC codes can still be accessed through the dash light.*

3.1 The ECU on 1990 and earlier Legend sedans and 1989 and earlier Integra models is located under the passenger front seat.

Clearing codes

1990 and earlier Legend, 1991 and earlier Integra

To erase the codes after making repairs, remove the Hazard fuse at the battery positive terminal (Integra) or Alternator Sense fuse in the under hood relay box (Legend) for at least ten seconds.

1991 and later Legend, 1992 and later Integra and Vigor models

To erase codes after making repair to these models, remove the BACK-UP fuse from the relay box under the hood (Integra, Vigor) or the ACG (fuse no. 15) from the fuse box under the left side of the dash (Legend) for at least 10 seconds. **Caution:** *If the stereo in your vehicle is equipped with an anti-theft system, make sure you have the correct activation code before removing the fuse.*

Acura

Code*	Probable cause
1	Oxygen sensor or circuit (Integra)
1	Front oxygen sensor (Legend)
2	Rear oxygen sensor (Legend)
3	Manifold absolute pressure (MAP) sensor or circuit
4	Crank angle sensor or circuit (Integra)
4	Crank angle sensor No. 1 (Legend)
5	Manifold absolute pressure (MAP) sensor or circuit
6	Coolant temperature sensor or circuit
7**	Throttle angle sensor or circuit
8	TDC sensor or circuit (Integra)
9	Crank angle sensor or circuit (CYL) (Integra)
9	Cylinder position sensor No. 1 (Legend)
10	Intake air temperature sensor or circuit
12	EGR control system
13	Atmospheric pressure sensor or circuit
14	Idle control system
15	Ignition output signal
16	Fuel injector
17**	Vehicle speed sensor or circuit
18	Ignition timing adjustment (Legend)
19	Lock-up control solenoid valve (Integra)
20	Electric load (Integra)
21	VTEC solenoid valve (Integra)
22	Front valve timing oil pressure switch (Integra)
23	Front knock sensor (Legend)
30	A/T FI signal A (Legend)
31	A/T FI signal B (Legend)
35	TC standby signal (Legend)
36	TC FC signal (Legend)

Acura
(continued)

Code*	Probable cause
41	Oxygen sensor heater (Integra)
41	Front oxygen sensor heater (Legend)
42	Rear oxygen sensor heater (Legend)
43	Fuel supply system (Integra)
43	Front fuel supply system (Legend)
44	Rear fuel supply system (Legend)
45	Front fuel metering (Legend)
46	Rear fuel metering (Legend)
47	Fuel pump (Legend)
51	Rear spool solenoid valve (Legend)
52	Rear valve timing oil pressure switch (Legend)
53	Rear knock sensor (Legend)
54	Crank angle B (Legend)
59	No. 1 cylinder position (Legend)
61	Upstream oxygen sensor, slow response
63	Downstream oxygen sensor, slow response
65	Downstream oxygen sensor heater
67	Low catalytic converter efficiency
70	Transaxle
71	Misfire, cylinder no. 1
72	Misfire, cylinder no. 2
73	Misfire, cylinder no. 3
74	Misfire, cylinder no. 4
75	Misfire, cylinder no. 5
76	Misfire, cylinder no. 6
76	Random misfire (all except 6-cylinder engines)
80	Low EGR flow
86	Coolant temperature sensor out of range
92	EVAP purge control solenoid

*If codes other than these are indicated, repeat self diagnosis. If code(s) reappear, substitute a known good ECM, and recheck codes.

** On Legend models, if S4 on the automatic transaxle indicator panel also blinks, automatic transaxle control unit may require diagnosis.

BMW

The EFI system control unit (computer) has a built-in self-diagnosis system which detects malfunctions in the system sensors and alerts the driver by illuminating a Check Engine warning light in the instrument panel. The computer stores the failure code until the diagnostic system is cleared by removing the negative battery cable for a period of five seconds or longer. The warning light goes out automatically (after five engine starts) when the malfunction is repaired.

Retrieving codes

There are two types of codes accessible on a BMW. The flash codes (listed here) and trouble codes that can be retrieved only with a BMW tester. This manual only addresses codes accessible without using a special BMW tool.

The Check Engine warning light should come on when the ignition switch is placed in the On position. When the engine is started, the warning light should go out. The light will remain on (with the engine running) once the diagnostic system has detected a malfunction or abnormality in the system. In order to read the codes, it is necessary to turn the key to the On position (engine not running), depress the accelerator pedal 5 times (6 times on 12-cylinder models) within 5 seconds (make sure the pedal reaches wide open throttle each time) and wait for any stored codes to be displayed.

The diagnostic code is the number of flashes indicated on the Check Engine light. If any malfunction has been detected, the light will blink the digit(s) of the code. For example on 1988 3-Series models, code 3 (coolant temperature sensor malfunction) will blink three flashes. There will be a pause (3 seconds) and then any other codes that are stored will be flashed. On 1989 and later 3, 5 and 7-Series models, code 1223 (coolant temperature sensor malfunction) will flash the first digit and then pause, flash the second digit (2 flashes) pause, flash the third digit (2 flashes) pause and finally flash the fourth digit (3 flashes). There will be another pause and the computer will start the next stored trouble code (if any) or it will repeat the code 1223. Once all the codes have been displayed, the Check Engine light will remain on. In order to re-check the codes, simply turn the ignition key Off and then back On (repeat procedure) and the codes will be repeated.

The following trouble code tables indicate the diagnostic code along with the system or component that is affected **Note**: *Diagnostic codes that are not emissions or engine control related (electronic transmission, ABS, etc.) will not be accessed by this system.*

Clearing codes

Caution: *If the stereo in your vehicle is equipped with an anti-theft system, make sure you have the correct activation code before disconnecting the battery.*

After repairs have been made, the diagnostic code can be canceled by disconnecting the negative battery cable for 5 seconds or longer. After cancellation, perform a road test and make sure the warning light does not come on. If desired, the check can be repeated.

1988 3-Series

Code	Probable cause
Code 1	Airflow meter
Code 2	Oxygen sensor
Code 3	Coolant temperature sensor
Code 4	TPS

Fuel Injection Diagnostic Manual

BMW
(continued)

1989 and later 3, 5 and 7-Series

Code	Probable cause
1000, 2000	End of diagnosis
1211, 2211	Electronic Control Unit (ECU)
1215, 2215	Airflow sensor
1216, 2216	Throttle Position Sensor
1221, 2221	Oxygen sensor
1222, 2222	Oxygen sensor regulation
1223, 2223	Coolant temperature sensor
1224, 2224	Intake air temperature sensor
1231, 2231	Battery voltage out of range
1232, 2232	Idle switch
1233, 2233	Full throttle switch
1251, 2251	Fuel injectors (final stage 1)
1252, 2252	Fuel injectors (final stage 2)
1253	Cylinder no. 3 fuel injector
1254	Cylinder no. 4 fuel injector
1255	Cylinder no. 5 fuel injector
1256	Cylinder no. 6 fuel injector
1261, 2261	Fuel pump relay
1262	Idle speed controller or idle air control valve
1263, 2263	EVAP canister purge valve
1264, 2264	Oxygen sensor heating relay
1444, 2444	No faults in memory

Note: *On 12-cylinder models, codes starting with 1 indicate problems on the right cylinder bank (cylinders 1 through 6). Codes starting with 2 indicate problems on the left cylinder bank (cylinders 7 through 12).*

Chrysler, Dodge and Plymouth - domestic cars and light trucks

Note: *On the models covered by this manual, the CHECK ENGINE light, located in the instrument panel, flashes on for three seconds as a bulb test when the engine is started. The light comes on and stays on when there's a problem in the EFI system.*

Retrieving codes

Note: *1996 models are all equipped with OBD II engine management systems, but Chrysler has continued the use of blinking light codes in addition to the mandated five-character codes accessible only with a scan tool.*

The self diagnosis information contained in the SBEC or SMEC (computer) can be accessed either by the ignition key or by using a special tool called the Diagnostic Readout Box (DRB II). This tool is attached to the diagnostic connector in the engine compartment and reads the codes and parameters on the digital display screen. The tool is expensive and most home mechanics prefer to use the alternate method. The drawback with the ignition method is that it does not access all the available codes for display. Most problems can be solved or diagnosed quite easily and if the information cannot be obtained readily, have the vehicle's self diagnosis system analyzed by a dealer service department or other properly-equipped repair shop.

To obtain the codes using the ignition key method, first set the parking brake and put the transaxle in Park (automatic) or Neutral (manual).

Raise the engine speed to approximately 2500 rpm and slowly let the speed down to idle.

Cycle the air conditioning system, if equipped (on briefly, then off).

If the vehicle is equipped with an automatic transmission, with your foot on the brake, select each position on the transmission (Reverse, Drive, Low etc.) and bring the shifter back to Park. This will allow the computer to obtain any fault codes that might be linked to any of the sensors controlled by the transmission, engine speed or air conditioning system.

To display the codes on the dashboard (POWER LOSS or CHECK ENGINE light), turn the ignition key On, Off, On, Off and finally On (engine not running). The codes will begin to flash. The light will blink the number of the first digit then pause and blink the number of the second digit. For example: Code 23, throttle body temperature sensor circuit, would be indicated by two flashes, then a pause followed by three flashes.

Certain criteria must be met for a fault code to be entered into the engine controller memory. The criteria may be a specific range of engine rpm, engine temperature or input voltage to the engine controller. It is possible that a fault code for a particular monitored circuit may not be entered into the memory despite a malfunction. This may happen because one of the fault code criteria has not been met. For example; The engine must be operating between 750 and 2000 rpm in order to monitor the Map sensor circuit correctly. If the engine speed is raised above 2400 rpm, the MAP sensor output circuit shorts to ground and will not allow a fault code to be entered into the memory. Then again, the exact opposite could occur: A code is entered into the memory that suggests a malfunction within another component that is not monitored by the computer. For example; A fuel pressure problem cannot register a fault directly but instead, it will cause a rich/lean fuel mixture problem. Consequently, this will cause an oxy-

Chrysler, Dodge and Plymouth

(continued)

gen sensor malfunction resulting in a stored code in the computer for the oxygen sensor. Be aware of the interrelationship of the sensors and circuits and the overall relationship of the emissions control and fuel injection systems.

The following table is a list of the typical trouble codes which may be encountered while diagnosing the system. If the problem persists after these checks have been made, more detailed service procedures will have to be performed by a dealer service department or other qualified repair shop.

Clearing codes

Caution: *If the stereo in your vehicle is equipped with an anti-theft system, make sure you have the correct activation code before disconnecting the battery.*

Trouble codes may be cleared by disconnecting negative battery cable for at least 15 seconds. However, on OBD II models the codes can only be cleared with the use of a scan tool.

Code	Probable cause
88	Start of test
11 (Dakota pick-up, 2.5L models)	Engine not cranked since battery was disconnected
11	Engine not cranked since battery was disconnected/no distributor input signal
12	Memory standby power lost
13*	MAP (Manifold Absolute Pressure) sensor vacuum circuit - slow or no change in MAP sensor input and/or output
14*	MAP (Manifold Absolute Pressure) sensor electrical circuit - high or low voltage
15**	Vehicle speed/distance sensor circuit
16*	Loss of battery voltage
16	Knock sensor
17	Engine running too cold
21**	Oxygen sensor circuit
22*	Coolant temperature sensor unit - high or low voltage
23	Throttle body air temperature sensor circuit - high or low voltage
24*	Throttle position sensor circuit - high or low voltage
25**	ISC (Idle Speed Control) motor driver circuit
25	AIS (Automatic Idle Speed) motor driver circuit
26*	Peak injector current has not been reached or injector circuits have high resistance
27*	Fuel Injector Control circuit or injector output circuit not responding

Code	Probable cause
31**	Canister purge solenoid circuit failure
32**	EGR (Exhaust Gas Recirculation) system open; short in transducer solenoid or failure; power loss to PCM during diagnostic test
33	Air conditioning clutch cutout relay circuit
34	Speed control vacuum or vent control solenoid circuits (or an open or shorted circuit at the EGR solenoid on 1987 models)
35	Cooling fan relay, high speed fan or low speed fan control relay(s)
35	Idle switch circuit; cooling fan relay circuit
36*	Air switching solenoid circuit (non-turbo) or wastegate solenoid circuit on turbocharged models
37	Part throttle unlock solenoid driver circuit (automatic transmission only) or shift indicator light circuit (lockup converter) - On 1996 models, no converter clutch engagement
41	Charging system excess or lack of field current
42	Automatic Shutdown relay driver circuit (ASD)
43	Ignition coil control circuit or spark interface circuit
44	Loss of FJ2 to logic board/battery temperature out of range or failure in the SMEC/SBEC
45	Overboost shut-off circuit on MAP sensor reading above overboost limit detected/overdrive solenoid (A-500 or A-518 automatic transmission) - On 1996 models, transmission fault present
46*	Charging system voltage too high
47	Charging system voltage too low
51**	Oxygen sensor indicates lean
52**	Oxygen sensor indicates rich
53	Module internal problem; SMEC/SBEC failure; internal engine controller fault condition detected
54	Problem with the distributor synchronization circuit - On 1995 and 1996 models, no cam signal at PCM
55	End of code output
61*	BARO solenoid failure
62	Emissions reminder light mileage is not being updated
63	EEPROM write denied - controller failure
64	Flexible fuel (methanol) sensor indicates concentration sensor input more than the acceptable voltage

Code	Probable cause
64	Flexible fuel (methanol) sensor indicates concentration sensor input less than the acceptable voltage
65	Manifold tune valve solenoid circuit open or shorted - On 1996 models, power steering switch failure
66	No message from the transmission control module (TCM) to the powertrain control module (PCM)
66	No message from the body control module (BCM) to the powertrain control module (PCM)
71	5-volt PCM output low
72	Catalytic converter efficiency failure
77	Speed control power relay circuit

* These codes light up Check Engine light
**These codes light up Check Engine light on vehicles with special California emissions controls

Eagle

Summit and Talon (1988 on)

Retrieving codes

Locate the diagnostic connector in or under the glove compartment. On some late-model Summit models, it may be next to the fuse box **(see illustration)**. Connect an analog voltmeter to the upper right (+) and lower left (-) connector terminals. On 1994 and later Summit models, connect the voltmeter (+) to the upper left terminal of the male, 12-pin connector and (-) to either of the upper-middle two of the female connector (on station wagon models, grounding the upper left terminal of the 16-pin connector is all that's necessary). Turn on the ignition On (engine Off) and watch the voltmeter needle. It will display the codes as long or short sweeps of the needle. For example, two long sweeps followed by three short sweeps is code 23. Count the number of long and short needle sweeps and write the codes down for reference. Continuous short pulses indicate that all is normal and there are no codes.

In 1995, some models appeared with OBD II systems, while others still had OBD I systems. Some of these models may not display codes on a voltmeter, but grounding the diagnostic connector should still provide codes through the MIL light on the dash. On all OBD II models from 1995 on, the OBD II codes can only be retrieved using a scan tool.

Clearing codes

Caution: *If the stereo in your vehicle is equipped with an anti-theft system, make sure you have the correct activation code before disconnecting the battery.*

After making repairs, disconnect the cable from the negative terminal of the battery to erase codes from the computer memory. **Caution:** *If you disconnect the battery from the vehicle to clear the codes, this will erase stored operating parameters from the computer and may cause the engine to run rough for a period of time while the computer relearns the information.*

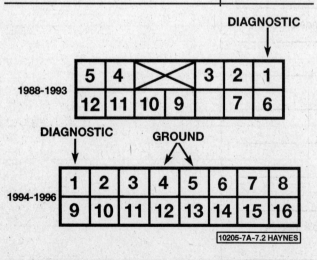

3.2 Diagnostic connectors for Eagle models

Code	Probable cause
11	Oxygen sensor
12	Airflow sensor
13	Intake air temperature sensor
14	Throttle position sensor
15	Idle speed motor position sensor
21	Coolant temperature sensor
22	Crank angle sensor
23	Top dead center sensor (camshaft position sensor)
24	Vehicle speed sensor
25	Barometric pressure sensor
31	Knock sensor (turbo models)
32	Faulty MAP sensor
36	Ignition timing adjustment signal (1.8L, 1991 on)
39	Faulty oxygen sensor
41	Injector
42	Fuel pump
43	EGR (California)
44	Ignition coil or ignition power transistor unit (cylinders 1 and 4)
52	Ignition coil (cylinders 2 and 5)
53	Ignition coil (cylinders 3 and 6)
55	Idle air control valve
59	Rear heated oxygen sensor
61	ECM-transaxle interlink
62	Warm-up valve position sensor (1993 on - Variable Induction Control valve position sensor)
71	Traction Control vacuum valve solenoid

Premier (1991 and 1992) and Vision

Retrieving codes

Turn the ignition switch On, Off, On, Off, On and watch the flashes of the Power Loss or Check Engine light on the dash. The codes will blink the number of the first digit, then pause and blink the number of the second digit. For example, Code 23 would be 2 blinks, pause, 3 blinks.

Clearing codes

Caution: *If the stereo in your vehicle is equipped with an anti-theft system, make sure you have the correct activation code before disconnecting the battery.*

After making repairs, disconnect the cable from the negative terminal of the battery to erase codes from the computer memory. **Caution:** *If you disconnect the battery from the vehicle to clear the codes, this will erase stored operating parameters from the computer and may cause the engine to run rough for a period of time while the computer relearns the information.*

Code	Probable cause
11	Ignition reference circuit
13	MAP sensor vacuum circuit
14	MAP sensor electrical circuit
15	Speed/distance sensor circuit
17	Engine running too cool
21	Oxygen sensor circuit
22	Coolant temperature sensor circuit
23	Charge temperature circuit
24	Throttle position sensor circuit
25	Automatic idle speed control circuit
26	Peak injector current not reached
26	Injector circuit
27	Fuel injection circuit control
32	EGR system
33	Air conditioner clutch relay
34	Speed control solenoid driver circuit

Code	Probable cause
35	Fan control relay circuit
42	Automatic shutdown relay circuit
43	Ignition coil circuit
51	Oxygen sensor lean
52	Oxygen sensor rich
53	Internal engine controller fault
54	No camshaft position sensor signal
55	End of message
63	EEPROM write denied
77	Speed control power relay

Ford, Lincoln and Mercury

Retrieving codes

Note: *Trouble codes are not retrievable on models with an EEC-V engine management system (a special scan tool must be used).*

The diagnostic codes for the EEC-IV systems are arranged in such a way that a series of tests must be completed in order to extract ALL the codes from the system. If one portion of the test is performed without the others, there may be a chance the trouble code that will pinpoint a problem in your particular vehicle will remain stored in the PCM without detection. The tests start first with a Key On, Engine Off (KOEO) test followed by a computed timing test then finally a Engine Running (ER) test. Here is a brief overview of the code extracting procedures of the EEC-IV system followed by the actual test:

Quick Test - Key On Engine Off (KOEO)

The following tests are all included with the key on, engine off:

Self test codes - These codes are accessed on the test connector by using a jumper wire and an analog voltmeter or the factory diagnostic tool called the Star tester. These codes are also called Hard Codes.

Separator pulse codes - After the initial Hard Codes, the system will flash a code 11 (separator pulse) (1990 and earlier) or code 111 (1991 and later) and then will flash a series of Soft Codes.

Continuous Memory Codes - These codes indicate a fault that may or may not be present at the time of testing. These codes usually indicate an intermittent failure. Continuous Memory codes are stored in the system and they will flash after the normal Hard Codes. These codes are either two digit (1988 through 1991) or three digit codes (1992 through 1995). These codes can indicate chronic or intermittent problems. Also called Soft Codes.

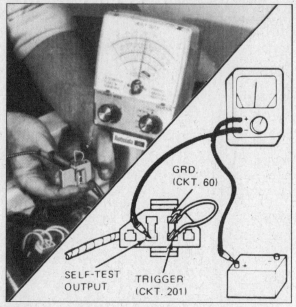

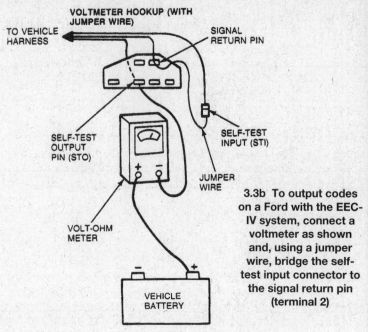

3.3a On 1984 and earlier Ford systems, hook up the volt/ohm meter as shown to read the trouble codes

3.3b To output codes on a Ford with the EEC-IV system, connect a voltmeter as shown and, using a jumper wire, bridge the self-test input connector to the signal return pin (terminal 2)

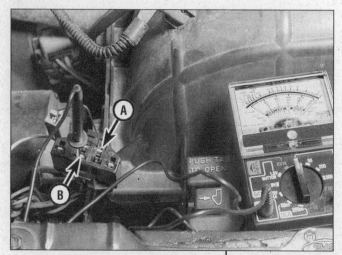

3.3c This is how it looks on a real vehicle - insert a jumper wire from terminal number 2 (A) to self-test input connector, then install the negative probe of the voltmeter into terminal number 4 (B) and position the positive probe to the battery positive terminal

Engine running codes (ER)

Running tests - These tests make it possible for the PCM to pick-up a diagnostic trouble code that cannot be set while the engine is in KOEO mode. These problems usually occur during driving conditions. Some codes are detected by cold or warm running conditions, some are detected at low rpms or high rpms and some are detected at closed throttle or wide open throttle.

I.D. Pulse codes - These codes indicate the type of engine (4, 6 or 8 cylinder) or the correct module and Self Test mode access.

Computed engine timing test - This engine running test determines base timing for the engine and starts the process of allowing the engine to store running codes.

Wiggle test - This engine running test checks the wiring system to the sensors and output actuators

Cylinder balance test - This engine running test determines injector balance as well as cylinder compression balance. **Note:** *This test should be performed by a dealer service department.*

Position the parking brake ON, Shift lever in PARK (NEUTRAL in manual transmission vehicles), block the drive wheels and turn off all electrical loads (air conditioning, radio, heater fan blower etc.). Make sure the engine is warmed to operating temperatures (if possible).

Perform the **KOEO tests:**

a) Turn the ignition key off for at least 10 seconds.

b) Locate the diagnostic Test connector inside the engine compartment **(see illustrations)**. Install the voltmeter leads onto the battery and pin number 4 (STO) of the test connector. Install a jumper wire from the test terminal to pin number 2 of the Diagnostic Test terminal (STI) **(see illustration)**.

c) Turn the ignition key On (engine not running) and observe the needle sweeps on the voltmeter. For example code 23, the voltmeter will sweep once, pause 1/2 second and sweep again. There will be a two second pause between digits and then there will be three distinct sweeps of the needle to indicate the second digit of the code number. On three digit codes, the sequence is the same except there will be an additional sequence of numbers (sweeps) to indicate the third digit in the code. Additional codes will be separated by a four second pause and then the indicated sweeps on the voltmeter. Be aware that the code sequence may continue into the continuous memory codes (read further). **Note:** *Later models will flash the Check Engine light on the dash in place of the voltmeter.*

Interpreting the continuous memory codes:

After the KOEO codes are reported, there will be a short pause and any stored Continuous Memory codes will appear in order. Remember that the "Separator" code is 11, or 111 on 1992 and later models. The computer will not enter the Continuous Memory mode without flashing the separator pulse code. The Continuous Memory codes are read the same as the initial codes or "Hard Codes". Record these codes onto a piece of paper and continue the test.

Perform the **Engine Running (ER) tests:**

a) Remove the jumper wires from the Diagnostic Test connector to start the test
b) Run engine until it reaches normal operating temperature
c) Turn the engine OFF for at least 10 seconds
d) Install the jumper wire onto Diagnostic Test connector and start the engine.
e) Observe that the voltmeter or Check Engine light will flash the engine identification code. This code indicates 1/2 the number of cylinders of the engine. For example, 4 flashes represent an 8 cylinder engine, or 3 flashes represent a six cylinder engine.
f) Within 1 to 2 seconds of the I.D. code, turn the steering wheel at least 1/2 turn and release. This will store any power steering pressure switch trouble codes.
g) Depress the brake pedal and release. **Note:** *Perform the steering wheel and brake pedal procedure in succession immediately (1 to 2 seconds) after the I.D. codes are flashed.*
h) Observe all the codes and record them on a piece of paper. Be sure to count the sweeps or flashes very carefully as you jot them down.

On some models the PCM will request a Dynamic Response check. This test quickly checks the operation of the TPS, MAF or MAP sensors in action. This will be indicated by a code 1 or a single sweep of the voltmeter needle (one flash on CHECK ENGINE light). This test will require the operator to simply full throttle ("goose") the accelerator pedal for one second. DO NOT throttle the accelerator pedal unless it is requested.

The next part of this test makes sure the system can advance the timing. This is called the Computed Timing test. After the last ER code has been displayed, the PCM will advance the ignition timing a fixed amount and hold it there for approximately 2 minutes. Use a timing light to check the amount of advance. The computed timing should equal the base timing plus 20 BTDC. The total advance should equal 27 to 33 degrees advance. If the timing is out of specification, have the system checked at a dealer service department.

Finally perform the **Wiggle Test:** (This test can be used to recreate a possible intermittent fault in the harness wiring system.)

a) Use a jumper wire to ground the STI lead on the Diagnostic Test connector.
b) Turn the ignition key On (engine not running).
c) Now deactivate the self test mode (remove jumper wire) and then immediately reactivate self test mode. Now the system has entered Continuous Monitor Test Mode.
d) Carefully wiggle, tap or remove any suspect wiring to a sensor or output actuator. If a problem exists, a trouble code will be stored that indicates a problem with the circuit that governs the particular component. Record the codes that are indicated.

Fuel Injection Diagnostic Manual

e) Next, enter Engine Running Continuous Monitor Test Mode to check for wiring problems only when the engine is running. Start first by deactivating the Diagnostic Test connector and turning the ignition key Off. Now start the engine and allow it to idle.

f) Use a jumper wire to ground the STI lead on the Diagnostic Test connector. Wait ten seconds and then deactivate the test mode and reactivate it again (install jumper wire). This will enter Engine Running Continuous Monitor Test Mode.

g) Carefully wiggle, tap or remove any suspect wiring to a sensor or output actuator. If a problem exists, a trouble code will be stored that indicates a problem with the circuit that governs the particular component. Record the codes that are indicated.

If necessary, perform the Cylinder Balance Test. This test should be performed by a qualified automotive service department.

Clearing codes

To clear the codes from the PCM memory, start the KOEO self test diagnostic procedure and install the jumper wire into the Diagnostic Test connector. When the codes start to display themselves on the voltmeter or Check Engine light, remove the jumper wire from the Diagnostic Test connector. This will erase any stored codes within the system.

Caution: *Do not disconnect the battery from the vehicle to clear the codes. This will erase stored operating parameters from the KAM (Keep Alive Memory) and cause the engine to run rough for a period of time while the computer relearns the information.*

EEC-IV 2-digit trouble codes (1991 and earlier models)

Code No.	Test Condition*	Probable cause
10	R	Cylinder #1 low during Cylinder Balance Test
11	O,R,C	System PASS
12	O,R,C	Cannot control RPM during high RPM test
13	O,R,C	Cannot control RPM during low RPM test
14	C	PIP circuit failure
15	O	EEC Read Only Memory failed
15	C	EEC Keep Alive Memory failed
16	O	Ignition Diagnostic Monitor Signal not received
16	R	RPM too low to perform HEGO test
16	R	Air/fuel mixture not within Self test range
17	R	RPM too low with ISC Retracted (1.9L CFI)

*0 = Key On, Engine Off; C = Continuous Memory; R = Engine Running

Code No.	Test Condition*	Probable cause
17	R	Air/fuel mixture not within Self test range
18	R	SPOUT circuit open
18	C	Loss of TACH input to ECA, SPOUT circuit grounded
19	O	Failure in EEC reference voltage
19	R	RPM for EGR test too low (1.9L CFI)
20	R	Cylinder #2 low during Cylinder Balance Test
21	O,R	ECT out of range during Self test
22	O,C, R	MAP/BP sensor out of range during Self test
23	O,R	TP sensor out of range during Self test
24	O,R	VAT sensor out of range during Self test (1.6L PFI and 2.3L Turbo)
24	O,R	ACT sensor out of range during Self test (except 1.6L PFI and 2.3L Turbo)
25	R	Knock not sensed during Dynamic Response Test
26	O, R	VAF sensor out of range during Self test (1.6L PFI and 2.3L Turbo)
27	R	Servo leaks down during Integrated Vehicle Speed Control Test
27	C	Insufficient input from VSS (2.3L Turbo)
28	R	Servo leaks up during Integrated Vehicle Speed Control Test
28	O, R	Intake air temperature at VAF meter out of range during Self test
30	R	Cylinder #3 low during Cylinder Balance Test
31	O,C,R	EVP voltage out of range during Self test (2.3L OHC and 3.8L CFI)
31	O,C,R	PFE/EPT/EVP below minimum voltage
32	R	EGR not controlling (2.3L OHC and 3.8L CFI)
32	C, R	EGR valve not seated (1.9L CFI, 2.9L and 3.0L)
32	O,C,R	PFE/EVP (sonic) voltage below closed limit
33	C,R	EGR valve not seated (2.3L OHC and 3.8L CFI)
33	C,R	EGR valve (PFE and Sonic) not opening

*0 = Key On, Engine Off; C = Continuous Memory; R = Engine Running

Fuel Injection Diagnostic Manual

EEC-IV 2-digit trouble codes (1991 and earlier models) (continued)

Code No.	Test Condition*	Probable cause
34	O	Defective PFE/EPT sensor (1.9L CFI, 2.9L and 3.0L)
34	C,R	Exhaust pressure high; Defective PFE/EPT sensor
35	R	RPM too low to perform EGR test (1983)
35	O,C, R	PFE/EPT/EVP circuit above maximum voltage
39	C	Automatic transaxle lock-up circuit failed (3.0L Cars)
40	R	Cylinder #4 low during Cylinder Balance Test
41	C, R	EGO sensor indicates system lean
42	C, R	EGO sensor indicates system rich
44	R	Thermactor Air System inoperative
45	R	Thermactor air upstream during Self test
46	R	Thermactor air not by-passed during Self test
50	R	Cylinder #5 low during Cylinder Balance Test
51	O,C	ECT sensor circuit open
52	O	Power Steering Pressure Switch circuit open
53	O,C	TP sensor circuit open, above maximum voltage
54	O,C	VAT sensor circuit open (1.6L PFI, 1.9L PFI and 2.3L Turbo)
54	O,C	ACT sensor circuit open (except 1.6L PFI, 1.9L PFI and 2.3L Turbo)
55	O,C, R	Key power circuit low
56	O,C	VAF circuit above maximum voltage (1.6L PFI, 1.9L PFI and 2.3L Turbo)
57	C	NPS circuit failed open (3.0L Car)
59	C	Automatic transaxle 4/3 circuit failed open (3.0L Car)
60	R	Cylinder #6 low during Cylinder Balance Test
61	O,C	ECT sensor circuit grounded
62	O, R	Automatic transaxle 3/2 or 4/3 circuit grounded (3.0L Car)

0 = Key On, Engine Off; C = Continuous Memory; R = Engine Running

Code No.	Test Condition*	Probable cause
63	O,C	TP sensor circuit below minimum voltage
64	O,C	ACT sensor out of range during Self test (1983 2.3L Turbo and 2.8L)
64	O,C	VAT sensor circuit grounded (1.6L PFI, 1.9L PFI and 2.3L Turbo)
64	O,C	ACT sensor circuit grounded (except 1.6L PFI, 1.9L PFI and 2.3L Turbo)
65	C, R	Key power low
66	O,C	VAF sensor circuit input voltage below minimum (1.6L PFI, 1.9L PFI and 2.3L Turbo)
67	O	NPS circuit open with Air conditioning on during Self test
67	C	Air conditioning clutch energized during Self test (1983 2.3L Turbo)
68	O	RPM not within Self test range
69	C	Automatic transaxle 3/4 input circuit failed open (3.0L Car)
70	R	Cylinder #7 low during Cylinder Balance Test
72	R	Insufficient MAP change during Dynamic Response Test
73	R	Insufficient TPS change during Dynamic Response Test
74	R	Brake on/off switch circuit open
75	R	Brake on/off switch circuit closed
76	R	Insufficient VAF change during Dynamic Response Test (1.6L PFI, 1.9L PFI and 2.3L Turbo)
77	R	Operator error during Dynamic Response Test or Cylinder Balance Test
80	R	Cylinder #8 low during Cylinder Balance Test
81	O	Air Management 2 circuit failure
82	O	Air Management 1 circuit failure
83	O	EGR Control circuit failure
83	O	High speed electro drive fan circuit failure (2.5L CFI and 3.0L Car)
84	O	EGR circuit failure
85	O,R	Canister Purge circuit failure
87	O,C,R	Fuel pump circuit failure

*O = Key On, Engine Off; C = Continuous Memory; R = Engine Running

Fuel Injection Diagnostic Manual

EEC-IV 2-digit trouble codes (1991 and earlier models) (continued)

Code No.	Test Condition*	Probable cause
87	O	Temperature Compensated pump fault (2.8L)
88	O	Idle speed not within Self test Range (5.0L CFI)
88	O	Electric cooling fan circuit failure (3.0L V6)
88	O	Variable Voltage Choke circuit failure (2.8L)
89	O	Clutch Converter Override circuit failure (2.3L PFI, 2.8L and 3.0L Truck)
89	O	Exhaust Heat Crossover circuit failure (3.8L CFI and 5.0L CFI)
89	O	Lock-up solenoid circuit failure (3.0L Car)
90	R	Pass Cylinder Balance Test
91	R	Air/Fuel mixture not within Self test range (3.8L CFI and 5.0L)
92	R	Air/Fuel mixture not within Self test range (3.8L CFI and 5.0L)
94/96	R	Thermactor Air System inoperative (3.8L CFI and 5.0L)
97/98	R	Air/Fuel mixture not within self test range (1985 3.8L CFI)
98	R	Hard Fault present
99	R	Idle not learned

EEC-IV 3-digit trouble codes (1992 to 1995)

Code No.	Test Condition*	Probable cause
111	O,C,R	Pass
112	O, R	Intake Air Temperature sensor circuit indicates circuit grounded - above 245-degrees F
113	O, R	Intake Air Temperature sensor circuit indicates open circuit - below -40-degrees F
114	O, R	Intake Air Temperature sensor out-of-self test range
116	O, R	Coolant Temperature sensor out-of-self test range
117	O,C	Coolant Temperature circuit below minimum voltage indicates above 245-degrees F.

*0 = Key On, Engine Off; C = Continuous Memory; R = Engine Running

Code No.	Test Condition*	Probable cause
118	O,C	Coolant Temperature sensor circuit above maximum voltage indicates below -40-degrees F
121	O,C, R	Throttle Position sensor out-of-self test range
122	O,C	Throttle Position sensor below minimum voltage
123	O,C	Throttle Position sensor above maximum voltage;
124	C	Throttle Position Sensor voltage higher than expected
125	C	Throttle Position Sensor voltage lower than expected
126	O,C, R	MAP/BARO sensor higher than expected (1993 to 1995)
128	C	MAP sensor vacuum hose damaged or disconnected (1993 to 1995)
129	R	Insufficient Manifold Absolute Pressure/Mass Air Flow change during Dynamic Response Check
136	R	Heated oxygen sensor indicates lean condition, left side
137	R	Heated oxygen sensor indicates rich condition, left side
139	C	No heated oxygen sensor switching detected, left side
144	C	No heated oxygen sensor switching detected, right side
157	R,C	Mass Air Flow Sensor below minimum voltage
158	O, R,C	Mass Air Flow Sensor above maximum voltage
159	O, R	Mass Air Flow Sensor out-of-self test range
167	R	Insufficient Throttle Position Sensor change during Dynamic Response Check
171	C	Heated oxygen sensor unable to switch, right side
172	R,C	Heated oxygen sensor indicates lean condition, right side
173	R,C	Heated oxygen sensor indicates rich condition, right side
174	C	Heated oxygen sensor switching slow, right side
175	C	Heated oxygen sensor unable to switch, left side
176	C	Heated oxygen sensor indicates lean condition, left side
177	C	Heated oxygen sensor indicates rich condition, left side
178	C	Heated oxygen sensor switching slow, left side

*0 = Key On, Engine Off; C = Continuous Memory; R = Engine Running

Fuel Injection Diagnostic Manual

EEC-IV 3-digit trouble codes (1992 to 1995) (continued)

Code No.	Test Condition*	Probable cause
179	C	Adaptive Fuel lean limit reached at part throttle, system rich, right side
181	C	Adaptive Fuel rich limit reached at part throttle, system lean, right side
182	C	Adaptive Fuel lean limit reached at idle, system rich, right side
183	C	Adaptive Fuel rich limit reached at idle, system lean, right side
184	C	Mass Air Flow higher than expected
185	C	Mass Air Flow lower than expected
186	C	Injector pulse-width higher than expected
187	C	Injector pulse-width lower than expected
188	C	Adaptive fuel lean limit reached, system rich, left side
189	C	Adaptive fuel rich limit reached, system lean, left side
191	C	Adaptive fuel lean limit reached at idle, left side
192	C	Adaptive fuel rich limit reached at idle, left side
193	O	Flexible fuel (FF) sensor circuit failure (1993 to 1995)
211	C	Profile Ignition Pick-up circuit fault
212	C	Ignition module circuit failure - SPOUT circuit grounded
213	R	SPOUT circuit open
214	C	Cylinder identification (CID) circuit failure
215	C	PCM detected coil 1 primary circuit failure
216	C	PCM detected coil 2 primary circuit failure
217	C	PCM detected coil 3 primary circuit failure (1994 and 1995)
219	C	Spark timing defaulted to 10 degrees SPOUT circuit open (EI)
221	C	Spark timing error (1993 to 1995)
222	C	Loss of ignition diagnostic monitor (IDM) signal - right side (dual plug) (1993 to 1995)
223	C	Loss of dual plug Inhibit (DPI) control (dual plug) (1993 to 1995)

*0 = Key On, Engine Off; C = Continuous Memory; R = Engine Running

Code No.	Test Condition*	Probable cause
224	C	PCM detected coil 1,2,3 or 4 primary circuit failure (dual plug EI) (1993 to 1995)
225	C	Knock sensor not detected during dynamic response test KOER
226	O	Ignition Diagnostic Module (IDM) signal not received (EI) (1993 to 1995)
232	C	PCM detected coil 1,2,3 or 4 primary circuit failure (EI) (1993 to 1995)
238	C	PCM detected coil 4 primary circuit failure (EI) (1993 to 1995)
241	C	ICM to PCM - IDM pulse width transmission error (EI) (1993 to 1995)
244	R	CID circuit fault present when cylinder balance test requested (1993 to 1995)
311	R	Thermactor Air System inoperative, right side
313	R	Thermactor Air not by-passed
314	R	Thermactor Air inoperative, left side
326	C,R	EGR circuit voltage lower than expected
327	O,C,R	EGR Valve Pressure Transducer; Position Sensor circuit below minimum voltage
328	O,C,R	EGR valve position sensor voltage below closed limit
332	C,R	EGR valve opening not detected
334	O,C,R	EGR valve position sensor voltage above closed limit
335	O	EGR Sensor voltage out-of-range
336	R	EGR circuit voltage higher than expected
337	O,C,R	EGR Valve Pressure Transducer; Position Sensor circuit above maximum voltage
341	O	Octane adjust circuit open (1993 to 1995)
381	C	Frequent air conditioning clutch cycling (1993 to 1995)
411	R	Unable to control RPM during Low RPM Self test
412	R	Unable to control RPM during High RPM Self test
415	R	Idle Air Control (IAC) system at maximum adaptive lower limit
416	C	Idle Air Control (IAC) system at upper adaptive learning limit
452	C	No input from Vehicle Speed Sensor

*O = Key On, Engine Off; C = Continuous Memory; R = Engine Running

Fuel Injection Diagnostic Manual

EEC-IV 3-digit trouble codes (1992 to 1995) (continued)

Code No.	Test Condition*	Probable cause
453	R	Servo leaking down (KOER IVSC test) (1993 to 1995)
454	R	Servo leaking up (KOER IVSC test) (1993 to 1995)
455	R	Insufficient rpm increase (KOER IVSC test) (1993 to 1995)
456	R	Insufficient rpm decrease (KOER IVSC test) (1993 to 1995)
457	O	Speed control command switch(s) circuit not functioning (KOEO IVSC test) (1993 to 1995)
458	O	Speed control command switch(s) stuck/circuit grounded (KOEO IVSC test) (1993 to 1995)
459	O	Speed control ground circuit open (KOEO IVSC test)
511	O	Read Only Memory test failed - replace PCM
512	C	Keep Alive Memory test failed
513	O	Internal voltage failure in PCM
519	O	Power steering pressure switch (PSP) circuit open (1993 to 1995)
521	R	Power steering pressure switch (PSP) circuit did not change states (1993 to 1995)
522	O	Manual Lever Position (MLP) sensor circuit open/vehicle in gear
525	O	Indicates vehicle in gear, air conditioning on
527	O	Manual Lever Position (MLP) sensor circuit open, air conditioning on during KOEO (1993 to 1995)
529	C	Data Communication link (DCL) or PCM circuit failure (1993 to 1995)
532	C	Cluster Control Assembly (CCA) circuit failure
533	C	Data Communications Link (DCL) or Electronic Instrument Cluster (EIC) circuit failure
536	C,R	Brake ON/Off (BOO) circuit failure/not activated during the KOER
538	R	Insufficient change in RPM; operator error in Dynamic Response Check
539	O	Air conditioning on during Self test
542	O,C	Fuel Pump circuit open; PCM to motor
543	O,C	Fuel Pump circuit open; Battery to PCM
551	O	Idle Air Control (IAC) circuit failure KOEO
552	O	Air Management 1 circuit failure

*O = Key On, Engine Off; C = Continuous Memory; R = Engine Running

Code No.	Test Condition*	Probable cause
552	O	Secondary Air Injection Bypass (AIRB) circuit failure (1993 to 1995)
553	O	Secondary Air Injection Diverter (AIRB) circuit failure (1993 to 1995)
554	O	Fuel Pressure Regulator Control (FPRC) circuit failure
556	O,C	Primary Fuel Pump circuit failure
557	O,C	Low speed fuel pump primary circuit failure (1993 to 1995)
558	O	EGR Vacuum Regulator circuit failure
559	O	Air Conditioning On (ACON) relay circuit failure (1993 to 1995)
563	O	High fan control (HFC) circuit failure (1993 to 1995)
564	O	Fan control (FC) circuit failure (1993 to 1995y)
565	O	Canister Purge circuit failure
567	O	Speed Control Vent (SCVNT) circuit failure (KOEO IVSC test)
568	O	Speed Control Vacuum (SCVAC) circuit failure (KOEO IVSC test)
569	O	Auxiliary Canister Purge (CANP2) circuit failure KOEO
571	O	EGRA solenoid circuit failure KOEO
572	O	EGRV solenoid circuit failure KOEO
578	C	Air conditioning pressure sensor circuit shorted
579	C	Insufficient air conditioning pressure change
581	C	Power to fan circuit over current
582	O	Fan circuit open
583	C	Power to fuel pump over current
584	C	VCRM Power ground circuit open (VCRM Pin 1)
585	C	Power to air conditioning clutch over current
586	C	Air conditioning clutch circuit open
587	O,C	Variable Control Relay Module (VCRM) communication failure
617	C	1 - 2 shift error
618	C	2 - 3 shift error

*0 = Key On, Engine Off; C = Continuous Memory; R = Engine Running

Fuel Injection Diagnostic Manual

EEC-IV 3-digit trouble codes (1992 to 1995) (continued)

Code No.	Test Condition*	Probable cause
619	C	3 - 4 shift error
621	O,C	Shift Solenoid 1 (SS 1) circuit failure KOEO
622	O	Shift Solenoid 2 (SS2) circuit failure KOEO
623	O	Transmission Control Indicator Light (TCIL) circuit failure
624	O,C	Electronic Pressure Control (EPC) circuit failure
625	O,C	Electronic Pressure Control (EPC) driver open in PCM
626	O	Coast Clutch Solenoid (CCS) circuit failure KOEO
627	O	Torque Converter Clutch (TCC) solenoid circuit failure
628	C	Excessive converter clutch slippage
629	O,C	Torque Converter Clutch (TCC) solenoid circuit failure
631	O	Transmission Control Indicator Lamp (TCIL) circuit failure KOEO
632	R	Transmission Control Switch (TCS) circuit did not change states during KOER
634	O,C,R	Manual Lever Position (MLP) sensor voltage higher or lower than expected
636	O,R	Transmission Fluid Temp (TFT) higher or lower than expected
637	O,C	Transmission Fluid Temp (TFT) sensor circuit above maximum voltage; -40°F indicated; circuit open
638	O,C	Transmission Fluid Temp (TFT) sensor circuit below minimum voltage; 290°F (143°C) indicated; circuit shorted
639	R,C	Insufficient input from Transmission Speed Sensor (TSS)
641	O,C	Shift Solenoid 3 (SS3) circuit failure
643	O,C	Torque Converter Clutch (TCC) circuit failure
645	C	Incorrect gear ratio obtained for first gear
646	C	Incorrect gear ratio obtained for second gear
647	C	Incorrect gear ratio obtained for third gear
648	C	Incorrect gear ratio obtained for fourth gear
649	C	Electronic Pressure Control (EPC) higher or lower than expected

*0 = Key On, Engine Off; C = Continuous Memory; R = Engine Running

Code No.	Test Condition*	Probable cause
651	C	Electronic Pressure Control (EPC) circuit failure
652	O	Torque Converter Clutch (TCC) solenoid circuit failure
653	R	Transmission Control Switch (TCS) did not change states during KOER
654	O	Transmission Range (TR) sensor not indicating PARK during KOEO
656	C	Torque Converter Clutch continuous slip error
657	C	Transmission over temperature condition occurred
659	C	High vehicle speed in park indicated
667	C	Transmission Range sensor circuit voltage below minimum voltage
668	C	Transmission Range circuit voltage above maximum voltage
675	C	Transmission Range sensor circuit voltage out of range
998	O	Hard fault present

0 = Key On, Engine Off; C = Continuous Memory; R = Engine Running

General Motors
Domestic cars and trucks (except Geo, Nova and Sprint)

All models except Cadillac with 4.1L, 4.5L, 4.6L, 4.9L and 6.0L engines and Oldsmobile Toronado (1988 to 1990, with CRT display)

Retrieving codes

The Check Engine light on the instrument panel will come on whenever a fault in the system has been detected, indicating that one or more codes pertaining to this fault are set in the Electronic Control Module (ECM). To retrieve the codes, you must use a short jumper wire to ground a diagnostic terminal. This terminal is part of an electrical connector known as the Assembly Line Diagnostic Link (ALDL) **(see illustrations)**. On most models the ALDL is located under the dashboard on the driver's side. If the ALDL has a cover, slide it toward you to remove it. Push one end of the jumper wire into the ALDL diagnostic terminal (B) and the other into the ground terminal (A), except on certain later

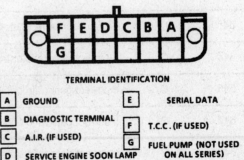

TERMINAL IDENTIFICATION

A GROUND	E SERIAL DATA
B DIAGNOSTIC TERMINAL	
C A.I.R. (IF USED)	F T.C.C. (IF USED)
D SERVICE ENGINE SOON LAMP	G FUEL PUMP (NOT USED ON ALL SERIES)

3.4a On most GM models (domestic) the ALDL connector is located under the dash, usually on the drivers side - to output trouble codes, jump terminals A and B with the ignition On

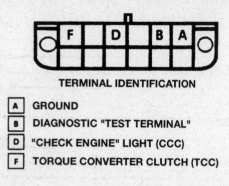

TERMINAL IDENTIFICATION

- **A** GROUND
- **B** DIAGNOSTIC "TEST TERMINAL"
- **D** "CHECK ENGINE" LIGHT (CCC)
- **F** TORQUE CONVERTER CLUTCH (TCC)

3.4b On early GM Computer Command Control (CCC) systems the terminal looks identical, except there are only four terminals used. A-to-B is still the connection to make to trigger the trouble codes to be output by the computer

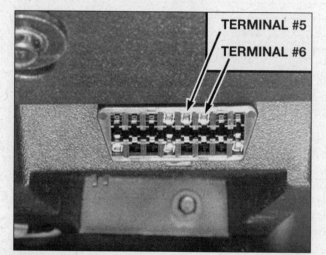

TERMINAL #5

TERMINAL #6

3.5 Some 1995 GM vehicles have the 16-pin connector like the OBD II system, but have accessible OBD I codes (check your emission decal for which system you have) - on this 1995 S-10 pickup with a 16-pin connector, bridge terminals 5 and 6 to extract trouble codes

models (see illustration 3.5). Caution: *Don't crank the engine with the diagnostic terminal grounded - the ECM could be damaged.*

When the diagnostic terminal is grounded with the ignition On and the engine stopped, the system will enter Diagnostic Mode and the Check Engine (or Service Engine Soon) light will display a Code 12 (one flash, pause, two flashes). The code will flash three times, display any stored codes, then flash three more times, continuing until the jumper is removed.

The new government-mandated OBD II diagnostic system was initially used on some GM models starting in 1994. Some other models switched in 1995, and all models use this system in 1996. This system uses five-character codes which can only be accessed with an expensive scan tool. To know if your model has the OBD II system, look at the VECI emission label on the radiator fan shroud. If it is OBD II, it should say "OBD II certified" somewhere on the decal.

Clearing codes

After checking the system, clear the codes from the ECM memory by interrupting battery power. Turn off the ignition switch (otherwise the expensive ECM will be damaged) disconnect the negative battery cable for at least 30 seconds, then reconnect it. **Caution:** *If you have an anti-theft radio, make sure you know the activation code before disconnecting the battery. An alternative method of clearing the codes is to disconnect the ECM's fuse from the fuse panel for 30 seconds.*

Cadillac 4.1L, 4.5L, 4.6L, 4.9L and 6.0L engines

Retrieving codes

To retrieve codes on these models, turn the ignition switch to On (engine not running), then press the Off and Warmer buttons on the climate control panel at the same time. Codes will be displayed on the climate control indicator with either an E or EO preceding them. Press the Reset and Recall buttons at the same time on 1984 to 1986 models, or Auto on 1987 and later models to exit the diagnostic mode.

Clearing codes

Clear codes by pressing the Off and High buttons at the same time.

Oldsmobile Toronado with CRT display (1988 to 1990)

Retrieving codes

To retrieve codes on these models, turn the ignition switch to On (engine not running), then press the Off and Warmer buttons on the climate control panel at the same time. Any stored codes will be displayed.

Clearing codes

To clear codes, press High to access the ECM system, then press Low after each message until "Clear Codes" is displayed. Press Bi-Level to exit the diagnostic mode.

Code	Probable cause
12	Diagnostic mode
13	Oxygen sensor or circuit
14	Coolant sensor or circuit/high temperature indicated
15	Coolant sensor or circuit/low temperature indicated
16	System voltage high/ECM voltage over 17.1 volts (could be alternator problem) (3.8L)
16	DIS (Distributorless Ignition System) circuit (Chevrolet cars only)
16	Low resolution pulse (engine VIN code P - 5.7L)
16	Transmission speed error (models equipped with 4L60-E transmission, or 4.3L "S" and "T" series utility vehicles with manual transmission)
16	System voltage high or low (3.8L)
17	Crank signal circuit (shorted) or faulty ECM
17	Camshaft position sensor circuit (3.4L)
18	Crank signal circuit (open) or faulty ECM
18	Injector circuit(s) (engine VIN code P - 5.7L)
18	Cam and crank sensor sync error (models with DIS ignition) (3.8L)
19	Fuel pump circuit (shorted)
19	Crankshaft position sensor (1988 to 91)
20	Fuel pump circuit (open)
21	Throttle Position Sensor (TPS) circuit or plunger
22	Throttle Position Sensor (TPS) out of adjustment
21/22	Grounded wide-open-throttle (WOT) circuit at same time
23	Manifold Absolute Temperature (MAT) sensor or circuit (fuel-injected models) (low temperature indicated)
23	Intake Air Temperature (IAT) sensor circuit (1995 models)
23	Electronic Spark Timing (EST) - bypass circuit problem (Cadillac DFI models)
24	Vehicle Speed Sensor (VSS) or circuit
25	Manifold Air Temperature (MAT) sensor or circuit (high temperature indicated)
25	Modulated displacement failure (1981 Cadillac V8-6-4 only)
25	Electronic Spark Timing (EST) (Cadillac HT4100 only)
26	Quad Driver Circuit (dealer serviced)

General Motors - domestic (continued)

Code	Probable cause
26	Evaporative emission (EVAP) purge solenoid circuit (VIN P - 5.7L)
26	Throttle switch circuit shorted
27	Throttle switch circuit open
27	Gear Switch Diagnosis (dealer serviced)
27	EGR vacuum control signal valve circuit (VIN P - 5.7L)
27 or 28	Quad-driver error (5.7L VIN P)
28	Pressure Switch Manifold check (PSM) vehicles with 4L80-E transmissions
28	Same as Code 27
29	Same as Code 27
29	Secondary Air Injection (AIR) pump circuit (VIN P - 5.7L)
30	ISC circuit problem (Cadillac TBI)
30	RPM error (Cadillac MFI)
31	Turbo over boost (Turbo models only)
31	Park/Neutral Switch (3.3L)
31	Manifold Air Temperature (MAT) sensor or circuit (Cadillac DFI models)
31	Canister purge solenoid circuit
31	Camshaft sensor or circuit
31	EGR circuit (1988 to 1990 TBI)
31	Shorted MAP sensor circuit
32	BARO sensor or circuit (carbureted models)
32	EGR circuit (fuel-injected models)
32	Digital EGR circuit (3.1L)
32	Open MAP sensor circuit
33	Manifold Absolute Pressure (MAP) sensor or circuit (low vacuum)
33	MAF (Mass Air Flow) sensor or circuit
33	Manifold Absolute Pressure (MAP) sensor signal voltage high
34	Manifold Absolute Pressure (MAP) sensor signal voltage low

Code	Probable cause
34	MAF (Mass Air Flow) sensor or circuit
34	Vacuum sensor or Manifold Absolute Pressure (MAP) sensor (high vacuum) or circuit (3.8L)
35	Idle Air Control (IAC) valve or circuit
35	Idle Speed Control (ISC) switch or circuit (shorted)
35	BARO sensor or circuit (shorted) (Cadillac DFI models)
36	BARO sensor or circuit (open) (Cadillac DFI models)
36	Mass Air Flow (MAF) sensor burn-off circuit
36	Distributorless Ignition System (DIS) (Quad-4)
36	Transaxle shift control (3.8L)
36	Closed throttle shift control (1991)
36	24X signal circuit error (3.4L - 1995)
36	DIS ignition circuit (Corvette and VIN P - 5.7L)
37	Manifold Absolute Temperature (MAT) sensor or circuit (shorted) (Cadillac HT4100)
37	MAT sensor temperature high (1984 to 1986)
37	Brake switch stuck on (4L60-E transmission)
38	Manifold Absolute Temperature (MAT) sensor or circuit (open) (Cadillac HT4100)
38	Brake Input Circuit (brake light switch)
38	MAT sensor temperature low (1984 to 1986)
38	Brake switch stuck off (4L60-E transmission)
39	Torque Converter Clutch (TCC)
39	Knock sensor circuit shorted (4.3L engine, manual transmission, "S" and "T" pick-up)
40	Power steering pressure switch circuit
41	No distributor signals to ECM, or faulty ignition module
41	Cam sensor or circuit (3.8L)
41	Cylinder select error
41	Quad 4 engine 1X Reference (check ignition module/ECM wiring)
41	Electronic Spark Timing (EST) circuit (Cadillac)
41	Opti-spark Electronic Spark Timing (EST) circuit open or grounded (5.7L "F" and "Y" bodies)

General Motors - domestic (continued)

Code	Probable cause
42	Opti-spark Electronic Spark Timing (EST) circuit grounded (5.7L "F" and "Y" bodies)
42	Electronic Spark Timing (EST) circuit
42	Front oxygen sensor lean (Cadillac MFI)
43	Electronic Spark Control unit (ESC)
43	Throttle Position Sensor (TPS) out of adjustment
43	Front oxygen sensor rich (Cadillac MFI)
43	Knock sensor signal
44	Oxygen sensor or circuit - lean exhaust detected
45	Oxygen sensor or circuit - rich exhaust detected
46	Power steering pressure switch (4 cylinder - air conditioned models)
46	Vehicle Anti-Theft System (VATS or PASS Key II)
46	Right to left fueling imbalance (Cadillac)
47	Air conditioning clutch and cruise circuit
48	Misfire diagnosis
48	EGR system fault (Cadillac)
51	PROM, MEM"CAL or ECM problem (3.1L)
52	CALPAK or ECM problem (3.1L)
53	System over-voltage (ECM over 17.7 volts)
53	EGR system (carbureted models)
53	Distributor signal interrupt (1983 and later Cadillac HT4100)
53	Alternator voltage out of range
53	Vehicle anti-theft circuit (5.0L TBI)
53	EGR fault (3.8L)
54	Fuel pump circuit (3.1L, 3.4L)
54	EGR fault (3.8L)
55	ECM/PCM error (except 5.7L PFI systems, Fuel Lean Monitor 5.7L - "F" and "Y" bodies)

Code	Probable cause
55	Oxygen sensor circuit or ECM
55	TPS out of range (Cadillac)
55	Fuel lean monitor (Corvette and F-body VIN P - 5.7L)
55	EGR fault (3.8L)
56	Vacuum sensor circuit
56	Quad driver B circuit (3.8L)
56	Anti-theft system (Cadillac)
58	PASS key fuel enable circuit
58	Transmission code -TTS high temperature (sensor or signal wire grounded)
59	Transmission code -TTS low temperature (sensor or signal wire open)
60	Transmission not in drive (Cadillac)
61	Oxygen sensor signal faulty
61	Cruise vent solenoid (3.8L)
61	Secondary part throttle valve (Corvette)
61	Air conditioning system performance (5.7L)
62	Transaxle gear switch signal circuits (3.1L V6/Quad-4 engines)
62	Engine oil temperature sensor (5.7L)
62	Cruise vacuum circuit (3.8L)
62	Engine oil temperature sensor (5.7L)
63	EGR flow check (3.8L)
63	MAP sensor voltage high
63	Right side oxygen sensor circuit open (5.7L)
64	Same as Code 63 (3.8L)
64	MAP sensor voltage low
64	Right side oxygen sensor lean (dual sensor models)
65	Same as Code 63 (3.8L)
65	Right side oxygen sensor rich (dual sensor models)
65	Cruise servo position sensor (3.8L)

Fuel Injection Diagnostic Manual

General Motors - domestic (continued)

Code	Probable cause
65	Fuel Injection Circuit (Quad-4 engines)
66	Air conditioning pressure sensor circuit
67	Air conditioning pressure sensor or clutch circuit (Chevrolet)
67	Cruise switch circuit
68	Air conditioning relay circuit (Chevrolet)
68	Cruise system problem
69	Air conditioning clutch circuit (Chevrolet)
69	Air conditioning head pressure switch circuit
69	Transmission code - Torque converter stuck on (4L60-E)
70	Intermittent TPS (Cadillac)
70	A/C refrigerant pressure sensor circuit (Chevrolet)
71	Intermittent MAP (Cadillac)
71	A/C evaporator temperature sensor circuit (low temperature)
72	Gear selector switch (Chevrolet)
72	Throttle switch circuit (Cadillac)
72	Transmission code - Vehicle Speed Sensor (VSS) signal loss (4L60-E)
73	Intermittent coolant sensor (Cadillac)
73	A/C evaporator pressure sensor circuit
74	Intermittent MAT (Cadillac)
74	Traction Control System (TCS) circuit voltage low (1995 F-body VIN P)
75	Intermittent speed sensor (Cadillac)
75	EGR circuit (1995)
75	System voltage low (charging system problem)
75	Transmission system voltage low (1995 F-body VIN P)
79	Transmission fluid temperature high (4L60-E)
80	TPS idle learn (Cadillac 4.6L)
80	Fuel system rich (Cadillac)

Code	Probable cause
80	Transmission slipping (F-body 3.4L)
81	Cam reference problem (Cadillac)
81	Transmission code - QDM solenoid "A" (1st and 2nd gear) current error
82	Reference signal high (Cadillac)
82	Transmission code - QDM solenoid "B" (2nd and 3rd gear) current error
83	Transmission code - QDM torque converter circuit fault (4L80-E)
83	Reverse Inhibit System (F-body, manual transmission, 5.7L)
85	Idle throttle angle high (Cadillac 4.6L)
85	Throttle body service required (Cadillac)
85	Undefined gear ratio (4L80-E)
85	PROM error (1995 3.4L)
86	Transmission code - Low gear ratio (4L80-E)
87	Transmission code - High gear ratio (4L80-E)
87	EEPROM error (1995 3.4L)
90	Transmission TCC solenoid circuit (manual transmission)
91	Skip shift lamp circuit (1995 F-body, VIN P)
93	PCS circuit current error (1995 3.4L)
95	Engine stall detected (Cadillac)
96	Transmission system voltage low (1995 F-body 3.4L)
97	VSS output circuit (1995 F-body VIN P)
98	Invalid PCM program (1995 F-body 3.4L)
99	Power management, cruise control system
99	TACH output circuit (1995 F-body VIN P)
99	Invalid PCM program
107	PCM/BCM data link problem
108	PROM checksum mismatch
109	PCM memory reset (Cadillac)
110	Generator L-terminal circuit (Cadillac)

General Motors - domestic (continued)

Code	Probable cause
112	EEPROM failure (Cadillac)
131	Knock sensor failure (Cadillac)
132	Same as 131

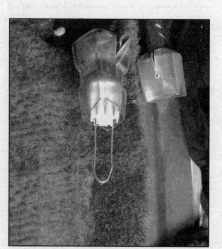

3.6 The Assembly Line Data Link (ALDL) is located under the passenger side glove box behind the kick panel - to activate the diagnostic codes, jump terminals 1 and 3 (the two outer terminals of the *white* connector)

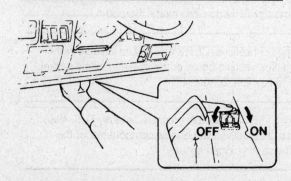

3.7 On 1987 and 1988 Sprint models, turn the diagnostic switch to the On position (with the ignition switch in the On position) to retrieve the trouble codes

General Motors imports
Geo (Metro, Prizm, Storm, Tracker), Chevrolet (Sprint, Nova and Spectrum)

Storm
Retrieving codes

You must use a short jumper wire to ground the white diagnostic connector. This terminal is part of the Assembly Line Diagnostic Link (ALDL), located under the dash near the ECM **(see illustration)**.

Turn the ignition switch to ON (engine not running). Jumper the two outer cavities of the three-terminal connector. The Check Engine light will flash a Code 12 three times, then display the stored codes.

Clearing codes

After making repairs, clear the memory by removing the ECM fuse for at least ten seconds.

Geo Storm - Electronic Control Module (ECM) - replacement

Note: *This system is equipped with an Engine Control Module (ECM) with an Erasable Programmable Read Only Memory (EEPROM). The calibrations (parameters) are stored in the ECM within the EEPROM. If the ECM must be replaced, it is necessary to have the EEPROM programmed with a special scanning tool (TECH 1) available only at dealership service departments. The EEPROM is not replaceable on these vehicles. In the event of any malfunction with the EEPROM (Code 51), the vehicle must be taken to a dealership service department for diagnosis and repair.*

Sprint
Retrieving codes

With the engine at normal operating temperature, turn the "diagnostic" switch located under the steering column to the On position **(see illustration)**.

The codes will then be flashed by the Check Engine light on the dashboard.

Clearing codes

After checking the system, clear the codes from the ECM memory by turning the "diagnostic" switch Off.

Code	Circuit or system	Probable cause
Code 12	No distributor reference pulses to ECM	This code will flash whenever the diagnostic terminal is grounded with the ignition turned On and the engine not running. If additional trouble codes are stored in the ECM they will appear after this code has flashed three times. If this code appears while the engine is running, no reference pulses from the distributor are reaching the ECM.
Code 13	Oxygen sensor circuit	Check for a sticking or misadjusted throttle position sensor (TPS). Check the wiring and connectors from the oxygen sensor (see Section 4). Replace the oxygen sensor.
Code 14	Coolant sensor - high or low temp	If the engine is experiencing cooling system problems the problem must be rectified before continuing. Check all wiring and connectors associated with the coolant temperature sensor. Replace the coolant temperature sensor.*
Code 21	Throttle position sensor - voltage high or low	Check for a sticking or misadjusted TPS plunger. Check all wiring and connections between the TPS and the ECM. Adjust or Replace the TPS (see Section 4).*
Code 23	Intake Air Temperature (IAT) sensor circuit voltage high or low	Check for continuity in the signal wire and the ground wire. Check the operation of the IAT sensor (see Section 4).
Code 24	Vehicle speed sensor	A fault in this circuit should be indicated only when the vehicle is in motion. Disregard Code 24 if it is set when the drive wheels are not turning. Check the connections at the ECM. Check the TPS setting.
Code 32	EGR (Exhaust gas recirculation)	EVRV shorted to ground on start-up, switch not closed after the ECM has commanded the EGR for a specified period of time or the EGR solenoid circuit is open for specified period of time. Replace the EGR valve.*
Code 33	MAP sensor voltage high or low	Check the vacuum hoses from the MAP sensor (see Section 4). Check the electrical connections at the ECM. Replace the MAP sensor.*
Code 42	Electronic Spark Timing circuit	Electronic Spark Timing (EST) bypass circuit or EST circuit is grounded or open. A malfunctioning HEI module can cause this code.
Code 44	O2 sensor indicates lean exhaust (heated type)	Check the ECM wiring connections. Check for vacuum leakage at the throttle body base gasket, vacuum hoses or the intake manifold gasket. Replace the oxygen sensor (see Section 4).*
Code 45	O2 sensor indicates rich exhaust	Possible rich or leaking injector, high fuel pressure or faulty TPS. Also, check the evaporative charcoal canister and its components for the presence of fuel. Replace the oxygen sensor.*
Code 51	ECM or EEPROM	Be sure that the ECM ground connections are tight. If they are, Replace the ECM (see Section 3).*

Component replacement may not cure the problem in all cases. For this reason, you may want to seek professional advice before purchasing replacement parts.

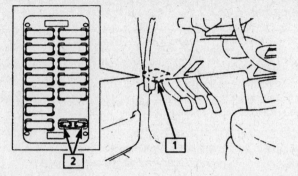

3.8 On 1989 and later Geo metro models, insert the spare fuse into the fuse block (1) diagnostic terminal (2) to retrieve the codes

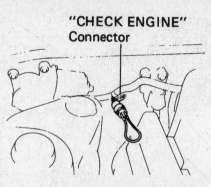

3.9 To display the codes on 1988 Nova (fuel injected) models, insert a jumper wire into the Check Engine connector with the ignition switch in the On position

Metro

Retrieving codes

Insert the spare fuse into the diagnostic terminal of the fuse block **(see illustration)**.

Turn the ignition switch On (engine Off).

Read the diagnostic codes as indicated by the number of flashes of the Check Engine light on the dashboard. Normal system operation is indicated by Code 12. If there are any malfunctions, the light will flash the requisite number of times to display the codes in numerical order, lowest to highest.

Clearing codes

After testing, remove the fuse from the diagnostic terminal and clear the codes by removing the tail light fuse (otherwise the clock and radio will have to be reset).

Nova (fuel-injected models only)

Retrieving codes

With the ignition switch On, use a jumper wire to bridge both the terminals of the Check Engine connector located near the wiper motor **(see illustration)**. The Check Engine light will flash any stored codes.

Clearing codes

After checking, clear the codes by removing the ECM fuse (with the engine Off) for at least ten seconds.

Prizm

Retrieving codes

With the ignition On (engine Off), use a jumper wire to bridge terminals T and E1 of the "diagnostic" connector in the engine compartment **(see illustration)**.

Start the engine; the Check Engine light will then flash any stored codes.

Clearing codes

After checking, clear the codes by removing the ECM fuse (with the engine Off) for at least ten seconds.

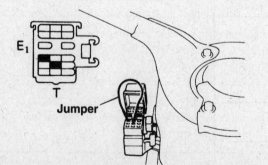

3.10 On 1989 and later Geo Prizm models, insert a jumper wire between terminals T (or TE1) and E1 of the diagnostic connector to retrieve the codes

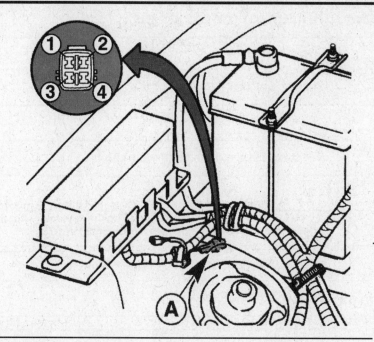

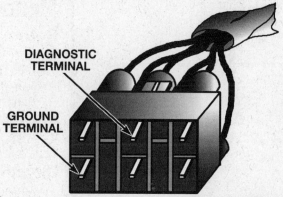

3.11a Obtain the codes on later Tracker models by using a jumper wire between the number 2 and 3 terminals of the test connector (A) located next to the battery

1   Duty check terminal
2   Diagnostic test terminal
3   Ground terminal
4   Test switch terminal

DIAGNOSTIC TERMINAL

GROUND TERMINAL

10205-7A-7.11B HAYNES

3.11b On 1995 Trackers with port fuel injection, bridge the diagnostic and ground terminals with a jumper wire

Tracker

Retrieving codes

On 1989 and 1990 models, insert the spare fuse into the diagnostic terminal of the fuse block.

On 1991 through 1994 (and 1995 TBI) models, use a jumper wire to bridge terminals 2 and 3 of the ECM check connector located in the engine compartment near the battery **(see illustration)**.

On 1995 models with port fuel injection, bridge the diagnostic and ground terminals of the check connector **(see illustration)**.

Turn the ignition switch On (engine Off).

Read the diagnosis codes as indicated by the number of flashes of the Check Engine light on the dashboard. Normal system operation is indicated by Code 12. Code 12 will flash three times, then if there are any malfunctions, the light will flash the requisite number of times to display the codes in numerical order, lowest to highest.

Clearing codes

After testing, remove the fuse or jumper wire and clear the codes by removing the tail light fuse (otherwise the clock and radio will have to be reset).

Spectrum (non-turbo)

Code	Probable cause
12	No distributor reference pulses to ECM
13	Oxygen sensor or circuit
14	Coolant sensor or circuit (shorted)

Fuel Injection Diagnostic Manual

Spectrum (non-turbo) (continued)

Code	Probable cause
15	Coolant sensor circuit (open)
16	Coolant sensor circuit (open)
21	Idle switch out of adjustment (or circuit open)
22	Fuel cut off relay or circuit (open)
23	Open or grounded Mixture Control (M/C) solenoid or circuit
25	Open or grounded vacuum switching valve or circuit
42	Fuel cut off relay or circuit
44	Oxygen sensor or circuit - lean exhaust indicated
45	Oxygen sensor or circuit - rich exhaust indicated
51	Faulty or improperly installed PROM
53	Shorted switching unit or faulty ECM
54	Mixture Control (M/C) solenoid or circuit shorted, or faulty ECM
55	Faulty ECM

Spectrum (turbo)

Code	Probable cause
12	No distributor reference pulses to ECM
13	Oxygen sensor or circuit
14	Coolant sensor or circuit (shorted)
15	Coolant sensor or circuit (open)
16	Coolant sensor or circuit (open)
21	Throttle Position Sensor (TPS) voltage high
22	Throttle Position Sensor (TPS) voltage low

Code	Probable cause
23	Manifold Air Temperature (MAT) sensor or circuit
24	Vehicle Speed Sensor or circuit
25	Air Switching Valve (ASV) or circuit
31	Wastegate control
33	Manifold Absolute Pressure (MAP) sensor voltage high
34	Manifold Absolute Pressure (MAP) sensor voltage low
42	Electronic Spark Timing (EST) circuit
43	Detonation (knock) sensor or circuit
45	Oxygen sensor - rich exhaust
51	Faulty PROM or ECM

Sprint (non-turbo)

Code	Probable cause
12	Diagnostic function working
13	Oxygen sensor or circuit
14	Coolant temperature sensor or circuit
21	Throttle position switches or circuit
23	Intake air temperature sensor or circuit
32	Barometric pressure sensor or circuit
51	Possible faulty ECM
52	Fuel cut solenoid or circuit
53	Secondary air sensor or circuit
54	Mixture control solenoid or circuit
55	Bowl vent solenoid or circuit

Fuel Injection Diagnostic Manual

1987 and 1988 Sprint Turbo, 1989 and later Metro, Tracker, Storm

Code	Probable cause
12	Diagnostic function working
13	Oxygen sensor or circuit
14	Coolant temperature sensor or circuit (open)
15	Coolant temperature sensor or circuit (shorted)
21	Throttle position sensor or circuit (open)
22	Throttle position sensor or circuit (shorted)
23	Intake air temperature sensor or circuit (open)
24	Vehicle Speed Sensor (VSS) or circuit
25	Intake air temperature sensor or circuit (shorted)
31	High turbocharger pressure (1987 and 1988 models)
31	Barometric pressure sensor or circuit (1989 through 1995 models)
32	Barometric pressure sensor or circuit (1989 through 1995 models)
32	EGR system (1991 through 1993 models)
33	Air flow meter (Turbo models)
33	Manifold Absolute Pressure (MAP) sensor (1990 and 1991 models)
41	Ignition signal problem
42	Crank angle sensor (except Storm)
42	Camshaft position sensor circuit (1994-1995)
42	Electronic Spark Timing (EST) (Storm)
44	ECM idle switch circuit open
44	Oxygen sensor or circuit - lean exhaust
45	Oxygen sensor or circuit - rich exhaust
45	Idle switch circuit grounded (1995 Tracker)
46	Idle speed control motor
51	EGR system (except Storm)
51	ECM (Storm)

Code	Probable cause
53	ECM ground circuit
On Steady	ECM fault

Prizm and Nova (with electronic fuel injection)

Code	Probable cause
Continuous Flashing	System normal
12	RPM signal
13	RPM signal
14	Ignition signal
21	Oxygen sensor or circuit
22	Coolant temperature sensor or circuit
24	Manifold Air Temperature sensor or circuit
25	Air/fuel ratio lean
26	Air/fuel ratio rich
27	Sub-oxygen sensor
31	Mass Air Flow (MAF) sensor or circuit
41	Throttle Position Sensor (TPS) or circuit
42	Vehicle Speed Sensor (VSS)
43	Starter signal
51	Air Conditioning Switch signal
71	EGR system

Honda

Retrieving codes

Accord (1985) and Civic (1985 through 1987)

The computer is located under the passenger's seat and displays the codes on four lights numbered, from left to right, 8-4-2-1. With the ignition On (engine Off), the lights will display the codes in ascending order.

Accord and Prelude (1986 and 1987)

The computer is located under the driver's seat. With the ignition switch On, the red light on the computer will display the codes by blinking (code 12 would be one blink, pause, two blinks) with a two second pause between codes.

1985 through 1987 models

	LED display	Symptom	Possible cause
1	○ ○ ○ ○ (Dash warning light on)	Engine will not start	Check for a disconnected control unit ground connector. Also check for a loose connection at the ECU main relay resistor. Possible faulty ECU
2	○ ○ ○ ○ (Dash warning light on)	Engine will not start	Check for a short circuit in the combination meter or warning light wire. Also check for a disconnected control unit ground wire. Possible faulty ECU
3	○ ○ ○ ● (1)	System does not operate	Faulty ECU
4	○ ○ ● ○ (2)	System does not operate	Faulty ECU
5	○ ○ ● ● (2 1)	Fuel-fouled spark plugs, engine stalls, or hesitation	Check for a disconnected MAP sensor coupler or an open circuit in the MAP sensor wire. Also check for a faulty MAP sensor
6	○ ● ○ ○ (4)	System does not operate	Faulty ECU
7	○ ● ○ ● (4 1)	Hesitation, fuel-fouled spark plugs or the engine stalls frequently	Check for disconnected MAP sensor vacuum hose
8	○ ● ● ○ (4 2)	High idle speed during warm-up, continued high idle or hard starting at low temperature	Check for a disconnected coolant temperature sensor connector or an open circuit in the coolant temperature sensor wire. Also check for a faulty coolant temperature sensor
9	○ ● ● ● (4 2 1)	Poor engine response when opening the throttle rapidly, high idle speed or engine does not rev-up when cold	Check for a disconnected throttle angle sensor connector. Also check for an open circuit in the throttle angle sensor wire. Possible faulty throttle angle sensor
10	● ○ ○ ○ (8)	Engine does not rev-up, high idle speed or erratic idling	Check for a short or open circuit in the crank angle sensor wire. Spark plug wires interfering with the crank angle sensor wire. Also the crank angle sensor could be faulty
11	● ○ ○ ● (8 1)	Same as above	Same as above
12	● ○ ● ○ (8 2)	High idle speed or erratic idling when very cold	Check for a disconnected intake air temperature sensor or an open circuit in the intake air temperature sensor wire. Possible faulty intake air temperature sensor
13	● ○ ● ● (8 2 1)	Continued high idle speed	Check for a disconnected idle mixture adjuster sensor coupler or an open circuit in the idle mixture adjuster sensor wire. Possible faulty idle mixture adjuster sensor
14	● ● ○ ○ (8 4)	System does not operate at all	Faulty ECU
15	● ● ○ ● (8 4 1)	Poor acceleration at high altitude when cold	Check for a disconnected atmospheric pressure sensor coupler or an open circuit in the atmospheric pressure sensor wire. Possible faulty atmospheric pressure sensor
16	● ● ● ○ (8 4 2)	System does not operate at all	Faulty ECU
17	● ● ● ● (8 4 2 1)	Same as above	Same as above

Accord, Civic and Prelude (1988 and 1990)

Pull back the carpeting on the passenger's side kick panel for access to the computer.

With the ignition On, the light on the computer will display the codes by flashing.

All models (1991 on)

Note 1: *The 1995 Accord V6 and all 1996 Honda models are equipped with OBD II diagnostics. The new, five-character codes are accessible only with an OBD II scan tool or Honda factory PGM tester, however, the basic two-digit trouble codes used on previous models can still be retrieved with the following procedures.*

Note 2: *The codes can be read by jumping the diagnostic connector and observing the Check Engine light on the instrument panel.*

To view self-diagnosis information from the computer memory, install a jumper wire onto the diagnostic terminal **(see illustration)** located in the upper corner under the dash. **Note:** *On 1991 Prelude models, the diagnostic connector is located in the engine compartment next to the fuse/relay block.* On 1992 and later Prelude models, it's located behind the center console, near the accelerator pedal. On Odyssey models it's located behind the center console on the left side. The codes are stored in the memory of the computer and when accessed, they blink a sequence on the Check Engine light to relay a number or code that represents a system component failure.

With the ignition On, the computer will display the coded flashes in a variety of combinations. The Check Engine light will blink a longer blink to represent the first digit of a two digit number and then will blink short for the second digit (for example, 1 long blink then 6 short blinks for the code 16 [fuel injector]). **Note:** *If the system has more than one problem, the codes will be displayed in sequence then a pause and the codes will repeat.*

When the computer sets a trouble code, the Check Engine light will come on and a trouble code will be stored in the memory. The trouble code will stay in the computer until the voltage to the computer is interrupted. To clear the memory, remove the Back-Up fuse from the relay box located in the right side of the engine compartment. **Note:** *Disconnecting the Back-Up fuse also cancels the radio preset stations and the clock setting. Be sure to make a note of the various radio stations that are programmed into the memory before removing the fuse.*

Caution: *To prevent damage to the computer, the ignition switch must be off when disconnecting or connecting power to the computer (this includes disconnecting and connecting the battery).*

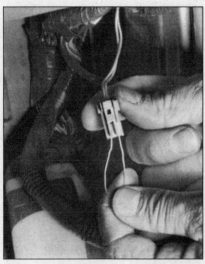

3.12 On most models, the diagnostic connector is located under the passenger side glove box behind the kick panel. To activate the diagnostic codes, bridge the terminals with a jumper wire or paper clip, then turn the ignition to the On position

Clearing codes

The procedure for clearing codes is the same for all systems. To clear the codes after making repairs, make sure the ignition is Off, then disconnect the negative battery cable for ten seconds.

1988 and later models

Code	Probable cause
0	Faulty ECU
1	Oxygen sensor or circuit
2	Faulty ECU

Honda
(continued)

Code	Probable cause
3/5	Manifold Absolute Pressure (MAP) sensor or circuit
4	Crank angle sensor or circuit
6	Coolant temperature sensor or circuit
7	Throttle angle sensor or circuit
8	TDC position/crank angle sensor or circuit
9	Crank angle sensor or circuit
10	Intake air temperature sensor or circuit
11	No particular symptom shown or system does not operate - faulty ECU
12	Exhaust Gas Recirculation (EGR) failure
13	Atmospheric pressure sensor circuit
14	Electronic Air Control Valve (EACV)
15	No ignition output signal - possible faulty igniter
16	Fuel injector circuit
17	Vehicle speed sensor or circuit
19	Lock-up control solenoid valve (automatic transmission)
20	Electric load detector - possible open or grounded circuit in ECU wiring
21	VTEC spool solenoid valve circuit (Civic & Civic Del-Sol)
22	VTEC oil pressure switch circuit (Civic & Civic Del-Sol)
23	Knock sensor (Prelude)
30	A/T control unit ECM fuel injection signal "A" (Accord and Prelude)
31	A/T control unit and ECM circuit signal "B"(Accord and Prelude)
41	Heated oxygen sensor - heater circuit
43	Fuel supply system circuit (except D15Z1 engine)
45	Fuel system out of range - rich or lean
48	Heated oxygen sensor circuit (D15Z1 engine)
50	Mass air flow sensor
61	Front oxygen sensor response slow

Code	Probable cause
63	Rear oxygen sensor circuit voltage out of range
65	Rear oxygen sensor circuit malfunction
67	Catalytic converter efficiency low
70	Automatic transaxle problem
71 - 76	Cylinder misfires
80	Insufficient EGR flow
86	Engine coolant temperature sensor circuit
92	Evaporative emission purge flow problem

Hyundai

1988 Stellar

Retrieving codes

With ignition off, connect an analog voltmeter to the diagnostic connector located in the engine compartment, behind the right strut tower. Turn the ignition On (engine Off) and watch the voltmeter needle.

It will display the codes as sweeps of the needle. The needle will sweep in long or short pulses over a ten-second period with each period separated by six-second intervals.

Short sweep = 0; Long sweep = 1

10000 = 1	00100 = 4	11100 = 7
01000 = 2	10100 = 5	00010 = 8
11000 = 3	01100 = 6	00000 = 9

Clearing codes

Clear the codes after repairs by disconnecting the negative battery cable for 15 seconds.

1988 Stellar

Code	Probable cause
4	Atmospheric pressure sensor or circuit
5	Throttle position sensor or circuit
6	Idle Speed Control (ISC) motor position sensor or circuit
7	Coolant temperature sensor or circuit
8	TDC sensor or circuit
9	Normal

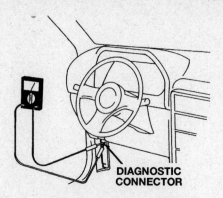

3.13a The self-diagnostic connector is located on the fuse panel (all models except 1989 Sonata)

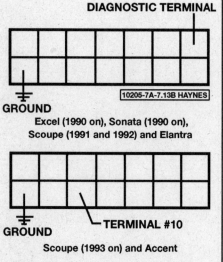

3.13b Diagnostic terminal positions

Sonata, Excel (1990 on), Scoupe (1991 and 1992) and Elantra

Retrieving codes

Locate the diagnostic connector. On 1989 Sonata models this is under the dash, to the left of the steering column. On all other models, it's under the driver's side kick panel **(see illustration)**.

Connect an analog voltmeter to the diagnostic connector ground terminal and MPI diagnostic terminal **(see illustration)**.

Turn the ignition On.

Count the voltmeter needle sweeps and write them down for reference. Long sweeps indicate the first digit in two-digit codes. The short sweeps indicate the second digit. For example, two long sweeps followed by one short sweep indicates a code 21

Clearing codes

To clear the codes, disconnect the negative battery cable for 15 seconds.

Sonata, Excel (1989 on), Scoupe (1991 and 1992), Elantra

Code	Probable cause
1	Electronic Control Unit (ECU) (one long needle sweep)
9	ECU normal state
11	Oxygen sensor or circuit
12	Airflow sensor or circuit
13	Intake air temperature sensor or circuit
14	Throttle Position Sensor (TPS) or circuit
15	Motor position sensor or circuit
21	Coolant temperature sensor or circuit
22	Crank angle sensor or circuit
23	TDC sensor or circuit
24	Vehicle Speed Sensor or circuit
25	Barometric pressure sensor or circuit
41	Fuel injector or circuit
42	Fuel pump or circuit
43	EGR system
44	Ignition coil
59	Oxygen sensor

Scoupe (1993 through 1995) and Accent

The diagnostic connector is still in the driver's kick panel area, but on these models, you must ground the #10 wire for three seconds to get the codes to display on the MIL light **(see illustration 3.13b)** . Do not ground for more than 4 seconds. If 4444 is displayed, there are no stored codes. The first stored code will be displayed over and over; to go to the next code, repeat the grounding procedure. Keep going through the procedure until 3333 is displayed which indicates the end of the self-diagnosis (all stored codes have been displayed).

Clearing codes

To clear the codes, disconnect the negative battery cable for 15 seconds.

Scoupe (1993 through 1995) and Accent

Code	Probable cause
1122	ECM failure (ROM/RAM)
1169	ECM failure
1233	ECM failure (ROM)
1234	ECM failure (RAM)
2121	Turbo boost sensor control valve
3112	No. 1 fuel injector
3114	Idle Air Control (opening failure)
3116	No. 3 fuel injector
3117	Mass Airflow sensor
3121	Turbo boost sensor failure
3122	Idle Air Control (closing failure)
3128	Heated oxygen sensor
3135	EVAP purge control solenoid valve
3137	Alternator output low
3145	Engine coolant temperature (ECT) sensor
3149	Air conditioning compressor
3152	Turbocharger overboost
3153	Throttle position switch (TPS)
3159	Vehicle speed sensor

Hyundai
(continued)

Scoupe (1993 through 1995) and Accent (continued)

Code	Probable cause
3211	Knock sensor
3222	Phase sensor
3224	ECM failure (knock evaluation circuit)
3232	Crankshaft position sensor
3233	Same as code 3224
3234	No. 2 fuel injector
3235	No. 4 fuel injector
3241	ECM failure (injector or purge solenoid)
3242	ECM failure (IAC or air conditioning relay)
3243	ECM failure
4133	ECM failure
4151	Air/fuel control
4152	Air/fuel adaptive failure
4153	Air/fuel multiple adaptive failure
4154	Air/fuel additive adaptive failure
4155	ECM failure (A/C relay, IAC, PCV or injector)
4156	Same as code 3121
4444	Normal
3333	End of trouble codes

Infiniti

All models are equipped with a Malfunction Indicator Light (MIL). As a bulb check, the light glows when the ignition is turned on and the engine is not running.

On **California** models, the MIL glows when a fault is detected with the engine running. A corresponding trouble code will set in the computer memory. The MIL also glows if the computer or crankshaft position sensor malfunctions.

On **Federal** models, the MIL glows only when the computer or crankshaft position sensor malfunctions with the engine running.

The self-diagnostic system can detect ECCS malfunctions and store related trouble codes. Intermittent codes are also stored. All codes are stored until cleared from memory. If an intermittent does not reoccur within 50 ignition key cycles, it will be cleared from memory.

Retrieving codes

Turn the ignition to the On position (don't start the engine).

Using a screwdriver, rotate the mode selector on the computer completely clockwise and wait approximately two seconds. After two seconds, turn the selector counterclockwise as far as it will go. This will put the computer in the diagnostic mode, causing the red LED to flash trouble codes, if any are present. For example, two long flashes, pause, followed by four short flashes indicates a code 24. If there is more than one code stored in memory, the codes will be displayed in numerical order; each code will be separated by a two second pause. **Note 1**: *On 1990 to 1995 models, it is the red LED on the computer which will flash. On 1996 models, it is the Malfunction Indicator Light (MIL) that will flash the codes.* **Note 2:** *Be sure the selector is in the fully counterclockwise position before driving the vehicle.*

Computer Location

On G20 models, the computer is located under the dash, in the center console. On J30 and Q45 models, the computer is located behind the right kick panel.

Clearing Codes

Note: *Ensure all diagnostic codes are accessed from the computer memory before disconnecting the battery.*

Stored memory can be erased by disconnecting the negative battery cable.

Code	System Affected	Probable Cause
11 (1)	Crankshaft Position Sensor	(2) No crank signal
12	Mass Airflow Sensor Circuit	Open/shorted circuit
13	Engine Coolant Temp Sensor	Open/shorted circuit
14	Vehicle Speed Sensor (VSS)	No VSS signal
16 (1)	Traction Control System	Open/shorted circuit
21 (1)	Ignition signal circuit	(2) Open/shorted circuit
31	ECM	Signals not normal
32 (3)	EGR function	No EGR operation
33	Oxygen sensor (Left)	Open/shorted circuit - high oxygen sensor signal
34 (1)	Knock sensor	Open/shorted circuit

Code	System Affected	Probable Cause
35 (3)	EGR temperature sensor	Open/shorted circuit
42	Fuel temperature sensor	Open/shorted circuit
43	Throttle Position Sensor	Open/shorted circuit
45 (3)	Injector leak	Leak at injectors
46 (1) (Q45 models with TCS)	Secondary Throttle Position Sensor	Open/shorted circuit
51	Injector circuit	Injector does not work
53	Oxygen sensor (right)	Open/shorted circuit - high for oxygen signal
54 (1)	Automatic transmission signal	Open signal - Transmission Control Unit
55 (1)	No malfunction	Normal condition

G20, J30 and Q45 models

(1) Trouble code will not activate Malfunction Indicator Light (MIL)
(2) If codes 11 and 21 are present at the same time, check items causing a malfunction of the crankshaft position sensor circuit
(3) California models

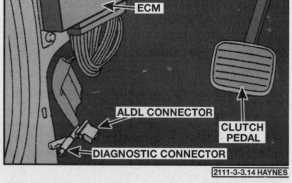

3.14 Location of the diagnostic connector, behind the drivers side kick panel

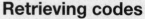

Isuzu

I-Mark (RWD), California pick-up (1982 on), Amigo, Trooper, Rodeo, Pick-up (1984 on), Impulse (1983 and later non-turbo)

Retrieving codes

The above models that have a Check Engine light on the dash will have the self-diagnostic feature.

To retrieve the codes, first find the diagnostic connectors. These can be located in the engine compartment, under the dash or near the computer. The connectors are usually found behind the drivers trim panel (see illustration) or under the dash, on the passenger side, tucked or taped out of the way in the harness (see illustration).

With the ignition switch On, connect the two leads of the diagnostic connectors together to ground them (see illustration).

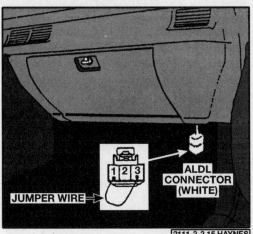

3.15 Location of the diagnostic connector, under the dash on the passenger side (on some models it is located to the left of the center console, near the accelerator pedal)

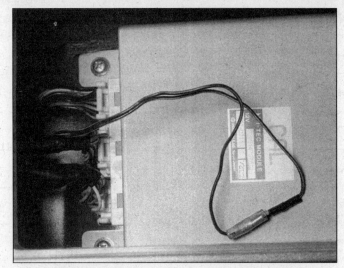

3.16 Typical diagnostic hook-up - make sure the ignition switch is On before connecting the terminals

Trooper and Rodeo V6 and I-Mark (FWD)

Retrieving codes

To retrieve the codes, use a short jumper wire to ground the diagnostic terminal. This terminal is part of an electrical connector known as the Assembly Line Diagnostic Link (ALDL). The ALDL is usually located under the dashboard or in the console near the computer **(see illustration)**.

Push one end of the jumper wire into the ALDL diagnostic terminal and the other into the ground terminal.

On I-mark models terminals A and C must be jumpered together (the two outer terminals on the three terminal connector).

On 1989 through 1991 V6 Trooper and Rodeo models, jumper terminals A and B. On 1992 and later models, jumper terminals 1 and 3 (on these models the connector is located to the right of the accelerator pedal).

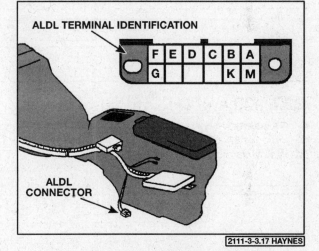

3.17 Location of the diagnostic connector on 1989 through 1991 Trooper models, next to the center console

All of the above models

With the diagnostic terminal now grounded and the ignition on with the engine stopped, the system will enter the Diagnostic Mode and the Check Engine light will display a Code 12 (one flash, pause, two flashes).

The code will flash three times, display any stored codes, then flash three more times, continuing until the jumper is removed.

Note 1: *On feedback carbureted models through 1989, after the code 12 is shown, disconnect the jumper and start the engine to display codes. On some models the codes 13, 15, 31, 44 and 45 will only show after the engine has run for five minutes at part throttle (after already reaching normal operating temperature).*

Note 2: *All 1996 models use the ODB II diagnostic system, which requires an expensive scan tool to access and clear the codes.*

Clearing codes

After checking the system, remove the jumper and clear the codes from the computer memory by removing the appropriate fuse (ECM on four-cylinder models, BLM on V6) for ten seconds.

Fuel Injection Diagnostic Manual

Code	Probable cause
12	No tach signal to ECM
13	Oxygen sensor or circuit
14	Coolant sensor shorted
15	Coolant sensor open
16	Same as 15
21/43/65	Throttle valve switch/Wide Open Throttle (WOT) position sensor; 1989 Manifold Absolute Pressure (MAP) circuit failure
21	Throttle Position Sensor (TPS) - V6 models
22	Starter signal system/1988 and 1989 fuel cut solenoid circuit failure
22	TPS signal (pickup models)
23	Mixture control solenoid circuit failure - 1987 and 1995 Amigo/Pick-up, 1989 to 1994 V6 models
23	Power transistor circuit - 1988 to 1994 four-cylinder models
23 or 25	Intake Air Temperature sensor voltage high - turbo, 1989-1995 1.6L, 1.8L, 3.2L
24	Vehicle Speed Sensor (VSS) circuit - V6 models
24	Pressure regulator vacuum switching valve - 1988- 1994 four-cylinder, Impulse non-turbo
25	AIR VSV circuit failure
26	Canister VSV (Vacuum Switching Valve) circuit failure
31	No ignition reference to ECM - 1988 and 1989 models
31	Wastegate control - turbo models
32	Exhaust Gas Recirculation (EGR) system failure
33	Injector circuit failure
33	Manifold Absolute Pressure (MAP) sensor voltage high - V6 models
34	Manifold Absolute Pressure (MAP) sensor voltage low - V6 models
34	Exhaust Gas Recirculation (EGR) sensor or circuit failure

Computer trouble codes

Code	Probable cause
35	Power transistor circuit failure
41	Crank angle sensor or circuit
42	Electronic spark timing circuit failure - V6 models
42	Fuel cut-off relay - four-cylinder models
43	Electronic spark control failure - V6 models
43	Idle contact switch always closed (1988-1994 four-cylinder, Impulse non-turbo)
43	Knock sensor (1989-1995 1.6L, 3.2L)
44	Oxygen sensor (lean condition indicated)
45	Oxygen sensor (rich condition indicated)
51	Fuel cut-off solenoid shorted - carbureted four-cylinder models
51/52	Electronic Control Module (ECM) failure (or prom error)
53	Faulty Electronic Control Module (ECM) or VCV (Vacuum Switching Valve)
54	Shorted vacuum control solenoid; Faulty Electronic Control Module (ECM) - 1988 and 1989 models
54	Fuel pump circuit failure - V6 models
54	Shorted mixture control solenoid - four-cylinder models
55	Faulty Electronic Control Module (ECM) or oxygen sensor
61/62	Air flow sensor circuit failure
63	Vehicle Speed Sensor (VSS) circuit
27/64	Fuel injector driver transistor
65	Full-throttle switch always on
66	Knock sensor failure
71	Throttle position switch signal abnormal
72	VSV for EGR system - short or open
73	Same as 72 transistor or ground

Jaguar XJS and XJ6 (1988 through 1994)

Note: *Trouble codes are not retrievable on 1995 and later models (a special scan tool must be used).*

All models are equipped with a Check Engine light. When the check engine light remains on, the self-diagnostic system has detected a system failure.

Hard Failures

Hard failures cause the check engine light to glow. Fault codes are stored in the Electronic Control Module (ECM) memory. All codes except Codes 26 and 44 will cause the check engine light to remain illuminated (with the ignition on) until the fault is corrected and the ECM memory is cleared.

Codes 26 and 44 - the check engine light will remain on only until the next ignition on/off cycle. The codes will no longer be indicated by a check engine light, but will still be stored in ECM memory.

If the light comes on and remains on during vehicle operation, the cause of malfunction can be determined using the diagnostic trouble code table.

If a sensor fails, the control unit will use a substitute value in its calculations to continue engine operation. In this condition, the vehicle is functional but poor driveability may occur.

Retrieving codes

To access any stored trouble codes, turn the ignition to the Off position and wait five seconds. Turn the ignition key to the On position, but don't crank the engine.

Locate the Vehicle Condition Monitor (VCM)/trip computer display panel near the speedometer and press the VCM button. Any stored trouble codes will be shown on the display panel. If the engine is started the code will disappear from the display, but the CHECK ENGINE light will stay on. **Note 1:** *On V12 models, the code will display without pushing the button.* **Note 2:** *Not every code is displayed through the dash light, and only the first priority code will display, until it is fixed and cleared. If there is a second code, it will not be displayed until the first is fixed and cleared.*

Clearing codes

Turn the ignition key to the Off position, then detach the cable from the negative terminal of the battery for at least 30 seconds.

Code	System Affected	Probable Cause
11	Idle Potentiometer	Not in Operating Range
12	Airflow meter	Not in Operating Range
14	Coolant Temperature sensor	Not in Operating Range
16	Air Temperature sensor	Not in Operating Range
17	Throttle Potentiometer	Not in Operating Range
18	Throttle Potentiometer/Airflow Meter	Signal Resistance Low At Wide Open Throttle
19	Throttle Potentiometer/Airflow Meter	Signal Resistance High At Idle

Code	System Affected	Probable Cause
22	Fuel Pump Circuit	Open or Short Circuit
23	Fuel Supply	Rich Exhaust Indicated
24	Ignition Amplifier Circuit	Open or Short Circuit
26	Oxygen Sensor Circuit	Lean Exhaust/Vacuum Leak
29	ECU	Self Check
33	Fuel Injector Circuit	Open or Short Circuit
34	Fuel Injector Circuit	Faulty Injector Indicated
37	EGR Solenoid Circuit	Short or Open Circuit
39	EGR Circuit	Faulty System Operation
44	Oxygen Sensor Circuit	Rich or Lean Condition
46	Idle Speed Control Valve - (Coil 1)	Open or Short Circuit
47	Idle Speed Control Valve - (Coil 2)	Open or Short Circuit
48	Idle Speed Control Valve	Not Within Specification
68	Vehicle Speed Sensor	Incorrect Signal Voltage
69	Neutral Safety Switch Circuit	Engine Cranks in Drive (adjust or replace switch)
89	Purge Control Valve Circuit	Open or Short Circuit

Jeep

Retrieving codes

1984 through 1986 four-cylinder and V6 models

To extract this information from the ECM memory, you must use a short jumper wire to ground terminals 6 and 7 on the diagnostic connector **(see illustration)**. The diagnostic connector is located in the engine compartment on the left (driver's side) fenderwell. **Caution:** *Do not start the engine with the terminals grounded.*

Turn the ignition to the On position - not the Start position. The CHECK ENGINE light should flash Trouble Code 12, indicating that the diagnostic system is working. Code 12 will consist of one flash, followed by a short pause, and then two flashes in quick succession. After a longer pause,

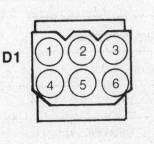
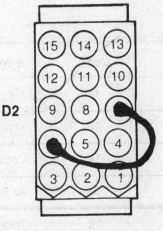

3.18 On 1984 through 1986 four-cylinder and V6 models, jump terminals 6 and 7 of the diagnostic connector to output trouble codes

Fuel Injection Diagnostic Manual

Jeep
(continued)

the code will repeat itself two more times.

If no other codes have been stored, Code 12 will continue to repeat itself until the jumper wire is disconnected. If additional Trouble Codes have been stored, they will follow Code 12. Again, each Trouble Code will flash three times before moving on.

Once the code(s) have been noted, use the Trouble Code chart to locate the source of the fault.

It should be noted that the self-diagnosis feature built into this system does not detect all possible faults. If you suspect a problem with the Computer Command Control System, but the CHECK ENGINE light has not come on and no trouble codes have been stored, take the vehicle to a dealer service department or other repair shop for diagnosis.

Furthermore, when diagnosing an engine performance, fuel economy or exhaust emissions problem (which is not accompanied by a CHECK ENGINE light) do not automatically assume the fault lies in this system. Perform all standard troubleshooting procedures, as indicated elsewhere in this manual, before turning to the Computer Command Control System.

Finally, since this is an electronic system, you should have a basic knowledge of automotive electronics before attempting any diagnosis. Damage to the ECM or related components can easily occur if care is not exercised.

1984 through 1986 V6 models

Trouble Code	Circuit or system	Probable cause
12 (one flash, pause, two flashes)	No reference pulses to ECM	This code should flash whenever the test terminal is grounded with the ignition On and the engine not running. If additional trouble codes are stored (indicating a problem), they will appear after this code has flashed three times. With the engine running, the appearance of this code indicates that no references from the distributor are reaching the ECM. Carefully check the four-terminal EST connector or the distributor.
13 (one flash, pause, three flashes)	Oxygen sensor circuit	Check for a sticking or misadjusted throttle position sensor. Check the wiring and connectors from the oxygen sensor. Replace oxygen sensor* (see Chapter 1).
14 (one flash, pause, four flashes) indicated)	Coolant sensor circuit (high temperature	If the engine is experiencing overheating problems the problem must be rectified before continuing (see Chapters 1 and 3). Check all wiring and connectors associated with the sensor. Replace the coolant sensor*.
15 (one flash, pause, five flashes)	Coolant sensor circuit (low temperature indicated)	See above.
21 (two flashes, pause, one flash)	TPS circuit (signal voltage high)	Check for sticking or misadjusted TPS. Check all wiring and connections at the TPS and at the ECM Adjust or replace TPS*.
23 (two flashes, pause, three flashes)	Mixture Control (M/C)	Check the electrical connections at the M/C solenoid (see Chapter 4). If solenoid circuit OK, clear the ECM memory and recheck for code(s) after driving the vehicle. Check wiring connections at the ECM. Check wiring from M/C solenoid.

Trouble Code	Circuit or system	Probable cause
34 (three flashes, pause, four flashes)	Manifold Absolute Pressure	Check the hose to the MAP sensor for a leak. Check the wiring from (MAP) sensor circuit the MAP sensor to the ECM. Check the connections at the ECM and the sensor. Replace the MAP sensor.*
41 (four flashes, pause, one flash)	No distributor signals	Check all wires and connections at the distributor. Check distributor pick-up coil connections (see Chapter 5).
42 (four flashes, pause, two flashes)	Bypass or EST problem	If the vehicle will start and run, check the wire leading to ECM terminal 12. An improper HEI module can also cause this trouble code.
44 (four flashes, pause, four flashes)	Lean exhaust	Check for a sticking M/C solenoid (Chapter 4). Check ECM wiring connections, particularly terminals 14 and 9. Check for vacuum leakage at carburetor base gasket, vacuum hoses or intake manifold gasket. Check for air leakage at air management system-to-exhaust ports and at decel valve. Replace oxygen sensor.*
44 and 45 at the same time	Oxygen sensor or circuit	Check the oxygen sensor circuit. Replace the oxygen sensor.*
45 (four flashes, pause, five flashes)	Rich exhaust	Check for a sticking M/C solenoid (Chapter 4). Check wiring at M/C solenoid connector. Check the evaporative charcoal canister and its components for the presence of fuel (Chapters 1, 6). Replace oxygen sensor.*
51 (five flashes, pause, one flash)	PROM problem	Diagnosis should be performed by a dealer service department or other repair shop.
54 (five flashes, pause, four flashes)	Mixture control (M/C) solenoid	Check all M/C solenoid and ECM wires and connections. Replace the M/C solenoid* (see Chapter 4).
55 (five flashes, pause, five flashes)	Reference voltage problem	Check for a short circuit to ground on the wire to ECM terminal 21. Possible faulty ECM or oxygen sensor.

Component replacement may not cure the problem in all cases. For this reason, you may want to seek professional advice before purchasing replacement parts.

1987 through 1990 models

A special scan tool is required to retrieve trouble codes on these models. Take the vehicle to a dealer service department or other qualified shop.

1991 on

The self-diagnostic capabilities of this system, if properly used, can simplify testing. The Powertrain Control module (PCM) monitors several different engine control system circuits.

Hard failures cause the Malfunction Indicator Light (MIL) (may also be referred to as "CHECK ENGINE" Light) to glow and flicker until the malfunction is repaired. If the light comes on and remains on (light may flash) during vehicle operation, determine the cause of malfunction using the self-diagnostic tests. If a sensor fails, the PCM will use a substitute value in its calculations, allowing the engine to operate in a "limp-in" mode. In this condition, the vehicle will run, but driveability may be poor.

Intermittent failures may cause the MIL to flicker or stay on until the intermittent fault goes away. However, the PCM memory will retain a corresponding fault. If a related fault does not reoccur within a certain time frame, the related fault will be erased from PCM memory. Intermittent failures can be caused by a faulty sensor, bad connector or wiring related problems.

Test the circuits and repair or replace the components as required. If the problem is repaired or ceases to exist, the PCM cancels the fault after 50 ignition on/off cycles. A specific fault results from a particular system failure. A fault does not condemn a specific component; the component is not necessarily the reason for failure. Faults only suggest the probable malfunction area.

Service precautions

1   When the battery is disconnected, vehicle computer and memory systems may lose memory data. Driveability problems may exist until the computer systems have completed a relearn cycle.
2   The vehicle must have a fully charged battery and a functional charging system.
3   Probe the PCM 60-pin connector from the pin side. **Caution:** *Do not backprobe PCM connector.*
4   Do not cause short circuits when performing any electrical tests. This will set additional faults, making diagnosis of the original problem more difficult.
5   When checking for voltage, **do not** use a test light - use a digital voltmeter.
6   When checking for spark, ensure that the coil wire is no more than 1/4-inch from a ground connection. If the coil wire is more than 1/4-inch from ground, damage to the vehicle electronics and/or PCM may result.
7   Do not prolong testing of the fuel injectors, or the engine may hydrostatically (liquid) lock.
8   Always repair the lowest fault code number first.
9   Always perform a verification test after repairs are made.

Retrieving codes

Note 1: *Although other scanners are available, the manufacturer recommends using Diagnostic Readout Box II (DRB-II).The malfunction indicator light (MIL) method can be used, without the need for the diagnostic scanner, but not all trouble codes can be accessed and has limited diagnostic capability. Due to the prohibitive cost of the Diagnostic Readout Box II, only the MIL method will be discussed here.*
Note 2: *Beginning in 1996, all models are equipped with the OBD II diagnostics system. Although a scan tool is required to retrieve and clear the new, five-character codes, the basic two-digit codes can still be retrieved from the MIL light.*

Start the engine, if possible, and shift the transmission through all of the gears. Place the shifter in the Park position, then turn the air conditioning on and off.

Stop the engine, then turn the ignition key to the On position, then Off, then On, then Off, then On again within three seconds. This will cause any stored trouble codes to be displayed by flashing the Malfunction Indicator Light (MIL or CHECK ENGINE light).

Code 55 indicates all of the trouble codes have been displayed.

Clearing codes

Caution: *If the stereo in your vehicle is equipped with an anti-theft system, make sure you have the correct activation code before disconnecting the battery.*

Trouble codes may be cleared by disconnecting the negative battery cable for at least 15 seconds.

1991 on

Code	Probable cause
11	Ignition
12	Battery disconnected in las 50 cycles
13	Manifold Absolute Pressure (MAP) sensor vacuum
14	Manifold Absolute Pressure (MAP) sensor electrical
15	Speed sensor or circuit
17	Engine running too cool
21	Oxygen sensor or circuit
22	Coolant temperature sensor or circuit
23	Air charge temperature
24	Throttle Position Sensor (TPS) sensor or circuit
25	Automatic Idle Speed (AIS) control
27	Fuel injector control
33	Air conditioning clutch relay
34	Speed control solenoid driver
35	Fan control relay
41	Alternator field
42	Automatic shutdown relay
43	Ignition coil Number 1-3 primary circuit; peak primary circuit current isn't reached with maximum dwell time
44	Battery temperature sensor
45	Overdrive solenoid - open or shorted condition detected in overdrive solenoid circuit
46	Battery over voltage
47	Battery under voltage
51	Oxygen sensor - lean condition indicated
52	Additive adaptive memory at lean limit.

1991 on (continued)

Code	Probable cause
52	Oxygen sensor - rich condition indicated
53	Internal engine controller fault
54	Crankshaft signal sync pick-up signal - no fuel sync signal during crankshaft rotation
54	No cam sync signal at PCM; open or shorted condition in cam sync signal circuit
55	End of self-diagnostic display
62	Emissions Maintenance Reminder (EMR) mileage accumulator
63	Controller failure EEPROM write denied
76	Fuel pump resistor bypass relay

Mazda

All models

Hard Failures

Hard failures cause the Check Engine light to illuminate and remain on until the problem is repaired.

If the light comes on and remains on (light may flash) during vehicle operation, the cause of the malfunction can be determined using the diagnostic code charts.

If a sensor fails, the computer will use a substitute value in its calculations to continue engine operation. In this condition, commonly known as "limp-in" mode, the vehicle will run but driveability will be poor.

Intermittent Failures

Intermittent failures may cause the Check Engine light to flicker or illuminate and go out after the intermittent fault goes away. However, the corresponding code will be retained in the computer memory. If a related fault does not reoccur within a certain time frame, the code will be erased from the computer memory. Intermittent failures may be caused by sensor, connector or wiring related problems.

Retrieving codes

1989 to 1991 models (except Miata); 1992 and 1993 MPV, 1993 and earlier pick-ups

The diagnostic connector is located in the engine compartment, back of left front strut tower **(see illustration)**.

Trouble codes are accessed by using a jumper wire to ground the single-pin, green-wire connector.

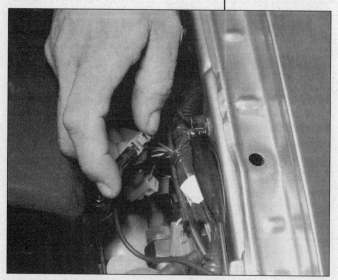

3.19a To retrieve the trouble code, use a jumper wire and ground the green 1-pin connector to a bolt on the body

1990 and 1991 Miata

On these models, a factory diagnostic tool must be used to retrieve codes.

1994 Pick-ups

Refer to the Ford trouble code retrieval procedure, and use the Ford EEC-IV three-digit code list. **Note:** *1995 and later pick-ups use the Ford EEC V engine management system; trouble codes on these models must be retrieved with a special scan tool.*

1992 to 1995 models, except pick-ups

Using a jumper wire, connect the self-diagnostic connector terminal TEN with the ground terminal **(see illustration)**. The connector is located near the left shock tower.

1995 Millennia

These models are equipped with OBD II diagnostic systems, which require the use of an expensive scan tool to retrieve the new, five-character diagnostic codes.

All models

With the ignition On and engine Off, observe the check engine light; any stored trouble codes will be displayed by flashes of the light. For example, two long flashes, pause, followed by four short flashes indicates a code 24.

If the light glows continuously, the check engine light circuit may be grounded or the computer may be defective **Note:** *If there is more than one code stored, they will be displayed in order from the lowest number to the highest number.*

Clearing codes

Disconnect the negative battery cable. Depress the brake pedal for at least 20 seconds. Reconnect the battery cable and reconnect the jumper wire. Turn the key to the ON position for at least six seconds, then start the engine and run it at a high idle (2000 rpm) for at least three minutes. If no codes are displayed on the MIL, the codes have been cleared successfully. Shut the engine off and disconnect the jumper wire.

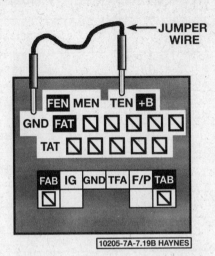

3.19b On 1992 through 1995 Mazdas (except pick-ups), bridge terminals TEN and GND to output trouble codes

Code	Probable cause
2	Crank position sensor - NE sensor
3/4	Crank position sensor - G sensor/cam position sensor
5/7	Left/right side knock sensor
6	Speedometer sensor
8	Mass Air Flow sensor
9	Water thermosensor
10	Intake air thermosensor
11	Intake air thermosensor
12	Throttle sensor - full range

Fuel Injection Diagnostic Manual

Code	Probable cause
13	Pressure sensor
14	Atmospheric pressure sensor (replace ECU)
15/23	Left/right side oxygen sensor
16	EGR switch - CA vehicles
17	Oxygen sensor - inaccurate
17/24	Left/right side feedback system
18	Throttle sensor - narrow range
20	Metering oil pump position sensor
23	Fuel thermosensor
25	Solenoid valve - pressure regulator control
26	Purge control solenoid valve
27	Metering oil pump (RX-7)
28	Solenoid Valve - EGR
29	Solenoid Valve - EGR vent
30	Solenoid valve - split air by-pass
31	Solenoid valve - relief 1
32	Solenoid valve - switching
33	Solenoid valve - port air by-pass
34	Solenoid valve - idle speed control
36/37	Right/left side oxygen sensor heater
37	Metering oil pump (RX-7)
39	Solenoid valve - relief 2
40	Solenoid valve - purge control
41	Variable Inertia Charging System (DOHC only)
42	Solenoid valve - turbo pre-control
43	Solenoid valve - wastegate control

Code	Probable cause
44	Solenoid valve - turbo control
45	Solenoid valve - charge control
46	Solenoid valve - charge relief control
50	Solenoid valve - double throttle control
51	Fuel pump relay
54	Air pump relay
65	Air conditioning signal
71	Injector - front secondary
73	Injector - rear secondary
76	Slip lock-up off signal
77	Torque reduced signal

Mercedes

Before retrieving codes the following pretest conditions must be met:
1 Start and run engine until engine oil temperature is 176°F (80°C).
2 Turn air conditioning **off**.
3 Make sure the shift lever is in **Park**.
4 Check all fuses and replace as necessary.
5 Verify battery voltage is 11-to-14 volts.

Retrieving codes:

HFM-SFI system (except C220, C280, 400, 190E and 500)

Turn the ignition On (engine not running).

Press the non-locking switch, located on diagnostic connector in right rear corner of the engine compartment **(see illustration),** for 2-to-4 seconds. HFM-SFI control unit will begin output of any fault codes present by flashing the LED light on diagnostic connector.

If the LED only flashes once, this indicates no fault codes are stored. If fault codes are stored, the LED will flash indicating fault code 3.

Press the push-button again for 2-to-4 seconds. If more fault codes are stored, the LED on the diagnostic connector will display the next code.

Continue pressing the push-button for 2-to-4 seconds at a time until the LED lights steadily, indicating the end of fault code display.

Record all fault codes and refer to the trouble code identification table. **Note:** *Other 1994 and later models are equipped with OBD II di-agnostic systems, which require the use of a special tool to retrieve trouble codes.*

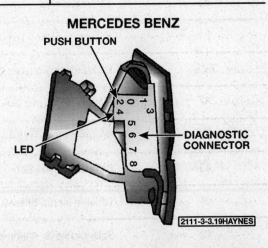

MERCEDES BENZ

3.20 Location of the diagnostic connector is in the right rear corner of the engine compartment

Clearing codes

On Federal vehicles, disconnect the negative battery cable. Stored trouble codes will be erased when the battery is disconnected.

On California vehicles, disconnecting the battery will not erase the codes. Each code that is stored in the CIS-E control unit will have to be erased individually.

Press the non-locking switch located on the diagnostic connector in the right rear corner of the engine compartment for 2-to-4 seconds.

When the fault is displayed, press the non-locking switch for 6-to-8 seconds. That code is now cleared. Repeat the procedure until all stored codes have been erased.

Press the Start button on the pulse counter for 2-to-4 seconds, maximum. The pulse counter will display the fault code. Press the start button again for 6-to-8 seconds. The fault code is erased when the pulse counter no longer displays the fault code.

Repeat the procedure for other stored fault codes. When the pulse counter displays "1", no faults are stored.

1990 through 1993 - 190E and 300 series (2.3L)

1	No System Malfunction
2	Throttle Valve Switch
3	Coolant Temperature Sensor
4	Airflow Sensor Position Indicator
5	Oxygen Sensor
6	Not Used
7	Td Signal
8	Altitude Correction Capsule
9	Electro-Hydraulic Actuator (EHA)
10	Throttle Valve Switch and/or Idle Speed Contact
11	Not Used
12	EGR Temperature Sensor

1991 and later - 300 series (2.8L and 3.2L)

No. of Flashes	Probable cause
1	No faults in system
2	Oxygen Sensor Inoperative
3	Lambda Control Inoperative

No. of Flashes	Probable cause
4	Air Injection inoperative
5	Exhaust Gas Recirculation (EGR) inoperative
6	Idle Speed Control Inoperative
7	Ignition System Failure
8	Coolant Temperature Sensor - Open Or Short Circuit
9	Intake Air Temperature Sensor - Open Or Short Circuit
10	Voltage At Air Mass Sensor Too High Or Low
11	TN (RPM) Signal Defective
12	Oxygen Sensor Heater Open Or Short Circuit
13	Camshaft Position Sensor Signal From - EZL/AKR Ignition Control Unit Defective
14	Intake Manifold Pressure At Start Too Low
15	Full Throttle Information Defective
16	Idle Speed Information Defective
17	Controller Area Network (CAN) Data Exchange - Malfunction Between Control Units
18	Adjustable Camshaft Timing Solenoid - Open Or Short Circuit
19	Fuel Injectors- Open Or Short Circuit, or Emission Control System Adaptation at Limit
20	Speed Signal Missing
21	Purge Switchover Valve - Open Or Short Circuit
22	Camshaft Position Sensor Signal Defective
23	Intake Manifold Pressure With Engine Running Too Low
24	Starter Ring Gear Segments Defective
25	Knock Sensors Defective
26	Upshift Delay Switch over Valve - Open Or Short Circuit
27	Coolant Temperature Sensor Deviation Between Sensor Circuit No. 1 and Sensor Circuit No. 2
28	Coolant Temperature Sensor (Coolant Temperature Change Monitor)

Fuel Injection Diagnostic Manual

1991 through 1993 - 190E and 300 series (2.6L and 3.0L)

No. of Flashes	Probable cause
1	No faults in system
2	Throttle Valve Switch (Full Throttle Contact)
3	Coolant Temperature Sensor
4	Airflow Sensor Potentiometer
5	Oxygen Sensor
6	Not assigned
7	TNA (Engine RPM) Signal
8	Altitude Pressure Signal From EZL Ignition Control Unit
9	Current To Electro-hydraulic Actuator
10	Throttle Valve switch (Idle Contact)
11	Air Injection System
12	Absolute Pressure Valves From EZL Ignition Control Unit
13	Intake Air Temperature Signal
14	Road Speed Signal At CIS-E Control Unit
15	Not assigned
16	Exhaust Gas Recirculation (EGR)
17	Oxygen Sensor Signal
18	Current To Idle Speed Air Valve
19	Not assigned
20	Not assigned
21	Not assigned
22	Oxygen Sensor Heating Current
23	Short Circuit To Positive In Regeneration Switch over Valve Circuit
24	Not assigned
25	Short Circuit To Positive in Start Valve Circuit
26	Short Circuit To Positive In Shift Point Retard Circuit

No. of Flashes	Probable cause
27	Data Exchange Fault Between CIS-E Control Unit and EZL Ignition Control Unit
28	Loose Contact In Coolant Temperature Sensor Circuit
29	Difference In Coolant Temperatures Between CIS-E Control Unit and EZL Ignition Control Unit
30	Not assigned
31	Loose Contact In Intake Air Temperature Sensor Circuit
32	Not assigned
33	Not assigned
34	Faulty Coolant Temperature Sensor Signal from EZL Ignition Control Unit

Mitsubishi

Retrieving codes

With the engine Off, locate the diagnostic connector. On most models, an analog voltmeter is connected to the diagnostic connector, the positive lead from the voltmeter to the test terminal, and the ground lead to the ground terminal **(see illustrations). Note:** *On all 1995 models (except the Expo, Summit wagon, and pickup models) the MIL lamp must be used, by jumping the test and ground terminals of the connector with a jumper wire and observing the flashes of the MIL lamp on the dash.* The location of the diagnostic connector varies with model and year:

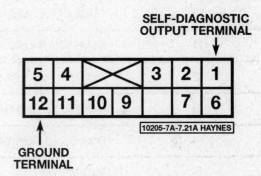

3.21a To put the ECU into code retrieval mode, connect an analog voltmeter to the indicated terminals of the connector - most models have this diagnostic connector

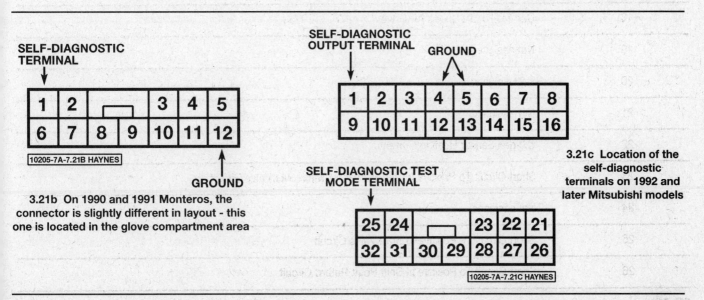

3.21b On 1990 and 1991 Monteros, the connector is slightly different in layout - this one is located in the glove compartment area

3.21c Location of the self-diagnostic terminals on 1992 and later Mitsubishi models

1983 through 1986 fuel-injected models

The diagnostic connector is located under the battery or on the right side firewall near the computer, depending on model.

1987 through 1989, except Galant and Mirage, 1990 through 1991 Montero

The diagnostic connector is in or under the glove compartment.

1987 through 1991 Galant and Mirage

The connector is behind the left side kick panel.

1990 through 1991 Eclipse and Pick-up, all 1992 through 1995 models

The diagnostic connector is located near the fuse block.

All models

Turn the ignition On and watch the voltmeter needle. It will display the codes as sweeps of the needle. Count the number of needle sweeps and write the codes down for reference. Long sweeps represent the tens digit, short sweeps represent the ones digit, i.e. one long and one short would be DTC code 11. Only continuous short sweeps indicates the system has no stored codes. On 1994 and 1995 models, the following models are accessed by using a voltmeter: Precis, Mirage, Eclipse, and pickup models. The Montero can be accessed with either a voltmeter *or* a jumper wire in place of the voltmeter connections, which indicates flashes on the MIL lamp instead of voltage sweeps. The following models are accessible only through the blinking MIL: Galant, Diamante, and 3000GT. **Note:** *1995 models are equipped with OBD II diagnostic systems, which require the use of an expensive scan tool to retrieve the new, five-character diagnostic codes, however, the basic MIL/voltmeter codes can still be obtained also.*

Clearing codes

Clear the codes by disconnecting the negative battery cable for 30 seconds.

All 1987 and 1988 models (except 1988 Galant)

Code	Probable cause
1	Exhaust gas sensor and/or ECU
2	Crankshaft angle sensor or ignition signal
3	Air flow sensor
4	Atmospheric pressure sensor
5	Throttle angle sensor
6	Idle Speed Control (ISC) motor position sensor
7	Engine coolant temperature sensor
8	Top Dead Center (TDC) sensor or vehicle speed sensor
9	Top Dead Center (TDC) sensor

All 1989 through 1995 fuel-injected models (including 1988 Galant)

Code	Probable cause
1	Electronic Control Unit (ECU) (one long needle sweep)
9	Normal state (continuous short flashes)
11	Oxygen sensor or circuit
12	Air flow sensor or circuit
13	Intake air temperature sensor or circuit
14	Throttle Position Sensor (TPS) or circuit
15	Idle speed control (ISC) motor position sensor or circuit fault
21	Coolant temperature sensor or circuit
22	Crank angle sensor or circuit
23	Top Dead Center sensor or circuit
24	Vehicle Speed Sensor or circuit
25	Barometric pressure sensor or circuit
31	Detonation (knock) sensor
32	Manifold Absolute pressure (MAP) sensor faulty
36	Ignition timing adjustment signal fault
39	Front oxygen sensor
41	Fuel injector failure
42	Fuel pump or circuit
43	Exhaust Gas Recirculation (EGR) system
44	Ignition coil (except DOHC V6)
44	Power transistor for coil (1-4) (DOHC V6)
52	Power transistor for coil (2-5) (DOHC V6)
53	Power transistor for coil (3-6) (DOHC V6)

All 1989 through 1995 fuel-injected models (including 1988 Galant)

Code	Probable cause
55	Idle air control (IAC)valve position sensor fault
59	Rear oxygen sensor fault
61	ECM and transmission interlock
62	Induction control valve position sensor
69	Right rear oxygen sensor
71	Traction control vacuum valve solenoid fault
72	Traction control vent valve solenoid fault

Nissan/Datsun cars and trucks

ECU location

To access the self-diagnostic procedures and extract trouble codes, the ECU (computer) must be located. Location varies with the year and model as follows:

Under dash, behind the center console

Maxima 1986 to 1994; Sentra 1991 to 1995; 200SX and 300SX, 1990 to 1995; 1993 to 1995 Altima

Behind glove box

Maxima, Quest 1995; 1991 to 1995 300ZX

Under passenger seat

Pick-up and Pathfinder, 1987 to 1995, Pulsar, Stanza, Sentra, 1987 to 1989

Under driver's seat

Stanza wagon, 1987, Sentra 4WD 1990

At kick panel under right side of dash

300ZX, 1986 to 1989; 240SX 1987 to 1995

At kick panel under left side of dash

200SX, 1987 to 1988

Retrieving codes, 1984 to 1989

Remove the computer. **Caution:** *Do not disconnect the electrical connector from the computer or you will erase any stored diagnostic codes.*

Turn the ignition switch to On. **Note:** *On 1984 to 1986 models (except pick-ups with TBI) start the engine and warm it to normal operating temperature.*

Turn the diagnostic mode selector on the computer fully clockwise or turn

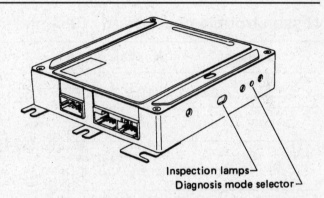

3.22a On all except TBI-equipped pick-ups and 1984 through 1986 300ZX, select the diagnostic mode by turning the ECU mode selector clockwise, gently, until it stops

3.22b On TBI-equipped pick-ups, activate the diagnostic mode by pushing the mode switch to the left - the red and green lights should begin flashing

the mode selector switch (a hand-operated switch on some models) to On **(see illustrations)**.

Wait until the inspection lamps flash. **Note:** *The LED-type inspection lamps are located on the side or top of the computer* **(see illustration)**. The inspection lamps flash once for each level of diagnostics, i.e. one flash is Mode I, two flashes is Mode II. After the inspection lamps have flashed three times (Mode III is the self-diagnostic mode that will display codes), turn the diagnostic mode selector fully counterclockwise or turn the mode selector to Off.

On 1984 to 1986 300ZX models, start the procedure by turning the screw *counter*clockwise, turn the ignition ON, make sure the bulbs stay on, then turn the screw clockwise. Later 300ZX models are diagnosed the same as other models.

The computer is now in the self-diagnostic mode. Now, count the number of times the inspection lamps flash.

First, the red lamp flashes, then the green lamp flashes. **Note:** *The red lamp denotes units of ten, the green lamp denotes units of one. Check the trouble code chart for the particular malfunction. For example, if the red lamp flashes once and the green lamp flashes twice, the computer is displaying the number 12, which indicates the air flow meter is malfunctioning.*

If the ignition switch is turned off at any time during a diagnostic readout, the procedure must be re-started. The stored memory or memories will be lost if, for any reason, the battery terminal is disconnected.

3.23 On 1984 through 1986 300ZX models, verify the diagnostic mode selector is turned fully counterclockwise using a small screwdriver

Retrieving codes, 1990 to 1995

Beginning with 1990 models, there are two types of diagnostics systems, the dual-LED type as described above, and a new single-LED system. The dual-LED system works the same as the previous models, with a red and a green light.

The single-LED system (Pathfinder and pick-up models) has only two Modes, with Mode II being the self-diagnostic mode for trouble code retrieval. The red LED will flash a long flash (.6 seconds) for the tens digit and short flashes (.3 seconds) for the single digits. **Note:** *All 1995 models have a Malfunction Indicator Lamp (Check Engine light), and instead of using the LED's on the computer to read codes, the MIL flashes the codes (except Pathfinder and pick-up models, which still have the dual-LED system). Also, most 1995 models are equipped with OBD II diagnostics systems. Although an expensive scan tool is required to retrieve the new, five-character diagnostic codes, the basic codes can still be obtained using the flashing MIL.*

Clearing codes

On early TBI-equipped pick-up models, to erase the memory after self-diag-

Fuel Injection Diagnostic Manual

nosis codes have been noted or recorded, turn the diagnostic mode selector to On. After the inspection lamps have flashed four times, turn the diagnostic mode selector to Off Turn the ignition switch to Off.

On all other early models, erase the memory by turning the diagnostic mode selector on the computer fully clockwise. After the inspection lamps have flashed four times, turn the mode selector fully counterclockwise. This will erase any signals the computer has stored concerning a particular component.

Note: *On all models, disconnecting the negative cable of the battery will clear all stored codes. On later models, unless the battery is disconnected, stored codes for problems that have been fixed will remain stored until the vehicle has made 50 restarts.*

Nissan trouble code chart - 1984 and later

Code	Probable cause
11	Crank angle sensor/circuit (1988 to 1990); Camshaft position sensor (1991 to 1996)
12	Air flow meter/circuit open or shorted
13	Cylinder head temperature sensor (Maxima and 300ZX models); coolant temperature sensor circuit (all other models)
14	Vehicle speed sensor signal circuit is open
15	Mixture ratio is too lean despite feedback control; fuel injector clogged
21	Ignition signal in the primary circuit is not being entered to the ECU during cranking or running
22	Fuel pump circuit (Maxima and 1987 and later 300ZX models); idle speed control valve or circuit (all other models)
23	Idle switch (throttle valve switch) signal circuit is open
24	Park/Neutral switch malfunctioning
25	Idle speed control valve circuit is open or shorted
26	Turbo boost
28	Cooling fan
29	Fuel system rich
31	1984 through 1986 EFI models: Problem in air conditioning system; all other models: ECU control unit problem
32 (California)	1984 through 1986 EFI models: check starter system. All other models: EGR function
33	Oxygen sensor or circuit (300ZX left side) - all other models: EGR function

Code	Probable cause
34	Detonation (knock) sensor
35 (California)	Exhaust gas temperature sensor
36	EGR transducer
37	Closed loop control/front oxygen sensor (Maxima)
41	Maxima and 1984 through 1987 300ZX models: fuel temp sensor circuit. All other models: air temperature sensor circuit
42	1988 and later 300ZX models: fuel temperature sensor circuit; all other models: throttle sensor circuit open or shorted
43 (1987 Sentra only)	The mixture ratio is too lean despite feedback control; fuel injector is clogged
43 (all others)	Throttle position sensor circuit is open or shorted
44	No trouble codes stored in ECU
45 (California)	Injector fuel leak
51 (California)	Fuel injector circuit open
53	Oxygen sensor (300ZX right side)
54	Short between automatic transmission control unit and ECU
55	Normal engine management system operation is indicated
63	Misfire detected - cylinder no. 6
64	Misfire detected - cylinder no. 5
65	Misfire detected - cylinder no. 4
66	Misfire detected - cylinder no. 3
67	Misfire detected - cylinder no. 2
68	Misfire detected - cylinder no. 1
71	Misfire detected (random)
72	Catalytic converter malfunction (right side)
74	EVAP pressure sensor
75	EVAP leak

Code	Probable cause
76	Fuel injection system
77	Rear oxygen sensor
81	Vacuum cut bypass valve
82	Crankshaft sensor
84	Automatic trans-to-fuel injection communication
85	VTC solenoid
87	EVAP canister purge control
91	Front oxygen sensor
95	Crankshaft sensor
98	Coolant temperature sensor
101	Camshaft sensor
103	Park/neutral switch
105	EGR and canister control valve
108	EVAP volume control

Porsche

The vehicle computer, the Digital Motor Electronics (DME) control unit, has the ability to store fault codes related to fuel injection and ignition systems. Detected faults are stored for at least 50 engine starts. If the positive battery cable or the DME control unit connector is disconnected, the fault code memory will be cleared.

Hard Failures

Hard failures cause the Check Engine light to illuminate and remain on until problem is repaired. If the light comes on and remains on (light may flash) during vehicle operation, the cause of malfunction must be determined using diagnostic code tables. If a sensor fails, the control unit will use a substitute value in its calculations to continue engine operation. In this condition, commonly known as limp-in mode, the vehicle will run but driveability will be poor.

Intermittent failures

Intermittent failures may cause the Check Engine light to flicker or illuminate. Light goes out after intermittent fault goes away. However, the corresponding trouble code will be stored in computer memory. If the fault does not reoccur within a certain time frame, related code(s) will be erased from computer memory. Intermittent failures may be caused by sensor, connector or wiring related problems.

Check engine light

The check engine light comes on if a component related to fuel injection and/or ignition system fails.

The check engine light is installed in oil the temperature/pressure gauge cluster. The light comes on as a self-test when the ignition switch is in the On position.

After the engine starts, the throttle valve closes, and the Check Engine light goes out to indicate that there are no codes stored in the computer memory.

If the check engine light remains on, a fault is present (hard failure) in the DME engine management system. If the check engine light comes on, or flickers, while driving, a fault in the DME engine management system has been identified (intermittent failure).

If the idle speed switch is open during the starting sequence, the check engine light will come on. As soon as the idle speed switch closes while driving, the check engine light goes out after a 4-second delay.

If the full throttle switch is faulty (shorted to ground), the check engine light will remain on constantly.

Some fault codes cannot be displayed using the check engine light. In such cases, retrieve the fault code(s) through the diagnostic connector, and repair the condition(s) causing the check engine light to come on.

Retrieving codes

Turn the ignition key to the On position, then depress the accelerator pedal to the floor and hold it there for five seconds. The CHECK ENGINE light should go out then come on again. At this point, take your foot off the accelerator pedal; the next series of flashes on the CHECK ENGINE light will represent the first trouble code. Write down the code number, then depress the accelerator pedal again for five seconds, then release the pedal and record the second trouble code. Repeat this procedure until all of the trouble codes have been output and code 1000 is displayed, indicating the end of the sequence.

Clearing codes

Ensure the fault that was causing the check engine light to come on has been corrected, then depress and hold the accelerator pedal at wide open throttle (WOT) for more than 12-seconds.

The check engine light will go out briefly after 3, 7 and 10-second intervals to indicate that fault code memory has been cleared.

To clear codes stored in memory, momentarily disconnect the electrical connector from the DME control unit The fault code memory will be cleared.

1990 and later

Code	System affected	Probable cause
1000		End of output
1111	DME power supply	Less than 10 volts
1112 (2)	Idle speed switch	Short in ground circuit
1113	Full throttle switch	Short in ground circuit

Fuel Injection Diagnostic Manual

Code	System affected	Probable cause
1114 (2)	Engine temperature sensor	Open circuit
1121 (2)	Airflow sensor	(3) signal not plausible
1122 (2)	Idle speed control	(3) signal not plausible
1123 (2)	Oxygen sensor	Air fuel/ mixture too rich or too lean
1124 (2)	Oxygen sensor	Open/shorted circuit or faulty sensor
1125	Intake air temperature sensor	Open/short circuit
1131	Knock sensor number 1	(3) signal not plausible
1132	Knock sensor number 2	(3) signal not plausible
1133	Knock regulation	Knock computer faulty
1134	Hall effect sensor	Open/short circuit
1141 (2)	DME control unit	Faulty unit
1143	Fuel tank vent solenoid	Open/short circuit
1144	Resonance plate	
1145	MIL lamp	Open circuit
1151 (2)	Fuel injector number 1	Open/short circuit
1152 (2)	Fuel injector number 2	Open/short circuit
1153 (2)	Fuel injector number 3	Open/short circuit
1154 (2)	Fuel injector number 4	Open/short circuit
1155 (2)	Fuel injector number 5	Open/short circuit
1156 (2)	Fuel injector number 6	Open/short circuit
1500 (2)	System operating properly	No faults codes stored in memory

(1) Except for codes 1000 and 1500, the second digit of all other codes can be a 2, indicating that the fault didn't exist during the last vehicle operation

(2) On 1991 models, these codes can also be displayed by **check engine light**. Other flashing codes are also possible but do not represent a warning regarding the check engine light

(3) Signal of a monitored component is not conforming with memory contents of DME control unit. The control unit recognizes that there is a faulty signal, but cannot always recognize the cause of the faulty signal

Saturn

The Computer Command Control (CCC) system consists of an Electronic Control Module (ECM) and information sensors which monitor various functions of the engine and send data back to the ECM.

This system is equipped with an Erasable Programmable Read Only Memory (EEPROM). The calibrations (parameters) are stored in the ECM within the EEPROM. If the ECM must be replaced, it is necessary to have the EEPROM programmed with a special scanning tool called TECH 1 available only at dealership service department. **Note:** *The EEPROM is not replaceable on these vehicles. In the event of any malfunction with the EEPROM (Code 51), the vehicle must be taken to a dealership service department for diagnosis and repair.*

The ECM controls the following systems:

Fuel control
Electronic spark timing
Exhaust gas recirculation
Canister purge
Engine cooling fan
Idle Air Control (IAC)
Transmission converter clutch
Air conditioning clutch control
Secondary air

Retrieving codes

Note: *A special tool is required to retrieve trouble codes on 1996 models.*

The CCC system has a built-in diagnostic feature which indicates a problem by flashing a Check Engine light on the instrument panel. When this light comes on during normal vehicle operation, a fault in one of the information sensor circuits or the ECM itself has been detected. More importantly, a trouble code is stored in the ECM's memory.

To retrieve this information from the ECM memory, you must use a short jumper wire to ground the diagnostic terminal. This terminal is part of an electrical connector known as the Assembly Line Data Link (ALDL) **(see illustration)**. The ALDL is located underneath the dashboard, to the left of the driver's foot area.

To use the ALDL, remove the plastic cover and with the electrical connector exposed to view, push one end of the jumper wire into the diagnostic terminal (B) and the other end into the ground terminal (A). When the diagnostic terminal is grounded, with the ignition On and the engine stopped, the system will enter the Diagnostic Mode. **Caution:** *Don't start or crank the engine with the diagnostic terminal grounded.*

In this mode the ECM will display a "Code 12" by flashing the Check Engine light, indicating that the system is operating. A code 12 is simply one flash, followed by a brief pause, then two flashes in quick succession. This code will be flashed three times. If no other codes are stored, Code 12 will continue to flash until the diagnostic terminal ground is removed.

After flashing Code 12 three times, the ECM will display any stored trouble codes. Each code will be flashed three times, then Code 12 will be flashed again, indicating that the display of any stored trouble codes has been completed.

When the ECM sets a trouble code, the Check Engine light will come on and a trouble code will be stored in memory. If the problem is intermittent, the light will go out after 10 seconds, or when the fault goes away.

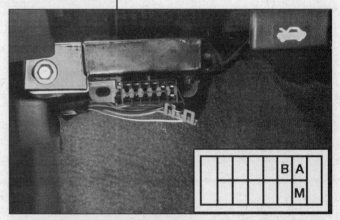

3.24 The Assembly Line Data Link (ALDL) is located under the driver's side dashboard near the kick panel. To activate the diagnostic codes, jump terminals B and A

Fuel Injection Diagnostic Manual

Clearing codes

The trouble code will stay in the ECM memory until the battery voltage to the ECM is interrupted. Removing battery voltage for 10 seconds will clear all stored trouble codes. Trouble codes should always be cleared after repairs have been completed. **Caution:** *To prevent damage to the ECM, the ignition switch must be Off when disconnecting or connecting power to the ECM.*

Code	Circuit or system	Probable cause
Code 11	Transaxle codes present	This indicates that there are trouble codes for the transaxle unit stored in the PCM. Read the codes after the engine code sequence on the SHIFT TO D2 light (1991 and 1992 models) or HOT light (1993 and later models).
Code 12	Diagnostic check only	Indicates the system is ready (ALDL grounded) and ready to flash the engine codes.
Code 13	Oxygen sensor circuit	Possible oxygen sensor ground loose; check the wiring and connectors from the oxygen sensor; replace the oxygen sensor.*
Code 14	Coolant sensor/high temperature	If the engine is experiencing cooling system problems, the problem must be rectified before continuing; check all the wiring and the connectors associated with the coolant temperature sensor; replace if necessary*.
Code 15	Coolant sensor/low temperature	See above, then check the wiring harness connector at the PCM for damage.
Code 17	PCM fault - Pull-up resistor	Faulty PCM resistor in PCM; replace PCM.
Code 19	6X signal fault (1992 to 1995 models)	PCM and/or ignition module may be defective; check all connections and grounds.
Code 21	Throttle position sensor voltage high	Check for a sticking or misadjusted TPS plunger; check all the wiring and connections between the TPS and the PCM; adjust or replace the TPS*.
Code 22	Throttle position sensor voltage low	Check the TPS adjustment; check the PCM connector; replace the TPS*.
Code 23	IAT circuit low	Intake air temperature sensor and/or circuit may be faulty; check sensor and replace if necessary.
Code 24	VSS circuit - no signal	A fault in this circuit should be indicated only when the vehicle is in motion. Disregard code 24 if it is set while the drive wheels are not turning (test situation) - check TPS and PCM.
Code 25	IAT circuit - temperature out of high range	Temperature range excessive causing a misreading by the PCM - check IAT sensor.

Code	Circuit or system	Probable cause
Code 26	Quad driver output fault	The PCM detects an improper voltage level on the circuit that is connected to the Quad Driver Module.
Code 32	EGR system fault	Vacuum switch shorted to ground on start-up, switch not closed after the PCM has commanded the EGR for a specified period of time or the EGR solenoid circuit is open for a specified amount of time; replace the EGR valve*.
Code 33	MAP circuit - voltage out of range high	Check the vacuum hoses from the MAP sensor - check the electrical connections at the PCM; replace the MAP sensor.
Code 34	MAP circuit - voltage out of range low	Signal voltage from MAP sensor too low - check MAP sensor circuit also TPS circuit.
Code 35	Idle air control (IAC) - rpm out of range	IAC motor possibly defective; idle control is high or low, possible PCM problem - have the system diagnosed by a dealer service department.
Code 41	Ignition control circuit open or shorted	Possible defective ignition module. Also check circuit to PCM from ignition module.
Code 42	Bypass circuit - open or shorted	Bypass circuit from ignition module to PCM possibly open or shorted.
Codes 41 and 42	IC control circuit grounded/bypass open	Bypass circuit and/or ignition control circuit shorted causing no feedback pulses for the ignition cycle.
Code 43	Knock sensor circuit - open or shorted	Possible loose or defective knock sensor, also check knock sensor circuit.
Code 44	Oxygen sensor indicates lean exhaust	Check for vacuum leaks near the throttle body gasket, vacuum hoses or the intake manifold gasket. Also check for loose connections on PCM, oxygen sensor etc. Replace oxygen sensor if necessary.*
Code 45	Oxygen sensor indicates rich exhaust	Possibly rich or leaking injector, high fuel pressure or faulty TPS or MAP sensor; also, check the charcoal canister and its components for the presence of fuel; replace the oxygen sensor if necessary.*
Code 46	Power steering pressure circuit (1991 models only) - open or shorted	Possible defective power steering pressure switch, also check the circuit to the switch.
Code 49	High idle indicates vacuum leak	Check all hoses to MAP sensor, PCV valve, brake booster, fuel pressure regulator, throttle body, intake manifold gasket and any other vacuum line.

Code	Circuit or system	Probable cause
Code 51	PCM memory error	Possible defective EEPROM, RAM or EPROM - have the vehicle diagnosed by a dealer service department or other qualified repair shop.
Code 53	System voltage error	Check charge voltage (see Chapter 5). If OK, have vehicle diagnosed by a dealer service department or other repair shop.
Code 55	A/D error	Defective PCM - have the vehicle diagnosed by a dealer service department or other qualified repair shop.
Code 58	Transmission fluid temperature too high	Sensor or signal wire grounded, radiator restricted
Code 59	Transmission fluid temperature too low	Sensor or signal wire open
Code 66 or 67	A/C pressure sensor	Have the vehicle diagnosed by a dealer service department or other qualified repair shop
Code 81	ABS message fault	Defective ABS controller - have the vehicle diagnosed by a dealer service department or other qualified repair shop.
Code 82	PCM internal communication fault	Defective PCM - have the vehicle diagnosed by a dealer service department or other qualified repair shop.

* *Component replacement may not cure the problem in all cases. For this reason, you may want to seek professional advice before purchasing replacement parts.*

Subaru
Retrieving codes

There are self-diagnostic connectors on all models which, when connected together with the key ON (engine off) flash diagnostic codes through the LED light on the oxygen monitor on the ECU. The connectors are under the steering wheel, to the left of the module **(see illustration)** on most models. On carbureted and SPFI injected 1989 models, the test connectors are located on the engine side of the firewall, on the driver's side. Impreza models have the ECU and test connectors located behind the right side of the dash instead of the left. On SVX models the connectors are located behind the driver's side kick panel.

There are four test modes. With *neither* test connector connected, and the ignition key ON (not running) the light will display codes that relate to starting and driving. With *only* the "Read Memory" connector connected, historic codes will be displayed. With *only* the "Test Mode" connector connected, a dealership technician can perform dynamic tests. The last mode is for clearing codes (see text below).

The codes are displayed as pulses of the Light Emitting Diode (LED) mounted on the module. The long pulses (1.2 seconds) indicate tens and the short pulses (.2 seconds) indicate ones. Pulses are separated by .3-second pauses, and codes are separated by 1.8-second pauses. **Note:**

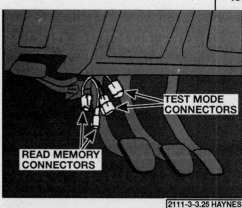

3.25 Location of the diagnostic connector, underneath the dash just to the left of the steering column

On 1989 MPFI models, the oxygen sensor monitor light and ECU are mounted under the rear seat package shelf, and are accessible only from the trunk.

On 1990 models, the trouble codes on the Justy are viewed on the oxygen monitor light only, while on other models, the codes can be viewed on either the oxygen monitor or the Malfunction Indicator Lamp (Check Engine light) on the dash.

1995 Impreza and Legacy models have OBD II diagnostics systems. The OBD II codes can be extracted and cleared with either a Subaru factory tool, called the Subaru Select Monitor, or with a universal OBD II scan tool. Although an expensive scan tool is required to retrieve these new, five-character diagnostic codes, the basic codes can still be obtained using the flashing MIL.

Clearing codes

Codes will clear only when the faulty system or circuit is repaired. After making the repairs, codes can be cleared by connecting *two* pairs of connectors, the self-diagnostic connectors, and the "Read Memory" connectors that are usually located right next to the diagnostic connectors. To begin, start with a warmed-up engine, turn the engine off, connect both pairs of connectors, then start the engine. This should clear the codes.

1983 carbureted models

Code	Probable cause
11, 12, 21, 22	Ignition pulse system
14, 24, 41, 42	Vacuum switches stay on or off
15, 51, 52	Solenoid valve stays on or off
23	Oxygen sensor or circuit
32	Coolant temperature sensor or circuit
33	Main system in feedback
34,43	Choke power stays on or off
42	Clutch switch or circuit

1984 through 1988 carbureted models

Code	Probable cause
11	Ignition pulse system
22	Vehicle Speed Sensor (VSS) or circuit
23	Oxygen sensor or circuit
24	Coolant temperature sensor or circuit
25	Manifold vacuum sensor or circuit (coolant temperature sensor or circuit on 1984 models)

1984 through 1988 carbureted models (continued)

Code	Probable cause
32	Duty solenoid valve or circuit
33	Main system in feedback
34	Back up system
42	Clutch switch or circuit
52	Solenoid valve control system
53	Fuel pump or circuit
54	Choke control system
55	Upshift control
62	Exhaust Gas Recirculation (EGR) solenoid valve control
63	Canister solenoid valve or circuit
64	Vacuum line control valve or circuit
65	Float chamber vent control valve or circuit
71, 73, 74	Ignition pulse system

1983 through 1985 carbureted models

Code	Probable cause
14	Duty solenoid or circuit (fuel control)
15	Coasting Fuel Cut (CFC) system
16	Feedback system
17	Fuel pump and automatic choke
21	Coolant temperature sensor or circuit
22	VLC solenoid valve or circuit
23	Pressure sensor or circuit
24	Idle-up solenoid valve or circuit
25	Float chamber vent solenoid valve or circuit

Code	Probable cause
32	Oxygen sensor or circuit
33	Vehicle speed sensor or circuit
34	EGR solenoid or circuit
35	Canister purge control solenoid or circuit
41	Feedback system (California models)
46	Radiator fan control
52	Clutch switch
53	Altitude compensator switch
55	EGR sensor
56	EGR system
62	Idle-up system (lighting and defogger switch)
63	Idle-up system (fan motor switch)

1984 through 1986 fuel-injected models

Code	Probable cause
11	Ignition pulse
12	Starter switch off
13	Starter switch on
14	Airflow meter or circuit
15	Atmospheric pressure switch - fixed value
16	Crank angle sensor or circuit
17	Starter switch or circuit
21	Seized air flow meter flap
22	Pressure or vacuum switches - fixed value
23	Idle switch - fixed value
24	Wide open throttle switch - fixed value

Fuel Injection Diagnostic Manual

1984 through 1986 fuel-injected models (continued)

Code	Probable cause
25	Throttle sensor idle switch or circuit
31	Speed sensor or circuit
32	Oxygen sensor or circuit
33	Coolant sensor or circuit
34	Abnormal aspirated air thermosensor (in airflow meter)
35	Air flow meter or EGR solenoid switch or circuit
41	Atmosphere pressure sensor or circuit
42	Fuel injector - fixed value
43, 55	KDLH control system
46	Neutral or parking switch or circuit
47	Fuel injector
53	Fuel pump or circuit
57	Canister control system
58	Air control system
62	EGR control system
88	TBI control unit

1987 fuel-injected models

Code	Probable cause
11	Ignition pulse/crank angle sensor
12	Starter switch or circuit
13	Crank angle sensor or circuit
14	Injectors 1 and 2
15	Injectors 3 and 4
21	Coolant temperature sensor or circuit

Code	Probable cause
22	Knock sensor or circuit
23	Air flow meter or circuit
24	Air control
31	Throttle sensor or circuit
32	Oxygen sensor or circuit
33	Vehicle Speed Sensor (VSS) or circuit
34	EGR solenoid valve stuck on or off
35	Purge control solenoid or circuit
41	Lean fuel mixture indicated
42	Idle switch or circuit
45	Kick-down relay or circuit
51	Neutral switch or circuit
61	Parking switch or circuit

1988 and later models with Single-Point Fuel Injection

Code	Probable cause
11	Crank angle sensor or circuit
12	Starter switch or circuit
13	Crank angle sensor or circuit
14	Fuel injector - abnormal output
21	Coolant temperature sensor or circuit
23	Air flow meter or circuit
24	Air control valve or circuit
31	Throttle sensor or circuit
32	Oxygen sensor or circuit

Fuel Injection Diagnostic Manual

1988 and later models with Single-Point Fuel Injection (continued)

Code	Probable cause
33	Vehicle Speed Sensor (VSS) or circuit
34	EGR solenoid or circuit
35	Purge control solenoid or circuit
42	Idle switch or circuit
45	Kick-down control relay or circuit
51	Neutral switch continuously in the on position
55	EGR temperature sensor or circuit
61	Parking switch or circuit

1988 and later models with Multi-Point Fuel Injection

Code	Probable cause
11	Crank angle sensor or circuit
12	Starter switch or circuit
13	Cam position sensor or circuit (TDC sensor on Justy)
14	Fuel injector no. 1 (Legacy, Impreza, Justy, SVX)
14	Fuel injector nos. 1 and 2 (XT, Loyale, GL, DL)
15	Fuel injector no. 2 (Legacy, Impreza, Justy, SVX)
15	Fuel injector nos. 3 and 4 (Loyale, GL, DL)
15	Fuel injector nos. 5 and 6 (XT6)
16	Fuel injector no. 3 (Legacy, Impreza, Justy, SVX)
16	Fuel injector nos. 3 and 4 (XT)
17	Fuel injector no. 4 (Legacy, Impreza, SVX)
17	Fuel injector nos. 1 and 2 (XT6)
18	Fuel injector no. 5 (SVX)

Code	Probable cause
19	Fuel injector no. 6 (SVX)
21	Coolant temperature sensor or circuit
22	Knock sensor or circuit (right side on SVX)
23	Airflow meter or circuit (exc. Justy)
23	Pressure sensor (Justy)
24	Air control valve or circuit (exc. Justy)
24	Idle Speed Control solenoid valve (Justy)
25	Fuel injector nos. 3 and 4 (XT6)
26	Air temperature sensor (Justy)
28	Knock sensor no. 2 (SVX, left side)
29	Crank angle sensor (SVX, no. 2)
31	Throttle position sensor or circuit
32	Oxygen sensor or circuit (no. 1, right side, on SVX)
33	Vehicle Speed Sensor (VSS) or circuit
34	EGR solenoid valve
35	Canister purge solenoid or circuit
36	Air suction solenoid valve (Impreza)
36	Igniter circuit (Justy)
37	Oxygen sensor (no. 2, left side, SVX)
38	Engine torque control (SVX)
41	Air/fuel adaptive control
42	Idle switch or circuit
43	Throttle switch (Justy)
44	Wastegate duty solenoid (turbo)
45	Pressure sensor duty solenoid (turbo)
45	Atmospheric pressure sensor or circuit (non-turbo)

1988 and later models with Multi-Point Fuel Injection (continued)

Code	Probable cause
49	Airflow sensor
51	Neutral switch (MT); inhibitor switch (AT)
52	Parking brake switch (exc. Justy)
52	Clutch switch (Justy)
55	EGR temperature sensor
56	EGR system
61	Parking brake switch (Loyale)
61	Fuel tank pressure control solenoid valve (Impreza)
62	Fuel temperature sensor (Impreza)
62	Electric load signal (Justy)
63	Fuel tank pressure sensor (Impreza)
63	Blower fan switch (Justy)
65	Vacuum pressure sensor

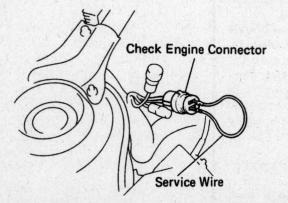

3.26a On 1984 Camrys, 1987 Corollas and 1986 and earlier pick-ups, bridge the terminals of the round Check Engine connector with a jumper wire to obtain the diagnostic codes (Corolla shown, others similar)

Toyota

The Check Engine warning light, which is located on the instrument panel, comes on when the ignition switch is turned to On and the engine is not running. When the engine is started, the warning light should go out. If the light remains on, the diagnosis system has detected a malfunction in the system.

Retrieving codes

To obtain an output of diagnostic codes, verify first that the battery voltage is above 11 volts, the throttle is fully closed, the transaxle is in Neutral, the accessory switches are off and the engine is at normal operating temperature.

Locate the diagnostic connector. The connector is located in several different places, depending on model. In most models it is near the left shock tower in the engine compartment, or near the master cylinder. In Previa models, it is under the driver's seat, In many later vehicles, it is mounted near the fuse/relay box in the engine compartment.

3.26b To access the self diagnostic system, locate the test terminal and using a jumper wire or paper clip, bridge terminals TE1 and E1. On later models, the test terminal is a multi-pin connector, usually with a protective plastic cover over it - using a jumper wire or paper clip, bridge terminals TE1 and E1

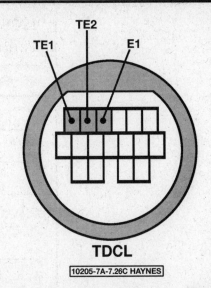

3.26c The 1989 to 1992 Cressida have a different type connector located behind the left dash area, which offers two types of testing modes

Turn the ignition On (engine not running), then use a jumper wire to bridge the terminals of the service electrical connector **(see illustration)**. Later models use a multi-pin connector **(see illustration)** for use with a factory scan tool, but a jumper wire between the TE1 and E1 terminals will make the MIL blink if there are codes. The connector is usually located in the engine compartment near one of the strut towers, or in the passenger compartment under the dash or near the driver's seat.

The 1989 to 1992 Cressida has a different-shaped connector **(see illustration)**, which performs both static and dynamic (vehicle running, see *Test mode* below) self-diagnostics. The 1993 to 1995 Camry and Supra have the same type connector, and the following 1993 models have the same dual-function self-diagnosis capability, but with a standard-looking connector: Corolla, Land Cruiser, MR2 and T100 (refer to the plastic cover for the positions of terminals TE1 and E1).

Read the basic diagnostic codes on all models by watching the number of flashes of the Check Engine light on the dash. Normal system operation is indicated by Code No. 1 (no malfunctions) for all models. The Check Engine light displays a Code No. 1 by blinking once every quarter-second consistently.

If there are any malfunctions in the system, their corresponding trouble codes are stored in computer memory and the light will blink the requisite number of times for the indicated trouble codes. If there's more than one trouble code in the memory, they'll be displayed in numerical order (from lowest to highest) with a pause interval between each one. The digits are simulated by half-second flashes, with 1.5-second pauses between numbers. For example, two flashes, pause, three flashes will indicate code 23. After the code with the largest number of flashes has been displayed, there will be another pause and then the sequence will begin all over again.

Note: *The diagnostic trouble codes 25, 26, 27 and 71 use a special diagnostic capability called "2 trip detection logic". With this system, when a malfunction is first detected, it is temporarily stored into the ECM on the first test drive or "trip". The engine must be turned off and the vehicle taken on another test drive "trip" to allow the malfunction to be stored permanently in the ECM. This will distinguish a true problem on vehicles with these particular codes entered into the computer. Normally the self diagnosis system will detect the malfunctions but in the event the home mechanic wants to double-check the diagnosis by canceling the codes* *and rechecking, then it will be necessary to go on two test drives to confirm any malfunctions with these particular codes.*

To ensure correct interpretation of the blinking Check Engine light, watch carefully for the interval between the end of one code and the beginning of the next (otherwise, you will become confused by the apparent number of blinks and misinterpret the display). The length of this interval varies with the model year.

Beginning in 1994, some Toyota models are equipped with the new OBD II diagnostic system, which requires an expensive Toyota or generic OBD II scan tool to access the new, five-character diagnostic codes. There is no consumer access to the codes through the MIL lamp. 1994 OBD II models include: Camry 3.0L, supercharged Previa, T100 2.7L; 1995 models include the Avalon, Camry 3.0L, Land Cruiser, supercharged Previa, Tacoma, Tercel, and the T100.

"Test" mode diagnostics

Those 1989 through 1993 models mentioned above as having the dynamic testing capability exhibit the standard codes on the MIL with the jumper wire connecting the E1 and TE1 pins. After such a self-diagnosis, turn the key OFF and connect the E1 to the TE2 pin. Now drive the vehicle (above 10 mph) around for about five minutes, trying if you can to simulate the driving conditions under which any driveability problems have occurred in the past.

Stop the vehicle, but keep it running. Switch the jumper wire from the TE2 terminal to the TE1 terminal and read the codes on the MIL. This procedure will self-diagnose some problems which do not show up on the basic static test.

Clearing codes

After the malfunctioning component has been repaired/replaced, the trouble code(s) stored in computer memory must be canceled. To accomplish this, simply remove the 15A EFI fuse for at least 30 seconds with the ignition switch off (the lower the temperature, the longer the fuse must be left out). On Corolla models before 1993, pull the STOP fuse.

Cancellation can also be affected by removing the cable from the negative battery terminal, but other memory systems (such as the clock) will also be canceled.

If the diagnosis code is not canceled, it will be stored by the ECM and appear with any new codes in the event of future trouble.

Should it become necessary to work on engine components requiring removal of the battery terminal, first check to see if a diagnostic code has been recorded.

Camry (1983 through 1986 models), Corolla (1987 models), Pick-ups and 4-Runner (1984 through 1987 models)

Code	Probable cause
1	Normal
2	Air Flow Meter Signal
3	Air Flow Meter Signal (1984 Trucks, 1983 through 1985 Camry)
3	No ignition signal from igniter
4	Coolant temperature sensor or circuit

Code	Probable cause
5	Oxygen sensor or circuit
6	No ignition signal (1984 trucks, 1983 through 1985 Camry)
6	RPM signal (no signal to ECU)
7	Throttle Position Sensor (TPS) or circuit
8	Intake Air Temperature sensor or circuit
9	Vehicle Speed Sensor (VSS) or circuit
10	Starter signal
11	Switch signal - air conditioning, TPS or Neutral start
11	ECU main relay (Cressida, Supra, Celica 3S-GE)
12	Knock sensor or circuit (distributor or circuit on Cressida, Supra, Celica 3S-GE)
13	Knock sensor/CPU (ECU) faulty
14	Turbocharger pressure (22R-TE/Turbo 22R models) - over-boost (abnormalities in air flow meter may also be detected)
14	Ignitor (Cressida, Supra, Celica 3S-GE)

Camry (1987 through 1990 models), all other models (1988 through 1990)

Code	Probable cause
11	Momentary interruption in power supply to ECU
12	RPM signal/no NE or G Signal to ECU within several seconds after engine is cranked
13	RPM Signal/no signal to ECU when engine speed is above 1500 RPM
14	No ignition signal to ECU
21	Oxygen sensor circuit or oxygen sensor heater circuit failure
22	Coolant temperature sensor circuit
23/24	Intake air temperature circuit
25	Air fuel ratio - lean condition indicated
26	Air fuel ratio - rich condition indicated
27	Oxygen sensor circuit (open or shorted)
31	Air flow meter or circuit

Fuel Injection Diagnostic Manual

Camry (1987 through 1990 models),
all other models (1988 through 1990) (continued)

Code	Probable cause
32	Air flow meter or circuit
41	Throttle position sensor or circuit
42	Vehicle Speed Sensor (VSS) or circuit
43	Starter signal/no start signal to ECU
51	Switch signal/Neutral start switch off or air conditioning on during diagnostic check
51	Switch signal - no IDL signal, NSW or air conditioning signal to ECU (1988 through 1990 Corolla, 1988-1/2 through 1990 Camry models)
52	Knock sensor circuit
53	Knock sensor signal/faulty ECU
71	Exhaust Gas Recirculation (EGR) system malfunction

All models (1991 on)

Code	Circuit or system	Diagnosis	Probable cause
Code 1	Normal	This appears when none of the other codes are identified.	
Code 12	RPM signal	No "Ne" signal to the ECM within several seconds after the engine is cranked. No "G" signal to the ECM two times in succession when engine speed is between 500 rpm and 4000 rpm.	Distributor circuit Distributor Igniter Igniter circuit Starter circuit ECM
Code 13	RPM signal	No "Ne" signal to the ECM engine speed is above 1500 rpm.	Distributor circuit Distributor Igniter Igniter circuit ECM
Code 14	Ignition signal	No "IGN" signal to the ECM 8 times in succession.	Igniter Igniter circuit ECM
Code 16	Transmission ECM	Fault in ECM signal.	Transmission ECM ECM
Code 21	Main oxygen sensor and heater	Problem in the main oxygen sensor circuit. Open or Short in the main oxygen sensor heater circuit.	Main oxygen sensor circuit ECM Main oxygen sensor heater

Code	Circuit or system	Diagnosis	Probable cause
Code 22	Coolant temperature sensor	Open or short in the coolant sensor circuit.	Coolant temperature sensor circuit Coolant temperature sensor ECM
Code 24	Intake air temperature sensor	Open or short in the intake air sensor circuit.	Intake air temperature sensor Intake air temperature sensor circuit
Code 25	Air/fuel ratio lean malfunction	The air/fuel ratio feedback correction value or adaptive control value continues at the upper (lean) or lower (rich) limit for a certain period of time.	Injector circuit Oxygen sensor or circuit ECM Oxygen sensor Fuel line pressure (injector blockage or leakage) Air temperature sensor or circuit Air leak Air flow meter Air intake system Ignition system
Code 26	Air/fuel ratio rich malfunction	The air/fuel ratio is overly rich. Open or short circuit in the oxygen sensor.	Injector or Injector circuit Coolant temperature sensor or circuit Air temperature sensor or circuit Airflow meter Oxygen sensor or circuit Cold start injector ECM
Code 27	Sub-oxygen sensor	Open or shorted circuit in the sub-oxygen sensor circuit.	Sub-oxygen sensor circuit ECM
Code 28	Oxygen sensor	Open or short in Oxygen sensor circuit.	Oxygen sensor Oxygen sensor circuit
Code 31	Airflow meter	Open or short circuit in Vc to E2.	Airflow meter circuit
Code 31	MAP sensor, vacuum sensor signal	Open or short circuit in Vc to E2.	MAP sensor-to-ECM circuit
Code 31	Volume Air Flow (VAF) sensor or circuit (1995)	No VAF signal for 2 seconds after starting	VAF sensor or circuit
Code 32	Airflow meter	Open or short circuit in Vs to Vc or E2.	Airflow meter circuit/ECM
Code 34/35	Turbocharger	Pressure abnormal	Open or short circuit in turbocharger pressure or BARO sensor(s)
Code 41	Throttle position sensor	Open or short in the throttle position sensor circuit.	Throttle position sensor or circuit ECM

Fuel Injection Diagnostic Manual

All models (1991 on)

Code	Circuit or system	Diagnosis	Probable cause
Code 42	Vehicle speed sensor	No "SPD" signal for 8 seconds when the engine speed is above 2000 rpm.	Vehicle speed sensor or circuit ECM
Code 43	Starter signal	No "STA" signal to the ECM until engine speed reaches 800 rpm with the vehicle not moving.	Starter signal circuit Ignition switch Main relay switch ECM
Code 47	TPS signal	Sub-throttle position sensor	Open or short circuit in sub-throttle position sensor
Code 51	Switch condition signal	No IDL signal or no NSW signal or A/C signal to the ECM when the test connector E1 and TE1 are connected.	A/C switch or circuit A/C amplifier Neutral start switch (A/T) Throttle position sensor Throttle position sensor circuit
Code 52	Knock sensor signal	Open or short circuit in knock sensor circuit.	Knock sensor ECM
Code 53	Knock control signal	Problem with knock control system in ECM.	ECM
Code 55	Knock control signal	Open or short circuit in knock sensor circuit	Knock sensor ECM
Code 71	EGR	EGR gas temperature signal is too low.	EGR system (EGR valve, hoses, etc.) EGR gas temperature sensor or circuit Vacuum switching valve for the EGR circuit ECM
Code 72	Fuel cut solenoid or circuit	Circuit open	Faulty solenoid or circuit
Code	Circuit or system	Diagnosis	Probable cause
Code 78	Fuel pump	Open or short circuit in fuel pump control circuit.	Fuel pump electronic control unit (ECM) Fuel pump control circuit
Code 81	Transmission to ECM	Open in ECT1 circuit for at least 2-seconds.	ECM Transmission control module (TCM)
Code 83	Transmission to ECM	Open in ESA1 circuit for 1/2-second after the engine idles at least 1/2-second.	ECM Transmission control module (TCM)
Code 84	Transmission to ECM	Open in ESA1 circuit for 1/2-second after the engine idles at least 1/2-second.	ECM Transmission control module (TCM)
Code 85	Transmission to ECM	Open in ESA1 circuit for 1/2-second after the engine idles at least 1/2-second.	ECM Transmission control module (TCM)

Volkswagen

Digifant I and II systems

Retrieving codes

Some vehicles equipped with the Digifant engine management system and sold in California have control units with a fault diagnosis capability.

This system indicates faults in the engine management system through a combination rocker switch/indicator light located to the right of the instrument cluster. **Note:** *Not all California models are equipped with a fault diagnosis system. Also, there are several variations among those so equipped. We recommend consulting with a VW dealer service department if you have any questions about the specific system used on your model.*

If it's operating properly, the light comes on briefly when you turn on the ignition. After a short period of driving, it also comes on to report any fault codes that might be stored in memory.

To display any stored fault codes, turn on the ignition - but don't start the engine - and depress the rocker switch for at least four-seconds. The indicator will display any stored fault codes in a series of flashes. For example, two flashes, followed by one flash, followed by four flashes, followed by two flashes, indicates the code 2-1-4-2, which means there's a problem with the knock sensor.

Clearing codes

To erase the fault codes from computer memory, make sure the ignition switch is turned off. Unplug the coolant temperature sensor harness connector.

Depress and hold the rocker switch and, with the switch depressed, turn on the ignition. The codes will then be erased.

Reconnect the coolant temperature sensor. Finally, test drive the vehicle for at least 10 minutes.

CIS-E Motronic systems

The CIS-E Motronic engine management system is used on vehicles equipped with the 2.0L 16-valve engine (engine code 9A). The Motronic system combines the fuel control of the CIS-E fuel injection system with the control of ignition timing, idle speed and emissions into one control unit.

The fuel injection and idle speed control functions of CIS-E Motronic are similar to those used on the CIS-E system. But the Motronic system uses "adaptive circuitry" in its oxygen sensor system. Adaptive circuitry enables the oxygen sensor system to adjust the operating range of fuel metering in accordance with subtle changes in operating conditions caused by such things as normal engine wear, vacuum leaks, changes in altitude, etc.

Retrieving codes

The CIS-E Motronic engine management system can detect faults, store these faults in coded form in its memory and, when activated, display the codes. Each code corresponds to a specific component or function of the Motronic system which should be checked, repaired and/or replaced. When a code is stored on a California vehicle, the "Check" light on the dashboard is illuminated.

You can access trouble codes by using the diagnostic connectors (located under the shifter boot) to activate the memory of the control unit, which displays any stored code(s) on an LED test light **(see illustration)**. Here's how to read the trouble codes on a CIS-E Motronic system.

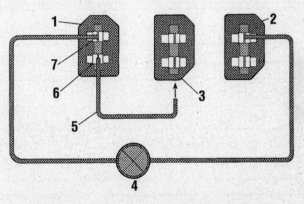

3.27 Here's how to bridge the terminals of the diagnostic connector with a jumper wire and an LED test light to output the codes on a CIS-E Motronic system (the connector is located under the shifter boot)

1	Black connector	5	Jumper wire
2	Blue connector	6	Negative terminal
3	White connector	7	Positive terminal
4	LED test light		

Make sure the air conditioning is switched off. Verify that fuse numbers 15 (engine electronics), 18 (fuel pump, oxygen sensor) and 21 (interior lights) are good. Inspect the engine ground strap (located near the distributor). Make sure it's in good shape and making a good connection.

Test drive the car for at least five minutes. Make sure the engine speed exceeds 3000 rpm at least once, the accelerator is pressed all the way to the floor at least once and the engine reaches its normal operating temperature.

After the test drive, keep the engine running for at least two minutes before shutting it off. Switch off the ignition. Connect an LED test light to the diagnostic connectors **(see illustration)**. Switch on the ignition.

Any stored fault codes are displayed by the LED as a sequence of flashes and pauses. For example, two flashes, a pause, one flash, a pause, two flashes, a pause and one flash indicates a code 2121, which means there's a problem in the idle switch circuit. A complete guide to the codes, their causes, the location of the faulty component and the recommended repair are contained in the accompanying tables.

To display the first code on 1988 to 1992 models, connect a jumper wire (as shown in illustration) for at least four seconds, then disconnect it. The LED will flash, indicating a four-digit code. To display the next code, connect the jumper wire for another four seconds, then detach it, and so on. Repeat this process until all stored codes have been displayed.

On 1993 and later models, a special scan tool is required to access all of the diagnostic information. However, using a VW jumper harness, the major four-digit codes can be displayed on the MIL.

Clearing codes

To erase trouble codes from the computer memory after all individual codes have been displayed as described in the previous steps, connect the jumper wire for more than four seconds - this erases the permanent fault storage memory of the control unit.

Code	Location or description of fault	Probable cause
1111	Control unit	a) Defective control unit
1231	Speed sender	a) Open circuit b) Faulty sender
2111	Engine speed sensor	a) Open circuit b) Faulty sender
2112	Ignition reference sensor	a) Open circuit b) Faulty sensor
2113	Hall sender	a) No signal or faulty signal from Hall sender
2121	Idle switch	a) Open circuit or short to ground b) Switch faulty or misadjusted
2141	Knock sensor I	a) Engine knock b) Fuel of incorrect octane c) Incorrect ignition timing d) damaged shield on knock sensor wiring

Code	Location or description of fault	Probable cause
2142	Knock sensor	a) Open or short circuit in knock sensor wiring b) Faulty knock sensor c) Faulty control unit
2142 (Eurovan)	Transmission control module	a) Open circuit to control module b) Faulty module
2144	Knock sensor II	a) Open or short circuit in knock sensor wiring b) Faulty knock sensor c) Faulty control unit
2212	Throttle Position Sensor	a) Open or short circuit to ground or battery voltage b) Faulty sensor
2214	Maximum rpm exceeded	a) Engine rpm exceeded fuel injection cut-off point b) Interference on signal wire
2222 (Eurovan)	Manifold Absolute Pressure	a) No vacuum to ECM (check the hose b) Faulty ECM
2231	Idle speed stabilizer system has exceeded adaptive range	a) Throttle valve basic adjustment incorrect b) Incorrect ignition timing c) Evaporative emission control system faulty d) Intake air leaks
2232	Air flow sensor Potentiometer	a) Open circuit or short to ground b) Potentiometer faulty
2234	System voltage out of range	a) Check battery b) Check charging system
2242	Throttle valve potentiometer	a) Open or short circuit b) Faulty potentiometer
2243	Fuel consumption signal	a) Short circuit to battery voltage in instrument panel
2312	Coolant temperature sensor	a) Faulty sensor b) Open circuit or short to ground
2314	Transmission control signal	a) Short to ground in transmission control module circuit
2322	Intake air	a) Open circuit or short to temperature sensor ground b) Sensor faulty
2324	Mass Airflow Sensor	a) Open or short circuit b) Faulty sensor

Fuel Injection Diagnostic Manual

Code	Location or description of fault	Probable cause
2341	Oxygen sensor control range exceeded	a) Idle mixture (%CO) incorrectly adjusted b) Faulty oxygen sensor wiring c) Leaking cold-start valve d) Evaporative emission control system faulty e) Intake air leaks
2342	Oxygen sensor system (faulty signal or exceeding adjustment range)	a) Open circuit b) Faulty oxygen sensor c) Incorrect idle speed d) Intake air leaks (leaking
2411	Exhaust Gas Recirculation (EGR) system (California cars only)	a) Intake air temperature sensor faulty b) Open circuit or short circuit to ground c) EGR system faulty or plugged
2413	Fuel mixture out of limit	a) Fuel pressure too low or high b) Fuel injector(s) faulty c) Leak in intake or exhaust system d) Faulty EGR frequency valve
4312	EGR frequency valve	a) Open or short circuit b) Faulty valve
4332	ECM	a) Connectors at ECM loose b) Faulty ECM
4343	EVAP frequency valve	a) Open or short circuit b) Faulty valve
4411 (exc. Eurovan)	Injector no. 1	a) Open or short circuit b) Faulty injector
4411 (Eurovan)	Injector driver circuit	a) Open or short circuit b) Faulty injector
4412	Injector no. 2	a) Open or short circuit b) Faulty injector
4413	Injector no. 3	a) Open or short circuit b) Faulty injector
4414	Injector no. 4	a) Open or short circuit b) Faulty injector
4415 (VR6)	Injector no. 5	a) Open or short circuit b) Faulty injector

Code	Location or description of fault	Probable cause
4416 (VR6)	Injector no. 6	a) Open or short circuit b) Faulty injector
4431	Idle air control valve	a) Open circuit or short circuit to ground b) Control unit faulty c) Faulty IAC valve
4433	Fuel pump relay	a) Open or short circuit b) Faulty relay
4444	No faults stored in memory	
0000	End of sequence	

Volvo, all models (1989 on)

There have been two basic systems used on Volvos with self-diagnostics. The 1989 through 1993 models, and some 1994 models, have used a system with a separate ECU for the fuel injection and another for the ignition system. Some 1994 and 1995 models are equipped with the new OBD II diagnostic system, which uses only one central computer.

1989 through 1993 models (and later non-turbo, non-OBD II models)

Locate the diagnostic unit behind left strut tower, and remove its cover (**see illustration**). Connect the selector cable to socket number 2, which tests the fuel system for codes. Turn the ignition switch to the On position (engine not running). Enter the diagnostic mode by pressing the push button on the diagnostic unit for at least one second, but not more than three seconds.

Watch the red LED, and count the number of flashes in 3-flash series. Flash series are separated by 3-second intervals. Write down all codes.

If no codes are stored, the LED will flash 1-1-1, indicating the fuel system is operating properly.

To access the ignition codes, repeat the above procedure, but with the selector cable plugged into the number 6 socket on the diagnostic unit. **Note:** *Most turbocharged models have separate codes for the turbo system which are accessed by hooking the diagnostic cable into socket number 5.*

1994 and later models with OBD II

The 850 Turbo and 960 models have the new, five-character OBD II codes, which are accessible only with the Volvo factory scan tool or a generic (still expensive) OBD II scan tool (used only in socket number 2). There are many more specific codes in the OBD II system than the previous three-digit codes. However, the three-digit codes can still be retrieved from the factory diagnostic unit as described above for earlier models.

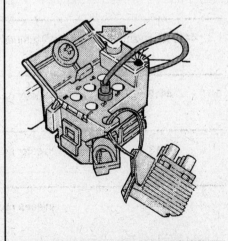

3.28 Locate the diagnostic connector box in the engine compartment at the left strut tower.

Fuel Injection Diagnostic Manual

Clearing codes

Once all the faults have been corrected, turn the ignition switch to the On position (engine not running). Read the codes again, then depress the button for five seconds and release. After three seconds the LED should light up. While the LED is lit, depress the button again for five seconds, after releasing the button the LED should stop shining.

Verify that the memory is erased by depressing the button for more than one second, but not more than three seconds. The LED should flash 1-1-1, indicating the memory is clear.

Code	Probable cause
1-1-1	No Faults
1-1-2	ECU
1-1-3	Fuel Injectors
1-1-3 (1994 on)	Heated oxygen sensor - maximum enrichment sensed
1-1-5	Injector no. 1
1-2-1	Mass Airflow Signal
1-2-2	Air temperature sensor signal
1-2-3	Coolant temperature sensor signal
1-2-5	Injector no. 2
1-3-1	Ignition System RPM signal
1-3-2	Battery Voltage
1-3-3	Throttle Switch signal (Idle)
1-3-5	Injector no. 3
1-4-2	ECU faulty
1-4-3	Knock sensor signal missing or sensor defective
1-4-4	Fuel system load signal (missing or defective)
1-4-5	Injector no. 4
1-5-3	Rear heated oxygen sensor signal
1-5-4	EGR system - leakage or excessive flow
1-5-5	Injector no. 5

Computer trouble codes

Code	Probable cause
2-1-2	Oxygen Sensor Signal (front sensor on 1994 and later models)
2-1-3	Throttle switch signal (wide open)
2-1-4	Ignition rpm signal erratic
2-2-1	Lambda Operation
2-2-1	Heated oxygen sensor (mixture too rich under part throttle)
2-2-2	Main relay
2-2-3	Idle Valve Signal
2-2-4	Coolant temperature sensor signal
2-2-5	A/C pressure sensor signal
2-3-1	Lambda adjustment
2-3-1 (1994 on)	Heated oxygen sensor (mixture too lean under part throttle)
2-3-2	Lambda adjustment
2-3-2 (1994 on)	Adaptive heated oxygen sensor control
2-3-3	Idle valve - closed, or intake air leak
2-3-4	Throttle switch signal missing
2-4-1	EGR malfunction
2-4-5	Idle Air Control valve - closing signal
3-1-1	Speedometer Signal
3-1-2	Knock/Fuel Enrichment signal missing
3-1-4	Camshaft position signal missing or defective
3-1-5	EVAP emission control system
3-2-1	Cold start valve - signal missing
3-2-2	Airflow meter hot wire
3-2-4	Camshaft position signal erratic
3-2-5	ECU memory failure

Fuel Injection Diagnostic Manual

Code	Probable cause
3-3-5	TCM request for MIL (CHECK ENGINE light)
4-1-1	Throttle switch signal faulty or missing
4-1-3	EGR temperature sensor signal incorrect or missing
4-1-4	Turbo boost regulation
4-1-6	Turbo boost reduction from TCM
4-2-5	Temperature warning level no. 1
4-3-1	EGR temperature sensor faulty or missing
4-3-2	High temperature warning inside ECU
4-3-3	No rear knock sensor signal
4-3-5	Front heated oxygen sensor - slow response
4-3-6	Rear heated oxygen sensor compensation
4-4-3	Catalytic converter efficiency
4-4-4	Acceleration sensor signal
4-5-1	Misfire, cylinder no. 1
4-5-2	Misfire, cylinder no. 2
4-5-3	Misfire, cylinder no. 3
4-5-4	Misfire, cylinder no. 4
4-5-5	Misfire, cylinder no. 5
5-1-1	Adaptive oxygen sensor control, provides leaner mixture at idle
5-1-2	Oxygen integrator at maximum lean running limit
5-1-3	High temperature warning inside ECU
5-1-4	Engine cooling fan - low speed signal faulty
5-2-1	Oxygen sensor preheating, front
5-2-2	Oxygen sensor preheating, rear
5-3-1	Power stage - group A

Code	Probable cause
5-3-2	Power stage - group B
5-3-3	Power stage - group C
5-3-4	Power stage - group D
5-3-5	TC control valve signal
5-4-1	EVAP valve signal
5-4-2	Misfire on more than one cylinder
5-4-3	Misfire on at least one cylinder
5-4-4	Misfire on more than one cylinder, catalytic converter damage
5-4-5	Misfire on at least one cylinder, catalytic converter damage
5-5-1	Misfire on cylinder no. 1, catalytic converter damage
5-5-2	Misfire on cylinder no. 2, catalytic converter damage
5-5-3	Misfire on cylinder no. 3, catalytic converter damage
5-5-4	Misfire on cylinder no. 4, catalytic converter damage
5-5-5	Misfire on cylinder no. 5, catalytic converter damage

4 Fuel system pressure relief

1 General information

Fuel injection systems operate under high pressure. This pressure can be as high as 50 or 60 psi on some models. The system can remain pressurized even when the engine is not running. With that much pressure, the possibility of fuel spray is a safety hazard for anyone working on the system. Most fuel injection systems must therefore be depressurized before any work is performed. The only exception is some Throttle Body Injection (TBI) (also called single point) systems, which automatically bleed down pressure shortly after the engine is shut off.

2 Fuel pressure relief procedure

Warning 1: *Gasoline is extremely flammable, so take extra precautions when you work on any part of the fuel system. Don't smoke or allow open flames or bare light bulbs near the work area, and don't work in a garage where a natural gas-type appliance (such as a water heater or clothes dryer) with a pilot light is present. If you spill any fuel on your skin, rinse it off immediately with soap and water. When you perform any kind of work on the fuel system, wear safety glasses and have a Class B type fire extinguisher on hand.*

Warning 2: *After the fuel pressure has been relieved, wrap shop towels around any fuel connection you'll be disconnecting. They'll absorb the residual fuel that may leak out, reducing the risk of fire and preventing contact with your skin.*

The procedure for depressurizing the fuel injection system is also covered in the Haynes Automotive Repair Manual for your specific vehicle. If the manual for your vehicle isn't available, follow the general depressurization procedure below.

Remove the fuel filler cap – this will release any pressure build-up in the tank.

Disconnect the battery power to the fuel pump (see below).

Start the engine and run it until it stalls, then turn the ignition key OFF.

The fuel system is now depressurized. Make sure all fuel in the system is exhausted by cranking the engine over for about five seconds, then turning the ignition key OFF.

Disconnecting battery power to the fuel pump

Disconnecting the electrical power to the fuel pump can be accomplished by a variety of methods, depending on model and manufacturer.

Fuel pump connector

The most effective way to disable the fuel pump is simply to unplug the harness connector at the fuel pump. On many models this is easily accessible from under the vehicle **(see illustration)**.

Fuel pump fuse

If the fuel pump harness connector isn't accessible, remove the fuel pump fuse (usually clearly marked in the fuse block) to disable the fuel pump **(see illustration)**. If the information is not marked on the fuse block, consult your owner's manual for the exact location. On some models the fuse may be located in the engine compartment **(see illustration)**. This procedure may not work on some models because the fuse may also control other functions so removing it won't allow the engine to start.

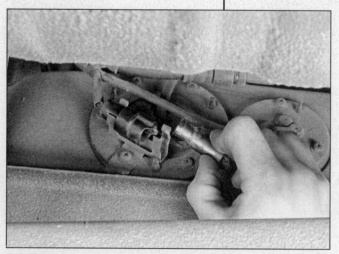

2.1 If the fuel pump electrical connector is accessible, simply unplug it to disable the fuel pump

2.2 The fuel pump fuse is usually clearly marked on the fuse block cover and it's a simple matter to remove it

2.3 On some models the fuel pump fuse is located in the engine compartment

Fuel pump relay

If the fuel pump connector or fuse isn't accessible or you can't locate them, the fuel pump can be disabled by removing the fuel pump relay **(see illustration)**.

Ford inertia switch

Ford models have an inertia switch that shuts off power to the fuel system in the event of an accident. This switch is found in the trunk, rear compartment or under the dash, depending on model and year. Look in your owners manual for the location of the "Fuel Pump Shutoff Switch". Unplugging the electrical connector from the inertia switch will disable the fuel pump **(see illustration)**.

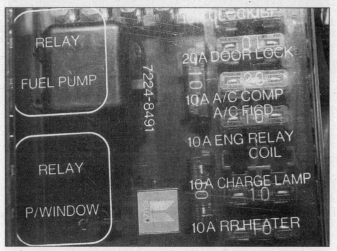

2.4 The fuel pump relay is usually clearly marked

Test-port valve

Some later models have a fuel pressure test-port valve located on the fuel rail that can also be used to depressurize the system.

Detach the cable from the negative battery terminal. Unscrew the cap from the test-port valve **(see illustration)**. Place shop towels or rags under, around and over the test-port to absorb the fuel when the pressure is released from the fuel rail. Wear safety goggles to protect your eyes from spraying fuel and use a small screwdriver or pin punch to push the test-port valve in to relieve the pressure **(see illustration)**. Clean up the spilled fuel with the towels or rags and install the test-port cap.

Residual fuel pressure

Remember that even a depressurized system may still retain some residual fuel and pressure. Before detaching a line, always wrap a rag around the connection to catch any fuel that may be expelled.

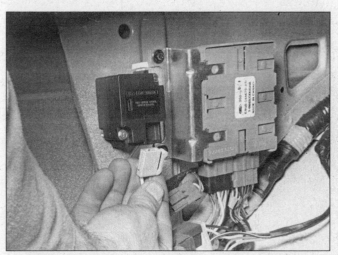

2.5 On Ford models, the fuel pump can be disabled by unplugging the inertia switch

2.6 Unscrew the fuel pressure test-port cap (arrow)

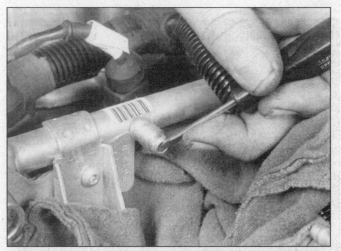

2.7 Use a small screwdriver or pin punch to depress the test-port valve and relieve the fuel pressure - this should be done under a layer of rags (removed here for clarity) to catch the fuel spray

Notes

5 Fuel filters, lines and fittings

1 General information

The fuel injection system circulates fuel from the tank through the filter and injection unit, then back to the tank by way of lines and fittings **(see illustration)**. The system operates under high pressure, so the fuel filter must be changed regularly or dirt can clog the filter and/or injectors, affecting system operation.

Damage to the lines and fittings not only affects the efficiency of the fuel injection system but can cause dangerous fuel leaks. Consequently, they should periodically be checked for damage and replaced if necessary.

2 Fuel filter replacement

Warning: *Gasoline is extremely flammable, so take extra precautions when you work on any part of the fuel system. Don't smoke or allow open flames or bare light bulbs near the work area, and don't work in a garage where a natural gas-type appliance (such as a water heater or clothes dryer) with a pilot light is present. Since gasoline is carcinogenic, wear latex gloves when there's a possibility of being exposed to fuel, and, if you spill any fuel on your skin, rinse it off immediately with soap and water. Mop up any spills immediately and do not store fuel-soaked rags where they could ignite. The fuel system is under constant pressure, so, before any lines are disconnected, the fuel system pressure must be relieved (see Chapter 4). When you perform any kind of work on the fuel system, wear safety glasses and have a Class B type fire extinguisher on hand.*

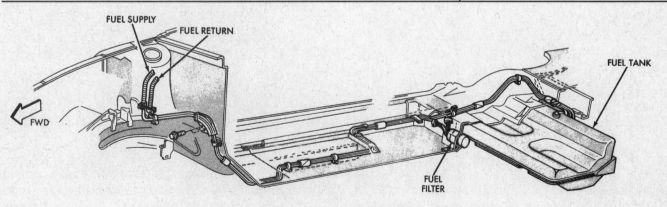

1.1 Typical fuel system layout

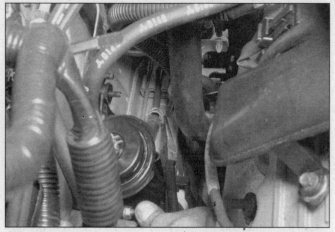

2.1a On this type of rubber fuel hose connection, use needle nose pliers to slide the clip off, then detach the hose

2.1b On threaded-type connections, steady the filter with one wrench and use a flare-nut wrench to unthread the fitting

Locating the filter

Fuel filters (there may be more than one on your vehicle) can be located anywhere in the fuel system, but are often mounted close to either the tank or the fuel injection unit. Begin your search for the filter canister in the engine compartment by following the fuel line from the fuel injection unit to the inlet line coming from the rear of the vehicle. If you can't find the filter in the engine compartment, raise the vehicle and support it securely on jackstands. Trace the fuel line back to the tank along the underside of the vehicle. After locating the filter, note it's type and mounting details. Have the proper replacement parts and the tools needed for removal ready before beginning the replacement procedure.

Removal

Relieve the fuel system pressure (see Chapter 4). If the filter is located in the engine compartment, mark the locations of any components that will interfere with removal and move them out of the way.

Disconnect the filter from the fuel lines **(see illustrations)**.

Remove the retaining nuts, bolts or clips and detach the filter from the vehicle **(see illustrations)**.

2.1c Support this type of filter with one wrench while using a box-end wrench to remove the banjo bolt

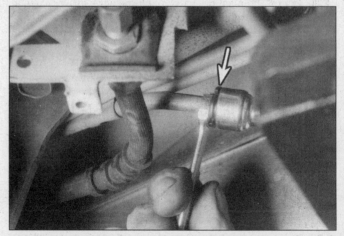

2.1d Use a small wrench to push on the black plastic ring (arrow) and release the connection

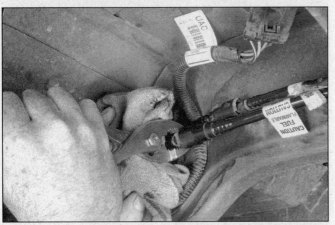

2.1e On this type of GM plastic quick-connect fitting, use pliers to gently depress the white plastic tabs and detach the fuel lines - always wrap a rag around the filter to soak up the fuel

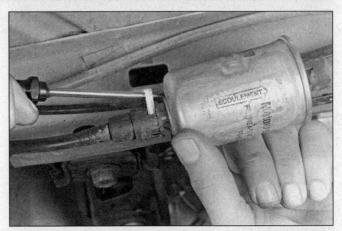

2.2a If the new clips are included with the new filter, pry off the old ones - if the clips are to be reused, remove them carefully by hand

Installation

Place the new filter in position. Make sure that any arrows or other markings on the filter indicating direction of flow face toward the fuel injection unit **(see illustration)**.Install the bracket nuts or bolts, then connect the fuel lines **(see illustrations on page 4)**.

2.2b Pry off the plastic rivet with a large screwdriver - use a sheet metal screw to install the new filter

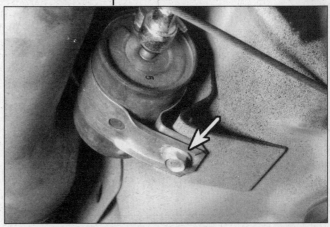

2.2c Filters are commonly secured with screws (arrow)

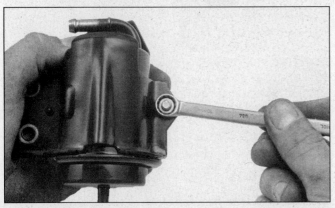

2.2d On some models a separate mounting bracket will have to be removed from the old filter and installed on the new one

2.3 Make sure the fuel filter outlet faces toward the fuel injection unit

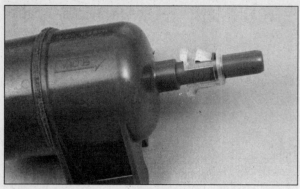

2.4a Install the new quick-disconnect clips on the new filter

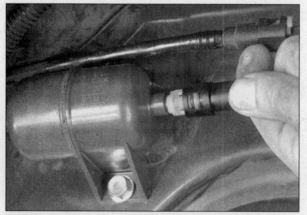

2.4b Push the fuel line onto the filter until it clicks in place

3.1 These are typical fuel feed and return line threaded fittings located in the engine compartment - check for loose mounting bolts and leaks

3 Fuel hoses and lines - check and replacement

Warning: *Gasoline is extremely flammable, so take extra precautions when you work on any part of the fuel system. Don't smoke or allow open flames or bare light bulbs near the work area, and don't work in a garage where a natural gas-type appliance (such as a water heater or clothes dryer) with a pilot light is present. Since gasoline is carcinogenic, wear latex gloves when there's a possibility of being exposed to fuel, and, if you spill any fuel on your skin, rinse it off immediately with soap and water. Mop up any spills immediately and do not store fuel-soaked rags where they could ignite. The fuel system is under constant pressure, so, before any lines are disconnected, the fuel system pressure must be relieved (see Chapter 4). When you perform any kind of work on the fuel system, wear safety glasses and have a Class B type fire extinguisher on hand.*

Check

Remember: the fuel lines are under pressure, so if any fuel lines are to be disconnected be prepared to catch spilled fuel.
Warning: *You must relieve the fuel system pressure before servicing the fuel lines. Refer to Chapter 4 for the fuel system pressure relief procedure.*

Some components of the fuel system, such as the fuel tank and part of the fuel feed and return lines, are underneath the vehicle and can be inspected more easily with the vehicle raised on a hoist. If that's not possible, raise the vehicle and support it securely on jackstands.

Check all hoses and pipes for cracks, kinks, deformation or obstructions. Make sure all hoses and pipe clips are securely attached to their associated hoses and the underside of the vehicle. Verify that all hose clamps attaching rubber hoses to metal fuel lines or pipes are snug enough to assure a tight seal between the hoses and pipes **(see illustration)**.

Rubber hose

Check all rubber fuel lines for deterioration and chafing. Inspect for cracks at hose bends and just before fittings, such as where a hose attaches to the fuel pump, fuel filter and fuel injection unit. High quality fuel line, usually identified by "Fluoroestomer" and the PSI rating printed on the hose, should be used for fuel line replacement. Never use unreinforced vacuum line, clear plastic tubing or water hose for fuel lines because they aren't designed for fuel or high pressure use.

Nylon lines

Many later models use nylon fuel line because of its flexibility and resistance to abrasion. Inspect along the length of each of these lines for cracks or damage.

Metal lines

Steel tubing is often used for fuel line between the fuel pump and the fuel injection unit. Check the entire length of line carefully to make sure it isn't bent, crimped or cracked. Replace sections of metal fuel line with seamless steel tubing only. Do not use copper or aluminum tubing because they can't withstand engine vibration.

The fuel feed, return and vapor lines extend from the fuel tank to the engine compartment. These lines are secured to the underbody with clip and screw assemblies and should be inspected for leaks, kinks and dents **(see illustration)**. Also check that the fittings and connectors securing the metal fuel lines to the fuel injection system and filter are tight and leak-free.

3.2 Make sure the lines are securely clipped to the frame

Replacement

Remember, before disconnecting any part of the fuel system, be sure to relieve the fuel system pressure (see Chapter 4). Also, make sure to cover the fitting being disconnected with a rag to absorb any fuel that may spray or spill out.

Rubber hose

Remove the fasteners attaching the lines to the vehicle body, detach the connectors that attach the rubber fuel hoses to metal lines (see below). After removing clamp-type fittings, twist the hose back and forth to make separation easier.

When attaching rubber hose to a metal line, make sure to correctly overlap them **(see illustration)**. Don't install the hose within four inches of any part of the exhaust system or within ten inches of the catalytic converter. Metal lines and rubber hoses must never be allowed to chafe against the frame. Maintain a minimum of 1/4-inch clearance around a line or hose to prevent contact with the frame.

Nylon line

Nylon replacement line will generally have to be obtained from a dealer since each length usually incorporates special connections specific to each manufacturer. Detach the fittings and install the new line.

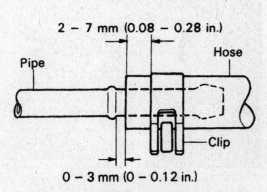

3.3 When connecting a rubber hose to a metal fuel line, be sure to overlap as shown here and use a new clamp to secure it

Steel tubing

Always use seamless steel tubing that meets the manufacturers specifications, or its equivalent, when replacing a metal fuel line or emissions line. Don't use copper or aluminum tubing to replace steel tubing because they can't withstand normal vehicle vibration. Disconnect the line at both ends (see *Connectors*), detach the retainers and remove the tubing from the vehicle. Replacement tubing is generally available in bulk form. Special bending and flaring tools will be needed to install the tubing into the vehicle, follow the manufacturers instructions for use of the tools. Using the original line as a pattern, form the new tubing to fit and attach it securely to the body or frame.

Connectors

Since the fuel lines are under constant pressure, a variety of connectors are used by the manufacturers in order to maintain leak-free connections. Some of these fuel line connector couplings are specific to a manufacturer and may require a special tool or technique for disconnection.

Clamp-type

Some models use clamps to secure rubber hoses onto metal fuel lines. Spring-type clamps should be replaced with new spring-type clamps or with screw-type clamps, anytime they are removed. Install a spring-clamp by sliding it onto the metal line, then push the hose in position. Squeeze the tabs together

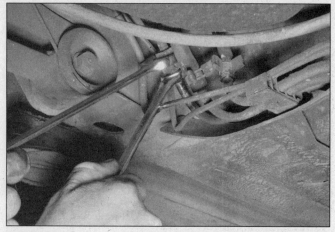

3.4 On threaded connections, use a backup wrench to steady the line while unthreading the fitting with another (preferably flare-nut) wrench

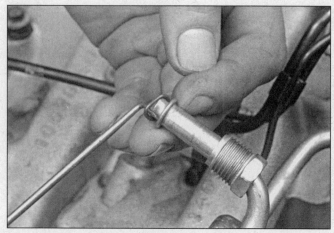

3.5 Always replace the fuel line O-ring (if equipped)

with pliers and slide the clamp over the hose. If installing screw-type clamps, tighten the screw securely.

Threaded-type

Probably the most common fuel injection line fitting is the threaded-type. On this type of connection, tightening the fitting draws the two lines, or line and component, together. The flare or sleeve compresses in the fitting to make a leak-free seal. Some threaded type fittings may also use an O-ring to seal the connection.

Use a backup wrench any time you loosen or tighten threaded-type fittings (see illustration). Check all O-rings for cuts, cracks and deterioration and replace any that appear worn or damaged (see illustration).

Chrysler quick-connect fittings

Late model fuel-injected Chrysler products use plastic quick-connect fittings. Disconnect this type of fitting by pushing in on the black plastic ring on the end of the fitting, then pull the lines apart (see illustration). When reconnecting, lubricate the ends of the fuel lines with clean engine oil, then push the fitting in until it clicks. Tug on the lines to ensure the connection is secure (see illustration).

Ford fittings

Late model Fords use several unique fuel line couplings, including the widely used spring-lock, hairpin and duck bill type.

Spring-lock coupling

This type of coupling is secured inside the male end by a garter spring that grips the flared end of the female fitting. For additional security, a tethered clip may also be used. Special tools (available at auto parts stores) are required to disconnect or connect the spring-lock coupling (see illustrations). These tools come in several different sizes depending on fuel line diameter.

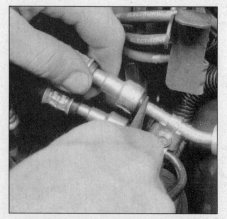

3.6 Disconnect the Chrysler quick-connect type of fitting by using needle nose pliers to depress the black plastic ring

3.7 After lubricating the end with clean engine oil, push the fitting in until it clicks, then tug to make sure its locked in place

3.8a These special tools (available at auto parts stores) are necessary when disconnecting or reconnecting some Ford spring-lock fuel lines

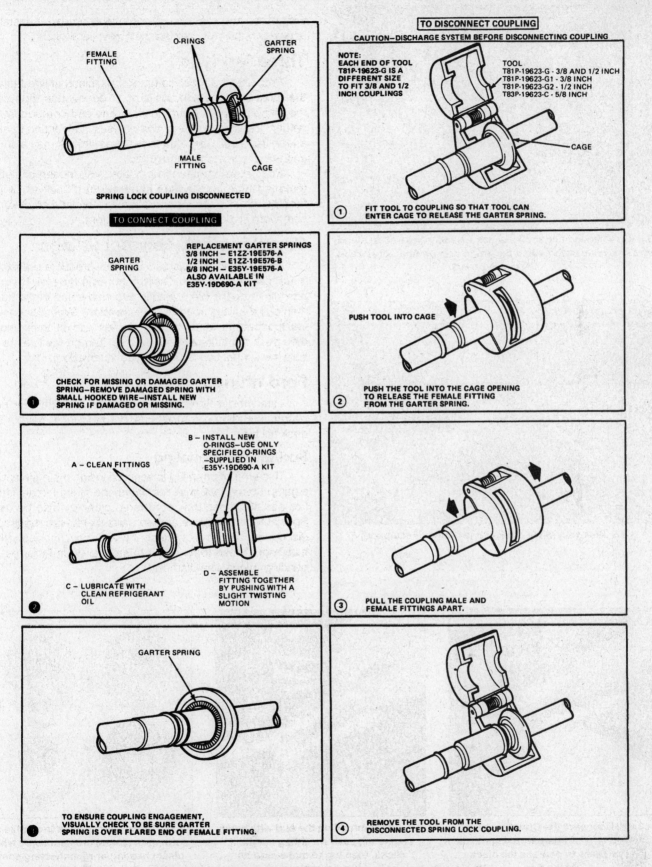

3.8b Ford spring-lock fuel line removal and installation details

3.9 Use a small screwdriver to pry off the safety clip

3.10a Open the spring lock coupling tool, place it in position around the coupling and close it securely

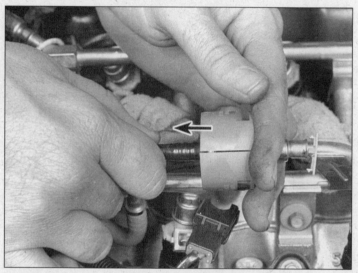

3.10b Disconnect the coupling by pushing the tool into the cage opening until the spring expands and the female fitting releases, then pull the fitting apart

Detach the tethered clip **(see illustration)**. Use the special tools to disconnect and reconnect the line **(see illustrations)**. Study the accompanying illustrations carefully before detaching any spring-lock coupling fitting.

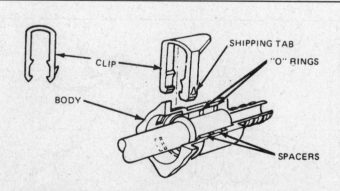

3.11 This exploded view shows how the hairpin clip fits into the connector

Hairpin clip

The plastic hairpin clip is used to lock the fitting securely over the fuel line.

Ford recommends discarding the clip after removal. Detach the clip by bending the shipping tab down until it clears the body coupling, then pry it off with a small screwdriver **(see illustration)**.

If you have to reuse the clip, carefully remove it by hand. First, gently spread each leg about 1/8-inch to disengage the body, then push the legs through the fitting. Pull lightly on the triangular end of the clip and work it clear of the line and fitting. Remember, don't use any tools to perform this procedure.

Once the clip is removed, grasp the fitting and hose and pull it straight off the fuel line.

Before installation, use a clean cloth to wipe off the line end. Check the inside of the line for dirt and/or obstructions, using aerosol carburetor cleaner to clean it out if necessary.

Install the fitting onto the line and push it into place until it clicks and pull on it to ensure that it's completely engaged **(see illustration)**. Insert the clip into any two adjacent openings in the fitting with the triangular portion of the clip pointing away from the fitting opening. Push the clip in with your finger until the legs are locked on the outside of the fitting.

Duck bill-type clip

The duck bill-type fitting uses an inner clip to secure it on the line **(see illustration)**. Look into the fitting to check for dirt and if you see any, use aerosol carburetor cleaner to wash it out before disconnecting the fitting. The seals may stick, so it's a good idea to twist the fitting on the line, then push and pull until it moves freely.

Disconnection

There are two ways to disconnect this type of fitting:

Using a special tool

The preferred method requires a special tool (available from your dealer or a auto parts store). To disengage the line from the fitting, align the slot in the push connect disassembly tool with either tab on the clip (90-degrees from the slots on the side of the fitting) and insert the tool **(see illustration)**. This disengages the duck bill from the line. Holding the tool and the line with one hand, pull the fitting off with the other **(see illustration)**. After disassembly, inspect and clean the line sealing surface. If any of the clip internal parts have been dislodged from the fitting, install them onto the fuel line prior to reconnecting.

Using pliers

You might have to use an alternate way to disconnect the clip because some fuel lines have a secondary bead that lines up with the outer surface making tool insertion difficult. Use small pliers with a jaw width of 3/16-inch or less. Line up the jaws with the openings in the side of the fitting, compress the part of the retaining clip that engages the body, then disengage the retaining clip (make sure both sides are disengaged).

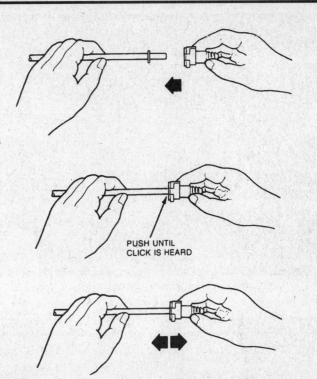

PUSH UNTIL
CLICK IS HEARD

3.12 Push the fittings together until you hear a click, then pull to make sure its engaged

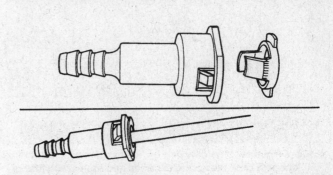

3.13 The duck bill-type clip snaps securely into the connector

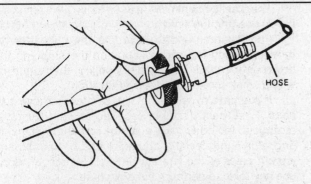

HOSE

3.14 Insert the special tool to disconnect the duck bill connector

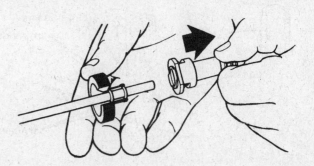

3.15 Once the tool has released the clip, pull the connector straight out of the fitting

3.16 Use aerosol carburetor cleaner or compressed air to wash or blow the dirt out of the fitting

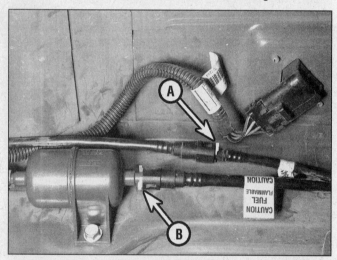

3.17 Disconnect this type of GM fitting by depressing the white tabs (arrows A and B) and pulling the lines apart

3.18 On this type of GM duck-bill connector, slide the plastic tool down into the fitting until it releases the internal clip, then pull the lines apart

Inspection

After removal, check the fitting and line for any internal parts that may have become dislodged from the fitting. The retaining clip should remain on the fuel line, but some internal parts may come off and these should be immediately inserted back on the line. Detach the clip from the line bead and discard it. Before reinstalling the fitting, wipe the line end with a clean cloth and check the inside of the fitting to make sure that it's clean.

Reconnection

Line up the fitting with the line and push it in until it clicks into place, then pull on it to make sure it's fully engaged. Install the new replacement clip by inserting one of the serrated edges on the duck bill portion into one of the openings. Push on the other side until the clip snaps into place.

General Motors fittings

Later GM models use both plastic quick connect and duck bill fuel line fittings. The quick connect fittings are easily released by pressing on the white plastic tabs, while the duck bill-type require a special plastic release tool available at a dealer or auto parts store.

Quick connect-type

On exposed fittings, keep dirt from getting into the fuel system by grasping the fittings securely and turning them a quarter-turn in each direction to loosen any dirt. Use compressed air or carburetor cleaner to blow or wash any dirt out of the fitting (see illustration).

Press on the white plastic tabs at the end of the fitting, then pull out to detach the fitting from the line or component (see illustration). Before reconnecting, lubricate the ends of the fuel lines with clean engine oil. Push the fitting in until it clicks, then pull on the line to check for a good connection.

Duck bill-type

A special tool (available from your dealer or an auto parts store) is necessary to disengage the duck bill from the line inside the fitting. Slide the tool over the line and down into the fitting, then push in until it disengages the clip. Holding the tool and the line with one hand, pull the fitting off with the other (see illustration).

Lubricate the line and fittings with clean engine oil, push the fitting in until it clicks, then make sure the connection is secure by pulling on the lines.

6 Component check and replacement

1 Introduction

Diagnosing fuel injection problems can be a very tedious and involved process unless the home mechanic can start with the basic system checks and look for the most obvious and simple answer to the problem. Although many driveability problems involve emissions systems, ignition systems and fuel system malfunctions, the diagnostic time can be reduced considerably once the basic structure or "backbone" of the system has been determined to be in good working order. For example, it is not a good idea to assume that the new fuel filter that was recently installed should be working fine and therefore the fuel pressure is sufficient. Many older vehicles will have corrosion in the fuel tank that constantly supplies debris to the fuel filter, fuel pump and injectors. With a few tools and some working knowledge of fuel injection systems, the home mechanic can repair a large percentage of the problems that occur. Don't feel overwhelmed by the process! Start with the most basic and obvious area of trouble and continue to look at each individual component of modern fuel injection systems. Here is a brief list to get started.

1) Check all the fuel lines and fittings for leaks and damage (see Section 2). This quick check will determine the presence of any leaking fuel lines (pressure drop), clogged fuel lines or damaged fuel fittings.
2) Check the fuel pump fuse and the fuel pump relay system for correct operation. This check will determine that the fuel pump electrical system is in working order. Electrical shorts, defective relays, broken fuses or defective fuel pumps are some of the most common fuel injection problems.
3) Check fuel pump pressure and transfer pump (if equipped) pressure. Now that the fuel pump is working or has been working, does it supply the correct fuel pressure at the injectors (end of line) from the fuel tank?
4) Check the fuel rail and the fuel injectors. This check will determine if the fuel is reaching the injectors and if the injectors are actually spraying fuel.
5) Check the throttle body and the throttle valve. This check will determine if the throttle body is regulating the amount of intake air that is allowed into the intake manifold.
6) Last, check the idle air control system for correct operation. Many modern fuel injection systems will not allow the home mechanic to adjust the idle speed but these checks will help to determine if the system is actually in need of repair.

These checks will give the home mechanic the knowledge that the basic fuel injection components are all up and working properly and from this point any diagnostic procedure for the emissions system or the ignition system can be easily accomplished. Remember that the fuel injection system on most vehicles consists of the fuel tank, fuel lines, fuel filter, fuel pump, fuel pressure regulator, fuel pump relay electrical system (fuses, relays, wiring harness, and the computer and related hardware.

2 Checking the fuel lines and fittings

Warning: *Gasoline is extremely flammable, so take extra precautions when you work on any part of the fuel system. Don't smoke or allow open flames or bare light bulbs near the work area, and don't work in a garage where a natural gas-type appliance (such as a water heater or a clothes dryer) with a pilot light is present. Since gasoline is carcinogenic, wear latex gloves when there's a possibility of being exposed to fuel, and, if you spill any fuel on your skin, rinse it off immediately with soap and water. Mop up any spills immediately and do not store fuel-soaked rags where they could ignite. The fuel system is under constant pressure, so, if any fuel lines are to be disconnected, the fuel pressure in the system must be relieved first (see Chapter 4 for more information). When you perform any kind of work on the fuel system, wear safety glasses and have a Class B type fire extinguisher on hand.*

Checking the fuel lines and the fittings may seem inconsequential but many fuel injection problems have been solved by replacing a fuel line or tightening up a leaking threaded fitting. There are, unfortunately, quite a few different types of fuel lines and fuel line arrangements on modern vehicles. Refer to Chapter 5 for a complete selection of procedures and illustrations for servicing the many different types of fuel line connectors and the specialized tools for separating them.

Always relieve the fuel pressure before disconnecting any fuel line or fitting! Refer to Chapter 4 for a complete list of procedures for the different automobiles. The fuel system is under high pressure (usually between 35 and 50 psi) and there is potential for fuel spraying the hands and face, manifold and electrical system or fender areas. Relieving the fuel pressure will save you and the vehicle from damage.

The typical modern fuel injection system uses a fuel feed line, return line and fuel vapor lines that extend from the fuel tank to the fuel injection components located near and on the engine. The fuel vapor lines extend to the throttle body and EVAP canister (most often located in the engine compartment). On some models it is located in the trunk area or in the panels in the rear section of a station wagon. It is very important that you recognize the different lines attached to the fuel tank. Refer to Chapter 5 for more information on fuel lines and how to check them.

Always check for contamination in the fuel when disconnecting and servicing the fuel lines, fittings or fuel filter. Look for excessive amounts of debris, rust or contaminants floating in the fuel. Also check for rotten-smelling fuel. This could be the result of old fuel, fuel that has been mixed with other harmful additives or the incorrect fuel (diesel fuel). Larger chunks of debris usually indicate severe rust or corrosion from inside the fuel tank. Be sure to have the fuel tank cleaned by a professional fuel tank service company. Many times it will be necessary to replace the old tank with a new one to avoid any further corrosion problems. Make sure the fuel system is free of any type of contamination before continuing with the fuel system checks!

The most important aspect of fuel line damage is the driveability problems that will occur as a result of the fuel line problem(s). Be sure to check the fuel pressure as part of the complete system inspection. Refer to Section 5 for checking the fuel pressure. Here is a brief list of all the possible symptoms:

1) Fuel pressure will increase if the fuel return line becomes pinched or soft and collapses. The best method is to follow the return line back to the fuel tank while carefully checking for damaged areas.
2) Fuel pressure will decrease if the fuel feed line becomes pinched, clogged or split (fuel leaks). Check carefully for damage all the way back to the fuel tank.
3) Damaged fuel lines will also show up as poor fuel mileage. Slight leaks from the fuel lines will decrease engine performance and fuel economy.
4) Clogged fuel lines will give erratic performance accelerating and under load, if the engine starts at all. Be sure to check the fuel tank for corrosion and debris.

3 Checking the fuel pump system

Now that the fuel tank and fuel lines are in good shape, the next most logical step is to check the fuel pump system. Most modern fuel injection systems use a single electric fuel pump, but some vehicles use a transfer fuel pump located in the fuel tank. The transfer fuel pump primes the main fuel pump (usually located next to the fuel tank) to assist in the long journey to the injectors. If the transfer pump becomes defective, the main fuel pump will continue to pump fuel to the engine but with a general lack of performance. This will be a large consideration when diagnosing fuel pressure problems (see Section 6). Most fuel pump systems are comprised of a fuel tank and lines, fuel pump(s), fuel filter and an electrical circuit that governs the fuel pump. This electrical circuit is constructed of a fuse, a relay (sometimes two relays) and the harness that connects the fuel pump to the fuse panel. Here is a list of the most logical steps to diagnose problems in the fuel pump system. These procedures are basic and can be accomplished using only a few special tools.

1) Check for sound coming from the fuel pump itself
2) Check the fuel pump fuse and/or circuit
3) Check fuel pump relay and/or circuit (check for power to the relay)
4) Check the fuel system operating pressure. This test will require activating the fuel pump from the relay connector or Diagnostic Test connector)
5) Check the fuel system rest pressure (bleed down)
6) Finally, check the direct fuel pump pressure (output pressure or "dead head pressure") and the direct fuel pump rest pressure (bleed down).

4 Fuel pump electrical circuit

The first test will determine if the fuel pump is actually operating. In the event the engine cranks but will not start, the most obvious test would be to find out if the fuel pump is pumping! The easiest place to hear the fuel pump in action is directly at the fuel filler cap. Simply remove the cap from the filler neck and have someone turn the ignition on and crank the engine over. Most electric fuel pumps will activate for a few seconds just by turning the ignition key to ON without the engine running. It should be relatively quiet when this test is performed. You should hear a whirring sound that lasts for at least a couple of seconds. If the pump is working and the engine still does not start, go back and check for a clogged fuel line or a defective ignition module or igniter. Remember, fuel, spark and compression are needed to make combustion! Most likely the engine will not start because of an ignition system problem. Refer to a *Haynes Automotive Repair Manual* for your vehicle for diagnostic procedures concerning the engine electrical and emissions control systems. If the fuel pump does not run, then you will need to continue down the list. Next check the fuel pump fuse.

The second test will determine if the fuse that governs the fuel pump circuit is blown **(see illustrations)** or corroded to the point of malfunctioning the fuel pump. Locate the fuse panel for your vehicle which is usually located under the dash area or in the engine compartment in a fuse/relay center. If necessary, consult your owner's manual or a *Haynes Automotive Repair Manual* for the correct location. Here are some typical fuel pump

4.1a To check for a blown fuse on the plastic type fuses, pull it out and inspect it visually for an open (1) or with the circuit activated, probe the exposed blades at the top of the fuse with a test light (2)

4.1b Ceramic fuses are often used on European cars (good fuse on the left, blown fuse on the right)

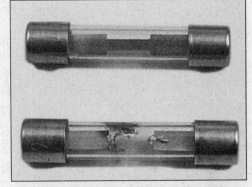

4.1c Traditional glass case fuse (good fuse on the top, blown fuse on the bottom)

4.2a Location of the fuel pump fuse on the Toyota Previa minivans

4.2b Location of the fuel pump fuse on a BMW 318i (fuse number 11)

fuse locations on some modern vehicles **(see illustrations)**. Carefully inspect the fuse to make sure it is intact. If the fuse is blown, replace it with a new one. Also check for corrosion on the fuel pump fuse terminals. Here is a good example of a fuse problem in a late model vehicle. Many Volvo 240 models will crank and turn over but not start until 20 or 30 seconds later. Down the road, the engine will hesitate slightly but continue to run. This intermittent problem gives the owner fits until the fuel pump fuse from the panel (driver's kick panel) is removed and cleaned. Carefully clean the blades on the fuse as well as the terminals on the panel.

The third test will determine if the fuel pump and/or circuit is operating properly. This check will involve a series of little checks and the process of elimination to resolve the problem. Simply remove the fuel pump relay and check for battery voltage to the relay connector, then jump the relay connector to apply battery voltage to the fuel pump and listen for the sound of the fuel pump activating. This will be the most common series of tests that must be performed on fuel injection systems.

4.2c The fuel pump fuse on the Saturn is located in slot number 12 adjacent to the relay panel under the center console

4.3a The fuel pump relay on a late model Ford Crown Victoria is located in a special relay assembly near the brake master cylinder. The designations are molded onto the cover

4.3b The fuel pump relay on many front-wheel drive GM vehicles is located on the right side of the engine compartment (1992 Pontiac Sunbird shown)

4.3c The GM Lumina APV minivan positions the fuel pump relay near the front of the engine compartment

A Fuel pump relay
B Cooling fan relay

C Air conditioning
   compressor relay

The only tough part of this step is finding the fuel pump relay. Many manufacturers have the fuel pump relay grouped together with other relays in a fuse/relay center usually located in the engine compartment or under the dash. They will have their designation stamped onto the cover (see illustrations). This is the easiest case. Now how about those models that have the relays UNMARKED and in small clumps throughout the entire engine compartment and under-dash area (see illustrations). These are the tough ones. In this situation it

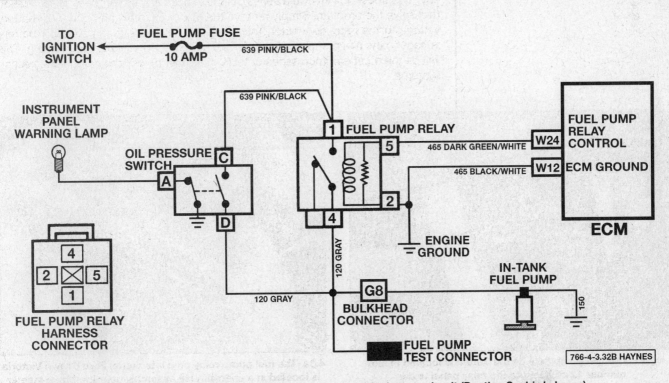

4.4a Schematic of a typical fuel pump relay, fuse and fuel pump circuit (Pontiac Sunbird shown)

Fuel Injection Diagnostic Manual

4.4b On GM Lumina APV minivans, check for battery voltage on the dark green/white wire on the fuel pump relay connector

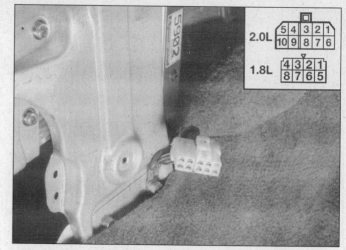

4.4c On Mitsubishi Eclipse, Chrysler Laser and Eagle Talon, remove the EFI relay under the center console and check for battery voltage on terminal number 10 (2.0L engine) or terminal number 8 (1.8L engine)

will be necessary to get additional information. Sometimes the owner's manual will have the location of the relays. If not; obtain a component location diagram from your *Haynes Automotive Repair Manual* or wiring diagram and compare the color of the wires to the ones listed.

Now that you have located the fuel pump relay, remove it from the connector, turn the ignition key ON (engine not running) and check for battery voltage. If you have a wiring schematic for the vehicle, follow the wire directly from the fuel pump relay connector to the ignition key. Check for battery voltage **(see illustrations)**. If you don't have a wiring schematic, probe the terminals of the fuel pump relay connector with the voltmeter or test light until battery voltage is found. If there is NO battery voltage present at the fuel pump connector then there is a bad fuse or a problem in the wiring harness somewhere between the fuse panel and the ignition key and/or battery. Diagnose the electrical short before continuing any further.

Now that battery voltage is present at the fuel pump relay connector, jump

4.4d It is a good idea to check for battery voltage using a voltmeter rather than a test light because it will determine the exact voltage or voltage drop at the relay connector (Crown Victoria shown)

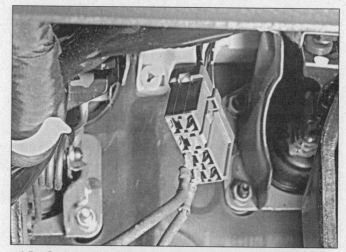

4.5a On late model Accords (1990 through 1994), install the jumper wire into terminals number 5 and number 7 of the fuel pump relay connector with the ignition key On (engine not running). They use an EFI relay located under the dash

4.5b On a BMW 325i, use a jumper wire across terminals number 30 and number 87

4.5c Remove the Saturn fuel pump relay located under the dash near the center console, and jump the top and bottom terminals of the panel

the connector to activate the fuel pump **(see illustrations)**. It will be necessary to check a wiring diagram to determine exactly which two terminals govern the fuel pump. It is possible to check for continuity between the fuel pump harness connector and the relay connector to determine the correct terminal. It is a bit awkward to stretch a jumper lead all the way from the fuel pump relay connector to the fuel pump but it is not impossible. **Caution**: *If the fuse blows when the jumper wire is installed in the relay connector, replace the fuse with a new one and double-check the terminal designation. Most likely, the jumper was inserted into the wrong terminal or it accidentally touched the wrong terminal and overloaded the circuit. You should hear a loud whirring sound from the fuel tank area or from under the body. A quick note on jumping the fuel pump - many manufacturers include a specialized test port to jump the fuel pump. This*

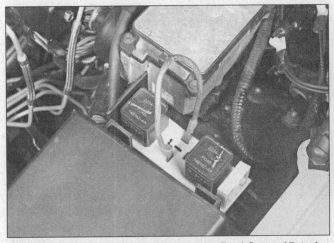

4.6a Fuel pump jumper location for the Ford Crown Victoria

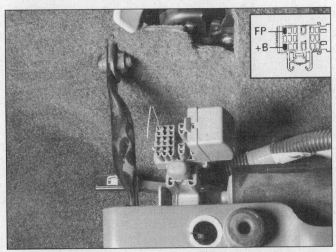

4.6b On Toyota Previa minivans, bridge terminals FP and B+ using a jumper wire or paper clip. The SST terminal box is located under the driver's seat

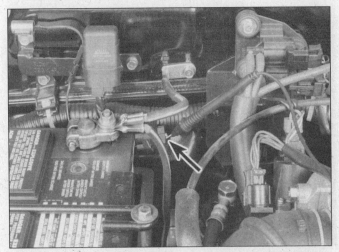

4.6c On Mitsubishi Eclipse, Chrysler Laser and Eagle Talon, install a jumper wire from the positive (+) terminal of the battery to the fuel pump check terminal taped to the wiring harness on the firewall behind the battery

4.6d The test terminal on many GM vehicles is located next to the battery

4.6e On Ford systems, ground terminal FP (top left terminal) to activate the fuel pump

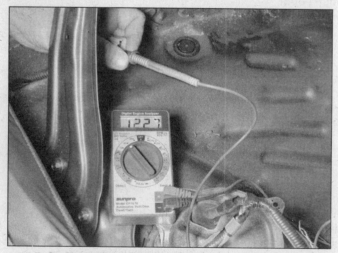

4.7 On late model Accords, remove the carpet from the trunk area and check for battery voltage to the fuel pump using a voltmeter

test connector is usually located in the engine compartment **(see illustrations)**. *Most require a jumper wire from the battery to the test port to power the fuel pump, but some use a simple jumper wire from a power source on the test connector. These test ports or test connectors are very handy to quick - check the fuel pump pressure but they do not check the working condition of the fuel pump relay. That is why it is a good idea to go ahead and make all the basic checks without using the test port unless necessary.*

If the fuel pump does not activate, it will be necessary to trace the wiring harness back to the fuel pump and check for battery voltage **(see illustration)**. If battery voltage is available to the fuel pump, replace the fuel pump with a new one. By carefully and methodically checking the relay and circuit all the way back to the fuel pump, the home mechanic can easily determine, by using the process of elimination, why the fuel pump does not work.

Before finishing the relay diagnostics, let us discuss what to do when battery voltage is available to the relay but the relay does not energize the circuit. In this situation it will be necessary to test the relay. The only easier method would be to replace the relay with a known working part and start the engine. If a test relay is not available and you want to be sure the part is bad before spending the non-refundable cost, here is a quick check.

The relay testing procedures are subheaded into three different categories; mechanical relays, multiple circuit relays and solid state relays. Mechanical relays that operate a single purpose fuel pump system usually have three or four terminals. The first category covers single circuit, mechanical relays. The second category covers relays that have more than one circuit involved in their control function. This category is called multiple circuit relays. Last category is the solid state relays. These relays operate on low voltage signals and they must be diagnosed using different methods. **Note**: *We recommend using the correct wiring diagram for your vehicle to determine the proper terminal designations for the relay you're testing. However, if wiring diagrams are not available, you may be able to determine the test hook-ups from the information that follows.*

Mechanical relays

Note: *The information that follows does not apply to polarity reversing relays, which are used in some power accessory circuits.*

Relays with four terminals

On most relays with four terminals, two of the four terminals are for the relay's control circuit (they connect to the relay's coil). The other two are for the relay's power circuit (they connect to the armature contact and the fixed contact).

If you have wiring diagrams for the vehicle, you can figure out which terminals hook up to which parts of the relay. Often, relay terminals are marked as an aid.

As a general rule, the two thicker gauge wires connected to the relay are for the power circuit; the two thinner gauge wires are for the control circuit.

Remove the relay from the vehicle and check for continuity between the relay's power circuit terminals. There should be no continuity.

Connect a fused jumper wire between one of the two control circuit terminals and the positive battery terminal. Connect another jumper wire between the other control circuit terminal and ground. When the connections are made, the relay should click. On some relays, polarity may be critical, so, if the relay doesn't click, try swapping the jumper wires on the control circuit terminals.

With the jumper wires connected, check for continuity between the power circuit terminals. Now there should be continuity.

If the relay fails any of the above tests, replace it.

Relays with three terminals

If the relay has three terminals, it's a good idea to check the vehicle's wiring diagram to determine which terminals connect to which of the relay's components. Most three-terminal relays are either case-grounded or externally-grounded.

On a case-grounded relay, one side of the relay's control circuit grounds through the relay case, eliminating the need for the fourth terminal. This type of relay requires the case to be securely connected to a good chassis ground. Check this type of relay the same way you would a four-terminal relay, noting that one of the control circuit's terminals is actually the relay case.

On an externally-grounded relay, one of the relay's terminals is connected to a positive power source. We'll call this the battery power terminal. Inside the relay, the battery power terminal is connected to one side of both the relay's power and control circuits. Another terminal is connected to the other side of the control circuit; the circuit is completed through a switch to ground. The third terminal is connected to the other side of the power circuit; it's grounded at the circuit's load component. This type of three-terminal relay is sometimes a plug-in type with no connection between the case and ground.

To check an externally-grounded relay, remove it from the vehicle and check for continuity between the relay's battery power terminal and it's power circuit terminal. There should be no continuity.

Hook up a fused jumper wire between the battery power terminal and the positive battery terminal. Connect another jumper wire between the relay's control circuit terminal and ground. The relay should click.

With the jumper wires in place, connect a test light between the relay's power circuit terminal and ground. The test light should light. If the relay fails any of these tests, replace it. This diagram **(see illustration)** shows how an externally-grounded three-terminal relay (a horn relay in this case) is connected to a vehicle's electrical system

Multiple circuit relays

Multiple circuit relays are checked the same way as relays with four terminals. It will be necessary to acquire a wiring diagram for the system to properly identify the exact terminals that govern the fuel pump system. Then it is just a matter of checking the relay within the relay. Follow the previous steps.

Solid state relays

A transistor can act as solid-state relay in a circuit, and this is one of the most important uses of a transistor in automotive electrical systems. They operate differently in theory but function the same as an electromagnetic type relay. The combination of diodes, resistors and zener diodes can control the switching action rapidly and efficiently. Have solid state relays checked by a dealer service department or an electronics repair shop.

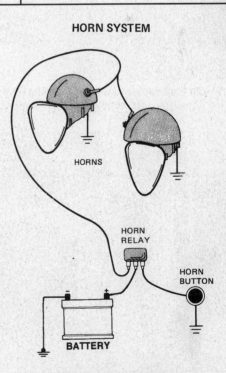

HORN SYSTEM

HORNS

HORN RELAY

HORN BUTTON

BATTERY

4.8 This diagram shows how an externally-grounded three terminal relay (a horn in this case) is connected to a vehicle's electrical system

5 Fuel pressure testing

This section will describe the testing procedures for checking the fuel pump pressure output and interpret the pressure readings to determine the actual problem within the fuel system. This section will be divided into two sections: mechanical fuel injection and electronic fuel injection. *Mechanical fuel injection* will cover the various Continuous Injection Systems (CIS) equipped on early European models while *Electronic fuel injection* will cover the remaining types. **Note**: *Throughout the testing procedures that follow concerning the CIS systems, K-basic and K-lambda will be referred to as the early CIS systems while KE and KE-Motronic will be referred to as CIS-E and CIS-E Motronic systems. This is a very important distinction that must be observed because several of the tests for the mechanical fuel injection system are similar and shared by both the early and later styles, while other tests are quite different and particular to only one type of CIS system. Electronic fuel injection covers throttle body injection systems as well as EFI systems installed on Ford's, General Motor's and Chrysler vehicles. Electronic Fuel Injection also covers the Bosch LH-Jetronic systems, PGM-FI systems on Hondas, and many other pulsed-type injection systems on modern fuel-injected engines. Read Chapter 1 to gain a complete understanding of your particular fuel- injection system. All the testing procedures will generally work on all models of vehicles. Refer to the appropriate Haynes Automotive Repair Manual for any additional fuel injection diagnostic procedures.*

Mechanical fuel injection

Warning: *Gasoline is extremely flammable, so take extra precautions when you work on any part of the fuel system. Don't smoke or allow open flames or bare light bulbs near the work area, and don't work in a garage where a natural gas-type appliance (such as a water heater or a clothes dryer) with a pilot light is present. Since gasoline is carcinogenic, wear latex gloves when there's a possibility of being exposed to fuel, and, if you spill any fuel on your skin, rinse it off immediately with soap and water. Mop up any spills immediately and do not store fuel-soaked rags where they could ignite. The fuel system is under constant pressure, so, if any fuel lines are to be disconnected, the fuel pressure in the system must be relieved first (see Chapter 4 for more information). When you perform any kind of work on the fuel system, wear safety glasses and have a Class B type fire extinguisher on hand.* **Note**: *Be sure to relieve the fuel pressure before performing any fuel system pressure checks. Refer to Chapter 4 for the procedure.*

Once you have confirmed that the fuel pump(s) is/are receiving power (see Section 4), proceed with the fuel pressure tests:

System pressure - the basic fuel pressure produced by the fuel pump and maintained by the pressure relief valve in the fuel distributor (CIS) or the diaphragm pressure regulator (CIS-E and CIS-E Motronic).

Control pressure - the difference between system pressure and lower chamber pressure in the fuel distributor as determined by the control pressure regulator (CIS) or the differential pressure regulator (CIS-E and CIS-E Motronic). It is used to counter system pressure and regulate the movement of the control plunger.

Residual pressure - the amount of pressure which remains in the closed system after the engine and fuel pump are shut off.

Differential pressure (CIS-E and CIS-E Motronic)

On CIS systems, connect the fuel pressure gauge between the control pressure regulator and the fuel distributor with the valve side of the gauge toward the control pressure regulator **(see illustration)**. On CIS-E and CIS-E Motronic systems, connect the above mentioned fuel pressure gauge (or equivalent) between the upper fuel distributor test port and the lower chamber test port **(see illustration)**. Install the shut-off valve toward the upper chamber test port. The position

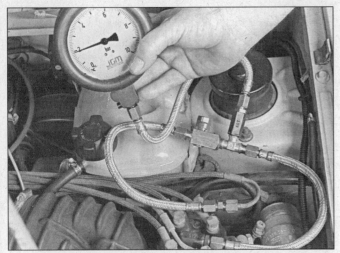

5.1 Be sure to connect the gauge with the valve on the control pressure regulator side on early CIS systems (VW Rabbit shown)

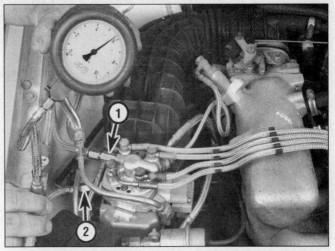

5.2 On CIS-E systems, connect the gauge to the fuel distributor test port upper chamber (1) and the lower chamber (2) (cold start valve supply line removed from the cold start valve). Be sure the shut-off valve is positioned between the upper chamber and the pressure gauge

of the shut-off valve is very important as it will allow testing of the lower chamber differential pressure by shutting off fuel to the upper chamber.

Checking system pressure (all CIS systems)

First check the system pressure. On early CIS systems, close the valve on the pressure gauge (this prevents fuel from entering the control pressure regulator). Also on early CIS systems, disconnect the electrical connectors to the auxiliary air valve and the control pressure regulator. This will prevent any warm-up conditions occurring before the cold control pressure is measured. Start the engine and observe the reading. System pressure should be about 65 to 85 psi for the early CIS systems.

On CIS-E and CIS-E Motronic systems, open the valve **(see illustration 5.2)** from the upper chamber on the fuel pressure gauge. Do not start the engine but instead remove the fuel pump relay and jump the fuel pump at the relay connector with a jumper lead (see Section 4). The system pressure should be between 75 to 95 psi on CIS-E and CIS-E Motronic systems (depending on the year, make and model). If the system pressure is too low, check for leaks, a clogged fuel filter or a damaged fuel line blocking the fuel flow. If no other cause can be found, the pressure on early CIS systems can be adjusted by adding shims to the pressure relief valve **(see illustrations)**. Refer to the *Fuel Distributor* procedure later in this section for more detailed information.

On early CIS systems, if the fuel pressure cannot be accurately adjusted, then the fuel distributor is faulty and must be replaced. On CIS-E and CIS-E Motronic systems, fuel pressure is not adjustable. If the fuel pressure is incorrect, replace the diaphragm pressure regulator.

Checking control pressure on early CIS systems

Next, check the control pressure. First check cold control pressure. Connect the electrical connectors onto the auxiliary air valve and the control pressure regulator. Turn the valve on the fuel

5.3a The system pressure regulator is located in the lower chamber of the fuel distributor

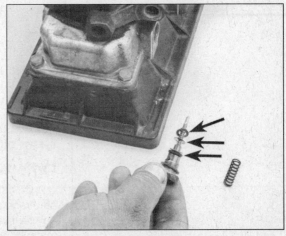

5.3b System pressure can be adjusted by removing or adding shims (arrows)

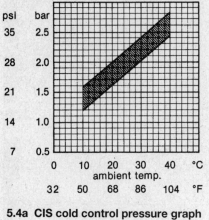

5.4a CIS cold control pressure graph for California models

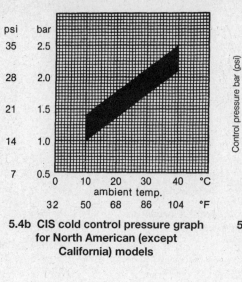

5.4b CIS cold control pressure graph for North American (except California) models

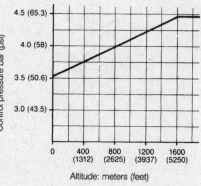

5.5 Graph of warm control pressure as affected by altitude (US cars except California) - example: at 800 meters (2625 feet) above sea level, warm control pressure should be approximately 58 psi

pressure gauge to the open position. Make sure the vehicle is cold (68-degrees F) in order to obtain an accurate pressure reading.

Start the vehicle and observe the gauge. The fuel pressure will increase as the temperature of the vehicle warms up **(see illustrations)**. Be sure to observe the pressure reading as soon as the engine is started. The first pressure reading will change very quickly as the engine warms up! The initial pressure value is called cold control pressure. The cold control pressure should be accurate according to the climate and altitude of the region. Most operate cold between 20 and 35 psi.

If the cold control pressure is too high, check for a fuel line that is blocked or kinked. Also, check the fuel union at the control pressure regulator for a plugged filter screen. If no problems are found in the fuel lines, replace the control pressure regulator. **Warning**: *Be sure to relieve the fuel pressure before disconnecting any fuel lines* (see Chapter 4).

To check the warm control pressure, run the engine until the control pressure is no longer increasing (approximately 2 minutes) and observe the gauge. The warm control pressure should be about 38 to 58 psi depending on the year make and model. Be sure to check your make and model for an alternate control pressure regulator for your area. Some models have control pressure regulators which compensate for changes in altitude. Refer to the chart to convert warm control pressure vs. altitude above sea level **(see illustration)**.

If the warm control pressure is too high, check for a blocked or kinked fuel line. Also, check the fuel union at the control pressure regulator for a plugged filter screen. If no problems are found, replace the control pressure regulator.

If warm control pressure is low, or takes more than 2 minutes to reach its highest value, test the resistance of the heating element and test for voltage reaching the harness connector at the control pressure regulator.

Checking differential pressure on CIS-E and CIS-E Motronic systems

Differential pressure, which is controlled by the differential pressure regulator, is the difference in pressure between the upper and lower chambers of the fuel distributor. The differential pressure regulator determines the pressure differential at the fuel distributor metering ports, which determines how much fuel flows to the injectors, which in turn determines the air/fuel mixture. Here's how to check it:

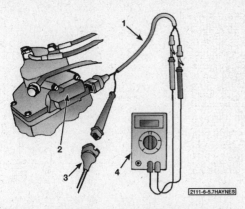

5.6 Special harness adapter for testing differential pressure actuator current with the engine running

1   Harness adapter
2   Fuel distributor
3   Engine electrical harness
4   Digital volt/ohm meter

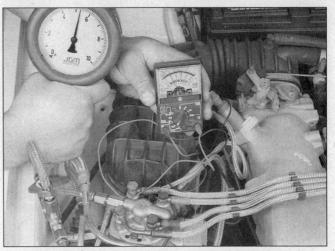

5.7 Check differential pressure with the valve closed, the ignition key On (engine not running) and the fuel pump relay connector jumped to power the fuel pump. Pressure should be approximately 70 to 85 psi (5.5bar [metric equivalent]) with 10 milliamps of current

First, install an ammeter into the circuit that controls the differential pressure regulator. This can easily be accomplished BY connecting an electrical adapter into the circuit **(see illustration)**. If the tool is not available, backprobe the electrical connector at the differential pressure regulator with the probes from the meter. Hook up the fuel pressure gauge, close the valve on the gauge **(see illustration)**, turn the ignition key ON (engine not running) and bypass the fuel pump relay so the fuel pump will run (refer to Section 4).

Note the indicated differential pressure (gauge valve closed) and the differential pressure actuator current. It should be between 70 and 85 psi fuel pressure and 10 milliamps of current. There should be approximately 5 psi fuel pressure difference between the system pressure and the differential pressure.

If the differential pressure is too low, measure the volume of fuel coming from the fuel distributor return line. Disconnect the fuel distributor fuel line from the lower test port (at the gauge) **(see illustration)** and put the detached line in a measuring container suitable for catching fuel. Make sure the fuel gauge valve is closed and run the fuel pump. After one minute, there should be 130 to 150 cc of fuel in the container. When you reattach the line, use new sealing washers and tighten the banjo fitting. If the quantity of fuel is correct, but the differential pressure tested below specifications, the differential pressure regulator is faulty. Replace it with a new part. If the quantity of fuel is incorrect, recheck the system pressure (see above). If the system pressure is within specification but the differential pressure and the measured fuel quantity aren't, the fuel distributor is probably faulty.

Now simulate the differential pressure of a cold engine. Hook up an ammeter to the differential pressure regulator as described above. On CIS-E (not CIS-E Motronic) systems, disconnect the temperature sending unit electrical connector and then the electrical connector for the coolant temperature sensor and connect a 15 k-ohm resistor across the connector terminals **(see illustration)**. Turn on the ignition (engine not running) and operate the fuel pump.

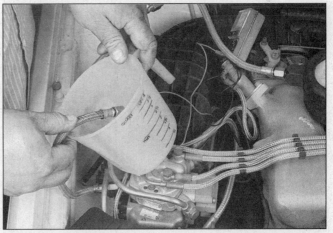

5.8 After one minute, there should be 130 to 150 cc of fuel collected in a graduated measuring cup

5.9 Connect a 15K ohm resistor between the coolant temperature sensor and the sending unit to simulate a cool running engine

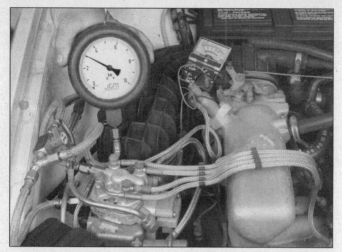

5.10 Residual pressure should not drop below 20 to 40 psi on most CIS systems

Differential pressure should be about 65 psi and differential pressure regulator current should be approximately 60 milliamps. There should be approximately 15 psi difference between the cold differential pressure versus the system pressure. If the differential pressure regulator current is within specifications, but the differential pressure isn't, the differential pressure regulator is faulty and must be replaced. If both the pressure and the regulator current are out of specifications, look for an electrical problem (see *Electrical tests*). But first, check all wires and connections. Check for a good ground connection at the cold-start valve. If you can't find any other faults, the electronic control unit is probably faulty.

Checking residual pressure (early CIS, CIS-E and CIS-E Motronic systems)

Finally, check the residual pressure. Check the residual pressure with the gauge connected as described in the previous fuel pressure tests **(see illustration)**.

When the engine is warm shut the engine off and leave the gauge connected. Wait ten minutes and observe the gauge. The fuel pressure should not have dropped off below 20 to 40 psi (depending on year, make and model).

If the pressure drops off excessively, check for leaks in the fuel lines, the fuel distributor, the injectors, the cold start valve and the oxygen sensor frequency valve. Also check residual pressure at the fuel supply line from the fuel pump. Disconnect the gauge from the fuel distributor and the control pressure regulator and reconnect those lines. Next, connect the gauge to the main supply line from the fuel pump and be sure to close the valve. Run the fuel pump with a jumper wire as described in Section 4 and pressurize the system until the gauge reads 49 to 55 psi. The pressure should not drop off below 38 psi within ten minutes.

If the pressure drops off excessively and there are no apparent leaks between the fuel pump and the gauge, pinch closed the fuel line between the tank and the fuel pump and observe the gauge. If residual pressure now remains steady, then the check valve in the fuel pump is faulty. If the residual pressure still drops off quickly, then the fuel accumulator is at fault.

On CIS systems, before changing the spacers in the fuel pressure regulator, be sure to double check the fuel pressure tests. This fuel pressure regulator can easily be changed to increase or decrease actual system pressure.

Electrical tests for CIS-E and CIS-E Motronic

Note: *The following electrical tests are presented in a specific sequence so you can logically isolate the cause of a problem, so it's imperative that you perform them in the order shown.*

Measuring differential pressure regulator current

Although the differential pressure regulator itself can't be diagnosed or repaired, the measurement of its current output during some of the following tests is the most important means by which you can check the operation of CIS-E and CIS-E Motronic fuel injection systems.

VW dealers use a special test harness **(see illustration)** to hook up a digital ammeter/multimeter to the differential pressure regulator. If you don't want to buy this special harness, you can fabricate your own leads and hook up an ammeter or multimeter between the corresponding terminals of the regulator and the harness connector. If you decide to make your own test leads, make sure all connections between the leads and the two sides of the connector, and the ammeter/multimeter itself are secure. Use male spade type terminals of the same dimensions as the terminals on the regulator for the harness end; use female terminals for the regulator ends of the leads. If you don't have good positive

5.11 This convenient test harness (VW 1315A/1) for checking the differential pressure regulator current on CIS-E Motronic systems is available through specialty tool distributors

connections, you'll get an erroneous current measurement - the current values you'll be measuring are in milliamps (mA), so good connections are essential. **Note**: *It is not possible to backprobe the electrical connector on the differential pressure regulator to obtain current values that require the engine to be running.*

After-start and cold-running enrichment

Note: *If the CIS-E system is functioning properly, it provides extra fuel to the engine when it's cold by increasing differential pressure regulator current for a brief period of time after starting and during warm-up. The control unit gets its information from two sources: When the starter is cranked, it signals the control unit to initiate after-start enrichment, a phase which lasts about 40 seconds. If the engine is still cold, a coolant temperature sensor prolongs this phase. Using the coolant temperature sensor as its monitor, the control unit gradually decreases the cold-running enrichment phase as the engine warms up. Here's how to test these two functions:*

Remove the fuel pump fuse and the electrical connector from the coolant temperature sensor to simulate an open circuit, i.e. a cold engine. To check cold-running enrichment, turn the ignition to On (engine not running). Hook up a digital ammeter to measure the differential pressure regulator current. Indicated current should be about 80 mA. **Note**: *Don't disconnect the ammeter - you'll need to measure differential regulator current again during some of the following tests.*

You must activate the starter to check after-start enrichment, but you don't want the engine to actually start, so disconnect the ignition coil wire from the distributor cap and use a jumper wire to ground it. Actuate the starter for two to three seconds, then leave the ignition turned on. The differential pressure regulator current should increase to more than 140 mA for 20 to 50 seconds **(see illustration)**, then return to the cold-running value above. When the test is completed, turn off the ignition and reconnect the coil wire, install the fuel pump fuse and the coolant temperature sensor electrical connector.

To test the coolant temperature sensor, disconnect the electrical connector and check the resistance across the sensor terminals. The resistance varies with the temperature of the engine coolant. If the indicated resistance doesn't match the value shown, replace the sensor. Refer to Section 16 for additional information on testing the coolant temperature sensor.

5.12 After cranking the engine for 2 to 3 seconds (coil wire disconnected and grounded), the differential pressure regulator current should increase to 140 mA for 20 to 50 seconds. This signal will allow for cold enrichment

Cold-acceleration enrichment

Note: *To maintain good throttle response while the engine is still warming up, the CIS-E system provides extra fuel when the throttle valve is suddenly opened. How does the control unit "know" when the throttle valve is opened? A potentiometer mounted on the side of the airflow sensor housing sends a voltage signal to the control unit. The strength of this voltage signal varies in accordance with the position of the air sensor plate. The potentiometer is adjusted at the factory and its mounting screws are sealed, so it shouldn't need adjustment. However, if the following test determines that it's faulty and must be replaced, you'll have to adjust the new unit. Here's how to check it:*

Unplug the electrical connector for the coolant temperature sensor and remove the black rubber boot for the air intake from the airflow sensor plate. Turn on the ignition and immediately raise the airflow sensor plate to its stop. The differential pressure regulator current should briefly exceed 140 milliamps - then return to - the cold-running enrichment value given in the previous test above. Turn off the ignition and plug in the electrical connector for the temperature sensor.

If the indicated current isn't as specified above, check the operation of the

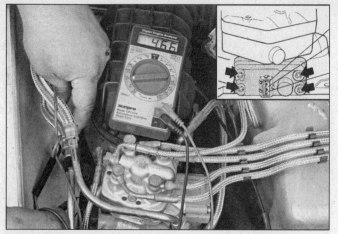

5.13 To check the potentiometer, install an ohmmeter onto the indicated terminals and observe the resistance changes as the throttle is activated from idle through wide open throttle

1 Terminal 1 (positive terminal)
2 Terminal 2
3 Terminal 3 (negative terminal)

potentiometer. Unplug the electrical connector for the potentiometer and use an ohmmeter to measure the resistance between the indicated terminals **(see illustration)**. The resistance between terminals should change immediately while slowly and evenly lifting the sensor plate. The resistance should steadily increase, without any flat spots. If the potentiometer doesn't exhibit change or there is a delay in the resistance change while the system is being accelerated, first try adjusting the potentiometer. If that does not work, replace it.

To replace the potentiometer, remove its mounting screws and pull it off the fuel distributor. Install the new potentiometer and mounting screws, but leave the screws just loose enough to permit adjustment of the potentiometer. Lift the airflow sensor plate until it's flush with the narrowest point in the air cone and hold the plate steady in this position. Adjust the position of the potentiometer until the voltage between the center and bottom terminals is approximately 0.2 volts (CIS-E) or 0.6 volts (CIS-E Motronic), then tighten the screws. Consult a *Haynes Automotive Repair Manual* for the exact adjusting procedure for the potentiometer for your vehicle.

Full-throttle enrichment

Note: *Full-throttle enrichment can only occur when the engine is warmed up, the engine speed is above 4000 rpm and the throttle is fully open. When the throttle is opened all the way, a full-throttle switch supplies a signal to the control unit. Here's how to check it*:

Unplug the electrical connector from the coolant temperature sensor. Using a jumper wire, bridge the connector terminals. Start the engine and let it warm up. Move the throttle until the engine speed exceeds 4,000 rpm and close the full-throttle switch on top of the throttle valve. The differential pressure regulator current should increase to about 14 mA.

If the indicated differential pressure regulator current is high, first verify that your jumper wire at the temperature sensor connector is fully seated into both terminals; if the current doesn't increase when you close the full-throttle switch, either the switch itself is faulty or the rpm signal from the ignition control unit is faulty. The full load switch can be checked with an ohmmeter. There should be continuity when the switch is closed.

Deceleration fuel shut-off

Note: *During deceleration, fuel flow to the injectors is shut off to enhance fuel economy. At normal operating temperature, fuel flow is cut off when the throttle is closed at engine speeds above 1600 rpm, and resumes when rpm drops below 1300 rpm (these limits are slightly higher when the engine isn't yet warmed up). The signal for a closed throttle is supplied to the control unit by an idle switch mounted under the throttle body. To check it*:

Unplug the electrical connector from the coolant temperature sensor and bridge the connector terminals with a jumper wire. Start the engine and let it warm up.

Increase engine speed to about 3,000 rpm, then release the throttle. The positive differential pressure regulator current should momentarily change to a negative reading (about -45 mA), then return to its normal value **(see illustration)**.

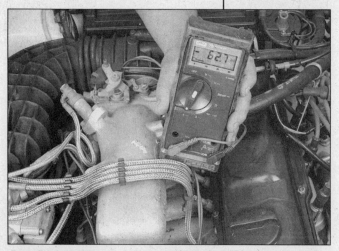

5.14 Deceleration fuel shut-off will be indicated by a negative mA value when the engine speed is raised to 3,000 rpm, then released (deceleration)

5.15a Be sure to clean all the sludge and carbon deposits from the inside of the sensor plate and funnel before checking clearances

5.15b The sensor plate is located at the bottom of the venturi

5.16 The airflow sensor plate must be centered in the venturi

If the current doesn't change to a negative value of about -45 mA, either the idle switch is incorrectly adjusted or the rpm signal from the control unit is faulty.

Component check and replacement for all CIS systems

Airflow sensor - description, check and adjustment

Description

The airflow sensor measures the air drawn in by the engine. As airflows past the airflow sensor plate, the plate is lifted, which lifts the control plunger in the fuel distributor to meter the fuel (see Chapter 1). The airflow sensor plate and its conical venturi are carefully machined to achieve an optimal ratio between air and fuel for every operating condition, from idle to full throttle. If the sensor plate is binding, or off-center, or the lever has too much resistance, the fuel distributor won't respond correctly to the airflow sensor plate.

Check

To check the position of the sensor plate it is necessary to remove the air intake casing, but before doing this, run the engine for a few minutes to build up pressure in the fuel lines. Loosen the clamp and take off the air intake duct. The sensor plate may now be seen **(see illustrations)**. Check the position of the plate relative to the venturi **(see illustration)**. There must be a gap of 0.004 in (0.10 mm) all around, between it and the venturi **(see illustration)**. The plate surface must also be even with the bottom of the air cone with the fuel line residual pressure removed **(see illustration)**.

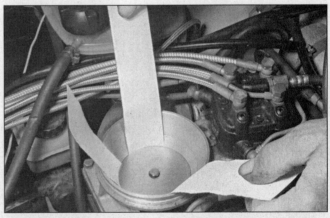

5.17 Use strips of regular typing paper positioned equally around the perimeter of the sensor plate to check for uneven clearances between the sensor plate and the air funnel

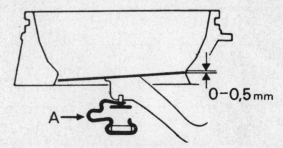

5.18 On early CIS systems, when the sensor plate is at rest (ignition off), the plate should be within 0.020 inches (0.5 mm) of the lower edge of the venturi

5.19a Location of the airflow sensor adjusting clip

5.19b Carefully pry the clip up or down to raise or lower the sensor plate while being very careful not to damage the mating surfaces of the sensor plate and the air funnel with the screwdriver

If the level is not correct, then the plate should be lifted with a magnet or pliers, being careful not to scratch the bore. The clip underneath may be bent to adjust the level, using small pliers **(see illustrations)**. Pull the plate up as far as it will come and the job can be done without dismantling anything else. The tolerance is 0.020 in (0.5 mm). On downdraft fuel distributors, the measurement is exactly the same except the situation is reversed.

Check-CIS-E and CIS-E Motronic

On CIS-E and CIS-Motronic, there are two sensor plate adjustments that must be checked:

1) **Zero position** (updraft fuel distributors) - In the zero position the updraft plate must rest below the edge of the funnel so you can see most of the vertical face of the air funnel **(see illustration)**. The plate must not rest part way up the face but if in doubt, consult a *Haynes Automotive Repair Manual* for the exact specification. Using a depth gauge, measure the zero position of the updraft plate with the gauge closest to the fuel distributor. The depth should be 0.075 inches (1.9 mm). Bend the wire clip to adjust the sensor plate as described previously.

Zero position (downdraft fuel distributors) - In the zero position the sensor plate must be above the edge of the funnel furthest from the fuel distributor so you cannot see most of the vertical face of the air funnel. The plate must not rest part way up the face but if in doubt, consult a *Haynes Automotive Repair Manual* for the exact specification. To adjust the position, it will be necessary to move the guide pin for the spring stop. This must be performed by a dealer service department.

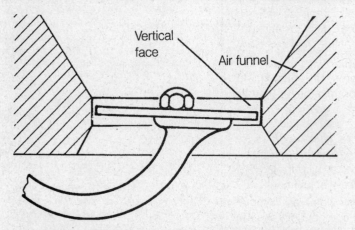

5.20 Notice on KE systems that the vertical face of the funnel is positioned almost at the lower edge of the face

5.21 Carefully touch the sensor plate lightly to drop it down into the basic position

2) **Basic position** (updraft fuel distributors) - Carefully lift the sensor plate until you feel the sensor level plate contact the control plunger. This checks the gap necessary for freeplay between the plunger and the seal. This gap should be no more than 0.08 inches (2 mm). If this clearance is incorrect, it may be possible to adjust the gap by turning the mixture screw on the arm. Take the fuel distributor to a dealer service department for the necessary adjustments.

Basic position (downdraft fuel distributors) - Carefully press the sensor plate down until you feel the sensor level plate contact the control plunger **(see illustration)**. Do not press excessively. You will not feel this resistance unless there is fuel pressure on the plunger. When you touch basic position, it will be near the bottom of the vertical face of the funnel. This gap should be no more than 0.08 inches (2 mm). If this clearance is incorrect, it may be possible to adjust the gap by turning the mixture screw on the arm. Take the fuel distributor to a dealer service department for the necessary adjustments.

Centering the plate can be easy or difficult. Try the easy way first. Remove the center bolt - it is fairly stiff as it is held by thread locking compound. Take the bolt out and clean the threads. Now try to center the plate with the bolt loosely in position. If this can be done, remove the bolt, put a drop of thread locking compound on the threads and reinstall it holding the plate centralized. Tighten the bolt securely.

5.22a Mixture control unit fuel line connections

5.22b Note the direction of the arrow on the fuel inlet when reconnecting the lines (make sure the feed line goes here)

5.22c Disconnect the air inlet hose from the air cleaner

If the plate will not center then the sensor unit must be removed from the vehicle (see illustrations). It is probably easier to remove the mixture control unit from the sensor unit than to remove all the fuel lines, but be careful that the plunger doesn't drop out when you separate the units. Disconnect the sensor unit from the top of the air cleaner. Take the sensor unit out and turn it upside down. Now check that the sensor beam is central in its bearings (see illustration). If it is not, loosen the clamp bolt on the counterweight and it may be possible to center the beam in its bearings and at the same time center the sensor plate in the cone. If this is possible, remove the bolt, clean the threads, put a drop of thread locking compound on them and reinstall the bolt with the beam and plate in the correct positions. If this doesn't work, a new sensor unit must be purchased, because if the plate is not centralized you will have major problems.

5.22d Crankcase ventilation hose location on the air cleaner

5.22e Removing the airflow sensor/air cleaner unit

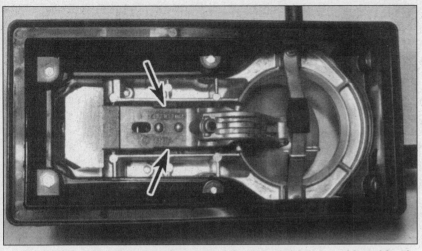

5.23 Bottom view of the airflow sensor unit - the clearance on either side of the sensor beam (arrows) should be even

Once the plate is centralized and level, the unit reassembled, the mixture control unit installed and the system recharged with fuel by turning the ignition on for a few seconds, it is possible to check the action of the airflow sensor. Turn the ignition off and, using a small magnet, lift the plate to the top of its movement. There must be a slight, even, resistance, but no hard spots. Now depress the plate quickly. This time there should be no resistance to movement.

If there is resistance to movement, or hard spots in both directions then the plate may not be centralized, so check it again. If the resistance or hard spot happens only when lifting the plate, then the problem is with the plunger of the fuel mixture unit. Remove the mixture unit from the sensor casing and carefully remove the plunger. Wash it with carburetor cleaner to remove any residue, reinstall it and try again. If this does not cure the problem then it is probable that a new mixture control unit is needed. DO NOT try to remove the hard spot with abrasives; this will only make matters worse. A visit to the dealer service department or other repair shop is indicated. They may be able to cure the problems but be prepared to purchase a new mixture control unit.

On CIS-E and CIS-E Motronic systems, a sensor plate potentiometer provides the control unit with information on the position of the sensor plate. On CIS-E systems, this signal is used for cold acceleration enrichment (see CIS-E electrical tests above); on CIS-E Motronic systems, the potentiometer's signal to the control unit is used to indicate load.

Fuel distributor - check and adjustment

The pressure regulating valve for the system pressure is included in the fuel distributor body **(see illustration)**. A hexagonal plug on the corner of the fuel distributor casing may be unscrewed and inside will be found a copper ring, shims for adjusting the pressure on the spring, the spring, a piston and a rubber ring. Be careful not to scratch the bore or the piston since these are mated on assembly and a new piston means a new distributor body. If the piston is stuck either blow it out with compressed air or work it out using a piece of soft wood. Do not attempt to adjust the system pressure by altering the shims. Always use new seals when refitting the plug.

Pressure can be adjusted by adding shims to the pressure relief valve. An additional 0.020-inch shim will increase system pressure by about 4 psi. A 0.040-inch shim will increase system pressure by about 8 psi.

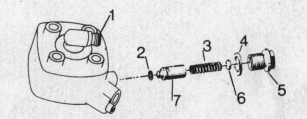

5.24 Exploded view of the pressure regulating valve on the fuel distributor body (early CIS system shown)

1	Fuel distributor body	5	Plug
2	Rubber ring	6	Shims for pressure
3	Spring		adjustment
4	Copper washer	7	Valve piston

If system pressure is too high, check for a blocked or damaged fuel return line. If the return line is good, the pressure can be lowered by reducing the thickness of the shims on the pressure relief valve. A reduction of a 0.020-inch shim thickness will decrease system pressure by about 4 psi. A reduction of 0.040-inch total shim thickness will decrease system pressure by 8 psi.

From the tests on·the air sensor plate movement, the operation of the plunger will have been checked. If it is suspect, then the fuel distributor body must be disconnected from the airflow sensor plate and lifted clear. Be careful that the plunger does not fall out and get damaged. Carefully extract the plunger and wash it in carburetor cleaner. When installing it, the small shoulder goes in first. Do not attempt to cure any hard spots by rubbing with abrasive. If washing it in carburetor cleaner does not cure the problem then a new assembly is required.

5.25 The control pressure regulator is located on the front side of the engine block

Control pressure regulator

Check

Disconnect the wiring from the control pressure (warm up) regulator **(see illustration)** and auxiliary air valve. Connect a voltmeter across the electrical connectors and operate the starter briefly - there should be a minimum of 11.5 volts. Connect an ohmmeter across the regulator heater element terminals - the resistance should be between 16 and 22 ohms. Replace the regulator if necessary and reconnect the wiring.

Replacement

Relieve the fuel pressure (see Chapter 4). Disconnect the electrical connector from the regulator. Use a box-end or socket wrench and disconnect the fuel lines from the regulator. Use a 6 mm Allen wrench and remove the two bolts that retain the regulator to the block **(see illustration)**. Installation is the reverse of removal.

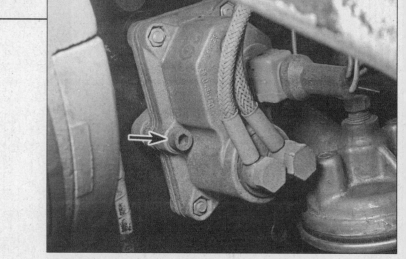

5.26 Use a 6 mm Allen wrench and remove the control pressure regulator mounting bolts

5.27a Thermo-time switch location on early CIS systems

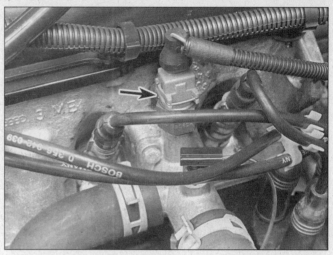

5.27b Thermo-time switch location on CIS-E systems

Thermo-time switch - check and replacement

Note: *This section applies to CIS systems equipped with a cold start injector*

Check

To test the switch, remove the plug from the cold start valve and bridge the contacts with a test light or a voltmeter. The test must be done with a cold (coolant below 95-degrees F, 35-degrees C) engine. Remove the coil wire from the center of the distributor and ground it with a jumper wire. Have an assistant operate the starter for ten seconds. Depending on the coolant temperature, the bulb should light or the voltmeter register for a period of between three and ten seconds and then cease to register. If the circuit is not broken in ten seconds the thermo-time switch must be replaced **(see illustrations)**. If the bulb does not light at all and you are sure the engine is cold, then check that there is voltage supplied to the switch. If there is no voltage, then the fuel pump relay must be checked.

Replacement

Warning: *The engine must be completely cool before beginning this procedure. Also, remove the radiator cap to relieve any residual pressure, then reinstall the cap.*

Prepare the new switch for installation by wrapping the threads with Teflon tape. Disconnect the electrical connector from the thermo-time switch. Unscrew the switch and install the new one as quickly as possible. Be prepared for coolant spillage. Installation is the reverse of removal, but wrap the threads of the switch with teflon tape before installing it.

Cold start valve

Check

Make sure the engine coolant is below 86-degrees F. Preferably the engine should sit for several hours. Disconnect the electrical connector from the cold start valve **(see illustration)** and move it aside, away from the work area - there will be fuel vapor present. Remove the two screws holding the valve to the intake chamber and take the valve out. The fuel line must be left connected to the valve. Wipe the nozzle of the valve. Pull the coil wire out of the center of the distributor and connect it to a good ground. Turn the ignition On and operate the fuel pump for one minute. There must be no fuel dripping from the nozzle. If there is, the valve is faulty and must be replaced. Switch off the ignition.

5.28 Disconnect the cold start valve electrical connector

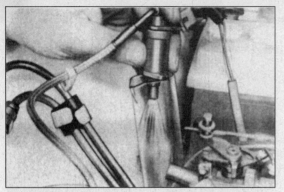

5.29 Check for proper cold start valve operation

Now put the stem of the valve in a container (an empty coffee can will do). Reconnect the plug to the valve. Unplug the electrical connector from the thermotime switch and connect a jumper lead over the plug terminals. Have an assistant turn the ignition On and operate the starter. The valve should squirt a conical shaped spray into the can **(see illustration)**. If the spray is correct the valve is working properly. If the spray pattern is irregular, the valve is damaged and should be replaced.

Replacement

Relieve the fuel pressure (see Chapter 4). Use a box end or socket wrench and remove the fuel line connected to the cold start valve. Remove the Allen bolts that retain the cold start valve to the air intake distributor and remove the valve. Installation is the reverse of removal, but be sure to clean the mating surfaces and use a new gasket.

Auxiliary air regulator

Check

The auxiliary air regulator allows air to bypass the throttle plate while the engine is cold. When the ignition is switched On the heater resistance causes a bi-metallic strip within the regulator to deform, slowly turning the rotating valve until the air passage is closed. It remains in this position during normal operation.

To check the operation of the auxiliary air regulator, remove it from the engine, disconnect the hoses and shine a flashlight into the port **(see illustration)**. If the unit is cold there must be a clear passage. Connect it to a 12-volt supply for five minutes and watch the operation through the inlet. At the end of the five min-

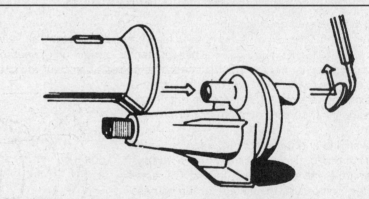

5.30 Shine a flashlight into the port of the regulator when the regulator is cold, it should open and light will pass through

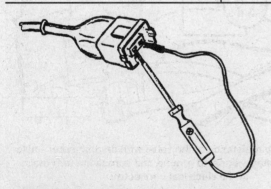

5.31 Use a test light to check for power to the auxiliary air regulator electrical connector while the engine is running

utes the valve should be closed. If it does not operate correctly check the resistance of the heater unit. This should be 30 ohms.

If the auxiliary air regulator resistance is in the correct range, disconnect the electrical connector from the control pressure regulator. Use a test light to determine whether the battery voltage is reaching the heating element while the engine is running **(see illustration)**. If it is not, test the fuel pump relay.

Replacement

Disconnect both air hoses from the auxiliary air regulator to the intake air chamber. Disconnect the electrical connector from the auxiliary air regulator. Remove the mounting screws that retain the auxiliary air regulator to the intake air chamber.

Installation is the reverse of removal.

Idle air stabilizer system

The idle air stabilizer system works to maintain engine idle speed within a 200 rpm range regardless of varying engine loads at idle. An electrically operated valve **(see illustration)** allows a small amount of air to flow past the throttle plate to raise the idle speed whenever the idle speed drops below 750 rpm. If the idle speed rises above 1050 rpm, the idle air stabilizer valve closes and stops extra air from bypassing the throttle plate, consequently reducing the idle speed. A second valve is used on air conditioned vehicles to boost the idle speed when the system is On.

Check - CIS fuel injection systems

The idle air stabilizer valve is governed by an electronic control relay that senses engine speed from the no. 1 terminal of the ignition coil. Clamp shut the hose from the valve to the air intake chamber.

Connect a tachometer to the engine. Start the engine and warm it up to normal operating temperature and disconnect the oxygen sensor electrical connector.

Adjust the idle speed to less than 750 rpm and listen for a clicking sound from the valve. Remove the clamp from the air supply hose and check to make sure the idle speed raises slightly. If the system is faulty, take the vehicle to a dealer service department or other repair shop for further diagnosis.

Check - CIS-E fuel injection systems

Whenever the throttle valve idle switch is closed, the idle air stabilizer valve receives a cycled voltage signal from the oxygen sensor control unit based on the engine rpm and other inputs. The voltage signal cycles on and off to incrementally open or close the valve to adjust idle speed. This on/off signal is referred to as the valve duty cycle and is measured with a duty cycle meter or a dwell meter.

Start the engine and make sure the valve is vibrating and humming slightly. If not, check for a voltage signal reaching the valve and check the valve's resistance. With the ignition On, the voltage at the harness connector should be approximately 12 volts (battery voltage) between the center terminal and ground and 10 volts between the center terminal and the outer two terminals **(see illustration)**. Check the resistance on the connector terminals of the idle air stabilizer valve. There should be continuity between the center terminal and each of the outer terminals. If the readings are incorrect, replace the valve. **Note:** *If the resistance of the idle air stabilizer valve is correct and the voltage is correct, have the oxygen sensor control unit tested by a dealer service department or other repair shop.*

Replacement

Remove the electrical connector and the bracket from the idle air stabilizer valve and remove the valve. Installation is the reverse of removal.

5.32 Location of the idle air stabilizer valve on CIS-E fuel injection systems - on early CIS systems it is usually positioned near the right strut tower with hoses leading to the intake air chamber

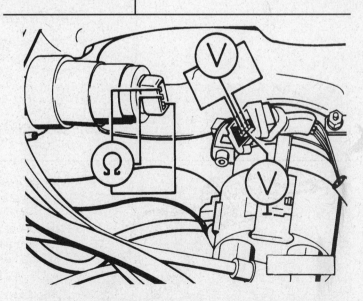

5.33 Check the resistance of the valve with an ohmmeter - also check the voltage signal to ground and across the terminals in the electrical connector

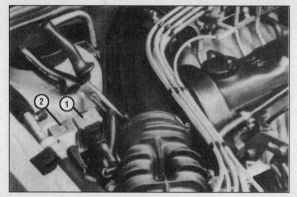

5.34 Location of the idle speed boost valve

1   Idle speed boost valve
2   Additional boost valve for vehicles with air conditioning

Idle speed boost valve

Check

The idle speed boost valve maintains the idle speed within a 300 rpm range. Vehicles with air conditioning have an extra boost valve. The electrically operated valves **(see illustration)** allow additional air to bypass the throttle plate and increase idle speed whenever the idle speed drops below 750 rpm. The idle speed boost valve is a solenoid valve that is controlled by an electronic control unit on the fuse/relay panel that turns the valve on and off according to an engine speed signal from the coil.

If the valve does not respond properly, check the voltage signal to the valve at the harness connector using a voltmeter. If the valve is receiving a voltage signal below 750 rpm and still does not open then the valve is faulty. If the valve is not receiving voltage below 750 rpm, take the vehicle to a dealer service department or other repair shop for further diagnosis.

Electronic fuel injection

Warning: *Gasoline is extremely flammable, so take extra precautions when you work on any part of the fuel system. Don't smoke or allow open flames or bare light bulbs near the work area, and don't work in a garage where a natural gas-type appliance (such as a water heater or a clothes dryer) with a pilot light is present. Since gasoline is carcinogenic, wear latex gloves when there's a possibility of being exposed to fuel, and, if you spill any fuel on your skin, rinse it off immediately with soap and water. Mop up any spills immediately and do not store fuel-soaked rags where they could ignite. The fuel system is under constant pressure, so, if any fuel lines are to be disconnected, the fuel pressure in the system must be relieved first (see Chapter 4 for more information). When you perform any kind of work on the fuel system, wear safety glasses and have a Class B type fire extinguisher on hand.*

The first step for checking fuel pressure on electronic fuel injection systems is to determine what type of fuel lines are on your vehicle and how to install the fuel pressure gauge to the fuel rail or fuel system. This may seem like a simple job but many of the major automobile manufacturers have changed their systems many times during the last ten years of the technology explosion in the automotive industry. Chapters 4 and 5 deal specifically with all the various fuel line disconnects and test ports available. Ford products use the spring-lock type couplers while GM products use the pinch type fuel line disconnects. GM also uses a smaller version of the spring-lock type system. Ford fuel line tools do not work on GM fuel lines. Nissan, Honda and Chrysler also have their own types and tools for removal.

Locate the test port for the fuel pressure gauge **(see illustration)**. The test port is usually located next to the fuel pressure regulator or on the fuel rail. If the system on your engine is not equipped with one, then it will be necessary to locate a convenient section of fuel line before the fuel pressure regulator to install the fuel pressure gauge. First, we will deal with fuel rails that are equipped with a test port for the fuel pressure gauge.

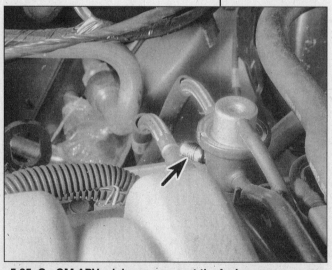

5.35 On GM APV minivans, connect the fuel pressure gauge to the Schrader valve (arrow) on the fuel pressure regulator (many other GM models share this arrangement)

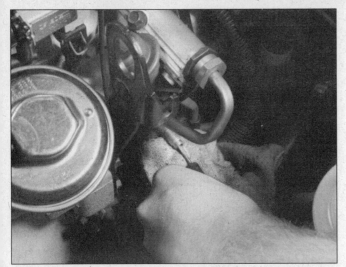

5.36 The Schrader valve fitting on the Saturn is located below the fuel pressure regulator near the fuel rail on both the TBI and Port fuel injected engines. Depress the valve to bleed off any excess fuel into a shop towel

5.37a If the wrenches are too wide to allow a secure grip, use a socket on the service bolt and a back-up wrench on the main bolt - before the bolt is loosened, cover the wrenches with a shop rag to catch the escaping fuel

Ideally, the test port will have a threaded Schrader valve **(see illustration)** that matches your fuel pressure gauge and installing the tool would be a matter of relieving the fuel pressure (see Chapter 4) and attaching the fuel pressure gauge. In the event your fuel pressure gauge requires a special fitting, it is possible to fabricate your own adapter for the fuel pressure test port. For example: On late model Honda Accords, go to the hardware store and purchase a 12 mm bolt with a 1.25 thread pitch. Cut the head off the bolt and drill a hole straight through the center to allow the fuel to enter the fuel pressure gauge. Attach the home-made tool to the fuel pressure gauge **(see illustrations)** and install it into the service port on the fuel rail. Start the engine and read the fuel pressure. Another example of a slightly more difficult fuel pressure test is the Toyota Previa. The easiest location for the fuel pressure gauge is on the fuel filter **(see illustration)**. The adapter will be a little tougher to build also. This particular tool is much like the Honda Accord. It will have the same thread pitch, diameter, bolt head and

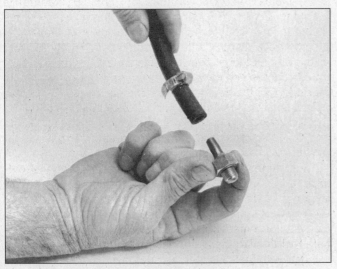

5.37b Install the hose end of the fuel pressure gauge onto the adapter and then . . .

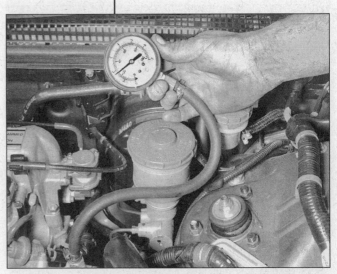

5.38 . . . install the fuel pressure gauge and adapter onto the fuel rail

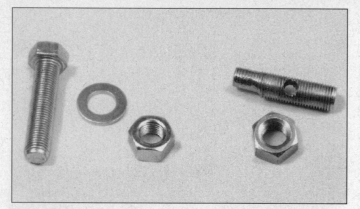

5.39a On Toyota Previa minivans, the fuel line adapter will be a bit different. Cut the head off the bolt (12 mm diameter/ 1.25 thread pitch) and drill a hole directly through the center (horizontal). Grind the end to form a slight taper and drill a vertical hole to allow system pressure to flow. It is important that the vertical hole is drilled in the correct location. The easiest method is to use the banjo bolt that was removed from the fuel filter and place it directly next to the tool for the correct alignment of the vertical passage for fuel flow

5.40a Install the fuel pressure gauge to the bottom of the fuel filter of the Previa

length. The difference is that a vertical hole must be drilled as well as the horizontal passage **(see illustration)**. This will allow system pressure to flow through the fuel rail. All in-line fuel pressure adapters will require the horizontal passage to be drilled into the bolt.

Now we will deal with fuel injection systems that are not equipped with a test port. Many throttle body injection (TBI) systems are not equipped with a test port or Schrader valve **(see illustrations)**. Remove the fuel inlet line from the throttle body and install a T-shaped fuel line adapter with the fuel pressure gauge attached to the center. Start the engine and record the fuel pressure. On engines equipped with quick-connect fittings or spring lock couplers, it will be necessary to purchase a special fuel line harness that will allow you to install a fuel pressure gauge into the fuel system. These tools are available from automotive specialty tool companies.

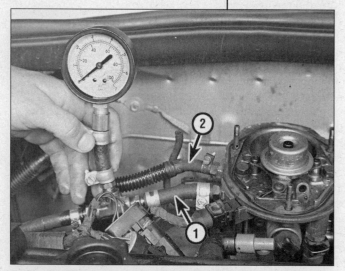

5.40b On TBI systems, install the fuel pressure gauge into the inlet line next to the throttle body unit using a T-fitting

5.40c On BMW 5-Series multi point fuel injection systems, install the tee fitting directly after the fuel pressure regulator. therefore you will be reading regulated fuel pressure

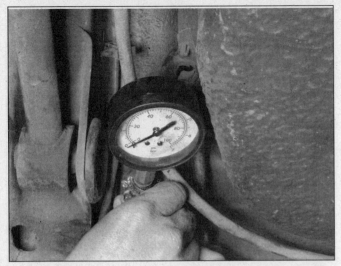

5.41a By installing the fuel pressure gauge directly after the fuel pump at the fuel tank, it is possible to observe "dead head" pressure. This is not quite as accurate as pinching the return line because the engine will quickly shut down because of the lack of fuel to the engine

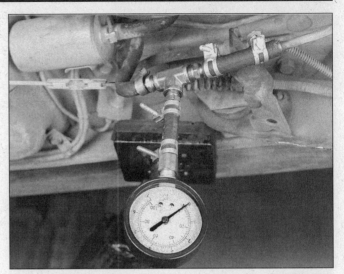

5.41b By installing the fuel pressure gauge directly after the fuel pump (before the fuel filter and fuel pressure regulator) but inline with the fuel system, you can determine if the fuel system pressure has increased or decreased and where the restriction is located by comparing the readings to the fuel pressure specifications taken at the engine (regulated fuel pressure)

Now that the fuel pressure gauge is in place and ready, install a jumper wire into the terminals located on the fuel pump relay connector to activate the fuel pump (see Section 4). Allow the fuel system to pressurize the gauge and check for leaks. Most MPFI (port) fuel injection systems will pressurize the system between 35 and 45 psi. Most TBI systems will pressurize the system between 10 and 20 psi. Be sure to consult your *Haynes Automotive Repair Manual* for the correct fuel pressure specification. Now, record this reading, install the fuel pump relay and start the engine. The running fuel pressure should be slightly lower. For example, many EEC-IV systems on the later model Fords will read 35 to 45 psi with the ignition key On (engine not running) (KOEO). Once the engine is running, the fuel pressure will drop to approximately 30 and 40 psi. Under running conditions, the fuel system will bypass a certain amount of fuel through the fuel pressure regulator thereby keeping pressure slightly lower. This is an important fuel pressure transition to observe and record.

The next test is for "dead head pressure". This test isolates the fuel pump from the fuel system to determine if the fuel pump will produce the correct pressure under operating conditions. The best method is to pinch the fuel return line using a hose clamping tool or a pair of pliers with a shop towel over the fuel line to prevent any damage. This test will prevent fuel from returning to the tank and in the process, build up direct pressure. This test can also be performed with the fuel pressure gauge attached to the fuel line directly at the tank outlet line **(see illustrations)**. In this position the engine will not run very long so it will be necessary to watch the gauge carefully. Start the engine and record the fuel pressure reading. The pressure should be approximately twice as much as running pressure or about 60 to 80 psi. Many Nissan 280ZX models will exhibit poor acceleration and occasional backfire problems through the vane airflow meter. After testing the "dead head pressure", the mechanic discovers the pressure is 50 psi or lower. In other words, under load, the fuel mixture becomes slightly lean because the fuel pump fails to deliver the proper volume of fuel to the injectors. The fuel pump must be replaced with a new part and retested. Checking "dead head pressure" will help diagnose fuel system problems that occur under load.

5.42 Carefully observe the fuel pressure gauge as vacuum is applied. Fuel pressure should DECREASE as vacuum is INCREASED

5.43 Now release vacuum from the pump. Fuel pressure should INCREASE as vacuum DECREASES

5.44 Make sure there is vacuum to the fuel pressure regulator hose when the engine is idling

Next, check the operation of the fuel pressure regulator. **Note**: *This test will not apply to engines equipped with TBI units. This component controls the fuel pressure during acceleration. When the engine speed increases, the manifold vacuum decreases as the demand for fuel increases. All fuel pressure regulators must increase fuel pressure on acceleration (low vacuum) and decrease fuel pressure on deceleration (high vacuum). To test the fuel pressure regulator, attach a vacuum pump to the fuel pressure regulator and observe the fuel pressure* **(see illustration)**. *Fuel pressure should decrease when vacuum is applied. Now release vacuum* **(see illustration)** *and confirm that fuel pressure increases. Another quick test, with the engine running at idle, simply remove the vacuum hose from the fuel pressure regulator and confirm that the fuel pressure increases.*

If the fuel pressure regulator is OK and you suspect fuel pressure problems, check for vacuum to the regulator. Install a vacuum gauge to the hose attached to the fuel pressure regulator **(see illustration)** and observe manifold vacuum. There should be approximately 14 to 21 inches Hg. at idle (high vacuum). Now throttle the valve and confirm that as the engine speed increases, manifold vacuum decreases. Check for a clogged port or damaged vacuum hose to the fuel pressure regulator if the vacuum readings are incorrect. Refer to Chapter 3 for additional information on vacuum testing.

Here are a few tips to remember if the fuel pressure is low:
1) Possible pinched inlet line from tank to the fuel filter. Move the fuel pressure gauge to rear and check pressure before the filter and then directly at the tank.
2) Inspect the fuel system for a fuel leak. Repair any leaks and recheck the fuel pressure.
3) Check the fuel pump output pressure.
4) Check for a faulty fuel accumulator, if equipped

Here are a few tips to remember if the fuel pressure is high:
1) Check for a restriction in the return line
2) Check for a faulty fuel pressure regulator

Turbocharged EFI engines are equipped with vacuum solenoids and electrical circuits that control the increase and decrease in fuel pressure at different rpm ranges to compensate for the high demand (turbo boost) and quick acceleration rates that drivers demand from their performance equipped engines. In the event of fuel pressure problems on a turbocharged engine, consult your *Haynes Automotive Repair Manual* or the dealer service department for additional information and repairs.

6 Fuel pump removal and installation

Warning: *Gasoline is extremely flammable, so take extra precautions when you work on any part of the fuel system. Don't smoke or allow open flames or bare light bulbs near the work area, and don't work in a garage where a natural gas-type appliance (such as a water heater or a clothes dryer) with a pilot light is present. Since gasoline is carcinogenic, wear latex gloves when there's a possibility of being exposed to fuel, and, if you spill any fuel on your skin, rinse it off immediately with soap and water. Mop up any spills immediately and do not store fuel-soaked rags where they could ignite. The fuel system is under constant pressure, so, if any fuel lines are to be disconnected, the fuel pressure in the system must be relieved first (see Chapter 4 for more information). When you perform any kind of work on the fuel system, wear safety glasses and have a Class B type fire extinguisher on hand.*

This section will describe the procedure for removing and installing the fuel pump mounted on the chassis of the vehicle or the fuel pump assembly located in the fuel tank. Some vehicles are equipped with both types of pumps. Others use one or the other. The first step is to determine the location of the fuel pump on your vehicle.

Just where is the fuel pump located on the vehicle? Locating the fuel pump may become difficult because of the many mounting locations manufacturers have chosen. Well, if it is not located outside the tank (external) then it is just a matter of checking inside the fuel tank! If the fuel pump does not operate or make any noise, then it may be slightly more difficult to confirm its location.

There are a few easy steps you can take to locate the fuel pump. First, follow the fuel lines all the way from the fuel rail to the fuel tank. Most externally mounted fuel pumps are mounted next to the fuel tank **(see illustrations)**. Some domestic pick-ups and heavy duty vehicles have the fuel pump mounted about

6.1a Externally mounted fuel pump on a BMW 318i

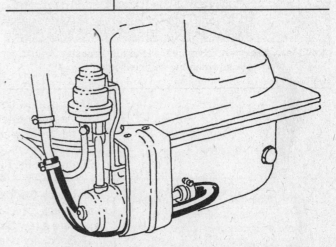

6.1b Volvo external fuel pump and fuel accumulator

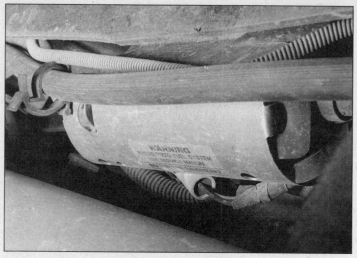

6.2 External fuel pump on a 1989 Ford Bronco

halfway between the fuel tank and fuel rail assembly **(see illustration)**. These type fuel pumps are easy to locate. Be aware that many of these type pumps are covered with a fuel pump protector plate to prevent rocks or road debris from damaging the case. Next, locate the fuel pump wiring harness. If the fuel pump is mounted in the fuel tank, then the harness for the fuel pump/fuel level sending unit should be directly above the fuel tank.

Externally mounted fuel pumps

Warning: *Be sure to relieve the fuel system pressure (see Chapter 4) before disconnecting any fuel lines.*
Note: *Many vehicles that are equipped with externally mounted fuel pumps are also equipped with a transfer fuel pump that is located in the fuel tank. This pump functions as an intermediate fuel pump that primes the main system. Be sure to test the transfer pump for correct operation before replacing the main fuel pump.*

To replace the external fuel pump is usually much easier than the internal type, especially if the internal type does not have an access plate in the trunk area. The first step in removing an external fuel pump is to raise the vehicle and support it securely on jackstands. Remove the rubber boots that cover the fuel pump electrical terminals and disconnect the wires from the fuel pump. Use line clamps to pinch the fuel lines shut before attempting to remove the hose clamps. This is very important to prevent fuel from spilling into your face or down your arms. If a specialized clamping tool is not available, wrap the fuel line carefully with a rag and use locking pliers to close off the fuel. Loosen the hose clamps on the fuel lines and remove the fuel lines. It is a good idea to have some extra rags directly in front of you as the fuel lines are being removed to soak up any excess fuel that may drip from the fuel line. Remove the fuel pump mounting bolt(s) and lift it away from the chassis of the automobile.

Internally mounted fuel pumps

Internally mounted fuel pumps can be removed either through the access plate in the trunk area or from the fuel pump cover after the fuel tank has been removed. If you are not sure if your particular model has an access plate, it is a good idea to take some time to look for it! It could mean the difference between a fairly easy job or a much more time consuming job. First, look through the trunk area for any obvious cover plates **(see illustration)** or removable sections of the floor of the trunk. It may be necessary to completely remove the trunk panels and carpet from the trunk area! Look thoroughly and remember, this search may save you a lot of time. If your vehicle does not have an access cover, refer to the appropriate *Haynes Automotive Repair Manual* for the fuel tank removal procedure, if necessary.

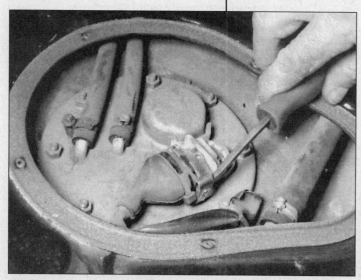

6.3 To expose the fuel pump on a 1990 BMW 535, remove the fuel pump cover screws (arrows) and lift the cover off the floor of the vehicle (under the back seat)

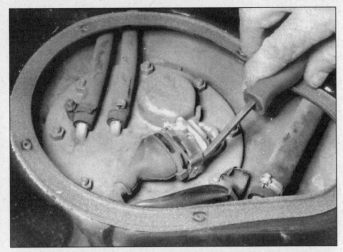

6.4a To unplug the electrical connector, pry the bracket until the notch aligns with the slot on the retaining clip and release the connector from the assembly

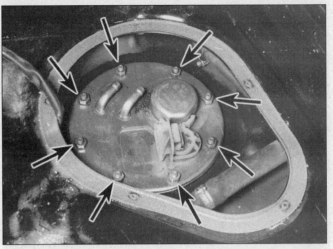

6.4b Remove the mounting nuts (arrows) from the perimeter of the fuel pump assembly

Remove the bolts or screws from the access cover. Now remove the bolts or screws from the fuel pump/fuel level sending unit assembly (see illustrations). If your particular assembly uses a lock ring instead of bolts, a special tool may be needed to release the lock ring (see Chapter 2). Rotate the cover to align and release the assembly from the fuel tank (see illustration). Carefully lift the assembly from the fuel tank (see illustration). Be careful not to bend or break the float or the sock filter that is attached to the end of the fuel pump assembly.

Next, remove the fuel pump from the assembly (see illustration). Many of the fuel pumps will have an electrical connector that must be removed first. Be sure to mark each wire appropriately to ensure correct installation.

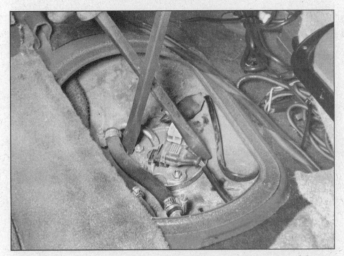

6.5 On models without mounting nuts, use two screwdrivers to rotate the assembly out of the notches (1990 BMW 525i shown)

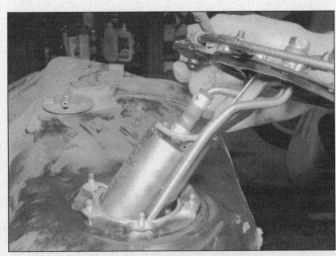

6.6 If the vehicle does not have an access plate, remove the fuel tank from the chassis and lift the fuel pump from the access hole on top of the fuel tank (1990 Honda Accord shown)

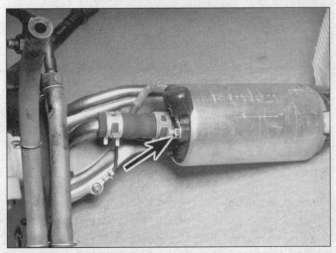

6.7 Remove the nut (arrow) and the electrical connector from the terminal on the fuel pump

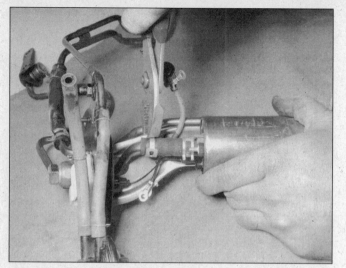

6.8 First, squeeze the hose clamps and slide them up the hose . . .

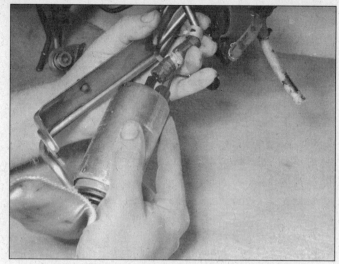

6.9 . . . and separate the pump from the bracket

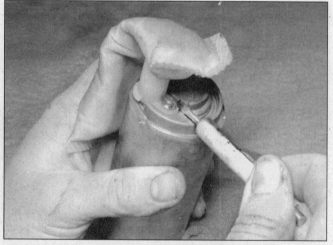

6.10 Pry off the retaining clip with a small screwdriver and detach the filter from the pump

Remove the clamps from the fuel line that connects the fuel pump to the assembly **(see illustration)**. Be careful not to bend or damage the metal fuel line. Carefully separate the fuel pump from the assembly **(see illustration)**. Remove the filter sock from the fuel pump body **(see illustration)**.

7 Fuel injectors

Warning: *Gasoline is extremely flammable, so take extra precautions when you work on any part of the fuel system. Don't smoke or allow open flames or bare light bulbs near the work area, and don't work in a garage where a natural gas-type appliance (such as a water heater or a clothes dryer) with a pilot light is present. Since gasoline is carcinogenic, wear latex gloves when there's a possibility of being exposed to fuel, and, if you spill any fuel on your skin, rinse it off immediately with soap and water. Mop up any spills immediately and do not store fuel-soaked rags where they could ignite. The fuel system is under constant pressure, so, if any fuel lines are to be disconnected, the fuel pressure in the system must be relieved first (see Chapter 4 for more information). When you perform any kind of work on the fuel system, wear safety glasses and have a Class B type fire extinguisher on hand.*

In this section we will discuss the different types of fuel injectors and how to determine if they are working properly. Modern fuel injection systems can easily become contaminated with sludge, rust debris or poor quality fuel and the injectors will suffer directly from the problem. Also, the electrical harness may become frayed or shorted and can cause problems with the necessary voltage reaching the injectors. Let's first discuss the different types of injectors and what to look for.

There are basically two types of injectors; the constant flow injectors on CIS systems (mechanical) or the solenoid-operated injectors on TBI and EFI (pulse

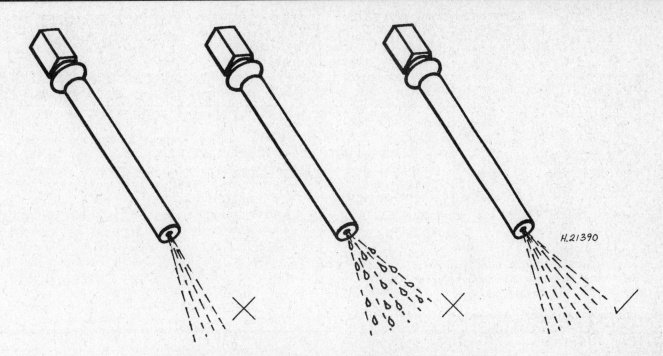

H.21390

7.1 Typical injector spray patterns on CIS type mechanical injectors

type) injection systems (electrical). The constant flow injectors are not electrically operated in any way, whereas the pulse injectors are grounded to the engine block or throttle body and are opened with a small (one to three volt) pulse from the computer. Even though the electrically operated fuel injectors are more complicated, both can become equally damaged due to contamination.

Check the constant flow injectors (mechanical) in the vehicle as well as on the bench. First, remove the injectors from the cylinder head without disconnecting the fuel lines. Carefully pry the assembly out of the seals without damaging the injector or retainer. It will be necessary to place a container or thick shop towels or rags below the injectors to catch the fuel during the testing procedure. Now to simulate the actual spray pattern. Remove the air intake boot from the airflow meter. With the ignition key On (engine not running), lift the sensor plate to activate the injectors. You should see a very even and constant flow of fuel from the injectors **(see illustration)**. Make sure the spray is not intermittent or off to one side. This would indicate some carbon buildup or debris stuck on one side of the injector. Also, make sure that the fuel is atomized evenly. There should not be intermittent droplets that change to mist. The size of the fuel molecules should be even and constant.

The next check on the constant flow type injectors (mechanical) should be performed on the bench. It will be necessary to use a specialized fuel injector tester **(see illustration)**. Mount the injector onto the tip of the injector tool and apply pressure to the injector. Observe the spray pattern. If the injector is clogged or contaminated, try running fuel through the injector under pressure to purge the debris from the tip. Sometimes this method will clean the injector, thereby saving the cost of a new one.

7.2 This injector tester requires a special fluid to pump through the injector for cleaning and testing purposes

Fuel Injection Diagnostic Manual

Also check the injector for leakdown. After the ignition key has been shut off, the system continues to apply residual pressure to the fuel injectors. Make sure the injectors hold pressure and do not allow any fuel to drip into the combustion chambers. This leakdown will cause rich starting problems and eventually ruin the piston rings by continually washing the walls of the cylinders with fuel. If you do not own this special fuel injector tool, have the injectors tested by a qualified repair shop. This test will finalize any defective mechanical type fuel injectors.

Check the pulse type fuel injectors (electrical) on the engine. On TBI systems, it is possible to observe the injector spray pattern while the engine is running. Remove the air cleaner assembly from the throttle body and while the engine is running, point the end of a strobe type timing light into the throat of the throttle body. Observe the spray pattern as the light illuminates the droplets of fuel passing into the manifold. The spray pattern should be an even, conical shaped pattern extending into the venturi area of the throttle body. Now accelerate the engine and observe how the pattern will surge slightly but not change shape or form. This is a very important test to determine how the throttle body injector is performing. **Warning**: *Be sure all loose clothing, ties, shop towels and other miscellaneous items are clear of the fan blades during the test procedure.*

Follow the same testing procedure for pulse type fuel injectors **(see illustration)**. The electrical injectors cannot be bench tested but instead they must be removed from the intake manifold and triggered while assembled to the fuel lines. Many of these type systems will require the engine to be cranked before fuel is fired through the fuel injectors. In this situation, be sure to ground the coil wire and have a container or shop rags to catch the fuel as the injectors spray. Also, the fuel rails on pulse type fuel injection systems are designed for very little clearance and maneuverability for testing purposes. If this type of test is impossible, have the fuel injector checked by a dealer service department.

Because some pulse type injectors are grounded through the engine block, it may not be possible to observe them spraying fuel while the engine is being cranked. If you suspect contamination in the injector and an incomplete spray pattern, try cleaning the tip of the injector with solvent. Also look into the cylinder head for any other obstruction that could be cleaned or removed. If the injector continues to malfunction, replace it with a new one.

If your engine is equipped with EFI port fuel injection, there are several alternative methods to check the performance of the fuel injectors. First, with the engine running, place the tip of an automotive type stethoscope on the main body of the injector **(see illustration)**. There should be a distinct clicking sound as the solenoid activates and deactivates

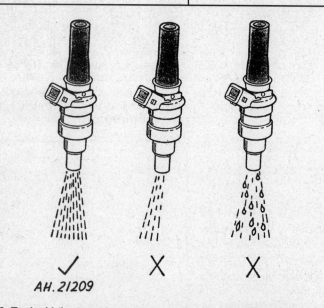

AH. 21209

7.3 Typical injector spray patterns on pulse type EFI injectors

7.4 Use an automotive type stethoscope to listen for the sounds of the injector solenoids cycling

from the voltage signal. If there is no sound heard, install a "noid light" into the fuel injector electrical connector and observe a flashing light **(see illustration)**. The noid light is simply a small bulb that lights up when the computer supplies voltage to the injector. This test will confirm the presence of power to the injector. If the noid light does not activate, there is a problem with the computer or wiring harness back to the computer. Tracking down a wiring problem may become difficult, so if necessary, have the fuel injection system wiring repaired by a dealer service department or qualified repair shop.

Cleaning

Fuel injector cleaners that can be added to the fuel tank are available at auto parts stores and are often very effective at cleaning injectors. These type of injector cleaners should be added periodically as part of a regular maintenance schedule.

A more immediate cleaning service can be performed by a qualified tune-up shop or other repair facility. This service is accomplished with special fuel line hook-ups and cleaning solvents **(see illustration)** that are directly injected into the fuel injection system while the engine is running. The engine is raised to a certain rpm level to aid in breaking up the excess sludge and carbon deposits in the injectors. These fuel injection kits are equipped with special fuel line adapters **(see illustration)**, hoses and other factory specific adapters to allow the tools to be attached to the fuel injection system. Compare the prices of the fuel injection service and the type of cleaners that are available at the repair facilities near you before choosing the one best for your engine.

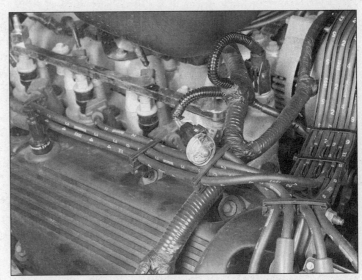

7.5 Plug a "noid light" into the fuel injector electrical connector and confirm that the light blinks as the engine is cranking or running

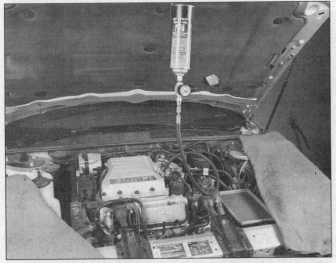

7.6 Fuel injector cleaning kits are equipped with a container of injector cleaner that is delivered to the fuel system without the aid of the vehicles fuel pump system. During the cleaning process, the fuel pump must be disabled to avoid fuel leaks while the engine is running

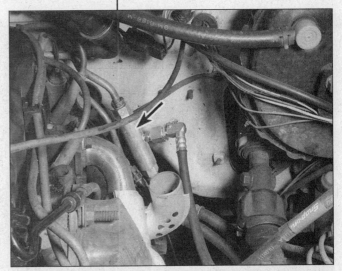

7.7 On TBI systems, install a special tee adapter (arrow) for the inlet fuel line that will accommodate the pressure fitting for the fuel injector cleaning procedure

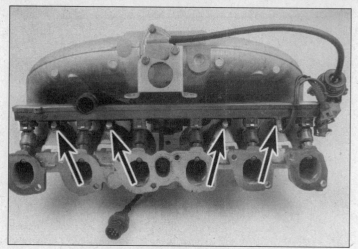

8.1 BMW 535i intake manifold, fuel injectors and fuel rail assembly

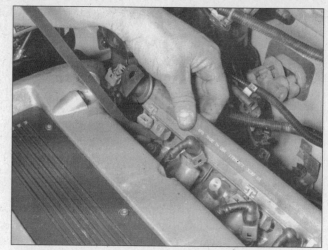

8.2 The fuel rail on a Geo Storm DOHC engine is made of solid cast aluminum and it can be removed from the engine compartment as a single component

8 Fuel rails

Warning: *Gasoline is extremely flammable, so take extra precautions when you work on any part of the fuel system. Don't smoke or allow open flames or bare light bulbs near the work area, and don't work in a garage where a natural gas-type appliance (such as a water heater or a clothes dryer) with a pilot light is present. Since gasoline is carcinogenic, wear latex gloves when there's a possibility of being exposed to fuel, and, if you spill any fuel on your skin, rinse it off immediately with soap and water. Mop up any spills immediately and do not store fuel-soaked rags where they could ignite. The fuel system is under constant pressure, so, if any fuel lines are to be disconnected, the fuel pressure in the system must be relieved first (see Chapter 4 for more information). When you perform any kind of work on the fuel system, wear safety glasses and have a Class B type fire extinguisher on hand.*

All port fuel injection systems are equipped with fuel rails. These fuel rails act as the plumbing to deliver the fuel to all the injectors. The injectors are usually mounted inside the fuel rail along with an O-ring seal **(see illustration)**. The fuel rails on many of the different type fuel injection systems are made of cast aluminum **(see illustration)**. Some are made of hardened plastic **(see illustration)**. G.M. uses a resin hardened plastic called 'Fluoroelastomer' for many of their fuel lines. These specialized fuel lines should only be replaced with the factory replacement material to ensure proper operating conditions under the extreme pressure and heat that fuel injected engines attain.

Replacement of the fuel rails usually requires quite a bit of disassembly to be able to lift it off the intake manifold. Many of the G.M. engines will require the removal of the air intake plenum **(see illustration)**. The Central Point Injection system is fairly easy to remove once the upper half of the air intake plenum is removed. Pinch the tabs on the poppet nozzle and lift

8.3 The Central Port Injection system on Chevy Blazers uses a hardened plastic material for the fuel injector delivery pipes

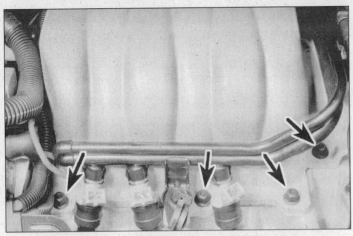

8.4 The Chevy Lumina is equipped with an intake plenum that must be removed before you're able to lift the fuel rail off the engine

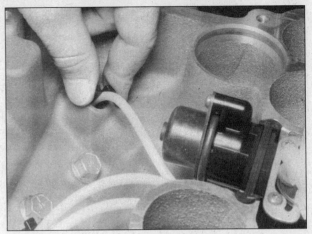

8.5 Squeeze the two tabs and lift the assembly to remove the poppet nozzle from the intake manifold

each nozzle from the intake manifold **(see illustration)**. Be sure to mark each vacuum line, electrical connector and engine component when removing them from the intake manifold **(see illustration)**. Once the fuel rail has been removed from the intake manifold **(see illustration)**, be sure to replace each O-ring with a new one. This will ensure a tight fit without fuel leaks.

9 Throttle body

The throttle body unit on most port fuel injection systems must be serviced to prevent sludge and dirt from clogging the vacuum ports or interfering with throttle plate operation. The throttle body should also be checked for vacuum leaks, cracks in the metal or stripped/broken bolts. Many idle control problems are the result of sludge deposits at the throttle shaft and edge of the throttle plate and the passageways of the idle air control valve. These deposits prevent the throttle valve from completely closing, thereby allowing excess intake air past the

8.6 On a Ford Crown Victoria, the wire loom and the plastic case must be removed before the fuel rail will separate

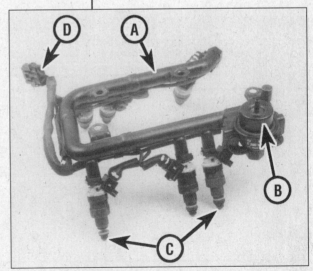

8.7 The fuel rail on the Chevy Lumina V6 engine can be removed with the injectors as a single unit

A   Fuel rail
B   Fuel pressure regulator
C   Fuel injectors
D   Fuel injector electrical connector

9.1a Clean the throttle body with carburetor cleaner to remove sludge deposits (a little scrubbing with a toothbrush may also be required)

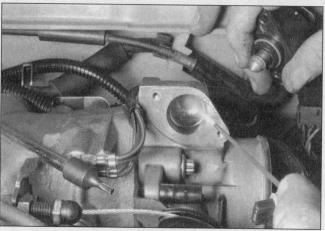

9.1b Spray carburetor cleaner into the IAC valve housing and check for clogged air passages in the air intake plenum

9.1c Remove the throttle body bolts (arrows) and lift the throttle body off the air intake plenum

throttle body. These excess volumes throw the computer off and many times cause an extreme or erratic idle condition.

If the throttle body is not excessively dirty, remove the air intake duct and service the unit with carburetor cleaner (**see illustrations**). However, it is a good idea to completely remove the throttle body and soak it in solvent or engine cleaner to remove all the dirt and sludge from the exterior as well as the interior of the unit.

10 G.M. Throttle Body Injection (TBI) Unit overhaul

Part A: Model 220 Throttle Body Injection (TBI)

Warning: *Gasoline is extremely flammable, so take extra precautions when you work on any part of the fuel system. Don't smoke or allow open flames or bare light bulbs near the work area, and don't work in a garage where a natural gas-type appliance (such as a water heater or a clothes dryer) with a pilot light is present. Since gasoline is carcinogenic, wear latex gloves when there's a possibility of being exposed to fuel, and, if you spill any fuel on your skin, rinse it off immediately with soap and water. Mop up any spills immediately and do not store fuel-soaked rags where they could ignite. The fuel system is under constant pressure, so, if any fuel lines are to be disconnected, the fuel pressure in the system must be relieved first (see Chapter 4 for more information). When you perform any kind of work on the fuel system, wear safety glasses and have a Class B type fire extinguisher on hand.*

Note: *Because of its relative simplicity, the throttle body assembly does not need to be removed from the intake manifold or disassembled for component replacement. However, for the sake of clarity, the following procedures are shown with the TBI assembly removed from the vehicle.*

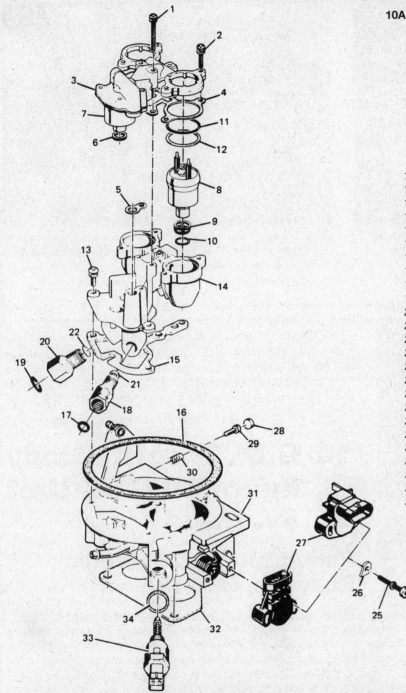

10A.5 Exploded view of the Model 220 TBI assembly on early GM systems

1   Long fuel meter cover attaching screw
2   Short fuel meter cover attaching screw
3   Fuel meter cover
4   Fuel meter cover gasket
5   Fuel meter outlet gasket
6   Pressure regulator seal
7   Pressure regulator
8   Fuel injector
9   Fuel injector inlet filter
10 Lower fuel injector O-ring
11 Upper fuel injector O-ring
12 Fuel injector washer
13 Fuel meter body-to-throttle body attaching screw
14 Fuel meter body
15 Throttle body-to-fuel meter body gasket
16 Air filter gasket
17 Fuel return line O-ring
18 Fuel outlet nut
19 Fuel inlet line O-ring
20 Fuel inlet nut
21 Fuel outlet nut gasket
22 Fuel inlet nut gasket
23 TPS lever attaching screw
24 TPS lever
25 TPS attaching screw
26 TPS attaching screw retainer
27 Throttle Position Sensor (TPS)
28 Idle stop screw plug
29 Idle stop screw
30 Idle stop screw spring
31 Throttle body
32 Flange gasket
33 Idle Air Control (IAC) valve
34 IAC valve gasket

1   Relieve system fuel pressure (see Chapter 4).
2   Detach the cable from the negative terminal of the battery.
3   Remove the air cleaner housing assembly, adapter and gaskets.

Fuel meter cover/fuel pressure regulator assembly

Note: *The fuel pressure regulator is housed in the fuel meter cover. Whether you are replacing the meter cover or the regulator itself, the entire assembly must be replaced. The regulator must not be removed from the cover.*

4   Unplug the electrical connectors to the fuel injectors.
5   Remove the long and short fuel meter cover screws **(see illustration)** and re-move the fuel meter cover.

10A.6 Carefully peel away the old fuel meter outlet passage gasket and fuel meter cover gasket with a razor blade

10A.7 Never remove the four pressure regulator screws (arrows) from the fuel meter cover

6   Remove the fuel meter outlet passage gasket, cover gasket and pressure regulator seal. Carefully remove any old gasket material that is stuck with a razor blade **(see illustration)**. **Caution**: *Do not attempt to re-use either of these gaskets.*

7   Inspect the cover for dirt, foreign material and casting warpage. If it is dirty, clean it with a clean shop rag soaked in solvent. Do not immerse the fuel meter cover in cleaning solvent - it could damage the pressure regulator diaphragm and gasket. **Warning**: *Do not remove the four screws* **(see illustration)** *securing the pressure regulator to the fuel meter cover. The regulator contains a large spring under compression which, if accidentally released, could cause injury. Disassembly might also result in a fuel leak between the diaphragm and the regulator housing. The new fuel meter cover assembly will include a new pressure regulator.*

8   Install the new pressure regulator seal, fuel meter outlet passage gasket and cover gasket.

9   Install the fuel meter cover using Loctite 262 or equivalent on the screws. **Note**: *The short screws go next to the injectors.*

10   Attach the electrical connectors to both injectors.

11   Attach the cable to the negative terminal of the battery.

12   With the engine off and the ignition on, check for leaks around the gasket and fuel line couplings.

13   Install the air cleaner, adapter and gaskets.

Fuel injector(s)

14   To unplug the electrical connectors from the fuel injectors, squeeze the plastic tabs and pull straight up **(see illustration)**.

15   Remove the fuel meter cover/pressure regulator assembly. **Note**: *Do not remove the fuel meter cover assembly gasket - leave it in place to protect the casting from damage during injector removal.*

10A.14 To remove either injector electrical connector, depress the two tabs on the front and rear of each connector and lift straight up

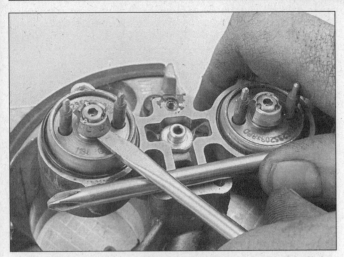

10A.16 To remove an injector, slip the tip of a flat-bladed screwdriver under the lip of the lug on top of the injector and, using another screwdriver as a fulcrum, carefully pry the injector up and out

10A.21 Slide the new filter onto the nozzle of the fuel injector

16   Use two screwdrivers **(see illustration)** to pry out the injector(s).

17   Remove the upper (larger) and lower (smaller) O-rings and filter from the injector(s).

18   Remove the steel backup washer from the top of each injector cavity.

19   Inspect the fuel injector filters for evidence of dirt and contamination. If present, check for the presence of dirt in the fuel lines and fuel tank.

20   Be sure to replace the fuel injector with an identical part. Injectors from other models can fit in the Model 220 TBI assembly but are calibrated for different flow rates.

21   Slide the new filter into place on the nozzle of the injector **(see illustration)**.

22   Lubricate the new lower (smaller) O-ring with automatic transmission fluid and place it on the small shoulder at the bottom of the fuel injector cavity in the fuel meter body **(see illustration)**.

23   Install the steel back-up washer in the injector cavity **(see illustration)**.

10A.22 Lubricate the lower O-ring (arrow) with transmission fluid then place it on the shoulder in the bottom of the injector cavity

10A.23 Place the steel back-up washer on the shoulder near the top of the injector cavity

10A.24 Lubricate the upper O-ring with transmission fluid then install it on top of the steel washer

10A.25 Make sure that the lug is aligned with the groove in the bottom of the fuel injector cavity

24   Lubricate the new upper (larger) O-ring with automatic transmission fluid and install it on top of the steel back-up washer **(see illustration)**. **Note:** *The backup washer and the large O-ring must be installed before the injector. If they aren't, improper seating of the large O-ring could cause fuel leakage.*

25   To install an injector, align the raised lug on the injector base with the notch in the fuel meter body cavity **(see illustration)**. Push down on the injector until it is fully seated in the fuel meter body. **Note:** *The electrical terminals should be parallel with the throttle shaft.*

26   Install the fuel meter cover assembly and gasket.

27   Attach the cable to the negative terminal of the battery.

28   With the engine off and the ignition on, check for fuel leaks.

29   Attach the electrical connectors to the fuel injectors.

30   Install the air cleaner housing assembly, adapter and gaskets.

Throttle Position Sensor (TPS)

31   Remove the two TPS attaching screws and retainers and remove the TPS from the throttle body.

32   If you intend to re-use the same TPS, do not attempt to clean it by soaking it in any liquid cleaner or solvent. The TPS is a delicate electrical component and can be damaged by solvents.

33   Install the TPS on the throttle body while lining up the TPS lever with the TPS drive lever.

34   Install the two TPS attaching screws and retainers.

35   Install the air cleaner housing assembly, adapter and gaskets.

36   Attach the cable to the negative terminal of the battery. **Note:** *See the non-adjustable TPS output check at end of this section.*

Idle Air Control (IAC) valve

37   Unplug the electrical connector from the IAC valve and remove the IAC valve **(see illustration)**.

38   Remove and discard the old IAC valve gasket. Clean any old gasket material from the surface of the throttle body assembly to insure proper sealing of the new gasket.

10A.37 The IAC valve can be removed with an adjustable wrench

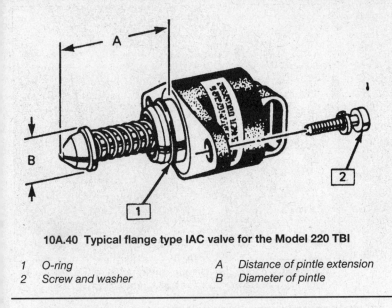

10A.40 Typical flange type IAC valve for the Model 220 TBI

1	O-ring	A	Distance of pintle extension
2	Screw and washer	B	Diameter of pintle

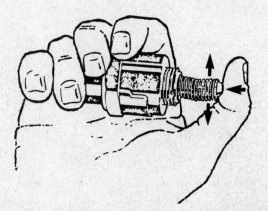

10A.41a To adjust an IAC valve with a collar, retract the valve pintle by exerting firm pressure while using a slight side-to-side movement on the pintle

39 All pintles in IAC valves on Model 220 TBI units have the same dual taper. However, the pintles on some units have a 12 mm diameter and the pintles on others have a 10mm diameter. A replacement IAC valve must have the appropriate pintle taper and diameter for proper seating of the valve in the throttle body.

40 Measure the distance between the tip of the pintle and the housing mounting surface with the pintle fully extended **(see illustration)**. If dimension "A" is greater than 1-1/8 inches, it must be reduced to prevent damage to the valve.

41 If the pintle must be adjusted, determine whether your valve is a Type I (collar around the electrical terminal) or a Type II (no collar around the electrical terminal).

a) To adjust the pintle of an IAC valve with a collar, grasp the valve and exert firm pressure on the pintle with the thumb. Use a slight side-to-side movement on the pintle as you press it in with your thumb **(see illustration)**.

b) To adjust the pintle of an IAC valve without a collar, compress the retaining spring while turning the pintle clockwise **(see illustration)**. Return the spring end to its original position with the straight portion aligned in the slot under the flat surface of the valve **(see illustration)**.

42 Install the IAC valve and tighten it securely. Attach the electrical connector.

43 Install the air cleaner housing assembly, adapter and gaskets.

44 Attach the cable to the negative terminal of the battery.

45 Start the engine and allow it to reach operating temperature, then turn it off. No adjustment of the IAC valve is required after installation. The IAC valve is reset by the ECM when the engine is turned off.

Fuel meter body assembly

46 Unplug the electrical connectors from the fuel injectors.

47 Remove the fuel meter cover/pressure regulator assembly, fuel meter cover gasket, fuel meter outlet gasket and pressure regulator seal.

48 Remove the fuel injectors.

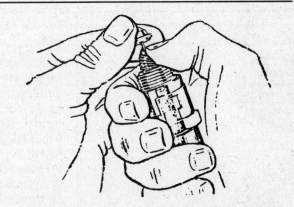

10A.41b To adjust an IAC valve without a collar, compress the valve retaining spring while turning the valve clockwise . . .

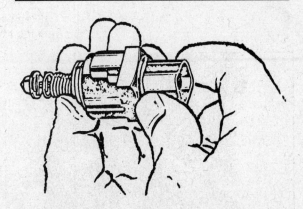

10A.41c . . . then return the spring to its original position with the straight portion aligned in the slot under the flat surface of the valve

10A.50 Remove the fuel inlet and outlet nuts from the fuel meter body

10A.52 Once the fuel inlet and outlet nuts are off, pull the fuel meter body straight up to separate it from the throttle body

49   Unscrew the fuel inlet and return line threaded fittings, detach the lines and remove the O-rings.

50   Remove the fuel inlet and outlet nuts and gaskets from the fuel meter body assembly **(see illustration)**. Note the locations of the nuts to ensure proper re-assembly. The inlet nut has a larger passage than the outlet nut.

51   Remove the gasket from the inner end of each fuel nut.

52   Remove the fuel meter body-to-throttle body attaching screws and remove the fuel meter body from the throttle body **(see illustration)**.

53   Install the new throttle body-to-fuel meter body gasket. Match the cut-out portions in the gasket with the openings in the throttle body.

54   Install the fuel meter body on the throttle body. Coat the fuel meter body-to-throttle body attaching screws with thread locking compound before installing them.

55   Install the fuel inlet and outlet nuts, with new gaskets, in the fuel meter body and tighten them securely. Install the fuel inlet and return line threaded fittings with new O-rings. Use a backup wrench to prevent the nuts from turning.

56   Install the fuel injectors.

57   Install the fuel meter cover/pressure regulator assembly.

58   Attach the cable to the negative terminal of the battery.

59   Attach the electrical connectors to the fuel injectors.

60   With the engine off and the ignition on, check for leaks around the fuel meter body, the gasket and around the fuel line nuts and threaded fittings.

61   Install the air cleaner housing assembly, adapters and gaskets.

Throttle body assembly

62   Unplug all electrical connectors - the IAC valve, TPS and fuel injectors. Detach the grommet with the wires from the throttle body.

63   Detach the throttle linkage, return spring(s), transmission control cable (automatics) and, if equipped, cruise control.

64   Clearly label, then detach, all vacuum hoses.

10A.65 When disconnecting the fuel feed and return lines from the fuel inlet and outlet nuts, be sure to use a backup wrench to prevent damage to the lines

10A.66 To remove the Model 220 throttle body from the intake manifold, remove the three bolts (arrows)

65   Using a backup wrench, detach the inlet and outlet fuel line nuts **(see illustration)**. Remove the fuel line O-rings from the nuts and discard them.

66   Remove the TBI mounting bolts **(see illustration)** and lift the TBI unit from the intake manifold. Remove and discard the TBI manifold gasket.

67   Place the TBI unit on a holding fixture (Kent-Moore J-9789-118 or BT-3553 or equivalent). **Note**: *If you don't have a holding fixture, and decide to place the TBI directly on a work bench surface, be extremely careful when servicing it. The throttle valve can be easily damaged.*

68   Remove the fuel meter body-to-throttle body attaching screws and separate the fuel meter body from the throttle body.

69   Remove the throttle body-to-fuel meter body gasket and discard it.

70   Remove the TPS.

71   Invert the throttle body on a flat surface for greater stability and remove the IAC valve.

72   Clean the throttle body assembly in a cold immersion cleaner. Clean the metal parts thoroughly and blow dry with compressed air. Be sure that all fuel and air passages are free of dirt or burrs. **Caution**: *Do not place the TPS, IAC valve, pressure regulator diaphragm, fuel injectors or other components containing rubber in the solvent or cleaning bath. If the throttle body requires cleaning, soaking time in the cleaner should be kept to a minimum. Some models have throttle shaft dust seals that could lose their effectiveness by extended soaking.*

73   Inspect the mating surfaces for damage that could affect gasket sealing. Inspect the throttle lever and valve for dirt, binds, nicks and other damage.

74   Invert the throttle body on a flat surface for stability and install the IAC valve and the TPS.

75   Install a new throttle body-to-fuel meter body gasket and place the fuel meter body assembly on the throttle body assembly. Coat the fuel meter body-to-throttle body attaching screws with thread locking compound and tighten them securely.

76   Install the TBI unit and tighten the mounting bolts securely. Use a new TBI-to-manifold gasket.

77   Install new O-rings on the fuel line nuts. Install the fuel line and outlet nuts by hand to prevent stripping the threads. Using a backup wrench, tighten the nuts securely.

78   Attach the vacuum hoses, throttle linkage, return spring(s), transmission control cable (automatics) and cruise control cable if equipped. Attach the grommet, with wire harness, to the throttle body.

79   Plug in all electrical connectors, making sure that the connectors are fully seated and latched.

80   Check to see if the accelerator pedal is free by depressing the pedal to the floor and releasing it with the engine off.

81   Connect the negative battery cable, and, with the engine off and the ignition on, check for leaks around the fuel line nuts.

82   Adjust the minimum idle speed and check the TPS output (see Steps 84 through 93).

83   Install the air cleaner housing assembly, adapter and gaskets.

Minimum idle speed adjustment

Note: *This adjustment should be performed only when the throttle body has been replaced. The engine should be at normal operating temperature before making the adjustment.*

84   Remove the air cleaner housing assembly, adapter and gaskets.

85   Plug any vacuum ports as required by the VECI label.

86   With the IAC valve connected, ground the diagnostic terminal of the ALDL connector. Turn on the ignition but do not start the engine. Wait at least 30 seconds to allow the IAC valve pintle to extend and seat in the throttle body. Disconnect the IAC valve electrical connector. Remove the ground from the diagnostic terminal and start the engine.

87   Remove the plug by first piercing it with an awl, then applying leverage.

88   Adjust the idle stop screw to obtain the idle speed specified on the VECI label, in neutral (manual) or in Drive (automatic).

89   Turn the ignition off and reconnect the IAC valve electrical connector.

90   Unplug any plugged vacuum line ports.

91   Install the air cleaner housing assembly, adapter and new gaskets.

Non-adjustable TPS output check

Note: *This check should be performed only when the throttle body or the TPS has been replaced or after the minimum idle speed has been adjusted.*

92   Connect a digital voltmeter from the TPS connector center terminal "B" to outside terminal "A" (you'll have to fabricate jumpers for terminal access).

93   With the ignition on and the engine off, TPS voltage should be less than one volt. If it's more than the specified voltage, check the minimum idle speed before replacing the TPS.

Part B: Model 300 Throttle Body Injection (TBI)

Warning: *Gasoline is extremely flammable, so take extra precautions when you work on any part of the fuel system. Don't smoke or allow open flames or bare light bulbs near the work area, and don't work in a garage where a natural gas-type appliance (such as a water heater or a clothes dryer) with a pilot light is present. Since gasoline is carcinogenic, wear latex gloves when there's a possibility of being exposed to fuel, and, if you spill any fuel on your skin, rinse it off immediately with soap and water. Mop up any spills immediately and do not store fuel-soaked rags where they could ignite. The fuel system is under constant pressure, so, if any fuel lines are to be disconnected, the fuel pressure in the system must be relieved first (see Chapter 4 for more information). When you perform any kind of work on the fuel system, wear safety glasses and have a Class B type fire extinguisher on hand.*

Note: *Because of its relative simplicity, a throttle body assembly does not need to be removed from the intake manifold nor completely disassembled for component replacement. However, for the sake of clarity, the following procedures are shown with the TBI unit removed from the vehicle.*

1   Relieve the fuel pressure (see Chapter 4).
2   Detach the cable from the negative terminal of the battery.
3   Remove the air cleaner housing assembly, adapter and gaskets.

Fuel meter cover and fuel injector

Disassembly

4   Remove the injector electrical connector (on top of the TBI) by squeezing the two tabs together and pulling straight up.
5   Unscrew the five fuel meter cover retaining screws and lockwashers securing the fuel meter cover to the fuel meter body. Note the location of the two short screws **(see illustration)**.

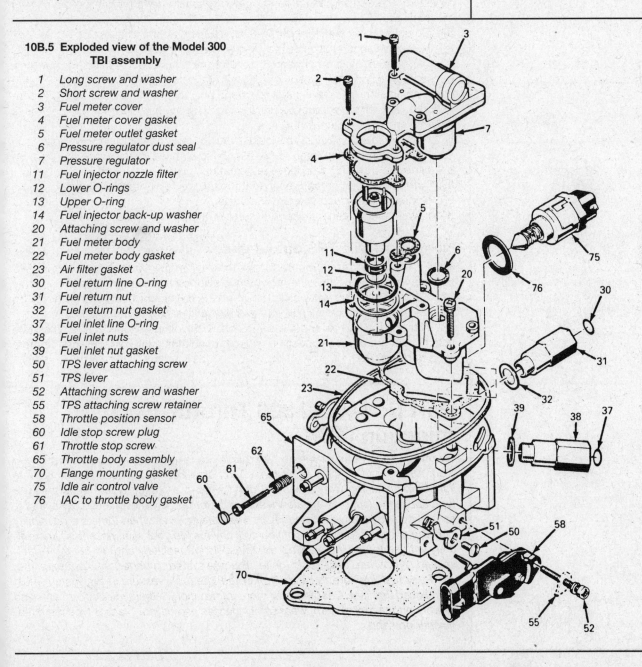

10B.5 Exploded view of the Model 300 TBI assembly

1	*Long screw and washer*
2	*Short screw and washer*
3	*Fuel meter cover*
4	*Fuel meter cover gasket*
5	*Fuel meter outlet gasket*
6	*Pressure regulator dust seal*
7	*Pressure regulator*
11	*Fuel injector nozzle filter*
12	*Lower O-rings*
13	*Upper O-ring*
14	*Fuel injector back-up washer*
20	*Attaching screw and washer*
21	*Fuel meter body*
22	*Fuel meter body gasket*
23	*Air filter gasket*
30	*Fuel return line O-ring*
31	*Fuel return nut*
32	*Fuel return nut gasket*
37	*Fuel inlet line O-ring*
38	*Fuel inlet nuts*
39	*Fuel inlet nut gasket*
50	*TPS lever attaching screw*
51	*TPS lever*
52	*Attaching screw and washer*
55	*TPS attaching screw retainer*
58	*Throttle position sensor*
60	*Idle stop screw plug*
61	*Throttle stop screw*
65	*Throttle body assembly*
70	*Flange mounting gasket*
75	*Idle air control valve*
76	*IAC to throttle body gasket*

10B.7 The fuel pressure regulator is installed in the fuel meter cover and pre-adjusted at the factory - don't remove the four retaining screws (arrows) or you may damage the regulator

10B.8a The best way to remove the fuel injector is to pry on it with a screwdriver, using a second screwdriver as a fulcrum

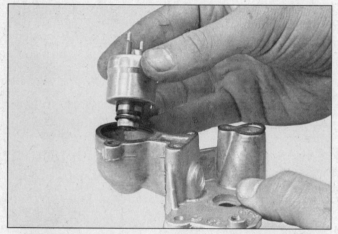

10B.8b Note the position of the terminals on top and the dowel pin on the bottom of the injector in relation to the fuel meter body when you lift the injector out of the body

6   Remove the fuel meter cover. **Caution**: *Do not immerse the fuel meter cover in solvent. It might damage the pressure regulator diaphragm and gasket.*

7   The fuel meter cover contains the fuel pressure regulator, which is pre-set and plugged at the factory. If a malfunction occurs, it cannot be serviced, and must be replaced as a complete assembly. **Warning**: *Do not remove the screws securing the pressure regulator to the fuel meter cover* (see illustration). *It has a large spring inside under heavy compression.*

8   With the old fuel meter cover gasket in place to prevent damage to the casting, carefully pry the injector from the fuel meter body with a screwdriver until it can be lifted free **(see illustrations). Caution**: *Use care in removing the injector to prevent damage to the electrical connector terminals, the injector fuel filter, the O-ring and the nozzle.*

9   The fuel meter body should be removed from the throttle body if it needs to be cleaned. To remove it, remove the fuel feed and return line fittings and the Torx screws that attach the fuel meter body to the throttle body.

10   Remove the old gasket from the fuel meter cover and discard it. Remove the large O-ring and steel back-up washer from the upper counterbore of the fuel meter body injector cavity **(see illustration).** Clean the fuel meter body thoroughly in solvent and blow it dry.

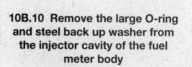

10B.10 Remove the large O-ring and steel back up washer from the injector cavity of the fuel meter body

1   *Fuel injector*
2   *Filter*
3   *Small O-ring*
4   *Large O-ring*
5   *Steel back-up washer*

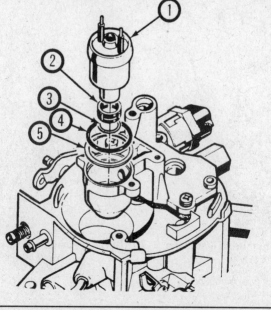

11   Remove the small O-ring from the nozzle end of the injector. Carefully rotate the injector fuel filter back and forth and remove the filter from the base of the injector **(see illustration)**. Gently clean the filter in solvent and allow it to drip dry. It is too small and delicate to dry with compressed air. **Caution**: *The fuel injector itself is an electrical component. Do not immerse it in any type of cleaning solvent.*

12   The fuel injector is not serviceable. If it is malfunctioning, replace it as an assembly.

Reassembly

13   Install the clean fuel injector nozzle filter on the end of the fuel injector with the larger end of the filter facing the injector so that the filter covers the raised rib at the base of the injector. Use a twisting motion to position the filter against the base of the injector.

14   Lubricate a new small O-ring with automatic transmission fluid. Push the O-ring onto the nozzle end of the injector until it presses against the injector fuel filter.

15   Insert the steel backup washer in the top counterbore of the fuel meter body injector cavity.

16   Lubricate a new large O-ring with automatic transmission fluid and install it directly over the backup washer. Be sure that the O-ring is seated properly in the cavity and is flush with the top of the fuel meter body casting surface. **Caution**: *The back-up washer and large O-ring must be installed before the injector or improper seating of the large O-ring could cause fuel to leak.*

17   Install the injector in the cavity in the fuel meter body, aligning the raised lug on the injector base with the cast-in notch in the fuel meter body cavity. Push straight down on the injector with both thumbs **(see illustration)** until it is fully seated in the cavity. **Note**: *The electrical terminals of the injector should be approximately parallel to the throttle shaft.*

18   Install a new fuel outlet passage gasket on the fuel meter cover and a new fuel meter cover gasket on the fuel meter body **(see illustration)**.

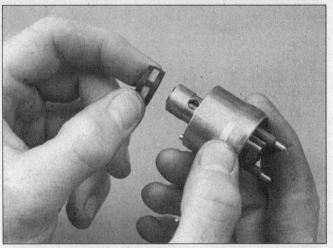

10B.11 Gently rotate the fuel injector filter back and forth and pull it off the nozzle

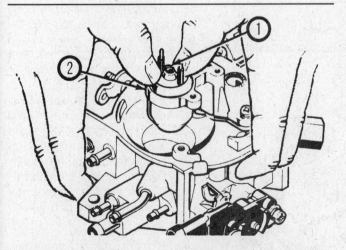

10B.17 Push straight down with both thumbs to install the injector in the fuel meter body

1   Fuel injector   2   Fuel meter body

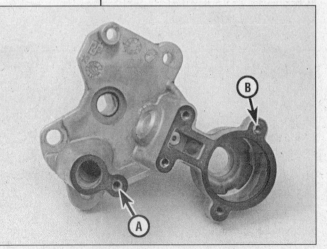

10B.18 Position the fuel outlet passage gasket (A) and the fuel meter cover gasket (B) properly

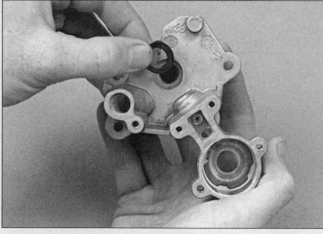

10B.19 Install a new dust seal into the recess of the fuel meter body

19   Install a new dust seal into the recess on the fuel meter body **(see illustration)**.

20   Install the fuel meter cover onto the fuel meter body, making sure that the pressure regulator dust seal and cover gaskets are in place.

21   Apply a thread locking compound to the threads of the fuel meter cover attaching screws. Install the screws (the two short screws go next to the injector) and tighten them securely. **Note**: *Service repair kits include a small vial of thread locking compound with directions for use. If this material is not available, use Loctite 262, GM part number 1052624, or equivalent. Do not use a higher strength locking compound than recommended, as this may prevent subsequent removal of the attaching screws or cause breakage of the screwhead if removal becomes necessary.*

22   Plug in the electrical connector to the injector.

23   Install the air cleaner.

Idle Air Control (IAC) valve

Removal

24   Unplug the electrical connector at the IAC valve.

25   Remove the IAC valve with a wrench on the hex surface only **(see illustration)**

Installation

26   Before installing a new IAC valve, measure the distance the valve is extended **(see illustration)**. The measurement should be made from the motor housing to the end of the cone. The distance should be no greater than 1-1/8 inch. If the cone is extended too far, damage may occur to the valve when it is installed.

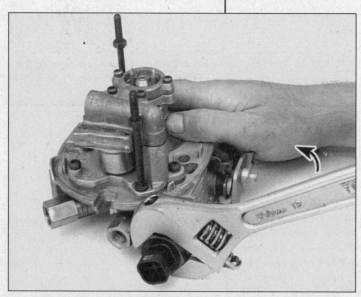

10B.25 Remove the IAC valve with a large wrench, but be careful - it's a delicate device

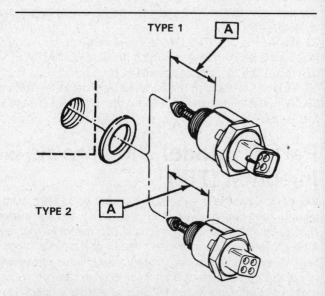

10B.26 Distance A should be less than 1-1/8 inch for either type of Idle Air Control valve - if it isn't, determine which kind of valve you have and adjust it accordingly

Type 1 - with electrical terminal collar
Type 2 - without electrical terminal collar

27   Identify the replacement IAC valve as either a Type I (with a collar at the electric terminal end) or a Type II (without a collar). If the measured dimension "A" is greater than 1-1/8 inch, the distance must be reduced as follows:

Type I - Exert firm pressure on the valve to retract it (a slight side-to-side movement may be helpful).

Type II - Compress the retaining spring of the valve while turning the valve in a clockwise direction. Return the spring to its original position with the straight portion of the spring aligned with the flat surface of the valve.

28   Install the new IAC valve to the throttle body. Use the new gasket supplied with the assembly.

29   Plug in the electrical connector.

30   Install the air cleaner.

31   Start the engine and allow it to reach normal operating temperature. The Electronic Control Module (ECM) will reset the idle speed when the vehicle is driven above 35 mph.

Throttle Position Sensor (TPS)

32   The Throttle Position Sensor (TPS) is connected to the throttle shaft on the TBI unit. As the throttle valve angle is changed (as the accelerator pedal is moved), the output of the TPS also changes. At a closed throttle position, the output of the TPS is below 1.25-volts. As the throttle valve opens, the output increases so that, at wide-open throttle, the output voltage is approximately 5-volts.

33   A broken or loose TPS can cause intermittent bursts of fuel from the injector and an unstable idle, because the ECM thinks the throttle is moving. A problem in any of the TPS circuits will set either a Code 21 or 22 (see "Trouble Codes," Chapter 6).

34   The TPS is not adjustable. The ECM uses the reading at idle for the zero reading. If the TPS malfunctions, it is replaced as a unit.

35   Unscrew the two Torx screws **(see illustration)** and remove the TPS.

36   Install the new TPS. **Note**: *Make sure that the tang on the lever is properly engaged with the stop on the TBI.*

37   Install the air cleaner assembly.

38   Attach the cable to the negative terminal of the battery.

39   With the ignition switch on and the engine off, check for fuel leaks.

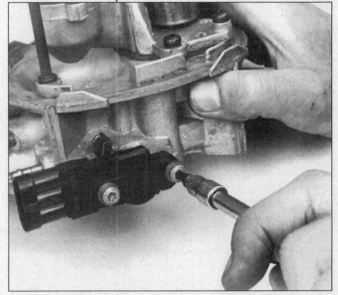

10B.35 The Throttle Position Sensor (TPS) is mounted to the side of the TBI with two Torx screws

Part C: Model 700 Throttle Body Injection (TBI)

Warning: *Gasoline is extremely flammable, so take extra precautions when you work on any part of the fuel system. Don't smoke or allow open flames or bare light bulbs near the work area, and don't work in a garage where a natural gas-type appliance (such as a water heater or a clothes dryer) with a pilot light is present. Since gasoline is carcinogenic, wear latex gloves when there's a possibility of being exposed to fuel, and, if you spill any fuel on your skin, rinse it off immediately with soap and water. Mop up any spills immediately and do not store fuel-soaked rags where they could ignite. The fuel system is under constant pressure, so, if any fuel lines are to be disconnected, the fuel pressure in the system must be relieved first (see Chapter 4 for more information). When you perform any kind of work on the fuel system, wear safety glasses and have a Class B type fire extinguisher on hand.*

10C.5 Exploded view of the Model 700 throttle body assembly

1   Air filter gasket
2   Fuel line inlet nut O-ring
3   Fuel line outlet nut O-ring
4   Flange gasket
5   Fuel meter assembly
6   Fuel meter body attaching screw and washer
7   Fuel meter body to throttle body gasket
8   Injector retainer screw
9   Injector retainer
10 Fuel injector
11 Upper fuel injector O-ring
12 Lower fuel injector O-ring
13 Injector filter
14 Pressure regulator cover
15 Pressure regulator attaching screw
16 Spring seat
17 Pressure regulator spring
18 Pressure regulator diaphragm
19 Fuel inlet nut
20 Fuel nut seal
21 Fuel outlet nut
22 Throttle body
23 Idle stop screw plug
24 Idle stop screw and washer
25 Idle stop screw spring
26 Throttle Position Sensor (TPS)
27 TPS attaching screw and washer
28 TPS screw
29 Idle Air Control (IAC) valve
30 IAC attaching screw
31 IAC O-ring
32 Tube module
33 Tube module screw
34 Tube module gasket

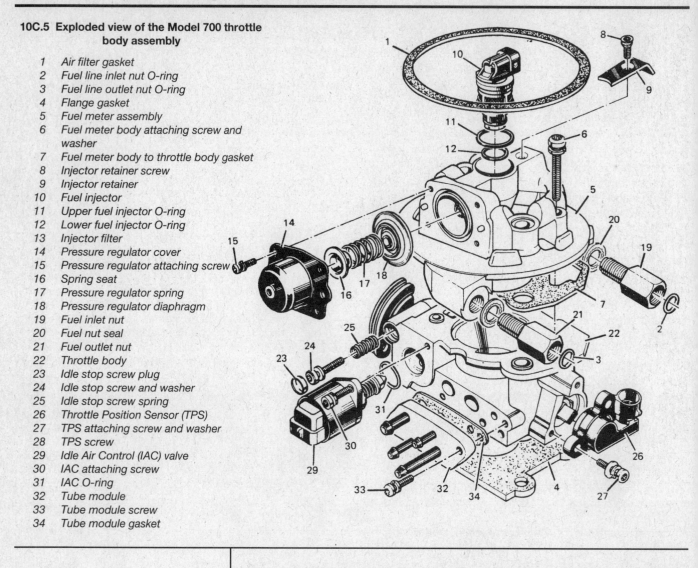

Note: *Because of its relative simplicity, the throttle body does not need to be removed from the intake manifold or disassembled for component replacement. However, for the sake of clarity, the following procedures are shown with the TBI removed from the vehicle.*

1   Relieve the fuel pressure (see Chapter 4)
2   Detach the cable from the negative terminal of the battery.
3   Remove the air cleaner housing assembly, adapter and gaskets.

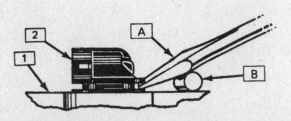

10C.6 To remove the fuel injector unit (2) from the fuel meter body (1) insert a screwdriver (A) under the fuel injector flange as shown, place a fulcrum (B) behind the tip and pry the injector loose

Fuel injector

4   Unplug the electrical connector from the fuel injector.
5   Remove the injector retainer screw and retainer **(see illustration)**.
6   To remove the fuel injector assembly, place a screwdriver blade under the ridge opposite the connector **(see illustration)** and carefully pry it out.
7   Remove the upper and lower O-rings from the injector and from the fuel injector cavity and discard them.
8   Inspect the fuel injector filter for evidence of dirt and contamination. If present, look for the presence of dirt in the fuel lines and the fuel tank.

9   Lubricate new upper and lower O-rings with transmission fluid and install them on the injector. Make sure that the upper O-ring is in the groove and the lower one is flush up against the filter.

10 To install the injector assembly, push it straight into the fuel injector cavity. Be sure that the electrical connector end on the injector is facing in the general direction of the cut-out in the fuel meter body for the wire grommet. **Note**: *If you are installing a new injector, be sure to replace the old unit with an identical part. Injectors from other models will fit in the Model 700 TBI assembly but are calibrated for different flow rates.*

11 Using thread locking compound on the retainer attaching screw, install the injector retainer and tighten the retaining screw.

12 Install the air cleaner housing assembly, adapter and gaskets.

13 With the engine off and the ignition on, check for fuel leaks.

Fuel pressure regulator

14 Remove the four pressure regulator attaching screws while keeping the pressure regulator compressed. **Caution**: *The pressure regulator contains a large spring under heavy compression. Use care when removing the screws to prevent personal injury.*

15 Remove the pressure regulator cover assembly.

16 Remove the pressure regulator spring, seat, and the pressure regulator diaphragm.

17 Using a magnifying glass, if necessary, inspect the pressure regulator seat in the fuel meter body cavity for pitting, nicks or irregularities. If any damage is present, the entire fuel body casting must be replaced.

18 Install the new pressure regulator diaphragm assembly. Make sure it is seated in the groove in the fuel meter body.

19 Install the regulator spring seat and spring into the cover assembly.

20 Install the cover assembly over the diaphragm while aligning the mounting holes. **Caution**: *Use care while installing the pressure regulator to prevent misalignment and possible leaks.*

21 While maintaining pressure on the regulator spring, install the four screw assemblies that have been coated with thread locking compound.

22 Reconnect the negative battery cable. With the engine off and the ignition on, check for fuel leaks.

Throttle Position Sensor (TPS)

23 Unplug the electrical connector from the TPS.

24 Remove the two TPS attaching screws and remove the TPS from the throttle body.

25 With the throttle valve closed, install the TPS on the throttle shaft. Rotate it counterclockwise to align the mounting holes.

26 Install the two TPS attaching screws.

27 Install the air cleaner housing assembly, adapter and gaskets.

28 Attach the cable to the negative terminal of the battery. **Note**: *See non-adjustable TPS output check at end of this Section.*

Idle Air Control (IAC) valve

29 Unplug the electrical connector from the IAC valve and remove the IAC valve mounting screws and the IAC valve.

30 Remove the O-ring from the IAC valve and discard it.

31 Clean the IAC valve seating surfaces on the throttle body to assure proper sealing of the new O-ring and proper contact if the IAC valve flange.

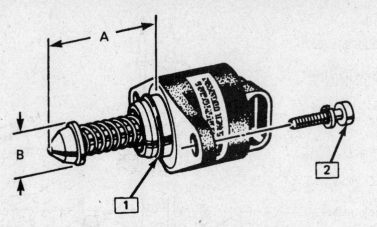

10C.32 The Idle Air Control valve pintle must not extend more than 1-1/8 inch - also, replace the O-ring if it is brittle

A   Distance of pintle extension
B   Diameter of pintle

1   O-ring
2   Screw and washer

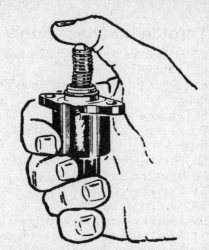

10C.33 To reduce the IAC valve pintle extension, grasp the valve and depress the pintle using a slight side-to-side motion

32   Before installing a new IAC valve, measure the distance between the tip of the valve pintle and the flange mounting surface when the pintle is fully extended **(see illustration)**. If dimension "A" is greater than 1-1/8 inches, it must be reduced to prevent damage to the valve.

33   To retract the IAC valve, grasp the IAC valve as shown and exert firm pressure with your thumb, using a slight side-to-side movement on the valve pintle **(see illustration)**.

34   Lubricate a new O-ring with transmission fluid and install it on the IAC valve.

35   Install the IAC valve to the throttle body. Coat the IAC valve attaching screws with thread locking compound. Install and tighten them securely. Plug in the IAC valve electrical connector.

36   Install the air cleaner housing assembly, adapter and gaskets.

37   Attach the cable to the negative terminal of the battery.

38   Start the engine, allow it to reach operating temperature, then take the vehicle for a drive. When the engine reaches normal operating temperature the ECM will set the proper idle speed.

Tube module assembly

39   Remove the tube module assembly attaching screws and remove the tube module.

40   Remove the tube module gasket and discard it. Clean any old gasket material from the surface of the throttle body to insure proper sealing of the new gasket.

41   Install the new tube module gasket.

42   Install the tube module and tighten the screws securely..

43   Install the air cleaner housing assembly, adapter and gaskets.

Fuel meter assembly

44   Remove the TBI unit (see Step 50).

45   Remove the two fuel meter body attaching screws and washers and remove the fuel meter assembly from the throttle body.

46   If you are installing a new fuel meter, remove the fuel pressure regulator and the fuel outlet nut and transfer them to the new fuel meter.

47   Remove the fuel meter body-to-throttle body gasket and discard it.

48   Install a new fuel meter-to-throttle body gasket. Match the cutout portions of the gasket with the openings in the throttle body.

49   Install the fuel meter onto the throttle body and tighten the attaching screws.

Throttle body assembly

50   Unplug the electrical connectors from the fuel injector, IAC and TPS.

51   Remove the throttle body mounting studs (see illustration).

52   Remove and discard the throttle body-to-intake manifold gasket. Place the TBI assembly on a clean work surface.

53   Remove the fuel injector, fuel meter assembly, TPS, IAC valve and the tube module.

54   Install the new tube module assembly, IAC valve and TPS on the new throttle body assembly.

55   Install a new fuel meter body-to-throttle body gasket.

56   Install the fuel meter assembly and fuel injector.

57   Install a new throttle body-to-intake manifold gasket and install the throttle body assembly on the intake manifold. Tighten the mounting studs securely.

Minimum idle speed adjustment

Note: *This adjustment should be performed only when the throttle body assembly has been replaced. The engine should be at normal operating temperature before making the adjustment.*

58   Plug any vacuum line ports as required (see the VECI label).

59   With the IAC valve connected, ground the diagnostic terminal of the ALDL connector.

60   Turn the ignition on but do not start the engine. Wait at least 30 seconds to allow the IAC valve pintle to extend and seat in the throttle body. Unplug the IAC valve electrical connector.

61   Remove the ground jumper from the diagnostic terminal and start the engine.

62   The throttle stop screw used for regulating minimum idle speed is adjusted at the factory. The screw is covered with a plug to discourage unauthorized adjustments (see illustration). To remove the plug, pierce it with an awl, then apply leverage.

63   With the transmission in Neutral (manual) or Park (automatic), adjust the idle stop screw to obtain the idle speed specified on the VECI label.

64   Turn the ignition off and reconnect the IAC valve electrical connector, unplug any plugged vacuum line ports and install the air cleaner housing assembly, adapter and gaskets.

Non-adjustable TPS output check

Note: *This check should be performed only when the throttle body or the throttle position sensor has been replaced or after the minimum idle speed has been adjusted.*

65   Connect a digital voltmeter from center terminal "B" to outside terminal "A" of the TPS connector.

66   With the ignition on and the engine stopped, the TPS voltage should be less than 1.25 volt. If the voltage is greater than specified, replace the TPS.

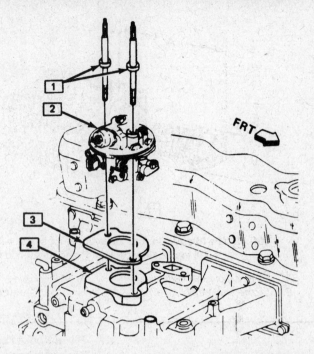

10C.51 Exploded view of the Model 700 mounting installation

1	Mounting studs	3	Gasket
2	TBI unit	4	Intake manifold

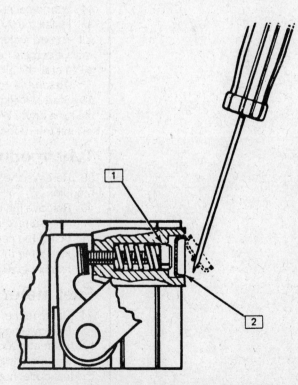

10C.62 To gain access to the factory sealed idle stop screw (1), remove the plug (2) by piercing it with an awl, then prying it loose

11 Ford Central Fuel Injection (CFI) Unit overhaul

Warning: *Gasoline is extremely flammable, so take extra precautions when you work on any part of the fuel system. Don't smoke or allow open flames or bare light bulbs near the work area, and don't work in a garage where a natural gas-type appliance (such as a water heater or a clothes dryer) with a pilot light is present. Since gasoline is carcinogenic, wear latex gloves when there's a possibility of being exposed to fuel, and, if you spill any fuel on your skin, rinse it off immediately with soap and water. Mop up any spills immediately and do not store fuel-soaked rags where they could ignite. The fuel system is under constant pressure, so, if any fuel lines are to be disconnected, the fuel pressure in the system must be relieved first (see Chapter 4 for more information). When you perform any kind of work on the fuel system, wear safety glasses and have a Class B type fire extinguisher on hand.*

Fuel Injector

Note: *If you're replacing the fuel injector, it isn't necessary to remove the fuel charging assembly from the intake manifold. If, however, you need to replace the base gasket, the spacer gasket between the main body and the throttle body or the idle speed control (ISC) throttle actuator, the fuel charging assembly must be removed from the intake manifold. Other than the components specifically mentioned here, we do not recommend further disassembly of the fuel charging assembly.*

1   Detach the cable from the negative terminal of the battery and relieve the fuel system pressure (see Chapter 4).

2   Unplug the fuel injector electrical connector and remove the screw and retainer **(see illustration)**.

3   Using a screwdriver, carefully pry the fuel injector out of the fuel charging assembly **(see illustration)**.

4   The injector has two O-rings; a large, upper O-ring and a small, lower one. The lower O-ring may stick to the wall of the fuel injector bore **(see illustration)**. Be sure to remove and discard it.

11.2 Before removing the fuel injector from the fuel charging assembly main body, unplug the electrical connector and set it aside, then remove the screw (arrow) and the retainer

11.3 Carefully pry the injector from the bore in the fuel charging assembly main body with a screwdriver

11.4 The small O-ring which seals the lower end of the injector will often come off the injector during removal and stick to the walls of the injector bore - be sure to remove it

11.5a If you're planning to reinstall the old injector, be sure to peel off the old injector O-rings with a small screwdriver and discard them

11.5b Note the position of the large (upper) O-ring and the small (lower) one - they must be attached properly before installing the injector

5   Whether you're replacing the injector or reinstalling the original, do not reuse the old O-rings. Carefully peel the O-rings off the old injector **(see illustration)**. Position the new O-rings as shown **(see illustration)** and lubricate them with clean engine oil.

6   Installation of the injector is the reverse of removal.

Base gasket

7   Relieve the fuel system pressure (see Chapter 4).

8   Detach the cable from the negative terminal of the battery.

9   Remove the air intake duct.

10   Clearly label the wires and terminals on the throttle body, then unplug and set aside all wires **(see illustration)**.

11   Detach the PCV hose from the throttle body.

12   Detach the fuel pressure and return lines from the fuel charging assembly **(see illustration)**. If necessary, refer to Section 3 for a detailed description of fuel line fitting removal.

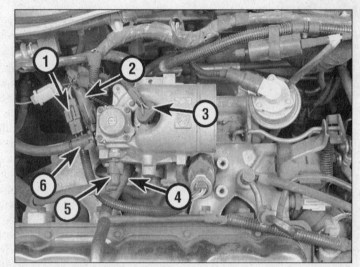

11.10 Disconnect the following items before removing the fuel charging assembly:

1	ISC connector	4	PCV valve vacuum hose
2	TPS connector	5	Fuel line fitting
3	Fuel injector connector	6	Fuel line fitting

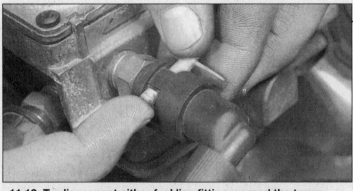

11.12 To disconnect either fuel line fitting, spread the tangs of the hairpin clip apart far enough to disengage them from the fitting body, then pull the clip out - the fitting can then be pulled off

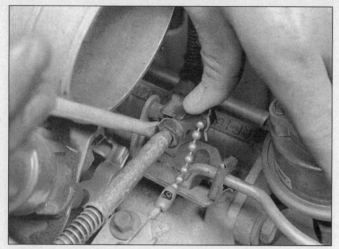

11.13 Using a screwdriver, pry the accelerator cable and, if equipped, the cruise control cable, from the throttle shaft linkage

11.14a If your vehicle is equipped with an automatic transmission or transaxle, pop the C-clip loose with a screwdriver. . .

13   Detach the throttle cable and (if equipped) cruise control cable assembly from the throttle rod **(see illustration)**.

14   If your vehicle is equipped with an automatic transmission or transaxle, re-move the C-clip **(see illustration)** and detach the transmission downshift rod from the throttle shaft. Push down on the rod to detach it **(see illustration)**.

15   Remove the two fuel charging assembly mounting nuts **(see illustration)** and detach the assembly and gasket from the intake manifold.

16   If the gasket was leaking, position a new gasket on the manifold, install the fuel charging assembly and tighten the mounting nuts.

17   The remainder of the installation procedure is the reverse of removal.

Idle speed control (ISC) throttle actuator

Note: *Handle the fuel charging assembly carefully when servicing it on the bench to avoid damage to the throttle plates.*

18   Remove the fuel charging assembly (see Steps 7 through 15).

19   Remove the three ISC bracket screws **(see illustrations)** and detach the ISC

11.14b . . . then disengage the downshift rod from the throttle shaft linkage

11.15 To detach the fuel charging assembly from the intake manifold, remove both mounting nuts (arrows)

11.19a To remove the ISC bracket, lay the fuel charging assembly upside down on a workbench and remove these two screws . . .

11.19b . . . followed by this one

and bracket assembly from the fuel charging assembly.

20 Remove the three ISC mounting screws **(see illustration)** and separate the ISC from the mounting bracket.

21 Installation is the reverse of removal.

Fuel charging body gasket

22 Remove the fuel charging assembly and ISC (Steps 7 through 15 and Step 19).

23 Turn the fuel charging assembly over and remove the four screws attaching the throttle body to the main body, then separate the two halves **(see illustration)**.

24 Remove and discard the old gasket. If it's necessary to use a gasket scraper, don't damage the mating surface.

25 With the main body resting upside down on the bench, place the new gasket in position, attach the throttle body, install the four screws and tighten them evenly and securely.

26 Install the ISC and fuel charging assembly.

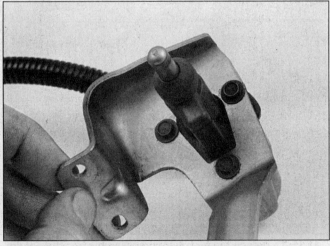

11.20 To detach the ISC motor from the bracket, remove the three mounting screws

11.23 To separate the throttle body from the main body of the fuel charging assembly, remove the four screws (arrows)

12 Chrysler Throttle Body Injection (TBI) Unit overhaul

Warning: *Gasoline is extremely flammable, so take extra precautions when you work on any part of the fuel system. Don't smoke or allow open flames or bare light bulbs near the work area, and don't work in a garage where a natural gas-type appliance (such as a water heater or a clothes dryer) with a pilot light is present. Since gasoline is carcinogenic, wear latex gloves when there's a possibility of being exposed to fuel, and, if you spill any fuel on your skin, rinse it off immediately with soap and water. Mop up any spills immediately and do not store fuel-soaked rags where they could ignite. The fuel system is under constant pressure, so, if any fuel lines are to be disconnected, the fuel pressure in the system must be relieved first (see Chapter 4 for more information). When you perform any kind of work on the fuel system, wear safety glasses and have a Class B type fire extinguisher on hand.*

Removal

1   Remove the air cleaner assembly .
2   Relieve the fuel system pressure (see Chapter 4).
3   Disconnect the negative cable from the battery.
4   Mark and disconnect the vacuum hoses and electrical connectors **(see illustration)**.

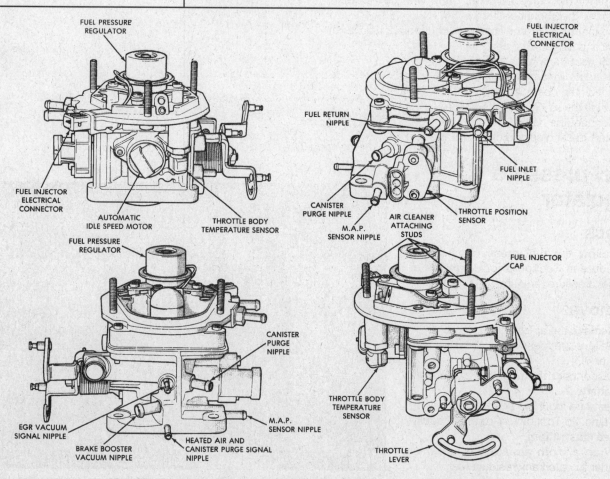

12.4 Single-point throttle body details (1989 models shown, others similar)

5   Disconnect the throttle linkage and (if equipped) the cruise control and transaxle kickdown cable.

6   Remove the throttle return spring.

7   Place rags or newspapers under the fuel hoses to catch the residual fuel. Loosen the clamps, wrap a cloth around each fuel hose and pull them off. Remove the copper washers from the hoses, noting their locations.

8   Remove the mounting bolts or nuts **(see illustration)** and lift the throttle body off the manifold. Remove all traces of old gasket material from the mating surfaces of the throttle body and intake manifold.

Installation

9   Inspect the mating surfaces of the throttle body and the manifold for nicks, burrs and debris that could cause air leaks.

10   Using a new gasket, place the throttle body in position and install the mounting bolts or nuts. Securely tighten the bolts or nuts following a criss-cross pattern.

11   Check all of the vacuum hoses and electrical connectors for damage, replacing them with new parts if necessary, then connect them.

12   Connect the throttle linkage and (if equipped) cruise control and kickdown cable.

13   Connect the throttle return spring.

14   Using new clamps, install the fuel hoses.

15   Check the operation of the throttle linkage.

16   Install the air cleaner assembly.

17   Connect the negative battery cable.

18   Start the engine and check for fuel leaks.

Fuel pressure regulator

Check

19   Follow the fuel pressure checking procedure in Section 5 for diagnosis of the fuel pressure regulator.

Removal

20   Remove the air cleaner assembly.

21   Relieve the fuel system pressure (see Chapter 4).

22   Disconnect the negative cable from the battery.

23   Remove the three screws (this will require a no. 25 Torx driver) from the regulator **(see illustration)**.

24   Wrap a cloth around the fuel inlet chamber to catch any residual fuel.

12.8 Remove the two long bolts (arrows) and the two short bolts (arrow) from the throttle body (the rear short bolt is hidden from view)

12.23 Use a Torx driver (no. 25) and remove the three screws from the regulator

12.25 If the regulator is still fastened to the throttle body after the bolts have been removed, wiggle the regulator to free-up the hardened rubber seal

25 Withdraw the pressure regulator from the throttle body **(see illustration)**.

26 Carefully remove the O-ring from the pressure regulator, followed by the gasket.

Installation

27 Place a new gasket in position on the pressure regulator and carefully install a new O-ring.

28 Place the pressure regulator in position on the throttle body, press it into position and install the three mounting screws. Tighten the screws securely.

29 Connect the negative battery cable. Check carefully for any fuel leaks.

30 Install the air cleaner assembly.

Fuel injector

Check

31 With the engine running, or cranking, listen to the sound from the injector with an automotive stethoscope and verify that the injector sounds as if it's operating normally. If you don't have a stethoscope, touch the area of the throttle body immediately above the fuel injector with your finger and try to determine whether the injector feels like it's operating smoothly. It should sound/feel smooth and uniform and its sound/feel should rise and fall with engine rpm. If the injector isn't operating, or sounds/feels erratic, check the injector electrical connector. If the connectors are snug, check for voltage to the injector using a special injector harness test light (available at most auto parts stores). If there's voltage to the injector and it isn't operating, or if it's operating erratically, replace it.

Removal

32 Remove the air cleaner assembly.

33 Relieve the fuel system pressure.

34 Disconnect the negative cable from the battery.

35 On some early model TBI units, it may be necessary to remove the fuel pressure regulator to access the fuel injector.

36 Remove the Torx screw that holds the injector cap.

37 Use two small screwdrivers and carefully pry the cap off the injector using the appropriate slots **(see illustration)**.

38 Place a small screwdriver into the hole in the injector and gently pry the injector from the throttle body unit **(see illustration)**.

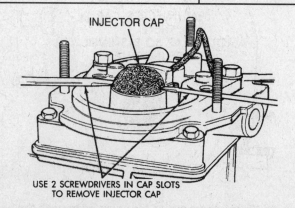

INJECTOR CAP

USE 2 SCREWDRIVERS IN CAP SLOTS
TO REMOVE INJECTOR CAP

12.37 Use two small screwdrivers to pry the injector cap off

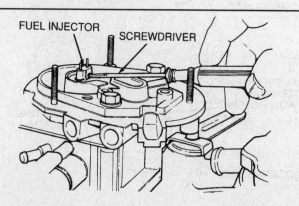

FUEL INJECTOR

SCREWDRIVER

12.38 Remove the fuel injector by inserting a small screwdriver into the slot on the injector and gently prying it up

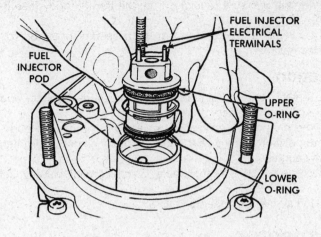

12.39 Fuel injector details

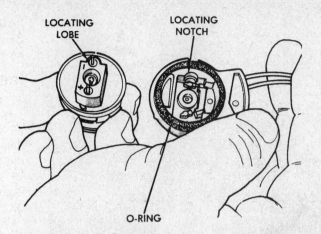

12.42a Alignment details of the cap and injector (early models)

39 Peel the upper and lower O-rings off the fuel injector **(see illustration)**. If the lower O-ring isn't on the injector, be sure to retrieve it from the throttle body.

Installation

40 Install new O-rings on the injector and a new O-ring on the injector cap.
Note: *New injectors come equipped with a new upper O-ring. Coat the O-rings with a light film of engine oil to help injector installation.*
41 Insert the injector into the throttle body.
42 Place the injector cap onto the injector. The injector and cap are keyed and must be aligned properly **(see illustrations)**.
43 Rotate the cap and injector to line up the attachment hole **(see illustration)**. Install the screws and tighten them securely.
44 Connect the negative battery cable, start the engine and check for leaks.
45 Turn off the engine and install the air cleaner assembly.

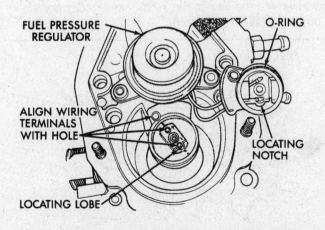

12.42b Alignment details of the cap and injector (later models)

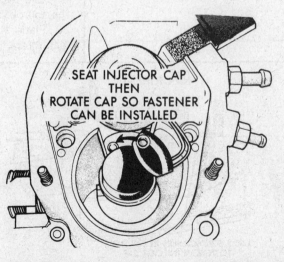

12.43 Rotate the cap so the screw aligns with the slot in the cap

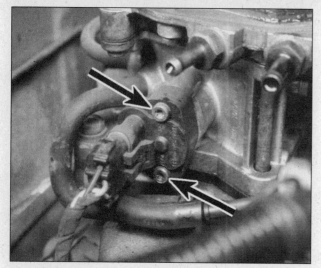

12.50 Use a Torx driver (no. 25) and remove the two bolts (arrows)

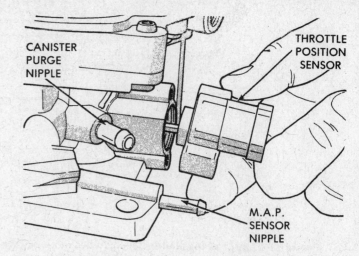

12.51 Remove the TPS carefully - don't strike it with a hammer or a hard object to loosen it from the throttle body

Throttle position sensor

Check

46   The Throttle Position Sensor (TPS) is monitored by the SMEC or SBEC (computer) located in the engine compartment. If the TPS malfunctions, a trouble code is stored in the logic module's memory. To get the computer to display any stored trouble codes, refer to the appropriate Section in Chapter 3. If a Code 24 is displayed, first check the circuit and, if necessary, replace the TPS.

Removal

47   Disconnect the negative cable from the battery.
48   Remove the air cleaner.
49   Unplug the electrical connector from the TPS.
50   Remove the two TPS-to-throttle body screws (a no. 25 Torx driver will be required) **(see illustration)**.
51   Separate the TPS from the throttle shaft **(see illustration)** and remove the O-ring.

Installation

52   Place the TPS with a new O-ring on the throttle body and install the retaining screws. Tighten the screws securely.
53   Plug in the electrical connector.
54   Install the air cleaner.
55   Connect the negative battery cable.

Automatic Idle Speed (AIS) motor

Check

56   The Automatic Idle Speed (AIS) motor is monitored by the SMEC or the SBEC (computer). If the AIS motor malfunctions, a trouble code is stored in the computer's memory. To get the computer to display any stored trouble codes, refer to the appropriate Section in Chapter 6. If a Code 25 is displayed, check the AIS motor circuit for problems. If necessary, replace the AIS motor.

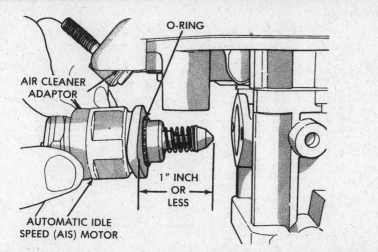

12.63 Measure the length of the pintle - if it protrudes more than one inch, take it to a dealer service department or other repair shop equipped with the necessary tool to have it retracted

Removal

57 Disconnect the negative cable from the battery.

58 Remove the air cleaner assembly.

59 Unplug the electrical connector on the AIS motor.

60 Remove the throttle body temperature sensor.

61 Remove the two retaining screws (no. 25 Torx) from the AIS motor.

62 Pull the AIS from the throttle body. Make sure the O-ring doesn't fall into the throttle body opening.

Installation

63 Prior to installation, make sure the pintle is in the retracted position. If the pintle protrudes more than one inch (25 mm), the AIS motor must be taken to a dealer service department to be retracted **(see illustration)**.

64 Install a new O-ring and insert the AIS motor into the housing, making sure the O-ring isn't dislodged.

65 Install the two retaining screws. Tighten the screws securely.

66 Plug in the electrical connector.

67 Install the throttle body temperature sensor.

68 Install the air cleaner assembly and connect the negative battery cable.

Throttle body temperature sensor
Check

69 The throttle body temperature sensor is monitored by the engine controller (computer). If the sensor malfunctions, a trouble code is stored in the computer's memory. To get the computer to display any stored trouble codes, refer to the appropriate section in Chapter 6. If a Code 23 is displayed, replace the sensor.

Removal

70 Disconnect the negative cable from the battery.

71 Remove the air cleaner assembly.

72 Disconnect the accelerator cable from the throttle body, remove the two cable bracket screws and lay the bracket aside **(see**

12.72 Remove the two bolts (arrows) that retain the cable bracket to the throttle body

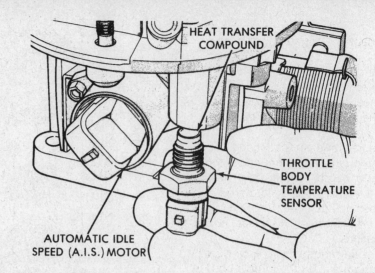

12.74 Carefully unscrew the sensor from the throttle body

illustration).

73 Unplug the electrical connector from the sensor.

74 Remove the sensor by unscrewing it **(see illustration)**.

Installation

75 Apply a thin coat of heat transfer compound (provided with the new sensor) to the tip of the sensor.

76 Screw the sensor into the throttle body and tighten it securely.

77 Plug in the electrical connector.

78 Connect the accelerator cable.

79 Install the air cleaner and connect the negative battery cable.

13 Honda Throttle Body Injection (TBI) Unit overhaul

Warning: *Gasoline is extremely flammable, so take extra precautions when you work on any part of the fuel system. Don't smoke or allow open flames or bare light bulbs near the work area, and don't work in a garage where a natural gas-type appliance (such as a water heater or a clothes dryer) with a pilot light is present. Since gasoline is carcinogenic, wear latex gloves when there's a possibility of being exposed to fuel, and, if you spill any fuel on your skin, rinse it off immediately with soap and water. Mop up any spills immediately and do not store fuel-soaked rags where they could ignite. The fuel system is under constant pressure, so, if any fuel lines are to be disconnected, the fuel pressure in the system must be relieved first (see Chapter 4 for more information). When you perform any kind of work on the fuel system, wear safety glasses and have a Class B type fire extinguisher on hand.*

Removal

1 Remove the air cleaner assembly .

2 Relieve the fuel system pressure (see Chapter 4).

3   Disconnect the negative cable from the battery.

4   Mark and disconnect the vacuum hoses and electrical connectors.

5   Disconnect the throttle linkage and (if equipped) the cruise control and transaxle kickdown cable.

6   Remove the throttle return spring.

7   Place rags or newspapers under the fuel hoses to catch the residual fuel. Loosen the clamps, wrap a cloth around each fuel hose and pull them off. Remove the copper washers from the hoses, noting their locations.

8   Remove the mounting bolts or nuts **(see illustration)** and lift the throttle body off the manifold. Remove all traces of old gasket material from the mating surfaces of the throttle body and intake manifold.

Installation

9   Inspect the mating surfaces of the throttle body and the manifold for nicks, burrs and debris that could cause air leaks.

10   Using a new gasket, place the throttle body in position and install the mounting bolts or nuts. Securely tighten the bolts or nuts following a criss-cross pattern.

11   Check all of the vacuum hoses and electrical connectors for damage, replacing them with new parts if necessary, then connect them.

12   Connect the throttle linkage and (if equipped) cruise control and kickdown cable.

13   Connect the throttle return spring.

14   Using new clamps, install the fuel hoses.

15   Check the operation of the throttle linkage.

16   Install the air cleaner assembly.

17   Connect the negative battery cable.

18   Start the engine and check for fuel leaks.

Fuel pressure regulator

Check

19   Follow the fuel pressure checking procedure in Section 5 for diagnosis of the fuel pressure regulator.

13.8 Exploded view of the throttle body assembly on a Honda Civic

1   *Air intake chamber*
2   *Throttle body assembly*
3   *O-ring*
4   *Insulator*

2111-6-13.8 HAYNES

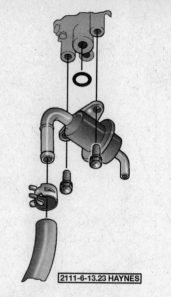

13.23 Fuel pressure regulator mounting details

Removal

20 Remove the air cleaner assembly.

21 Relieve the fuel system pressure (see Chapter 4).

22 Disconnect the negative cable from the battery.

23 Remove the bolts from the fuel pressure regulator **(see illustration)**.

24 Place shop towels under the fuel pressure regulator to catch any residual fuel.

25 Withdraw the pressure regulator from the throttle body.

26 Carefully remove the O-ring from the pressure regulator, followed by the gasket.

Installation

27 Place a new gasket in position on the pressure regulator and carefully install a new O-ring.

28 Place the pressure regulator in position on the throttle body, press it into position and install the three mounting bolts. Tighten the screws securely.

29 Connect the negative battery cable. Check carefully for any fuel leaks.

30 Install the air cleaner assembly.

Fuel injector(s)

Check

31 With the engine running, or cranking, listen to the sound from the injector with an automotive stethoscope and verify that the injector sounds as if it's operating normally. If you don't have a stethoscope, touch the area of the throttle body immediately above the fuel injector with your finger and try to determine whether the injector feels like it's operating smoothly. It should sound/feel smooth and uniform and its sound/feel should rise and fall with engine rpm. If the injector isn't operating, or sounds/feels erratic, check the injector electrical connector. If the connectors are snug, check for voltage to the injector using a special injector harness test light (available at most auto parts stores). If there's voltage to the injector and it isn't operating, or if it's operating erratically, replace it.

Removal

32 Remove the air cleaner assembly.

33 Relieve the fuel system pressure.

34 Disconnect the negative cable from the battery.

35 Remove the screws that hold the injector retainers **(see illustration)**.

36 Gently remove the injector(s) from the throttle body unit.

37 Peel the O-rings off the fuel injector(s). If the lower O-ring isn't on the injector, be sure to retrieve it from the throttle body.

Installation

38 Install new O-rings on the injector and a new O-ring on the injector. **Note:** *Coat the O-rings with a light film of engine oil to help injector installation.*

39 Insert the injector(s) into the throttle body.

40 Install the injector retainers.

41 Connect the negative battery cable, start the engine and check for leaks.

42 Turn off the engine and install the air cleaner assembly.

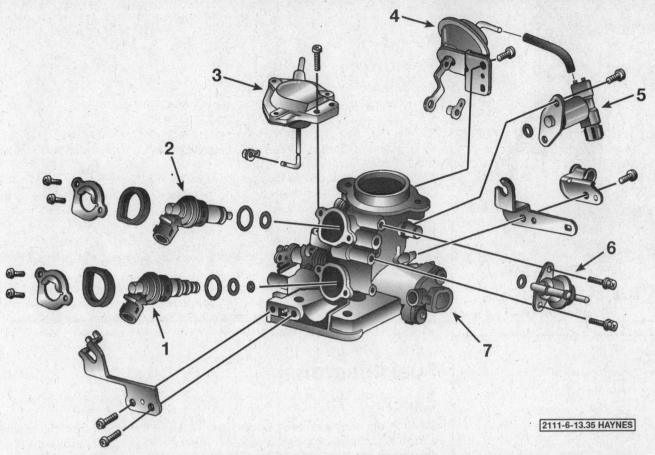

13.35 Be sure to replace all the O-rings with new ones after removing the fuel injector assemblies from the throttle body (this throttle body is from a 1988 Honda Civic)

1   Auxiliary injector
2   Main injector
3   Dashpot diaphragm
4   Tandem valve control diaphragm

5   Tandem valve control solenoid valve
6   Pressure regulator
7   Throttle angle sensor

14 Nissan Throttle Body Injection (TBI) Unit overhaul

Warning: *Gasoline is extremely flammable, so take extra precautions when you work on any part of the fuel system. Don't smoke or allow open flames or bare light bulbs near the work area, and don't work in a garage where a natural gas-type appliance (such as a water heater or a clothes dryer) with a pilot light is present. Since gasoline is carcinogenic, wear latex gloves when there's a possibility of being exposed to fuel, and, if you spill any fuel on your skin, rinse it off immediately with soap and water. Mop up any spills immediately and do not store fuel-soaked rags where they could ignite. The fuel system is under constant pressure, so, if any fuel lines are to be disconnected, the fuel pressure in the system must be relieved first (see Chapter 4 for more information). When you perform any kind of work on the fuel system, wear safety glasses and have a Class B type fire extinguisher on hand.*

14.5a To remove the throttle body, unplug the electrical connector to the airflow meter, detach the coolant hoses from the fast idle cam, detach the throttle cable and, if equipped, the ASCD (cruise control) cable (arrows) . . .

14.5b . . . unplug the connectors at the ends of the pigtail leads for the FICD solenoid valve, the idle-up solenoid valve and the injectors, detach the fuel hoses (arrows) from the pressure regulator (lower hose not shown), unplug the electrical connector (not shown - in back) to the throttle sensor and idle switch, remove all four throttle body mounting nuts and lift off the throttle body

Throttle body - removal and installation

Removal

1   Relieve the fuel pressure (see Chapter 4).
2   Detach the cable from the negative terminal of the battery.
3   Drain approximately 1-1/8 quart of engine coolant.
4   Remove the air cleaner housing assembly.
5   Detach the electrical connectors for the throttle sensor, the idle switch, the injectors and the airflow meter (see illustrations).
6   Detach the throttle cable from the throttle linkage.
7   Detach the Automatic Speed Control Device (ASCD) cable, if equipped, from the throttle linkage.
8   Detach the fuel hoses from the pressure regulator.
9   Detach the coolant hoses from the fast idle cam.
10 Remove the injection body-to-intake manifold mounting nuts.
11 Remove the injection body assembly and gasket from the manifold.

Installation

12 Installation is the reverse of removal. Tighten the throttle body mounting nuts securely. Make sure that all cables, wires and hoses are properly reattached.
13 Start the engine and make sure that there is no fuel leakage from the clearance between the injector cover and the throttle body. Stop the engine and make sure that the fuel vapor sprayed on the throttle valve is not dripping (if it is, there is a leak). Also be sure that the engine is idling steadily at the idle speed specified on the VECI label. After the engine is warmed up, add approximately 1-1/8 quart of engine coolant.

Fuel injector - replacement

14 Relieve the fuel pressure (see chapter 4).
15 Remove the throttle body (see illustration).

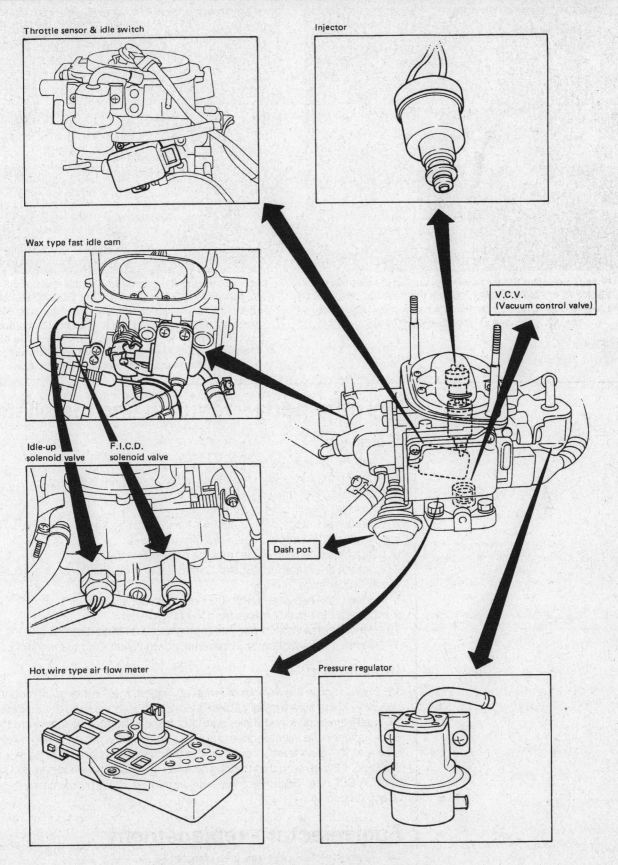

14.15 Nissan throttle body details (early model shown)

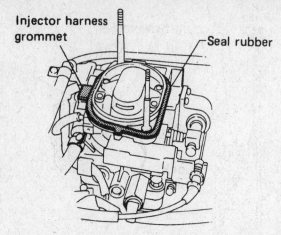

14.16 Remove the seal rubber and the injector harness grommet from the throttle body

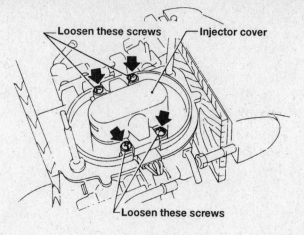

14.17 Remove the injector cover screws (arrows) and detach the injector cover

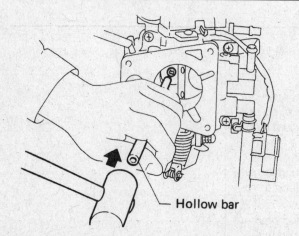

14.18a With the throttle valve fully open, tap the bottom of the injector with a hollow bar as shown

16   Remove the seal rubber and the injector harness grommet from the injection body (see illustration).

17   Remove the injector cover (see illustration).

18   With the throttle valve kept fully open, carefully tap the bottom of the fuel injector with a hollow bar (see illustration). Note: The hollow bar must have an inside diameter of no less than 7/32-inch (see illustration). Be careful not to damage the injector nozzle tip. If the tip is deformed by the bar during removal, the injector must be replaced.

19   If you are simply removing a leaking injector that is otherwise okay, remove the old large and small O-rings and the rubber ring (see illustration) and install new ones. Be sure to apply some silicone oil to both of the new O-rings when installing them on the injector.

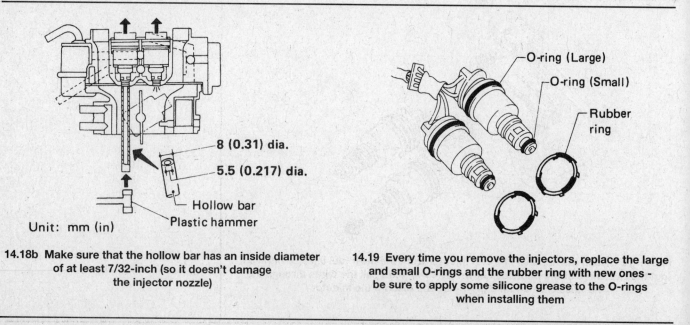

14.18b Make sure that the hollow bar has an inside diameter of at least 7/32-inch (so it doesn't damage the injector nozzle)

14.19 Every time you remove the injectors, replace the large and small O-rings and the rubber ring with new ones - be sure to apply some silicone grease to the O-rings when installing them

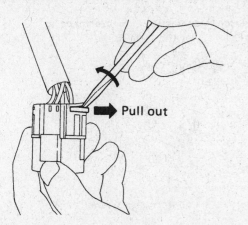

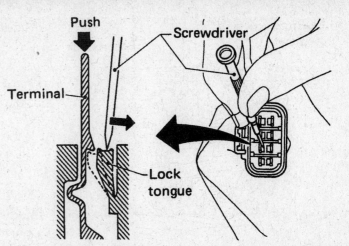

14.20a Before unplugging the terminal from the harness connector, remove the retainer - the best way to get the retainer out is to pry it loose with a small screwdriver, pick or scribe

14.20b To get a terminal out of the connector, tilt the tongue lock with a small screwdriver, pick or scribe as shown and simultaneously push out the terminal

20   If you are replacing a faulty injector, disconnect the harness of the bad injector from the harness connector and remove it as follows:

a) Remove the terminal retainer **(see illustration)**.

b) With a small screwdriver, tilt the lock tongue and, at the same time, push out the terminal **(see illustration)**. **Caution**: *When extracting a terminal, do not pull the wire harness. Always push the tip of the terminal. Be careful not damage or spill gasoline on the seal boot unless you intend to replace it with a new one.*

c) Cut the wire boots as indicated **(see illustration)**. **Caution**: *Before cutting either wire, be sure you are cutting the wires for the injector you intend to replace by referring to the accompanying charts in Step 9.*

21   Push the harness of the new injector through the injector harness grommet and the harness tube. **Note**: *The harness grommet should be replaced with a new one every time it is removed.*

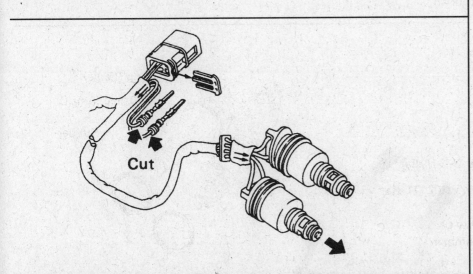

14.20c To detach the harness of a bad injector from the main fuel injector harness, cut the two wires at the boots as shown (arrows), then pull the wires through the harness tube and the grommet and discard the injector

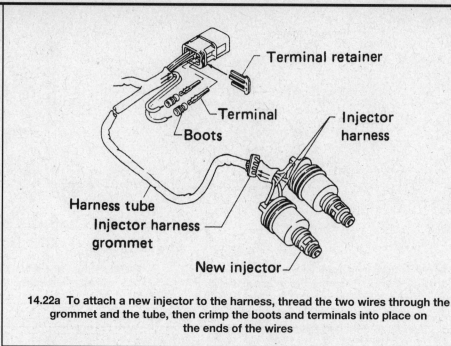

14.22a To attach a new injector to the harness, thread the two wires through the grommet and the tube, then crimp the boots and terminals into place on the ends of the wires

22 Attach the boots and terminals to the harness with terminal pliers, then, referring to the accompanying chart, plug the harness terminals into the connector **(see illustrations). Caution:** *Be extremely careful when connecting the terminals to the connector. Pay attention to the harness colors and terminal numbers and positions. Otherwise, the injector(s) will be damaged.*

23 Push the terminal retainer back into the connector.

24 Install new large and small O-rings and a new rubber ring on the injector.

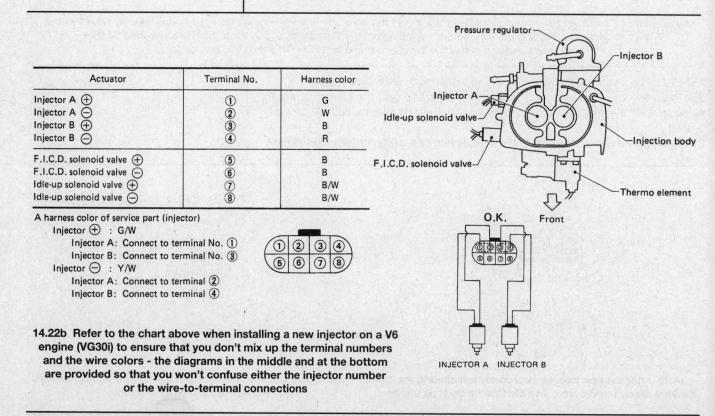

Actuator	Terminal No.	Harness color
Injector A ⊕	①	G
Injector A ⊖	②	W
Injector B ⊕	③	B
Injector B ⊖	④	R
F.I.C.D. solenoid valve ⊕	⑤	B
F.I.C.D. solenoid valve ⊖	⑥	B
Idle-up solenoid valve ⊕	⑦	B/W
Idle-up solenoid valve ⊖	⑧	B/W

A harness color of service part (injector)
  Injector ⊕ : G/W
    Injector A: Connect to terminal No. ①
    Injector B: Connect to terminal No. ③
  Injector ⊖ : Y/W
    Injector A: Connect to terminal ②
    Injector B: Connect to terminal ④

14.22b Refer to the chart above when installing a new injector on a V6 engine (VG30i) to ensure that you don't mix up the terminal numbers and the wire colors - the diagrams in the middle and at the bottom are provided so that you won't confuse either the injector number or the wire-to-terminal connections

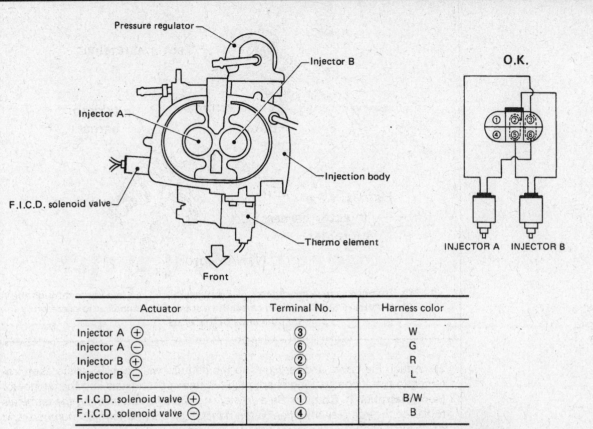

Actuator	Terminal No.	Harness color
Injector A ⊕	③	W
Injector A ⊖	⑥	G
Injector B ⊕	②	R
Injector B ⊖	⑤	L
F.I.C.D. solenoid valve ⊕	①	B/W
F.I.C.D. solenoid valve ⊖	④	B

A harness color of service part (injector)
Injector ⊕ : G/W   Connect terminal No. ② or ③
Injector ⊖ : Y/W   Connect terminal No. ⑤ or ⑥

14.22c Refer to the chart above when installing a new injector on a four-cylinder engine (Z24i) to ensure that you don't mix up the terminal numbers and the wire colors - the diagrams in the middle and at the bottom are provided so that you won't confuse either the injector number or the wire-to-terminal connections

25 Place the injector assembly into the injection body **(see illustration)**.
26 Push the injectors into the throttle body by hand until the O-rings are fully seated. Invert the injection body and make sure that the injector tips are properly seated.
27 Apply some silicone sealant to the injector harness grommet **(see illustration)**.

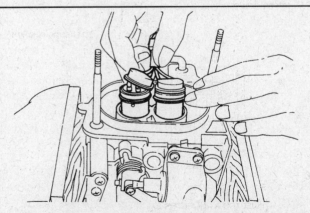

14.25 After the new injector is properly attached to the harness, place the injectors into the throttle body as shown

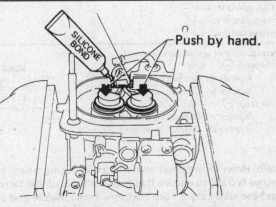

14.27 Apply silicone sealant to the injector harness grommet, then push the grommet into place

28 Install the injector cover. Be sure to use non-hardening locking compound on the screw threads. Tighten the screws in a criss-cross pattern to ensure proper seating of the injector and cover.

29 Attach the seal rubber to the top face of the injection body with silicone sealant. **Caution**: *Be sure to apply some silicone sealant to the bottom of the seal rubber so that the rubber adheres to the throttle body. Do not reinstall the air cleaner housing assembly until this sealant has hardened.*

30 Install the throttle body on the intake manifold.

31 Have the mixture ratio feedback system inspection performed by a dealer service department (or other repair shop) to make sure that there is no fuel leakage at the injector top seal (this procedure requires several special, expensive tools and is beyond the scope of this manual).

15 G.M. Central Point Injection (CPI) system

General information

1 The function of the Central Port Injection (CPI) unit is to control fuel delivery to the engine. The CPI system is controlled by the Electronic Control Module (ECM) located in the passenger compartment. The ECM is the control center of the Computer Command Control system (CCCS).

2 The ECM monitors voltage from several sensors to determine how much fuel the engine needs. When the key is first turned On, the ECM turns on the fuel pump relay for two seconds and the fuel pump builds up pressure to the CPI unit. The ECM monitors the Coolant Temperature Sensor (CTS), the Intake Air Temperature Sensor (IATS), Throttle Position Sensor (TPS) and Manifold Absolute Pressure (MAP) sensor and then determines the proper air/fuel ratio for starting.

3 The fuel control system has an electric fuel pump, located in the fuel tank on the fuel gauge sending unit. The pump provides pressure above the regulated pressure needed by the CPI injector.

4 The intake manifold is designed with an upper and lower manifold assembly. The upper manifold is a variable-tuned split-plenum design that also includes an intake manifold tuning valve, MAP sensor and a throttle valve attached to the plenum.

5 The throttle valve is used to control airflow into the engine and consequently engine output. During engine idle, the throttle valve is almost completely closed and airflow control is handled by the Idle Air Control (IAC) valve.

6 Most of the CPI components are housed directly under the air intake plenum **(see illustration)**. In order to service the CPI unit, it will be necessary to remove

15.6 Central Port Injection (CPI) details

1   Poppet nozzle
2   Distributor
3   Fuel pressure regulator
4   Central Port Injection unit
5   Schrader valve (fuel pressure test port)
6   Return fuel line
7   Inlet fuel line
8   Fuel inlet and return line clip

the air intake plenum from the intake manifold. The pressure regulator assembly consists of a fuel meter body, gasket seal, fuel pressure regulator, fuel injector and six poppet nozzles with fuel tubes. The CPI unit is not repairable and must be replaced as an assembly if found to be defective. Be sure to contact a dealer service department for any warranties that might cover the repair of the fuel system before attempting it on your own.

7   The CPI system has a low gain fuel pressure regulator to maintain pressure at the fuel injector through a range of fuel recirculation rates from the in-tank fuel pump. With the ignition On and the engine NOT running, the fuel pressure should be 54 to 62 psi. Fuel enters the fuel meter body through the inlet line and flows directly into the injector cavity. When the ECM de-energizes the injector solenoid, fuel is recirculated through the pressure regulator. Fuel pressure applied to the regulator diaphragm acts against the spring force and opens the valve from its seat. This allows fuel to return to the fuel tank by way of the fuel meter body outlet and the return line. When the ECM energizes the injector solenoid, the armature lifts off the six fuel tube seats and delivers fuel through the fuel meter body out to the six poppet nozzles.

8   When the ECM energizes the injector solenoid, pressurized fuel flows through the fuel tubes to each poppet nozzle. There are six poppet nozzles (one for each cylinder). An increase in fuel pressure will cause the poppet nozzle ball to lift from its seat against spring force and spray fuel at approximately 52 psi. De-energizing the injector solenoid closes the armature and reduces the fuel pressure on the poppet nozzle ball.

CPI unit removal and installation

Note: *Do not attempt to disassemble the CPI unit. It is a non-serviceable part.*

Removal

9   Relieve the fuel pressure (see Chapter 4). Remove the Torx screws and lift off the plastic cover from the air intake plenum.

10   Disconnect the electrical connectors on the TPS, IAC motor, MAP sensor and intake manifold tuning valve assembly **(see illustration)**.

11   Disconnect the Throttle Valve (TV) linkage, cruise control cable and accelerator cable **(see illustrations)** from the throttle valve assembly.

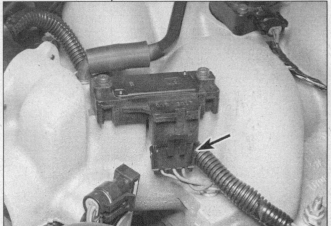

15.10 Disconnect the MAP sensor electrical connector (arrow)

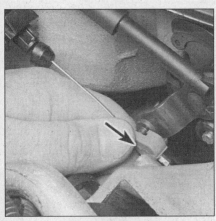

15.11a Push the TV cable forward and off the throttle valve

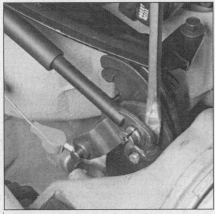

15.11b Carefully pry the cruise control cable off the throttle valve

15.11c While pulling the throttle back, lift the accelerator cable from the notch on the throttle valve

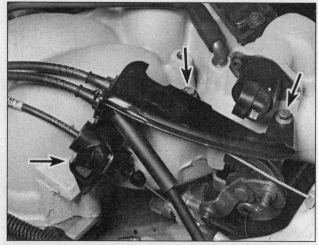

15.12 Remove the three bolts (arrows) from the plenum and lift the bracket assembly off the plenum

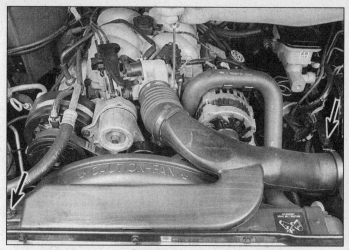

15.13a Loosen the clamps and wing nut (arrows) and . . .

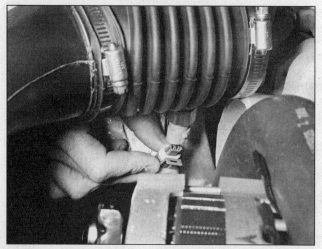

15.13b . . . disconnect the electrical connector from the air intake sensor - then, lift the air intake tube from the engine compartment

12 Remove the bolts (see illustration) that retain the bracket to the air intake plenum.

13 Remove the intake air ducts from the plenum and the fan shroud (see illustrations).

14 Remove the ignition coil (see illustration).

15 Disconnect the PCV hose from the plenum and the valve cover.

16 Disconnect the vacuum lines from the front and rear of the air intake plenum.

17 Remove the ignition wire and harness bracket from the plenum. Be sure to mark the position of each stud and nut (see illustration).

18 Remove the bolts and nuts from the air intake plenum. Start on the front bolt and work your way counterclockwise (standing directly in front of the engine compartment) around the circumference of the plenum.

15.14 Remove the nuts (arrows) from the air intake plenum mounting studs (right side shown)

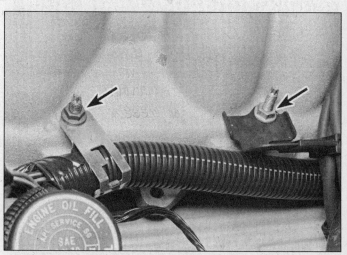

15.17 Remove the nuts (arrows) from the mounting studs located on the air intake plenum and lift the brackets (left side shown)

15.19 Lift the gasket off the intake manifold

15.22 Squeeze the tab (arrow) to disconnect the injector electrical connector

19 Lift the air intake plenum from the intake manifold. Remove the gasket from the intake manifold **(see illustration)**.

20 Inspect the gasket surface on the plenum and the intake manifold for any chips, burrs or cracks. If the plenum is damaged, replace it with a new unit.

21 Clean the gasket surface on the plenum and the intake manifold with a soft cloth and solvent.

22 Detach the electrical connector from the CPI assembly **(see illustration)**.

23 Disconnect the fuel fitting clip and dispose it.

24 Disconnect the fuel inlet and outlet lines from the CPI assembly **(see illustration)**. Remove the O-ring seals and dispose them. Use new seals for assembly.

25 Squeeze the poppet nozzle locking tabs **(see illustration)** while lifting the nozzle out of the intake manifold.

26 After disconnecting the six poppet nozzles, lift the CPI assembly out of the intake manifold as a single unit.

15.24 Carefully remove the inlet and return line from the injector assembly

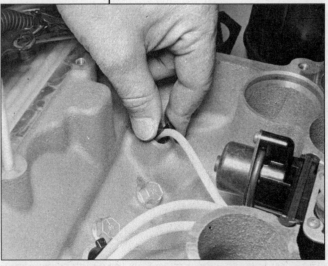

15.25 Squeeze the two tabs and lift the assembly to remove the poppet nozzle from the intake manifold

Installation

27 Align the CPI assembly grommet with the casting grommet slots and push down until it is seated at the bottom of the guide hole.

28 Push the poppet nozzles into the casting sockets. **Caution**: *Be sure the poppet nozzles are seated and secured in the casting sockets before installing the plenum. Check by pulling each poppet nozzle firmly until it is in its correct place. This will prevent fuel leaks and fire danger.*

29 Connect the fuel inlet and outlet lines to the CPI assembly. Be sure to install new O-rings. Coat the new O-rings with clean engine oil.

30 Install the new fuel fitting clip.

31 Be sure the fuel pump relay is connected and pressurize the fuel pump by turning the ignition key On. Do not start the engine. Check all the fittings for fuel leaks before installing the air intake plenum.

32 Install the air intake plenum. Be sure to use a new gasket. Tighten the plenum fasteners. **Note**: *Be sure the plenum does not pinch any fuel lines or nozzles.*

16 Engine management sensors and output actuators

Note: *Some of the procedures in this Section require you to operate the vehicle after disconnecting a portion of the engine management system (such as a sensor or a vacuum line). This may set trouble codes in the computer. Be sure to clear any trouble codes (see Chapter 3) before returning the vehicle to normal service.*

This Section deals with the engine management systems used on modern, computer-controlled vehicles to meet new low-emission regulations. The system's computer, information sensors and output actuators interact with each other to collect, store and send data. Basically, the information sensors collect data (such as the intake air mass and/or temperature, coolant temperature, throttle position, exhaust gas oxygen content, etc.) and transmit this data, in the form of varying electrical signals, to the computer. The computer compares this data with its "map," which tells what the data should be under the engine's current operating conditions. If the data does not match the map, the computer sends signals to output actuators (fuel injectors or throttle body injector, Electronic Air Control Valve (EACV), Idle Speed Control (ISC) motor, etc.) which correct the engine's operation to match the map **(see illustration)**.

When the engine is warming up (and sensor input is not precise) or there is a malfunction in the system, the system operates in an "open loop" mode. In this mode, the computer does not rely on the sensors for input and sets the fuel/air mixture rich so the engine can continue operation until the engine warms up or repairs are made. **Note**: *The engine's thermostat rating and proper operation are critical to the operation of a computer-controlled vehicle. If the thermostat is rated at too low a temperature, is removed or stuck open, the computer may stay in "open loop" operation and emissions and fuel economy will suffer.*

The automotive computer

Automotive computers come in all sizes and shapes and are generally located under the dashboard, around the fenderwells or under the front seat. The Environmental Protection Agency (EPA) and the Federal government require all automobile manufacturers to warranty their emissions systems for 5 years or 50,000 miles. This broad emissions warranty coverage will allow most com-

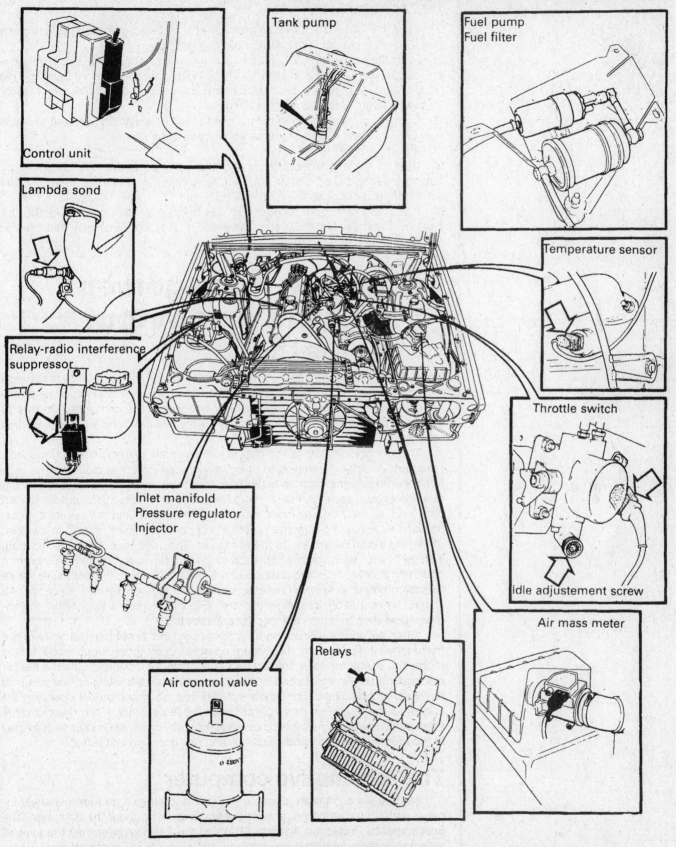

Control unit

Lambda sond

Relay-radio interference suppressor

Tank pump

Fuel pump
Fuel filter

Temperature sensor

Throttle switch

Idle adjustement screw

Inlet manifold
Pressure regulator
Injector

Air mass meter

Relays

Air control valve

16.1 Overall view of a fuel injection system, including the computer, information sensors and output actuators
(Bosch LH-Jetronic system shown)

puter malfunctions to be repaired by the dealership at their cost. Keep this in mind when diagnosing and/or repairing any fuel injection/emissions systems problems.

Computers have delicate internal circuitry which is easily damaged when subjected to excessive voltage, static electricity or magnetism. When diagnosing any electrical problems in a circuit connected to the computer, remember that most computers operate at a relatively low voltage (about 5 volts).

Observe the following precautions whenever working on or around the computer and engine management system circuits:

1) Do not damage the wiring or any electrical connectors in such a way as to cause it to ground or touch another source of voltage.
2) Do not use any electrical testing equipment (such as an ohmmeter) that is powered by a six-or-more-volt battery. The excessive voltage might cause an electrical component in the computer to burn or short. Use only a ten mega-ohm impedance digital multimeter when working on engine management circuits.
3) Do not remove or troubleshoot the computer without the proper tools and information, because any mistakes can void your warranty and/or damage components.
4) All spark plug wires should be at least one inch away from any sensor circuit. An unexpected problem in a computer circuit can be caused by magnetic fields that send false signals to the computer, frequently resulting in hard-to-identify performance problems. Although there have been cases of high-power lines or transformers interfering with the computer, the most common cause of this problem in the sensor circuits is the position of the spark plug wires (too close to the computer wiring).
5) Use special care when handling or working near the computer. Remember that static electricity can cause computer damage by creating a very large surge in voltage (see *Static electricity and electronic components* below).

Static electricity and electronic components

Caution: *Static electricity can damage or destroy the computer and other electronic components. Read the following information carefully.*

Static electricity can cause two types of damage. The first and most obvious is complete failure of the device. The other type of damage is much more subtle and harder to detect as an electrical component failure. In this situation, the integrated circuit is degraded and can become weakened over a period of time. It may perform erratically or appear as another component's intermittent failure.

The best way to prevent static electricity damage is to drain the charge from your body by grounding your body to the frame or body of the vehicle. A static-control wrist strap (available at electronic supply stores) properly worn and grounded to the frame or body of the vehicle will drain the charges from your body, thereby preventing them from discharging into the electronic components.

Remember, it is often not possible to feel a static discharge until the charge level reaches 3,000 volts! It is very possible to have damaged the electrical component without even knowing it!

Information sensors

The information sensors are a series of highly specialized switches and temperature-sensitive electrical devices that transform physical properties of the engine such as temperature (air, coolant and fuel), air mass (air volume and density), air pressure and engine speed into electrical signals that can be translated into workable parameters by the computer.

Each sensor is designed specifically to detect data from one particular area of the engine; for example, the mass airflow sensor is positioned inside the air intake system and it measures the volume and density of the incoming air to help the computer calculate how much fuel is needed to maintain the correct air/fuel mixture.

Diagnosing problems with the information sensors can easily overlap other management systems because of the inter-relationship of the components. For instance, if a fuel-injected engine is experiencing a vacuum leak, the computer will often release a diagnostic code that refers to the oxygen sensor and/or its circuit. The first thought would be that the oxygen sensor is defective. Actually, the intake leak is forcing more air into the combustion chamber than is required and the fuel/air mixture has become lean. The oxygen sensor relays the information to the computer which cannot compensate for the increased amount of oxygen and, as a result, the computer will store a fault code for the oxygen sensor.

The test information in the following sections is generalized and applies to most fuel injection components. In order to solidify your diagnosis, it may be necessary to consult a factory service manual for the exact specification(s) for your vehicle.

Manifold Absolute Pressure (MAP) sensor

What it is and how it works

The MAP sensor reports engine load to the computer, which uses the information to adjust spark advance and fuel enrichment **(see illustration)**. The MAP sensor measures intake manifold pressure and vacuum on the absolute scale (from zero instead of from sea-level atmospheric pressure [14.7 psi] as most gauges and sensors do). The MAP sensor reads vacuum and pressure through a hose connected to the intake manifold. A pressure-sensitive ceramic or silicon element and electronic circuit in the sensor generates a voltage signal that changes in direct proportion to pressure. There are two types of MAP sensors; one that varies signal voltage and another that varies frequency. The former can easily be read on a digital or analog voltmeter while the latter (frequency varying type) must be measured using a frequency meter, or you can use a tachometer set on the 6-cylinder scale. If you are not sure exactly which type of MAP sensor is installed on your vehicle, perform the check for the voltage signal first and if the MAP sensor does not react, use a tachometer to check for a frequency signal.

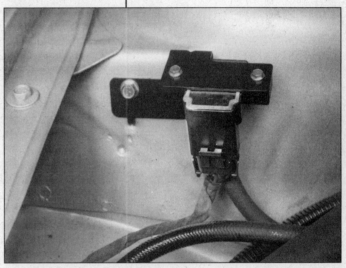

16.2 Here's a typical MAP sensor (voltage varying type) - this one is from a Plymouth Sundance

Under low-load, high-vacuum conditions, the computer leans the fuel/air mixture and advances the spark timing for better fuel economy. Under high-load, low-vacuum conditions, the computer richens the fuel/air mixture and retards timing to prevent detonation. The MAP sensor serves as the electronic equivalent of both a vacuum advance on a distributor and a power valve in the carburetor.

Checking the MAP sensor

Anything that hinders accurate sensor input can upset both the fuel mixture and ignition timing. This includes the MAP sensor itself as well as shorts or opens in the sensor wiring circuit and/or vacuum leaks in the intake manifold or vacuum hose to the sensor. Some of the most typical driveability symptoms associated with problems in the MAP sensor circuit include:

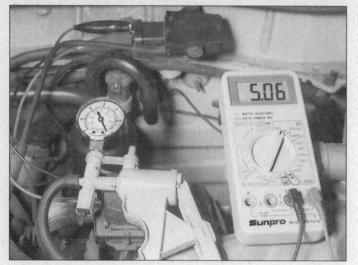

16.3 The MAP sensor voltage (measured at the signal wire) will decrease as vacuum is applied to the sensor

1) Detonation and misfire due to increased spark advance and a lean fuel mixture.
2) Loss of power and/or fuel economy and sometimes even black smoke due to retarded ignition timing and a very rich fuel mixture.
3) Poor fuel economy.
4) Hard starts and/or stalling.

When a MAP sensor trouble code is detected, be sure to first check for vacuum leaks in the vacuum hose, loose electrical connectors or wiring damage in the MAP sensor circuit. Check for anything that is obvious and easily repaired before actually replacing the sensor itself.

To check the MAP sensor it will be necessary to install the negative probe of the voltmeter or tachometer onto the ground wire of the MAP sensor connector and the positive probe onto the signal wire. The ground wire is typically black in color. The signal wire can be distinguished from the reference wire by checking for a 5.0 volt reference signal (ignition key On [engine not running]) and by the process of elimination. Remember, the signal wire will vary voltage or frequency as vacuum is applied to the MAP sensor. If there is any doubt, consult a wiring diagram for the correct terminal designations.

A MAP sensor will typically produce a voltage signal that will drop with decreasing manifold pressure (rising vacuum). Test specifications will vary according to the manufacturer and engine type. A typical MAP sensor (voltage varying type) will read 4.6 to 4.8 volts with 0 in-Hg vacuum applied to it **(see illustration)**. Raise it to 5 in-Hg vacuum and the reading should drop to about 3.75 volts. Raise it up again to 20 in-Hg and the reading should drop to about 1.1 volts. A typical MAP sensor (frequency varying type) will read 300 to 320 rpm with 0 in-Hg vacuum applied to it **(see illustration)**. Raise it to 5 in-Hg vacuum and the reading should drop to about 275 to 295 rpm. Raise it up again to 20 in-Hg and the reading should drop to about 200 to 215 rpm **(see illustration)**. All tests should be performed with the ignition key On, engine NOT running.

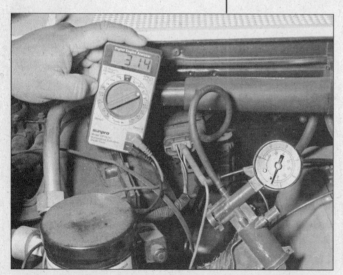

16.4 To check a frequency varying MAP sensor, with no vacuum applied, the sensor should read between 300 and 320 rpm on the tachometer scale (6-cylinder selection)

16.4 Now apply vacuum (20 inches Hg) and the tach should read between 200 and 230 rpm

Mass Air Flow (MAF) sensor

What it is and how it works

The MAF sensor is positioned in the air intake duct (**see illustration**), and it measures the amount of air entering the engine. Mass airflow sensors come in two basic varieties; hot wire and hot film. Both types work on the same principle, though they are designed differently. They measure the volume and density of the air entering the engine so the computer can calculate how much fuel is needed to maintain the correct fuel/air mixture. MAF sensors have no moving parts. Contrary to the vane airflow sensors that use a spring-loaded flap, MAF sensors use an electrical current to measure airflow. There are two types of sensing elements; platinum wire (hot wire) or nickel foil grid (hot film). Each one is heated electrically to keep the temperature higher than the intake air temperature. In a hot-film MAF sensor, the film is heated 170-degrees F warmer than the incoming air temperature. On hot-wire MAF sensors, the wire is heated to 210-degrees F above the incoming air tempera-

16.6 Here's a typical airflow sensor (this one's from a Nissan Maxima) - to remove it, remove the bolts (arrows)

ture. As airflows past the element it cools the element and thereby increases the amount of current necessary to heat it up again. Because the necessary current varies directly with the temperature and the density of the air entering the intake, the amount of current is directly proportional to the air mass entering the engine. This information is fed into the computer and the fuel mixture is directly controlled according to the conditions.

Checking the MAF sensor

The most effective method for testing the MAF sensor is measuring the sensor's output or its effect on the injector pulse width. On Bosch or Ford hot-wire systems, the voltage output can be read directly with a voltmeter by probing the appropriate sensor terminals (**see illustrations**). Refer to a factory service manual for the correct terminal designations and specifications. If the voltage readings are not within range or the voltage fails to INCREASE when the throttle is OPENED with the engine running, the sensor is faulty and must be replaced with

16.7a The signal voltage on a typical Bosch MAF sensor will read 0.60 to 0.80 volts at idle and . . .

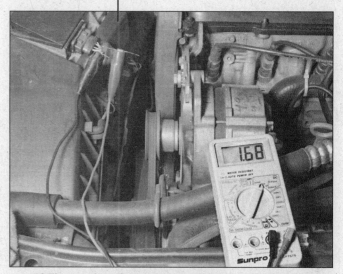

16.7b . . . when the engine speed is raised to 2,500 to 3,500 rpm, the voltage increases to approximately 1.50 to 2.20 volts

16.8 Checking a MAF sensor (this one's on a Ford) - this test requires a special multimeter that detects pulse width variations

a new part. A dirty wire or a contaminated wire (a direct result of a faulty self-cleaning circuit) will deliver a slow response to the changes in airflow. Also, keep in mind that the self-cleaning circuit is controlled by relays. So, check the relays first if the MAF sensor appears to be sluggish or not responsive. Proper diagnosis of the MAF sensor is very important because this part is usually somewhat expensive. Be sure to check for diagnostic codes, if possible. If the wiring checks out and all other obvious areas are checked carefully, replace the sensor.

Another way to check MAF sensor output is to see what effect it has on injector pulse width (if this specification is available). Using a multimeter or oscilloscope that reads milliseconds, connect the positive probe directly to any injector signal wire and the negative probe to a ground terminal **(see illustration)**. Remember that one injector terminal is connected to the supply voltage (battery voltage) and the other is connected to the computer (signal wire) which varies the amount of time the injector is grounded. **Note**: *Typically, if by chance you connect to the wrong side of the injector connector, one wire will give you a steady reading (battery voltage) while the signal wire will fluctuate slightly. Look at the pulse width at idle or while cranking the engine. The injector pulse width will vary with different conditions. If the MAF sensor is not producing a signal, the pulse width will typically be FOUR times longer than the correct width. This will indicate an excessively rich fuel/air mixture.*

Vane Air Flow (VAF) sensor

What it is and how it works

VAF sensors are positioned in the air intake stream ahead of the throttle, and they monitor the volume of air entering the engine by means of a spring-loaded flap **(see illustration)**. The flap is pushed open by the air entering the system and a potentiometer (variable resistor) attached to the flap will vary the voltage signal to the computer according to the volume of air entering the engine (angle of the flap). The greater the airflow, the further the flap is forced open.

VAF sensors are used most commonly on Bosch L-Jetronic fuel injection systems, Nippondenso multi-port fuel injection systems and certain Ford multi-port fuel injection systems.

Checking the VAF sensor

Diagnosing VAF sensors is quite different from diagnosing MAF or MAP sensors. Vane airflow sensors are vulnerable to dirt and grease. Unfiltered air that gets by a dirty or torn air filter will build up on the flap hinge or shaft, causing the flap to bind or hesitate as it swings. Remove the air intake boot and gently push open the flap with your finger; it should open and close smoothly. If necessary, spray a small amount of carburetor cleaner on the hinge and try to loosen the flap so it moves freely.

Disconnect the electrical connector to the VAF sensor.

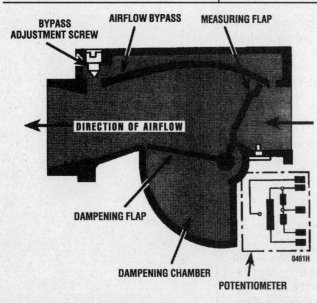

16.9 A cross-sectional diagram of a vane airflow sensor

Connect an ohmmeter to the electrical connector on the VAF sensor; the resistance should vary evenly as the flap opens and closes. If the resistance changes erratically or skips and jumps, you will have to replace the VAF with a new unit. **Note**: *Be sure to use an ANALOG ohmmeter for this check, since a digital meter will not usually register the rapid resistance changes that occur during this test.*

Another common problem to watch out for with VAF sensors is a bent or damaged flap caused by backfiring in the intake manifold. Some VAF sensors incorporate a "backfire" valve in the sensor body that prevents damage to the flap by venting any explosion away from the sensor. If the "backfire" valve leaks, it will cause the sensor to read low, consequently causing the engine to run on a rich fuel/air mixture.

The VAF sensor is manufactured as a sealed unit, preset at the factory with nothing that can be serviced except the idle mixture screw. Do not attempt to disassemble the unit if it is still under warranty, because tampering with the unit will void the warranty.

Air temperature sensor

What it is and how it works

The air temperature sensor is also known a Manifold Air Temperature (MAT) sensor, an Air Charge Temperature (ACT) sensor, a Vane Air Temperature (VAT) sensor, a Charge Temperature Sensor (CTS), an Air Temperature Sensor (ATS) and a Manifold Charging Temperature (MCT) sensor. The sensor is located in the intake manifold or air intake plenum **(see illustration)** and detects the temperature of the incoming air. The sensor usually consists of a temperature sensitive thermistor which changes the value of its voltage signal as the temperature changes. The computer uses the sensor signal to richen or lean-out the fuel/air mixture, and, on some applications, to delay the EGR valve opening until the manifold temperature reaches normal operating range.

16.10 Here's a typical MAT sensor (1985 Corvette shown) - it is located in the underside of the air intake plenum

Checking the ATS

The easiest way to check an air temperature sensor is to remove it from the manifold, then hook up an ohmmeter to its terminals and check the resistance when the sensor is cold. Then warm up the tip of the sensor with a heat gun or blow drier (never a propane torch!) and watch for a decrease in resistance. No change in resistance indicates the sensor is defective. When reinstalling the sensor, be sure to use sealant on the threads so you don't end up with a vacuum leak.

On most GM vehicles equipped with the MAT sensor, a Code 23 or 25 will indicate a fault in the sensor (see Chapter 3). Be aware that problems with the EGR system might be caused by a defective MAT sensor.

Throttle Position Sensor (TPS)

What it is and how it works

The TPS is usually mounted externally on the throttle body. Some are inside the throttle body. The TPS is attached directly to the throttle shaft and varies simultaneously with the angle of the throttle. Its job is to inform the computer about the rate of throttle opening and relative throttle position. A separate Wide

Open Throttle (WOT) switch may be used to signal the computer when the throttle is wide open. The TPS consists of a variable resistor that changes resistance thereby varying the voltage signal as the throttle changes its opening. By signaling the computer when the throttle opens, the computer can richen the fuel mixture to maintain the proper air/fuel ratio. The initial setting of the TPS is very important because the voltage signal the computer receives tells the computer the exact position of the throttle at idle.

Checking the TPS

Throttle position sensors typically have their own types of driveability symptoms that can be distinguished from other information sensors. The most common symptom of a faulty or misadjusted sensor is hesitation or stumble during acceleration (the same symptom of a bad accelerator pump in a carbureted engine).

There are basically two voltage checks you can perform to test the TPS. **Note**: *It is best to have the correct wiring diagram for the vehicle when performing the following checks.*

The first test is for the presence of voltage at the TPS supply wire with the ignition key On. The throttle position sensor cannot deliver the correct signal without the proper supply voltage. You can determine the function of each individual wire (ground, supply, signal wire) by probing each one with a voltmeter and checking the different voltages. The voltage that remains constant when the throttle is opened and closed will be the supply voltage. If there's no voltage at any of the wires, there's probably an open or short in the wiring harness to the sensor. Most systems use 5.0 volts on the supply wire.

The second check is for the proper voltage change that occurs as the throttle opens and closes (signal voltage). As the throttle goes from closed-to-wide open, the voltage at the signal wire should typically increase smoothly from 1 volt to 5 volts **(see illustration)**. **Note**: *An alternate method for checking the range is the resistance test. Hook up an ohmmeter to the supply and signal wires. With the ignition key OFF, slowly move the throttle through the complete range* **(see illustration)**. *Observe carefully for any unusual changes in resistance (the change should be smooth) as it increases from low to high.*

Also, check your diagnostic codes for any differences in the circuit failures versus the actual sensor failure. Be sure you have checked all the obvious items before replacing the throttle position sensor.

16.11 On a typical TPS, the voltage should range from 0.45 to 5.0 volts. Position the positive probe of the voltmeter to the signal wire and the negative probe on the ground wire and slowly open the throttle completely

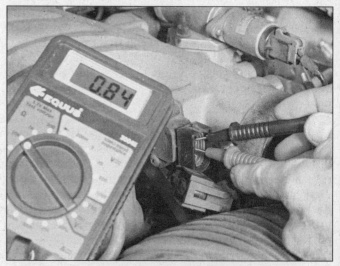

16.12 Slowly move the throttle and observe the resistance readings on the display - there should be a smooth transition as the resistance increases

Adjusting

TPS's seldom need adjustment. However, many TPS's must be adjusted when they are replaced. Since different makes and models of vehicles have different specifications and procedures for adjusting the TPS, we recommend you refer to a factory service manual for your specific vehicle to adjust the TPS. Also, dealer service departments or other qualified shops can usually adjust the TPS for you for a nominal fee. **Note**: *The adjustment information in the following paragraph may not be applicable to your vehicle. It is only intended to familiarize you with a typical procedure.*

Normally, you'll only need a voltmeter to adjust the TPS. Hook the meter up to the signal (return) and ground terminals (not the five-volt reference) and loosen the mounting screws **(see illustration)**. With the throttle in the specified position (usually against the throttle stop), rotate the sensor clockwise or counterclockwise until the specified voltage is obtained (normally about 0.5-volt). Retighten the mounting screws and check the voltage again.

16.13 On a BMW 318i, the TPS is located under the air intake plenum. Both mounting screws must be loosened to adjust the sensor

Oxygen sensor

What it is and how it works

The oxygen sensor (also known as a Lambda or EGO sensor) is located in the exhaust manifold (or in the exhaust pipe, near the exhaust manifold) and produces a voltage signal proportional to the content of oxygen in the exhaust **(see illustration)**. A higher oxygen content across the sensor tip will vary the oxygen differential, thereby lowering the sensor's output voltage. On the other hand, lower oxygen content will raise the output voltage. Typically the voltage ranges from 0.10 volts (lean) to 0.90 volts (rich). The computer uses the sensor's input voltage to adjust the air/fuel mixture, leaning it out when the sensor detects a rich condition or enriching it when it detects a lean condition. When the sensor reaches operating temperature (600-degrees F), it will produce a variable voltage signal based on the difference between the amount of oxygen in the exhaust (internal) and the amount of oxygen in the air directly surrounding the sensor (external). The ideal stoichiometric fuel/air ratio (14.7:1) will produce about 0.45 volts.

16.14 This oxygen sensor (arrow) is screwed into the exhaust manifold (GM V6 engine shown)

There are basically two types of oxygen sensors on the market. The most popular type uses a zirconia element in its tip. The latest type of oxygen sensor uses a titania element. Instead of producing its own voltage, the titania element resistance will alter a voltage signal that is supplied by the computer itself. Although the titania element works differently than the zirconia element, the results are basically identical. The biggest difference is that the titania element responds faster and allows the computer to maintain more uniform control over a wide range of exhaust temperatures.

Contamination can directly affect the engine performance and life span of the oxygen sensor. There are basically three types of contamination; carbon, lead and silicon. Carbon buildup due to a rich-running condition will cause inaccurate readings and increase the problem's symptoms. Diagnose the fuel injection system for correct fuel adjustments. Once the system is repaired, run the engine at high rpm without a load (parked in the driveway) to remove the carbon deposits. Avoid leaded gasoline as it causes contamination of the oxygen sensor. Also, avoid using old-style silicone gasket sealant (RTV) that releases volatile compounds into the crankcase which eventually wind up on the sensor tip. Always check to make sure the RTV sealant you are using is compatible with modern emission systems. Before an oxygen sensor can function properly it must reach a minimum operating temperature of 600-degrees F. The warm-up period prior to this is called "open loop." In this mode, the computer detects a low coolant temperature (cold start) and wide open throttle (warm-up) condition. Until the engine reaches operating temperature, the computer ignores the oxygen sensor signals. During this time span, the emission controls are not precise! Once the engine is warm, the system is said to be in "closed loop" (using the oxygen sensor's input). Some manufacturers have designed an electric heating element to help the sensor reach operating temperature sooner. A typical heated sensor will consist of a ground wire, a sensor output wire (to the computer) and a third wire that supplies battery voltage to the resistance heater inside the oxygen sensor. Be careful when testing the oxygen sensor circuit! Clearly identify the function of each wire or you might confuse the data and draw the wrong conclusions.

Checking the oxygen sensor

Sometimes an apparent oxygen sensor problem is not the sensor's fault. An air leak in the exhaust manifold or a fouled spark plug or other problem in the ignition system causes the oxygen sensor to give a false lean-running condition. The sensor reacts only to the content of oxygen in the exhaust, and it has no way of knowing where the extra oxygen came from.

When checking the oxygen sensor it is important to remember that a good sensor produces a fluctuating signal that responds quickly to the changes in the exhaust oxygen content. To check the sensor you will need a 10 megaohm digital voltmeter. Never use an ohmmeter to check the oxygen sensor and never jump or ground the terminals. This can damage the sensor. Connect the meter to the oxygen sensor circuit. Select the mV (millivolt) scale. If the engine is equipped with a later style (heated oxygen sensor), be sure you are connected to the signal wire and not one of the heater or ground wires.

Start the engine and let it idle. Observe the reading on the voltmeter. It should be fixed at approximately 0.2 volts. Allow the engine to warm up and enter "closed loop" operation. This period of time is usually 2 to 3 minutes. **Note**: *Typically once in "closed loop", the meter will respond with a fluctuating millivolt reading (0.1 to 0.9 volts) when connected properly. If the oxygen sensor is slow to respond to the "closed loop" mode, the sensor is not operating efficiently therefore it is termed "lazy". Keep watching the voltmeter. If the oxygen sensor waits more than 1 or 2 minutes after "closed loop" mode (3 to 4 minutes total), replace the oxygen sensor. Be very careful the engine is completely warmed up and actually operating in "closed loop" mode and there is not a problem with the thermostat or cooling system. "Lazy" oxygen sensors will quite often fail emissions testing and if there is any doubt, replace it with a new one.*

Watch very carefully as the voltage oscillates. The display will flash values ranging from 100 mV to 900 mV (0.100 to 0.900 V). The numbers will flash very quickly, so be observant. Record the high and low values over a period of one minute **(see illustration)**. The way the

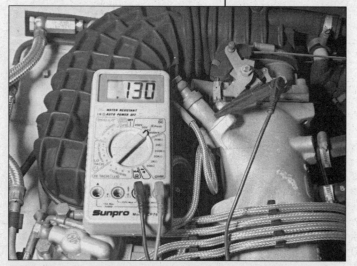

16.15 .Very carefully observe the readings as the oxygen sensor cycles - note on paper the high and low values and try to come up with an average - also, if the VOM does not have a millivolt scale, just move the decimal point over; for example, 0.130 volts = 130 millivolts

oxygen sensor responds is very important in determining the condition of the sensor. Start the test when the engine is cold (open loop) and observe that the oxygen sensor is steady at approximately 0.5 to 0.9 volts. As the sensor warms up (closed loop) it will switch suddenly back and forth between 0.1 and 0.9 volts. These signals should be constant and within this range or the sensor is defective. Also, if the engine warms up and the sensor delays before entering into closed loop readings (fluctuating between 0.1 and 0.9 volts), the sensor is defective. Also, if the sensor does not output a voltage signal greater than 0.5 volts, replace it.

To further test the oxygen sensor, remove a vacuum line and observe the readings as the engine stumbles from the excessively LEAN mixture. The voltage should LOWER to an approximate value of 200 mV (0.200 V). Install the vacuum line. Now, obtain some propane gas mixture (bottled) and connect it to a vacuum port on the intake manifold. Start the engine and open the propane valve (open the propane valve only partially and do so a little at a time to prevent over-richening the mixture). This will create a RICH mixture. Watch carefully as the readings INCREASE. **Warning:** *Propane gas is highly flammable. Be sure there are no leaks in your connections or an explosion could result. If the oxygen sensor responds correctly to the makeshift lean and rich conditions, the sensor is working properly.*

EGR Valve Position (EVP) sensors

What it does and how it works

The EGR Valve Position (EVP) sensor **(see illustration)** monitors the position of the EGR valve and keeps the computer informed on the exact amount the valve is open or closed. From this data, the computer can calculate the optimum EGR flow for the lowest NOx emissions and the best driveability, then control the EGR valve to alter the EGR flow by means of the EGR solenoid.

The EVP sensor is a linear potentiometer that operates very much like a Throttle Position Sensor (TPS). Its electrical resistance changes in direct proportion to the movement of the EGR valve stem. When the EGR valve is closed, the EVP sensor registers maximum resistance. As the valve opens, resistance decreases until it finally reaches a minimum value when the EGR valve is fully open.

Checking the EVP sensor

Typical symptoms of a malfunctioning EGR valve position sensor include hesitating during acceleration, rough idling and hard starting. Be sure to distinguish between an EGR valve problem and an EGR valve position sensor problem. Consult the section on EGR valves for additional information on testing the EGR valve itself.

Generally, the EGR valve position sensor should change resistance smoothly as the EGR valve is opened and closed. Be sure to check the appropriate factory service manual to determine which terminals of the sensor to hook the ohmmeter up to (there's often more than two). A typical Ford EVP sensor should have no more than 5,500 ohms resistance when the EGR valve is closed and no less than 100 ohms when the valve is fully open.

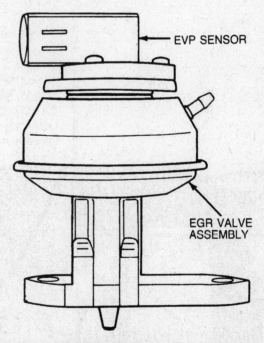

16.16 The EVP sensor is mounted directly on top of the EGR valve

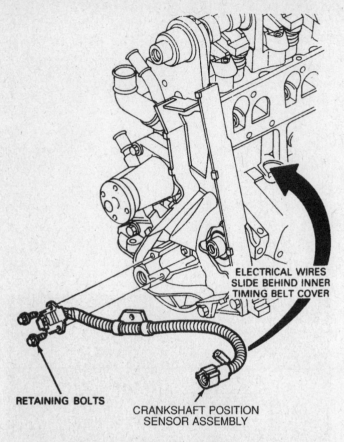

16.17 Typical crankshaft position sensor mounting details (Ford 2.3L shown)

Crankshaft position sensor

What it is and how it works

A crankshaft position sensor works very similarly to an ignition pick-up coil or trigger wheel in an electronic distributor **(see illustration)**. The crankshaft position sensor provides an ignition timing signal to the computer based on the position of the crankshaft. The difference between a crankshaft position sensor and a pick-up coil or trigger wheel is that the crankshaft position sensor reads the ignition timing signal directly off the crankshaft or harmonic balancer instead of from the distributor. This eliminates timing variations from backlash in the timing chain or distributor shaft. Crankshaft position sensors are necessary in most modern distributorless ignition (DIS) systems. Basically, the sensor reads the position of the crankshaft by detecting breaks in the magnetic field created by pulse rings on the crankshaft or harmonic balancer **(see illustrations)**.

Checking the crankshaft position sensor

Most crankshaft position sensor problems can be traced to a fault in the wiring harness or connectors. These problems can cause a loss of the timing signal and consequently the engine will not start. When troubleshooting a crankshaft position sensor problem, it is advisable to follow the diagnostic flow chart in a factory service manual to isolate the faulty component. The problem could be in the ignition module, computer, wiring harness or crankshaft position sensor. Be aware of the interrelationship of these components.

If it is necessary to replace the sensor, be sure to install it correctly, paying attention to the alignment. Any rubbing or interference will cause driveability

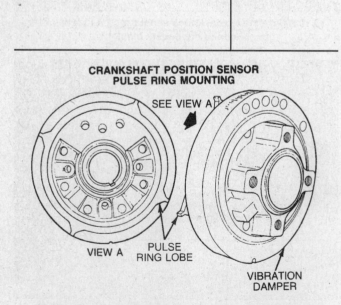

16.18a The crankshaft position sensor pulse rings are mounted on the harmonic balancer (vibration damper) on Ford V8 engines

16.18b On Ford V6 engines, the pulse rings are directly behind the crankshaft pulley, easily detected by the sensor

problems. Also, on variable reluctance type crankshaft position sensors, be sure to adjust the air gap properly. Consult a factory service manual for the correct specification.

Vehicle Speed Sensor (VSS)

What it is and how it works

Vehicle Speed Sensors (VSS) are used in modern vehicles for a number of different purposes. One purpose is to monitor the vehicle speed so the computer can determine the correct time for torque converter clutch (TCC) lock-up. The sensor may also provide input to the computer to control the function of various other emissions systems components based on vehicle speed. On some GM vehicles, the signal from the VSS is used by the computer to reset the Idle Air Control valve as well as the canister purge valve. Another purpose is to assist with the power steering. Here, the sensor input is used by the electronic controller to vary the amount of power assist according to the vehicle speed. The lower the speed, the greater the assist for easier maneuverability for parking. The higher the speed, the less the assist for better road feel. Another purpose is to change the position of electronically adjustable shock absorbers used in ride control systems. The ride control systems in Mazda 626's and Ford Probes automatically switch the shocks to a "firm" setting above 50 mph in the AUTO mode and "extra firm" in the SPORT mode. Also, vehicle speed sensors replace the mechanical speedometer cable in some modern vehicles.

Checking the VSS

The driveability symptoms of a faulty vehicle speed sensor depend on what control functions require an accurate speed input. For example, on some GM vehicles, the idle quality may be affected by a faulty sensor. Other symptoms include hard steering with increased speed, premature torque converter lock-up or fluctuating or inaccurate speedometer readings.

Different vehicles require different testing techniques. It is best to consult a factory service manual for the specific test procedures for your particular vehicle. Also, it is rare, but sometimes the input shaft on the transmission has broken or missing teeth that affect the accuracy of the sensor's reading.

Knock sensor

What it is and how it works

The knock sensor (sometimes called an Electronic Spark Control [ESC] sensor) is an auxiliary sensor that is used to detect the onset of detonation **(see illustrations)**. Although the knock sensor influences ignition timing, it doesn't have direct impact on the fuel and emission systems. It affects ignition timing only.

The sensor, which is usually mounted on the intake manifold or engine block, generates a voltage signal when the engine vibrations are between 6 to 8 Hz. The location of the sensor is very critical because it must be positioned so it can detect any vibrations from the most detonation-prone cylinders. On some engines, it is necessary to install two knock sensors.

16.19a Here's a typical knock sensor mounted low on the side of the engine block

16.19b On many GM models, information from the knock sensor is sent to the Electronic Spark Control (ESC) module (arrow), which retards ignition timing if detonation is evident

When the knock sensor detects a pinging or knocking vibration, it signals the computer to momentarily retard ignition timing. The computer then retards the timing a fixed number of degrees until the detonation stops.

This system is vital on turbocharged vehicles to achieve maximum performance. When the knock control system is working properly, the maximum timing advance for all driving conditions is achieved.

Checking the knock sensor

The most obvious symptom of knock sensor failure will be an audible pinging or knocking, especially during acceleration under a light load. Light detonation usually does not cause harm, but heavy detonation over a period of time will cause engine damage. Knock sensors sometimes are fooled by other sounds such as rod knocks or worn timing chains. Reduced fuel economy and poor performance result from the constantly retarded timing.

Another thing to keep in mind is that most engine detonation has other causes than the knock sensor. Some causes include:

1) Defective EGR valve
2) Too much compression due to accumulated carbon in the cylinders
3) Overadvanced ignition timing
4) Lean fuel/air mixture; Possible vacuum leak
5) Overheated engine
6) Low-octane fuel

To check the knock sensor, use a wrench to rap on the intake manifold (not too hard or you may damage the manifold!) or cylinder block near the sensor while the engine is idling. Never strike the sensor directly. Observe the timing mark with a timing light. The vibration from the wrench will produce enough of a shock to cause the knock sensor to signal the computer to back off the timing. The timing should retard momentarily. If nothing happens, check the wiring, electrical connector or computer for any obvious shorts or problems. If the wiring and connectors are OK, the sensor is probably faulty.

The knock sensor is a sealed unit. If it is defective, replace it with a new part.

Output actuators

The output actuators receive commands from the computer and actuate the correct engine response after all the data and parameters have been analyzed by the computer. Output devices can be divided into three categories: Solenoids, electric motors and controller modules.

Solenoids include the EGR solenoid, Canister Purge (CANP) solenoid, carburetor feedback solenoid (FBC), Electronic Air Control Valve (EACV), Torque Converter Clutch (TCC) solenoid and fuel injectors.

Electric motors include the Idle Speed Control motor (ISC), the fuel pump and cooling fan.

Controller modules are used to control more than one device. Modules can control air conditioner and cooling fan response as well as ignition functions.

The following discusses operation and diagnosis of the most common types of output actuators.

Fuel injectors

Note: *Refer to Section 7 for all the general information and diagnostic procedures for testing the fuel injectors.*

EGR valve solenoid

What it is and how it works

On computer-controlled vehicles, the action of the EGR valve is usually controlled by commanding the EGR control solenoid(s). Refer to the information earlier in this Chapter on EGR valve position sensors for additional information concerning these systems. The EGR valve solenoid is computer controlled and located in the vacuum line between the EGR valve and vacuum source. It opens and closes electrically to maintain finer control of EGR flow than is possible with ported-vacuum-type systems. The computer uses information from the coolant temperature, throttle position and manifold pressure sensors to regulate the EGR valve solenoid.

During cold operation and at idle, the solenoid circuit is grounded by the computer to block vacuum to the EGR valve. When the solenoid circuit is not grounded by the computer, vacuum is allowed to the EGR valve.

Checking the EGR valve solenoid

First, inspect all vacuum hoses, wires and electrical connectors associated with the EGR solenoid and system. Make sure nothing is damaged, loose or disconnected.

Locate the vacuum line that runs from the vacuum source to the EGR solenoid. Disconnect it at the solenoid and hook up a vacuum gauge to the hose. Start the engine, bring it to normal operating temperature and observe the vacuum reading. There should be at least ten in-Hg of vacuum. If not, repair the hose to the vacuum source. Disconnect the gauge and re-connect the hose.

If there is at least ten in-Hg vacuum to the EGR solenoid, locate the vacuum hose running from the EGR solenoid to the EGR valve. Disconnect and plug the hose at the solenoid and hook up a vacuum gauge to the solenoid. Open the EGR solenoid by starting the engine and raising the speed to about 2,000 rpm. With the solenoid open, the vacuum gauge should read at least ten in-Hg **(see illustration)**. If there is no vacuum, either the solenoid valve is defective or there is a problem in the wiring circuit or computer.

To check the wiring circuit, disconnect the electrical connector from the EGR solenoid. With the ignition on and the engine off, connect a test light across the two terminals of the connector **(see illustration)**. The test light should come on. If it does not, there is a problem in the wiring or computer. If the light does come on, but there is no vacuum from the EGR solenoid to the EGR valve, the solenoid is probably defective. Check the solenoid's resistance. Normally, it should not be less than about 20 ohms.

Electronic Air Control Valve (EACV)

What it is and how it works

The EACV (sometimes called an Idle Air Control [IAC] valve) changes the amount of air bypassed (not flowing through the throttle valve) into the intake manifold in response to the changes in the electrical signals from the computer. EACVs are usually located on the throttle body, although some are mounted remotely.

16.20 Hook up a vacuum gauge to the EGR valve side of the solenoid - with the engine running at about 2,000 rpm, the gauge should register at least ten inches-Hg of vacuum

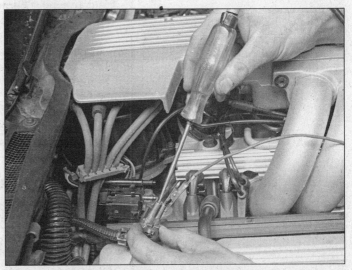

16.21 Connect a test light across the EGR solenoid connector terminals with the ignition key ON (engine not running) - the light should come on

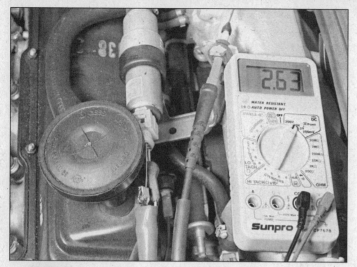

16.22 Observe the voltage reading at the EACV connector

After the engine starts, the EACV opens, allowing air to bypass the throttle and thus increases idle speed. While the coolant temperature is low, the EACV remains open to obtain the proper fast idle speed. As the engine warms up, the amount of bypassed air is controlled in relation to the coolant temperature. After the engine reaches normal operating temperature, the EACV is opened, as necessary, to maintain the correct idle speed.

Checking the EACV

To check the EACV valve circuit, connect the positive probe of a voltmeter to the signal wire in the EACV connector and the negative probe to the ground **(see illustration)**. Check the voltage as the engine starts to warm up from cold to warm conditions. Most EACV valves will indicate an increase in voltage as the system warms and the valve slowly cuts off the additional air. Consult a factory service manual for the correct voltage specifications for your vehicle. If the voltage is correct, but the EACV valve is not opening or closing to provide the correct airflow, replace the valve.

Torque Converter Clutch (TCC) solenoid

What it is and how it works

Lock-up torque converters are installed on newer vehicles to help eliminate torque converter slippage and thus reduce power loss and increase fuel economy. The torque converter is equipped with a clutch that is activated by a solenoid valve. The computer determines the best time to lock up the clutch device based on data it receives from various sensors and switches.

When the vehicle speed sensor indicates speed above a certain range and the coolant temperature sensor is warm, the Throttle Position Sensor (TPS) determines the position of the throttle (acceleration or deceleration) and the transmission sensor relays the particular gear the transmission is operating in to the computer for a complete analysis of operating parameters. If all parameters are within a certain range, the computer sends an electrical signal to the clutch, telling it to lock up. Needless to say, diagnosing a problem in this system can become complicated.

Checking the TCC solenoid

One symptom of TCC failure is a clutch that will not disengage, causing the engine to stall when slowing to a stop. Another symptom is an increase in engine rpm at cruising speed, resulting in decreased fuel economy (this usually means the converter is not locking up). If the converter is not locking up, the driver might not notice any differences unless he/she checks fuel consumption and the increase in tachometer readings. Without the TCC operating, the engine will turn an additional 300 to 500 rpm at cruising speed to maintain the same speed. Also, when the converter is not locking up, there is a chance the transmission will overheat and become damaged due to the higher operating temperatures.

Before diagnosing the TCC system as defective, make some preliminary checks. Check the transmission fluid level, linkage adjustment and the condition of the vacuum lines. After you've checked that all the basics are in order, check for any trouble codes (see Chapter 3). Further diagnosis should be referred to a dealer service department or other qualified repair shop.

Glossary

A

Absolute pressure - Pressure measured from the point of total vacuum. For instance, absolute atmospheric pressure at sea level is 14.5 psi (1 bar).

Accumulator - A device, installed in-line between the fuel pump and the fuel filter on many fuel injection systems, which dampens the pulsations of the fuel pump. The accumulator also maintains residual pressure in the fuel delivery system, even after the engine has been turned off, to prevent vapor lock.

Actuator - One name for any computer-controlled output device, such as a fuel injector, an EGR solenoid valve, an EVAP solenoid purge valve, etc. The term also refers to a specific component, the pressure actuator, used on Bosch KE-Jetronic and KE-Motronic continuous injection systems. See *pressure actuator*.

Adaptive control - The ability of a control unit to adapt its closed-loop operation to changing operating conditions - such as engine wear, fuel quality or altitude - to maintain proper air-fuel mixture control, ignition timing or idle rpm. Also referred to as self-learning.

Air-Flow Controlled (AFC) - A Bosch term for early L-Jetronic fuel injection systems, used to distinguish L-Jet from the earlier D-Jetronic, which was a pressure-controlled system. AFC also refers to many other fuel injection systems that measure the amount of air flowing past a sensor to determine engine fuel requirements

Airflow meter - In Bosch systems, any device that measures the amount of air being used by the engine. The control unit uses this information to determine the load on the engine. The two most common examples of airflow meters are the airflow sensor used in the Bosch L-Jetronic and the air mass sensor used in the Bosch LH-Jetronic systems. See *airflow sensor* and *air mass sensor*.

Airflow sensor - A sensor used to measure the volume of air entering the engine on many fuel injection systems. Continuous injection systems use an airflow sensor *plate* to measure airflow volume; electronic systems use a *vane* or flap-type airflow sensor.

Air mass sensor - An airflow meter that uses the changing resistance of a heated wire in the intake airstream to measure the mass of the air being drawn into the engine. Also referred to as a hot-wire sensor.

Air vane - The pivoting flap inside an L-Jetronic or Motronic airflow sensor that swings open in relation to the amount of air flowing through the airflow sensor.

Ambient temperature - The temperature of the surrounding air.

Armature - The spring-loaded part in an injector that's magnetically attracted by the solenoid coil when it is energized. Also another name for the solenoid itself.

Atmospheric pressure - Normal pressure in the surrounding atmosphere, generated by the weight of the air pressing down from above. At sea level, atmospheric pressure is about 1 bar, or 14.5 psi, above vacuum, or zero absolute, pressure. See *barometric pressure*.

Atomize - To reduce to fine particles or spray.

Auxiliary air valve - A special valve which bypasses the closed throttle valve. The auxiliary air valve provides extra air into the intake manifold during cold engine starting for a higher idle speed during warm-up.

B

Bar - The metric unit of measurement used in the measurement of both air and fuel. One bar is about 14.5 psi, or 100 kPa.

Barometric pressure - Another term for atmospheric pressure, expressed in inches of Mercury (in-Hg). Barometric pressure is determined by how high atmospheric pressure (relative to zero absolute pressure) forces Mercury up a glass tube. 14.5 psi = 29.92 inches.

Bimetal - A spring or strip made of two different metals with different thermal expansion rates. A rising temperature causes a bimetal element to bend or twist one way when it's cold and the other way when it's warm.

Bypass - A passage inside a throttle body casting that allows air to go around a closed throttle valve.

C

Carbon monoxide (CO) - A harmful gas produced during combustion when there's insufficient oxygen in the air/fuel mixture.

Cavitation - The formation of gas or vapor-filled cavities in a liquid, fuel for example, when the pressure is reduced to a critical value while ambient temperature remains constant. If the velocity of the flowing liquid exceeds a certain value, the pressure can be reduced to such an extent that Bernoulli's theorem breaks down. It is at this point that cavitation occurs, causing a restriction on the speed at which hydraulic machinery, a fuel pump, for instance, can be run without noise, vibration, erosion of metal parts or loss of efficiency).

CIS - Continuous Injection System. A Bosch fuel injection system which injects a steady stream of pressurized fuel into each intake port. CIS was once widely used throughout the industry.

CIS-E - A CIS system with electronic controls.

CIS-Lambda - A CIS system with an oxygen sensor.

CFI - Central Fuel Injection. A Ford Motor Company fuel injection system that uses an injector-mounted throttle body assembly

Closed loop - The mode of operation that a system with an oxygen sensor goes into once the engine is sufficiently warmed up. When the system is in closed-loop operation, an oxygen sensor monitors the oxygen content of the exhaust gas and sends a varying voltage signal to the control unit, which alters the air/fuel mixture ratio accordingly.

Cold-start injector - A solenoid-type injector, installed in the intake plenum, that injects extra fuel during cold-engine starts. Also referred to as a cold start valve.

Cold-start valve - See *cold-start injector*.

Computer Controlled Coil Ignition (C3I) - General Motors' computerized ignition coil system, used on many different engine applications.

Continuous Injection System (CIS) - A Bosch-developed fuel injection system that injects fuel continuously. Unlike an electronic injection system, which uses a computer to control the pulse-width of electronic solenoid injectors, CIS uses hydraulic controls to alter the amount of fuel injected. There are four basic types of CIS: K-Jetronic, K-Jetronic with Lambda (oxygen sensor), KE-Jetronic and KE-Motronic.

Control module - One of several names for a solid-state micro-computer which monitors engine conditions and controls certain engine functions, i.e. air/fuel ratio, injection and ignition timing, etc.

Control plunger - In Bosch CIS, the component inside the fuel distributor that rises and falls with the airflow sensor plate lever, which controls fuel flow to the injectors.

Control pressure - In Bosch CIS, the pressurized fuel used as a hydraulic control fluid to apply a counterforce to the control plunger in Bosch CIS. Control pressure alters the air-fuel ratio through the operation of the control-pressure regulator.

Control pressure regulator - In Bosch CIS, the control-pressure regulator is a thermal-hydraulic device that alters the control pressure by returning the excess fuel from the control pressure circuit to the fuel tank. The control-pressure regulator controls the counterforce pressure on top of the control plunger. Also referred to as the warm-up regulator.

Control unit - An electronic computer that processes electrical inputs and produces electrical outputs to control a series of actuators which alter engine operating conditions. Also referred to as an electronic control assembly (ECA), electronic control module (ECM), electronic control unit (ECU), logic module, or simply, the computer.

Counterforce - The force of the fuel-pressure applied to the top of the control plunger to balance the force of the airflow pushing against the sensor plate. See *control pressure*.

CPI - Central Point Injection. A General Motors fuel injection system that uses a centralized fuel injector delivering fuel through lines to injector nozzles located at each cylinder.

D

Density - The ratio of the mass of the mass of something (air, in this book) to the volume it occupies. Air has less density when it's warm, and when the vehicle is operating at higher altitude. It has more density when it's cool, and at lower altitude.

Detonation - See *knock*.

Differential pressure - In Bosch KE-Jetronic systems, the difference between actuator fuel pressure in the lower chambers of the differential-pressure valves and the system pressure entering the pressure actuator. See *pressure-drop*.

Differential-pressure regulator - See *pressure actuator*.

Differential-pressure valves- Inside the Bosch CIS fuel distributor, these valves (there's one for each cylinder) maintain a constant pressure drop at each of the control-plunger slits, regardless of changes in the quantity of fuel flow.

Distributor pipe - Another (archaic) name for the fuel rail.

D-Jetronic - D-Jetronic is the term used by Bosch to describe a fuel injection system controlled by manifold pressure. The D is short for *druck*, the German word for "pressure." Manifold pressure is measured to indicate engine load (how much air the engine is using). This pressure is an input signal to the control unit (ECU) for calculation of the correct amount of fuel delivery.

Differential pressure - In Bosch KE-Jetronic and KE-Motronic systems, the difference between actuator pressure in the lower chambers and system pressure entering the pressure actuator.

Differential-pressure valve - In a continuous injection system, differential-pressure valves maintain a constant pressure drop at the slits for the entire range of plunger lift.

Digifant - Volkswagen collaborated with Bosch to develop this electronic injection system. Digifant is similar to a Motronic system, except that its timing control map is less complicated than the Motronic map. And it doesn't have a knock sensor.

Digifant II - A refined version of Volkswagen's Digifant. This system has some control improvements and uses a knock sensor for improved timing control.

Digital Fuel Injection (DFI) - A General Motors system, similar to earlier electronic fuel injection systems, but with digital microprocessors. Analog inputs from various engine sensors are converted to digital signals before processing. The system is self-monitoring and self-diagnosing. It also has the capabilities of compensating for failed components and remembering intermittent failures.

DIS - Direct Ignition System. A distributorless ignition system similar to the C3I system, using two coils on four-cylinder engines.

Driveability - A Condition describing a car in which it starts easily, idles, accelerates and shifts smoothly with adequate power for varying temperatures and conditions.

Duty cycle - Many solenoid-operated metering devices cycle on and off. The duty cycle is a measurement of the amount of time a device is energized, or turned on, expressed as a percentage of the complete on-off cycle of that device. In other words, the duty cycle is the ratio of the pulse width to the complete cycle width.

Dwell - The amount of time that primary voltage is applied to the ignition coil to energize it. Dwell is also a measurement of the duration of time a component is on, relative to the time it's off. Dwell measurements are expressed in degrees (degrees of crankshaft rotation, for example). See *duty cycle*.

E

ECA - Electronic Control Assembly. See *control unit*.

ECM - Electronic Control Module. See *control unit*.

ECU - Electronic Control Unit. See *control unit*.

EFI - Electronic Fuel Injection. A fuel injection system which uses a microcomputer to determine and control the amount of fuel required by, and injected into, a particular engine.

EGI - Electronic Gasoline Injection. Mazda's fuel injection system for the RX7, RX7 Turbo, 323 and 626 models.

Electro-hydraulic pressure actuator - See *pressure actuator*.

Electronic control unit - One (of many) names for the system computer. Often referred to as simply the "control unit."

F

False air - Any air leak that introduces unmeasured air into the intake system between the airflow meter and the intake valves is "false air."

Frequency valve - In Bosch CIS, a device that regulates pressure in the lower chamber of the differential-pressure valve, in response to a signal from the lambda (oxygen) sensor. Also referred to as a Lambda valve (Bosch's term) or a timing valve.

Fuel distributor - On Bosch CIS, the device that supplies the injectors with pressurized fuel in proportion to air volume, measured by the airflow sensor plate. The fuel distributor houses the control plunger and the differential-pressure valves. All fuel metering takes place inside the fuel distributor.

Fuel filter - Filters fuel before delivery to protect injection system components.

Fuel injector - In all systems (except CIS, CIS/Lambda and CIS-E systems), a spring-loaded, solenoid (electromagnetic) valve which delivers fuel into the intake manifold, in response to electrical signals from the control module. In CIS, CIS/Lambda and CIS-E systems, a spring-loaded, pressure sensitive valve which opens at a preset value.

Fuel pump - Delivers fuel from the fuel tank to the fuel injection system and provides system pressure. On fuel-injected vehicles, the pump is always electric.

Fuel rail - The hollow pipe, tube or manifold that delivers fuel at system pressure to the injectors. The storage volume of the fuel rail influences the stability of the fuel pressure in the system. The fuel rail also serves as the mounting point for the upper ends of the injectors, and for the damper (if equipped) and the pressure-regulator.

Full-load - The load condition of the engine when the throttle is wide open. Full-load can occur at any rpm.

Full-load enrichment - The extra fuel injected during acceleration to enrich the mixture when the throttle is wide open. On some systems, the computer goes open-loop during full-load enrichment.

G

Galvanic battery - The principle of operation of an oxygen sensor; a galvanic battery generates voltage as a result of a chemical reaction.

H

Hertz (Hz) - A measure of the frequency, measured in cycles per second.

Hot start - Starting the engine when it's at or near its normal operating temperature.

Hot-wire sensor - See *air mass sensor*.

I

Ideal air-fuel ratio - See *stoichiometric ratio*.

Idle-speed stabilizer - An electronically-controlled air bypass around the throttle. Also referred to as an idle speed actuator or a constant idle system.

In-Hg - Inches-of-mercury. See *barometric pressure*.

Injection pressure - In Bosch CIS, the pressure of the fuel in the lines between the differential-pressure valves and the injectors. Also referred to as injector fuel.

Injection valve - See *injector*.

Injector - This device opens to spray fuel into the throttle bore (throttle body injection) or into the intake port (electronic port injection systems and continuous injection systems). Electronic injectors are opened by an electric solenoid and closed by a spring; continuous injectors are opened by fuel pressure and closed by a spring. Injectors are also referred to as injection valves.

Injector fuel - See injection pressure.

K

K-Jetronic - K-Jetronic is the term used by Bosch to describe the original continuous injection system. The K is short for *kontinuerlich*, the German word for "continuous." Airflow is measured by a circular plate inside the airflow sensor part of the mixture control unit. Fuel delivery was purely mechanical, in relation to airflow, until 1980, i.e. there were no electronics used in the K-Jet system. VW, Audi and Mercedes refer to K-Jet as CIS.

K-Jetronic with Lambda - This second-generation K-Jet system, which began in 1980, uses a feedback loop consisting of an oxygen sensor and a control unit to provide some electronic control of the air-fuel mixture. This system is also referred to as "CIS with Lambda." "Lambda" is the Bosch term for an oxygen sensor.

KE-Jetronic - This third-generation K-Jet system combines mechanical control with electronic regulation of the mixture. Many of the sensors it uses are the same as those used in L-Jetronic systems. VW, Audi and Mercedes refer to it as CIS-E.

KE-Motronic - This Bosch system is similar to KE-Jetronic, except that it has ignition-timing control and all the other features as any other Motronic system. See *Motronic*.

Kilohertz (kHz) - 1000 Hertz (Hz), the unit of frequency. See *Hertz*.

Knock - A sudden increase in cylinder pressure caused by preignition of some of the air-fuel mixture as the flame front moves out from the spark plug ignition point. Pressure waves in the combustion chamber crash into the piston or cylinder walls. The result is a sound known as knock or pinging. Knock can be caused by using fuel with an octane rating that's too low, by excessively advanced ignition timing, or by a compression ratio that's been raised by hot carbon deposits on the piston or cylinder head.

Knock sensor - A vibration sensor mounted on the cylinder block that generates a voltage when the knock occurs. The voltage signals the control unit, which alters the ignition timing (and, on turbocharged vehicles, limits boost) to stop the knock.

L

Lambda (l) - The Greek symbol engineers use to indicate the ratio of one number to another. Expresses the air-fuel ratio in terms of the stoichiometric ratio compared to the oxygen content of the exhaust. At the stoichiometric ratio, when all of the fuel is burned with all of the air in the combustion chamber, the oxygen content of the exhaust is said to be at lambda = 1. If there's excess oxygen in the exhaust (a lean mixture), then lambda is greater than 1 (l > 1); if there's an excess of fuel in the exhaust (a shortage of air - a rich mixture), then lambda is less than 1 (l < 1).

Lambda control - Bosch's term for a closed-loop system that adjusts the air-fuel ratio to lambda = 1, based on sensing the amount of excess oxygen in the exhaust.

Lambda control valve - See *frequency valve*.

Lambda sensor - Bosch's term for the oxygen sensor. See *oxygen sensor*.

Lean - A mixture that has more air than required for a stoichiometric ratio. Oxygen is left over after the fuel is burned. In Bosch terms, lambda is greater than one; the air-fuel ratio is greater than 14.7:1.

L-Jetronic - L-Jetronic is the term used by Bosch to describe a fuel injection system controlled by the air flowing through a sensor with a movable vane, or flap, which indicates engine load. The L is short for *luft*, the German word for "air." Later versions of L-Jet are equipped with a Lambda (oxygen) sensor for better mixture control. Bosch originally used the term Air-Flow Controlled (AFC)

Injection to denote L-Jet systems in order to differentiate them from pressure-controlled D-Jetronic systems.

LH-Jetronic - Bosch LH-Jetronic systems measure air mass (weight of air) with a hot-wire sensor instead of measuring airflow with a vane, or flap, type air *volume* sensor used on L-Jet systems. The H is short for *heiss*, the German word for "hot."

LH-Motronic - This Bosch system is the same as any other Motronic system, except that it uses a hot-wire air-mass sensor (L is short for *luft*, the German word for "air" and H is short for *heiss*, which means "hot," hence hot wire). LH-Motronic systems also have idle stabilization.

"Limp-in" or "limp-home" - This term is used by many manufacturers to explain the driveability characteristics of a failed computer system. Many computer systems store information that can be used to get the vehicle to a repair facility. In this mode of operation, driveability is greatly reduced.

Load - The amount of work the engine must do. When the vehicle accelerates quickly from a stop, or from a low speed, the engine is placed under a heavy load.

Logic module - See *control module*.

Lucas Bosch - This system, used in Jaguars and Triumphs, is a Bosch L-Jetronic system licensed for production by Lucas.

M

Manifold absolute pressure (MAP) - Manifold pressure measured on the absolute pressure scale, an indication of engine load. At sea level, MAP equals 1 bar (14.5 psi).

Manifold Pressure Controlled (MPC) - A fuel injection system which determines engine load based on intake manifold pressure.

Map - A pictorial representation of a series of data points stored in the memory of the control unit of systems with complete engine management. The control unit refers to the map to control variables such as fuel injection pulse width and ignition timing.

MAP sensor - A device that monitors manifold absolute pressure and sends a varying signal to the control unit, which alters the air-fuel mixture accordingly.

Mass - The amount of matter contained in an object or a volume. In the field of earth gravity, mass is roughly equivalent to the weight of the object or volume. In fuel injection terms, a measured air volume is corrected for temperature and density to determine its mass.

Mass Air Flow (MAF) Sensor - See *Air mass sensor*.

Metering slits - In Bosch CIS, the narrow slits in the control-plunger barrel of the fuel distributor. Fuel flows through the slits in accordance with the lift of the control plunger and the pressure drop at the slits.

Mixture control unit - In Bosch CIS, the collective term for the airflow sensor plate and the fuel distributor, which are integrated into a single component.

Motronic - This term is used by Bosch to denote its engine management systems. The original Motronic system combined L-Jetronic with electronic ignition timing control in one control unit. Most Motronic-equipped engines also have electronic idle stabilization. Around 1986, Motronic systems received: knock regulation by ignition timing of individual cylinders; adaptive circuitry, which adapts fuel delivery and ignition timing to actual conditions; diagnostic circuitry which enables the control unit to recognize system faults and store fault information in its memory. Motronic has also been integrated with KE-Jetronic systems, and is referred to as KE-Motronic.

Multi-Point Fuel Injection (MPFI) - A fuel injection system that uses one injector per cylinder, mounted on the engine to spray fuel near the intake valve area or the combustion chamber. Also referred to as Multi-Port Injection.

N

Negative Temperature Coefficient (NTC) - A term used to describe a thermistor (temperature sensor) in which the resistance decreases as the temperature increases. The thermistors used on fuel injection systems are nearly all NTCs.

O

Open loop - An operational mode during which "default" (preprogrammed) values in control unit memory are used to determine the air/fuel ratio, injection timing, etc., instead of "real" sensor inputs. The system goes into open loop during cold-engine operation, or when a particular sensor malfunctions.

Orifice - The calibrated fuel delivery hole at the nozzle end of the fuel injector.

Oxygen sensor - A sensor, mounted in the exhaust manifold or exhaust pipe, that reacts to changes in the oxygen content of the exhaust gases. The voltage generated by the oxygen sensor is monitored by the control unit.

P

Part-load - The throttle opening between idle and fully-open.

Part-load enrichment - Extra fuel injected during throttle opening to enrich the mixture during transition. Usually occurs during closed-loop operation.

PGM-FI - Programmed Fuel Injection. Honda's fuel injection system for the Accord, Civic, Civic CRX and Prelude models

Pintle - In an injector, the tip of the needle that opens to allow pressurized fuel through the spray orifice. The shape of the pintle and the orifice determines the spray pattern of the atomized fuel.

Plunger - See *control plunger*.

Port injection - A fuel injection system in which the fuel is sprayed by individual injectors into each intake port, upstream of the intake valve.

Positive Temperature Coefficient (PTC) - A term used to describe a thermistor (temperature sensor) in which the resistance increases as the temperature increases. The thermistors used on most fuel injection systems are negative tem-

Fuel Injection Diagnostic Manual

perature coefficient (NTC) but a few Chryslers and some mid-80s Cadillacs used PTCs.

Potentiometer - A variable resistor element that acts as a voltage divider to produce a continuously variable output signal proportional to a mechanical position.

Power module - On Chryslers, the power module works in conjunction with the logic module. The power module is the primary power supply for the EFI system.

Pressure actuator - On Bosch KE-Jetronic and KE-Motronic systems, an electronically-controlled hydraulic valve, affixed to the mixture-control unit, that regulates fuel flow through the lower chambers of the differential-pressure valves. The pressure actuator controls all adjustments to basic fuel metering and air-fuel ratio to compensate for changing operating conditions. Also referred to as a differential-pressure regulator and as an electro-hydraulic pressure actuator.

Pressure drop - The difference in pressure where fuel metering occurs. In electronic injection systems, this is the difference between fuel system pressure and intake manifold pressure. In Bosch CIS, it's the difference between system pressure inside the control plunger and the pressure outside the slits, in the upper-chamber of the differential-pressure valves.

Pressure regulator - A spring-loaded diaphragm-type pressure-relief valve which controls the pressure of fuel delivered to the fuel injector(s) by returning excess fuel to the tank.

Pressure tap - Another name for the fuel-injection system test port.

Pressure relief - What you must do to all fuel-injection systems before cracking a line and opening up the system.

Pressure relief valve - Another name for the fuel-injection system test port.

Primary pressure - Another name for system pressure in a continuous injection system.

Pulsed injection - A system that delivers fuel in intermittent pulses by the opening and closing of solenoid-controlled injectors. Also referred to as electronic fuel injection (EFI).

Pulse period - The time available, depending on engine speed, for opening the solenoid injectors.

Pulse width - The amount of time that a fuel injector is energized, measured in milliseconds. The duration of the pulse width is determined by the amount of fuel the engine needs at any time. Also referred to as pulse time.

Push valve - In a continuous injection system, the push valve controls the return of fuel from the control-pressure regulator to the system-pressure regulator. When engine is shut off, push valve closes control pressure circuit.

R

Relative pressure - In electronic injection systems, the difference in pressure between fuel pressure in the injector(s) and pressure in the intake manifold.

Residual pressure - Fuel pressure maintained within the system after engine shutdown.

Resistor - Any electrical circuit element that provides resistance in a circuit.

Rich - Not enough air or too much fuel is drawn into the engine to maintain a stoichiometric ratio. There's still fuel left after all the oxygen has been burned in the combustion process. Lambda is less than one, and the air-fuel mixture is less than 14.7:1.

S

Sensor - A device which monitors an engine operating condition and sends a voltage signal to the control unit. This variable voltage signal varies in accordance with the changes in the condition being monitored. There can be anywhere from half a dozen to two dozen sensors on an engine, depending on the sophistication of the system.

Sensor plate - In Bosch CIS, the flat, round plate, bolted to a lever arm, which rises and falls with the flow of air through the airflow sensor, raising and lowering the control plunger in the fuel distributor.

Sequential Electronic Fuel Injection (SEFI), or Sequential Fuel Injection (SFI) - A fuel injection system which uses a micro-computer to determine and control the amount of fuel required by, and injected into, a particular cylinder in the same sequence as the engine firing sequence.

Slit - See *metering slits*.

Solenoid - An electromagnetic actuator consisting of an electrical coil with a hollow center and an iron piece, the armature, that moves into the coil when it is energized. Solenoids are used to open fuel injectors and many other output actuators on fuel-injected vehicles.

Solenoid valve - A valve operated by a solenoid.

Stoichiometric - The ideal air/fuel mixture ratio (14.7:1) at which the best compromise between engine performance (richer mixture) and economy and low exhaust emissions (leaner mixture) is obtained. All of the air and all of the fuel is burned inside the combustion chamber.

System pressure - The fuel pressure in the fuel lines and at the pressure regulator, created by the fuel pump.

System pressure regulator - In a continuous injection system, holds system fuel pressure constant.

T

Temperature sensor - A special type of solid-state resistor, known as a thermistor. Used to sense coolant and, on some systems, air temperature. See *thermistor*.

Test port - The Schrader valve fitting located on the fuel rail of a port injection system. Used for relieving fuel pressure and for hooking up a fuel-pressure gauge.

Timing valve - See *frequency valve*.

Thermistor - A special kind of resistor whose resistance decreases as its temperature increases. Thermistors are used for air and coolant temperature sensors. Also referred to as a Negative Temperature Coefficient (NTC) resistor. See *temperature sensor*.

Throttle body - The carburetor-like aluminum casting that houses the throttle valve, the idle air bypass (if equipped), the throttle position sensor (TPS), the idle air control (IAC) motor, the throttle linkage and, on TBI systems, one or two injectors.

Throttle Body Injection (TBI) - . Any of several injection systems which have the fuel injector(s) mounted in a centrally located throttle body, as opposed to positioning the injectors close to the intake ports.

Throttle valve - The movable plate, inside the throttle body, which is controlled by the accelerator pedal. The throttle valve controls the amount of air that can enter the engine.

Tuned port injection (TPI) - A General Motors fuel injection system that uses tuned air intake runners for improved airflow.

V

Vacuum - Anything less than atmospheric pressure.

Vapor lock - A condition which occurs when the fuel becomes so hot that it vaporizes, slowing or stopping fuel flow in the fuel lines.

W

Warm-up regulator - On Bosch CIS, the original name for the control-pressure regulator.

Z

Zero absolute pressure - A total vacuum. Zero on the absolute pressure scale.

Index

Fuel Injection Diagnostic Manual

Haynes Automotive Manuals

NOTE: New manuals are added to this list on a periodic basis. If you do not see a listing for your vehicle, consult your local Haynes dealer for the latest product information.

ACURA
*1776 Integra '86 thru '89 & Legend '86 thru '90

AMC
Jeep CJ - see JEEP (412)
694 Mid-size models, Concord, Hornet, Gremlin & Spirit '70 thru '83
934 (Renault) Alliance & Encore '83 thru '87

AUDI
615 4000 all models '80 thru '87
428 5000 all models '77 thru '83
1117 5000 all models '84 thru '88

AUSTIN-HEALEY
Sprite - see MG Midget (265)

BMW
*2020 3/5 Series not including diesel or all-wheel drive models '82 thru '92
276 320i all 4 cyl models '75 thru '83
632 528i & 530i all models '75 thru '80
240 1500 thru 2002 except Turbo '59 thru '77

BUICK
Century (front wheel drive) - see GM (829)
*1627 Buick, Oldsmobile & Pontiac Full-size (Front wheel drive) all models '85 thru '95
Buick Electra, LeSabre and Park Avenue;
Oldsmobile Delta 88 Royale, Ninety Eight and Regency; Pontiac Bonneville
1551 Buick Oldsmobile & Pontiac Full-size (Rear wheel drive)
Buick Estate '70 thru '90, Electra '70 thru '84, LeSabre '70 thru '85, Limited '74 thru '79
Oldsmobile Custom Cruiser '70 thru '90, Delta 88 '70 thru '85, Ninety-eight '70 thru '84
Pontiac Bonneville '70 thru '81, Catalina '70 thru '81, Grandville '70 thru '75, Parisienne '83 thru '86
627 Mid-size Regal & Century all rear-drive models with V6, V8 and Turbo '74 thru '87
Regal - see GENERAL MOTORS (1671)
Riviera - see GENERAL MOTORS (38030)
Skyhawk - see GENERAL MOTORS (766)
Skylark '80 thru '85 - see GM (38020)
Skylark '86 on - see GM (1420)
Somerset - see GENERAL MOTORS (1420)

CADILLAC
*751 Cadillac Rear Wheel Drive all gasoline models '70 thru '93
Cimarron - see GENERAL MOTORS (766)
Eldorado - see GENERAL MOTORS (38030)
Seville '80 thru '85 - see GM (38030)

CHEVROLET
*1477 Astro & GMC Safari Mini-vans '85 thru '93
554 Camaro V8 all models '70 thru '81
866 Camaro all models '82 thru '92
Cavalier - see GENERAL MOTORS (766)
Celebrity - see GENERAL MOTORS (829)
24017 Camaro & Firebird '93 thru '96
625 Chevelle, Malibu & El Camino all V6 & V8 models '69 thru '87
449 Chevette & Pontiac T1000 '76 thru '87
550 Citation all models '80 thru '85
*1628 Corsica/Beretta '87 thru '96
274 Corvette all V8 models '68 thru '82
*1336 Corvette all models '84 thru '91
1762 Chevrolet Engine Overhaul Manual
704 Full-size Sedans Caprice, Impala, Biscayne, Bel Air & Wagons '69 thru '90
Lumina - see GENERAL MOTORS (1671)
Lumina APV - see GENERAL MOTORS (2035)
319 Luv Pick-up all 2WD & 4WD '72 thru '82
626 Monte Carlo all models '70 thru '88

241 Nova all V8 models '69 thru '79
*1642 Nova and Geo Prizm all front wheel drive models, '85 thru '92
420 Pick-ups '67 thru '87 - Chevrolet & GMC, all V8 & in-line 6 cyl, 2WD & 4WD '67 thru '87; Suburbans, Blazers & Jimmys '67 thru '91
*1664 Pick-ups '88 thru '95 - Chevrolet & GMC, all full-size pick-ups, '88 thru '95; Blazer & Jimmy '92 thru '94; Suburban '92 thru '95; Tahoe & Yukon '95
831 S-10 & GMC S-15 Pick-ups '82 thru '93
*24071 S-10 & GMC S-15 Pick-ups '94 thru '96
*1727 Sprint & Geo Metro '85 thru '94
*345 Vans - Chevrolet & GMC, V8 & in-line 6 cylinder models '68 thru '96

CHRYSLER
25025 Chrysler Concorde, New Yorker & LHS, Dodge Intrepid, Eagle Vision, '93 thru '96
2114 Chrysler Engine Overhaul Manual
*2058 Full-size Front-Wheel Drive '88 thru '93
K-Cars - see DODGE Aries (723)
Laser - see DODGE Daytona (1140)
*1337 Chrysler & Plymouth Mid-size front wheel drive '82 thru '95
Rear-wheel Drive - see Dodge (2098)

DATSUN
647 200SX all models '80 thru '83
228 B - 210 all models '73 thru '78
525 210 all models '79 thru '82
206 240Z, 260Z & 280Z Coupe '70 thru '78
563 280ZX Coupe & 2+2 '79 thru '83
300ZX - see NISSAN (1137)
679 310 all models '78 thru '82
123 510 & PL521 Pick-up '68 thru '73
430 510 all models '78 thru '81
372 610 all models '72 thru '76
277 620 Series Pick-up all models '73 thru '79
720 Series Pick-up - see NISSAN (771)
376 810/Maxima all gasoline models, '77 thru '84
Pulsar - see NISSAN (876)
Sentra - see NISSAN (982)
Stanza - see NISSAN (981)

DODGE
400 & 600 - see CHRYSLER Mid-size (1337)
*723 Aries & Plymouth Reliant '81 thru '89
1231 Caravan & Plymouth Voyager Mini-Vans all models '84 thru '95
699 Challenger/Plymouth Saporro '78 thru '83
Challenger '67-'76 - see DODGE Dart (234)
610 Colt & Plymouth Champ (front wheel drive) all models '78 thru '87
*1668 Dakota Pick-ups all models '87 thru '96
234 Dart, Challenger/Plymouth Barracuda & Valiant 6 cyl models '67 thru '76
*1140 Daytona & Chrysler Laser '84 thru '89
Intrepid - see CHRYSLER (25025)
*30034 Neon all models '94 thru '97
*545 Omni & Plymouth Horizon '78 thru '90
*912 Pick-ups all full-size models '74 thru '93
*30041 Pick-ups all full-size models '94 thru '96
*556 Ram 50/D50 Pick-ups & Raider and Plymouth Arrow Pick-ups '79 thru '93
2098 Dodge/Plymouth/Chrysler rear wheel drive '71 thru '89
*1726 Shadow & Plymouth Sundance '87 thru '94
*1779 Spirit & Plymouth Acclaim '89 thru '95
*349 Vans - Dodge & Plymouth V8 & 6 cyl '71 thru '96

EAGLE
Talon - see Mitsubishi Eclipse (2097)
Vision - see CHRYSLER (25025)

FIAT
094 124 Sport Coupe & Spider '68 thru '78
273 X1/9 all models '74 thru '80

FORD
10355 Ford Automatic Trans. Overhaul
*1476 Aerostar Mini-vans all models '86 thru '96

268 Courier Pick-up all models '72 thru '82
2105 Crown Victoria & Mercury Grand Marquis '88 thru '96
1763 Ford Engine Overhaul Manual
789 Escort/Mercury Lynx all models '81 thru '90
*2046 Escort/Mercury Tracer '91 thru '96
*2021 Explorer & Mazda Navajo '91 thru '95
560 Fairmont & Mercury Zephyr '78 thru '83
334 Fiesta all models '77 thru '80
754 Ford & Mercury Full-size, Ford LTD & Mercury Marquis ('75 thru '82); Ford Custom 500, Country Squire, Crown Victoria & Mercury Colony Park ('75 thru '87); Ford LTD Crown Victoria & Mercury Gran Marquis ('83 thru '87);
359 Granada & Mercury Monarch all in-line, 6 cyl & V8 models '75 thru '80
773 Ford & Mercury Mid-size, Ford Thunderbird & Mercury Cougar ('75 thru '82); Ford LTD & Mercury Marquis ('83 thru '86); Ford Torino, Gran Torino, Elite, Ranchero pick-up, LTD II, Mercury Montego, Comet, XR-7 & Lincoln Versailles ('75 thru '86)
231 Mustang II 4 cyl, V6 & V8 models '74 thru '78
357 Mustang V8 all models '64-1/2 thru '73
*654 Mustang & Mercury Capri all models Mustang, '79 thru '93; Capri, '79 thru '86
*36051 Mustang all models '94 thru '97
788 Pick-ups & Bronco '73 thru '79
*880 Pick-ups & Bronco '80 thru '96
649 Pinto & Mercury Bobcat '75 thru '80
1670 Probe all models '89 thru '92
*1026 Ranger/Bronco II gasoline models '83 thru '92
*36071 Ranger '93 thru '96 & Mazda Pick-ups '94 thru '96
*1421 Taurus & Mercury Sable '86 thru '95
*1418 Tempo & Mercury Topaz all gasoline models '84 thru '94
1338 Thunderbird/Mercury Cougar '83 thru '88
*1725 Thunderbird/Mercury Cougar '89 and '96
344 Vans all V8 Econoline models '69 thru '91
*2119 Vans full size '92-'95

GENERAL MOTORS
*10360 GM Automatic Transmission Overhaul
*829 Buick Century, Chevrolet Celebrity, Oldsmobile Cutlass Ciera & Pontiac 6000 all models '82 thru '96
*1671 Buick Regal, Chevrolet Lumina, Oldsmobile Cutlass Supreme & Pontiac Grand Prix front wheel drive models '88 thru '95
*766 Buick Skyhawk, Cadillac Cimarron, Chevrolet Cavalier, Oldsmobile Firenza & Pontiac J-2000 & Sunbird '82 thru '94
38020 Buick Skylark, Chevrolet Citation, Olds Omega, Pontiac Phoenix '80 thru '85
1420 Buick Skylark & Somerset, Oldsmobile Achieva & Calais and Pontiac Grand Am all models '85 thru '95
38030 Cadillac Eldorado '71 thru '85, Seville '80 thru '85, Oldsmobile Toronado '71 thru '85 & Buick Riviera '79 thru '85
*2035 Chevrolet Lumina APV, Olds Silhouette & Pontiac Trans Sport all models '90 thru '95
General Motors Full-size Rear-wheel Drive - see BUICK (1551)

GEO
Metro - see CHEVROLET Sprint (1727)
Prizm - '85 thru '92 see CHEVY Nova (1642), '93 thru '96 see TOYOTA Corolla (1642)
*2039 Storm all models '90 thru '93
Tracker - see SUZUKI Samurai (1626)

GMC
Safari - see CHEVROLET ASTRO (1477)
Vans & Pick-ups - see CHEVROLET (420, 831, 345, 1664 & 24071)

(Continued on other side)

* Listings shown with an asterisk (*) indicate model coverage as of this printing. These titles will be periodically updated to include later model years - consult your Haynes dealer for more information.

Haynes North America, Inc., 861 Lawrence Drive, Newbury Park, CA 91320 • (805) 498-6703

NOTE: New manuals are added to this list on a periodic basis. If you do not see a listing for your vehicle, consult your local Haynes dealer for the latest product information.

HONDA

351	Accord CVCC all models '76 thru '83
1221	Accord all models '84 thru '89
2067	Accord all models '90 thru '93
42013	Accord all models '94 thru '95
160	Civic 1200 all models '73 thru '79
633	Civic 1300 & 1500 CVCC '80 thru '83
297	Civic 1500 CVCC all models '75 thru '79
1227	Civic all models '84 thru '91
*2118	Civic & del Sol '92 thru '95
*601	Prelude CVCC all models '79 thru '89

HYUNDAI

*1552	Excel all models '86 thru '94

ISUZU

*1641	Trooper & Pick-up, all gasoline models Pick-up, '81 thru '93; Trooper, '84 thru '91 Hombre - see CHEVROLET S-10 (24071)

JAGUAR

*242	XJ6 all 6 cyl models '68 thru '86
*49011	XJ6 all models '88 thru '94
*478	XJ12 & XJS all 12 cyl models '72 thru '85

JEEP

*1553	Cherokee, Comanche & Wagoneer Limited all models '84 thru '96
412	CJ all models '49 thru '86
50025	Grand Cherokee all models '93 thru '95
50029	Grand Wagoneer & Pick-up '72 thru '91 Grand Wagoneer '84 thru '91, Cherokee & Wagoneer '72 thru '83, Pick-up '72 thru '88
*1777	Wrangler all models '87 thru '95

LINCOLN

2117	Rear Wheel Drive all models '70 thru '96

MAZDA

648	626 (rear wheel drive) all models '79 thru '82
*1082	626/MX-6 (front wheel drive) '83 thru '91
370	GLC Hatchback (rear wheel drive) '77 thru '83
757	GLC (front wheel drive) '81 thru '85
*2047	MPV all models '89 thru '94 Navajo - see Ford Explorer (2021)
267	Pick-ups '72 thru '93 Pick-ups '94 thru '96 - see Ford Ranger (36071)
460	RX-7 all models '79 thru '85
*1419	RX-7 all models '86 thru '91

MERCEDES-BENZ

*1643	190 Series four-cyl gas models, '84 thru '88
346	230/250/280 6 cyl sohc models '68 thru '72
983	280 123 Series gasoline models '77 thru '81
698	350 & 450 all models '71 thru '80
697	Diesel 123 Series '76 thru '85

MERCURY

See FORD Listing

MG

111	MGB Roadster & GT Coupe '62 thru '80
265	MG Midget, Austin Healey Sprite '58 thru '80

MITSUBISHI

*1669	Cordia, Tredia, Galant, Precis & Mirage '83 thru '93
*2097	Eclipse, Eagle Talon & Plymouth Laser '90 thru '94
*2022	Pick-up '83 thru '96 & Montero '83 thru '93

NISSAN

1137	300ZX all models including Turbo '84 thru '89
*72015	Altima all models '93 thru '97
*1341	Maxima all models '85 thru '91
*771	Pick-ups '80 thru '96 Pathfinder '87 thru '95
876	Pulsar all models '83 thru '86
*982	Sentra all models '82 thru '94
*981	Stanza all models '82 thru '90

OLDSMOBILE

	Achieva - see GENERAL MOTORS (1420)
	Bravada - see CHEVROLET S-10 (831)
	Calais - see GENERAL MOTORS (1420)
	Custom Cruiser - see BUICK RWD (1551)
*658	Cutlass V6 & V8 gas models '74 thru '88
	Cutlass Ciera - see GENERAL MOTORS (829)
	Cutlass Supreme - see GM (1671)
	Delta 88 - see BUICK Full-size RWD (1551)
	Delta 88 Brougham - see BUICK Full-size FWD (1551), RWD (1627)
	Delta 88 Royale - see BUICK RWD (1551)
	Firenza - see GENERAL MOTORS (766)
	Ninety-eight Regency - see BUICK Full-size RWD (1551), FWD (1627)
	Ninety-eight Regency Brougham - see BUICK Full-size RWD (1551)
	Omega - see GENERAL MOTORS (38020)
	Silhouette - see GENERAL MOTORS (2035)
	Toronado - see GENERAL MOTORS (38030)

PEUGEOT

663	504 all diesel models '74 thru '83

PLYMOUTH

	Laser - see MITSUBISHI Eclipse (2097)
	For other PLYMOUTH titles, see DODGE.

PONTIAC

	T1000 - see CHEVROLET Chevette (449)
	J-2000 - see GENERAL MOTORS (766)
	6000 - see GENERAL MOTORS (829)
	Bonneville - see Buick FWD (1627), RWD (1551)
	Bonneville Brougham - see Buick (1551)
	Catalina - see Buick Full-size (1551)
1232	Fiero all models '84 thru '88
555	Firebird V8 models except Turbo '70 thru '81
867	Firebird all models '82 thru '92 Firebird '93 thru '96 - see CHEVY Camaro (24017)
	Full-size Front Wheel Drive - see BUICK, Oldsmobile, Pontiac Full-size FWD (1627)
	Full-size Rear Wheel Drive - see BUICK Oldsmobile, Pontiac Full-size RWD (1551)
	Grand Am - see GENERAL MOTORS (1420)
	Grand Prix - see GENERAL MOTORS (1671)
	Grandville - see BUICK Full-size (1551)
	Parisienne - see BUICK Full-size (1551)
	Phoenix - see GENERAL MOTORS (38020)
	Sunbird - see GENERAL MOTORS (766)
	Trans Sport - see GENERAL MOTORS (2035)

PORSCHE

*264	911 except Turbo & Carrera 4 '65 thru '89
239	914 all 4 cyl models '69 thru '76
397	924 all models including Turbo '76 thru '82
*1027	944 all models including Turbo '83 thru '89

RENAULT

141	5 Le Car all models '76 thru '83
	Alliance & Encore - see AMC (934)

SAAB

247	99 all models including Turbo '69 thru '80
*980	900 all models including Turbo '79 thru '88

SATURN

2083	Saturn all models '91 thru '96

SUBARU

237	1100, 1300, 1400 & 1600 '71 thru '79
*681	1600 & 1800 2WD & 4WD '80 thru '89

SUZUKI

*1626	Samurai/Sidekick &Geo Tracker '86 thru '96

TOYOTA

1023	Camry all models '83 thru '91
92006	Camry all models '92 thru '95
935	Celica Rear Wheel Drive '71 thru '85
*2038	Celica Front Wheel Drive '86 thru '93
1139	Celica Supra all models '79 thru '92
361	Corolla all models '75 thru '79

961	Corolla all rear wheel drive models '80 thru '87
1025	Corolla all front wheel drive models '84 thru '92
*92036	Corolla & Geo Prizm '93 thru '96
636	Corolla Tercel all models '80 thru '82
360	Corona all models '74 thru '82
532	Cressida all models '78 thru '82
313	Land Cruiser all models '68 thru '82
*1339	MR2 all models '85 thru '87
304	Pick-up all models '69 thru '78
*656	Pick-up all models '79 thru '95
*2048	Previa all models '91 thru '95
2106	Tercel all models '87 thru '94

TRIUMPH

113	Spitfire all models '62 thru '81
322	TR7 all models '75 thru '81

VW

159	Beetle & Karmann Ghia '54 thru '79
238	Dasher all gasoline models '74 thru '81
96017	Golf & Jetta all models '93 thru '97
*884	Rabbit, Jetta, Scirocco, & Pick-up gas models '74 thru '91 & Convertible '80 thru '92
451	Rabbit, Jetta & Pick-up diesel '77 thru '84
082	Transporter 1600 all models '68 thru '79
226	Transporter 1700, 1800 & 2000 '72 thru '79
084	Type 3 1500 & 1600 all models '63 thru '73
1029	Vanagon all air-cooled models '80 thru '83

VOLVO

203	120, 130 Series & 1800 Sports '61 thru '73
129	140 Series all models '66 thru '74
*270	240 Series all models '76 thru '93
400	260 Series all models '75 thru '82
*1550	740 & 760 Series all models '82 thru '88

TECHBOOK MANUALS

2108	Automotive Computer Codes
1667	Automotive Emissions Control Manual
482	Fuel Injection Manual, 1978 thru 1985
2111	Fuel Injection Manual, 1986 thru 1996
2069	Holley Carburetor Manual
2068	Rochester Carburetor Manual
10240	Weber/Zenith/Stromberg/SU Carburetors
1762	Chevrolet Engine Overhaul Manual
2114	Chrysler Engine Overhaul Manual
1763	Ford Engine Overhaul Manual
1736	GM and Ford Diesel Engine Repair Manual
1666	Small Engine Repair Manual
10355	Ford Automatic Transmission Overhaul
10360	GM Automatic Transmission Overhaul
1479	Automotive Body Repair & Painting
2112	Automotive Brake Manual
2113	Automotive Detailing Manual
1654	Automotive Eelectrical Manual
1480	Automotive Heating & Air Conditioning
2109	Automotive Reference Manual & Dictionary
2107	Automotive Tools Manual
10440	Used Car Buying Guide
2110	Welding Manual
10450	ATV Basics

SPANISH MANUALS

98903	Reparación de Carrocería & Pintura
98905	Códigos Automotrices de la Computadora
98910	Frenos Automotriz
98915	Inyección de Combustible 1986 al 1994
99040	Chevrolet & GMC Camionetas '67 al '87 Incluye Suburban, Blazer & Jimmy '67 al '91
99041	Chevrolet & GMC Camionetas '88 al '95 Incluye Suburban '92 al '95, Blazer & Jimmy '92 al '94, Tahoe y Yukon '95
99042	Chevrolet & GMC Camionetas Cerradas '68 al '95
99055	Dodge Caravan & Plymouth Voyager '84 al '95
99075	Ford Camionetas y Bronco '80 al '94
99077	Ford Camionetas Cerradas '69 al '91
99083	Ford Modelos de Tamaño Grande '75 al '87
99088	Ford Modelos de Tamaño Mediano '75 al '86
99095	GM Modelos de Tamaño Grande '70 al '90
99118	Nissan Sentra '82 al '94
99125	Toyota Camionetas y 4-Runner '79 al '95

Listings shown with an asterisk (*) indicate model coverage as of this printing. These titles will be periodically updated to include later model years - consult your Haynes dealer for more information.

Over 100 Haynes motorcycle manuals also available

5-97

Haynes North America, Inc., 861 Lawrence Drive, Newbury Park, CA 91320 • (805) 498-6703